# REFLECTIONS AND REVELATIONS

## THE LATER YEARS

**THOMAS KANNATTUMADOM**

INDIA • SINGAPORE • MALAYSIA

ISBN

Paperback 979-8-89556-391-5
Hardcase 979-8-89699-298-1

# Contents

# 58

# In the New Job

After booking the railway tickets to Bangalore, a great message came from the heavens above. Leelamma knew and informed me that she, too, heard the silent statement - 'I want to be a member of your happy family,' which was the pulse of another new life growing within. The notice given to us was a delightful surprise. In recent years, there has been a row of small successes for which we received a gift as beautiful as the supreme blessing from the Heavens!

Leelamma knew and informed me that she had received the message, the pulse of another new life.

When the job order came, I decided to go to Bangalore and join the job as soon as possible. Let Leelamma and the children stay in their current accommodation for another two months. It was a good relief that Babu was also there in Pune to help my family. Within that time, I had to get a house to rent in Bangalore and go to Pune to bring everyone. Tony was in UKG class and would study in Bangalore from the 1st standard. Nita can also be admitted to the KG class. It was essential to reach Bangalore early to find a place to stay and seek admission to the school before the schools reopened after the summer vacation.

The medical certificate required to join the new job was also obtained from the district hospital in Pune. Before certifying my fitness for the latest employment, the doctor suggested wearing power lenses to improve my vision. So, I started wearing glasses.

Achayan wrote and conveyed the happy news even before we moved from Pune to Bangalore. "The agricultural land was sold, the gold chain on my mother's neck was restored using the money obtained through the receipt of the advance amount, and the debt of the previous farm was settled. Even a small farm labourer has a little crop in Kuttanad," Achayan felt sad to lose the land. Everyone else was happy. Regarding the good hopes for the future, Raju failed again and paid fees for the next exam. Babychan keeps going to Champakulam and learning typing. With the hope that everything is for good," Achayan concluded his letter.

Before leaving for Bangalore, I wrote to Kuryachan, 'It would be great if you have some acquaintance in Bangalore who could help me find a house to rent. I was told to meet MLC Manohar and make the request to him.

Raghavan Nair, an Ammunition Factory employee, lived in the old quarters opposite my residence in the Range Hills. His family had become good family friends to us. His Son Vijayan studied in Pune like me, got a job, married a Christian girl who was a friend, and was living in another house. Other children work in private companies in industrial estates in Pune.

Raghavan Nair told me that his son got a job in Bangalore and has already moved to Bangalore.

"Vijayan is now in Bangalore. It looks like Vijayan is also in the same government department where you got your new job. He lives in Bangalore with his wife and two children. You can stay with them, join your job, and look for a house nearby." He also gave Vijayan Nair's address.

So, I boarded the train to Bangalore with many burgeoning hopes.

As planned, Vijayan Nair visited the railway station and took me to his residence. Vijayan Nair's wife Monica and children Deepa and

Ruby welcomed me with love and hospitality. Like a brother, Vijayan suggested we could go to our office together. I could stay with them until I left for Pune to bring my family to Bangalore.

Vijayan took me to our Bangalore office the next day. A new shirt and a new leather belt wide enough for the pants, with a metal buckle, were kept for going to the new office for the first time. I had already started using my new glasses.

Deepa and Ruby came to say good luck to Uncle, who was joining for a new job. They desired a kiss on their cheek just as their daddy gave them. Deepa was tall like her mother. Bowing slightly, I could accept a kiss on my cheek from Deepa while the little girl Ruby stood aside, waiting for her chance. No matter how much I bent down, catching up with Ruby's height was difficult. So I picked up Ruby in my hands. Ruby cried with pain! Making her stand, I found Ruby had a small gash on her stomach caused by the metal buckle of my belt. The sadness of hurting that child remained in my mind the whole day.

I reported to the new office on 12 Mar 1981. I had the first sight of an aircraft manufacturing factory. None of the workers had come to the factory, as they were on strike. All aircraft manufacturing factories were locked out for an indefinite period. Although no work was happening, all government departments inside the factory were allowed access during the lock-out period. In those days, it was possible to leave the compound and do personal work without affecting routine work.

I met MLC Manohar at the MLA Hostel, near Vidhan Soudha. The Rent Controller had a house available. I applied for it in Indiranagar since going to the aircraft factory was convenient. All applicants were heard in the Rent Controller Court. MLC Manohar could get a directive - a recommendation from the Karnataka Revenue Dept - in my favour. It was said that an advocate could be appointed to present the applicant's case in court. Seeing that it would cost a lot, I thought - who was there better than me to show my case in front of the judge in court if the advocate's uniform or qualification was not required? I went to court on the appointed day. A large number of applicants and their lawyers came. When the court considered my application, I politely presented the matter to the judge. (25 March 1981).

"Central Govt does not have adequate quarters for the employees. My family is in Pune and should be brought to Bangalore. My children are of school-going age and should be admitted to small classes. I do not have sufficient savings to give the advance deposit of ten months' rent. "And so on.

The judge was merciful. The house was allotted to me. The owner of the house also came to the court.

"Let's go and drink tea together," I told the owner. One month's rent was paid in advance. I collected the house key. (09 Apr 1981). The next day, I took a month's leave and left for Pune. To come back with family.

Globalisation began after the Second World War, which ended in 1945. The primary purpose of globalisation was to develop trade relations among countries. In the 1990s, the then Indian Finance Minister Dr. Manmohan Singh launched the economic liberalisation programme, and in India, we felt the awakening of globalisation. Exports increased. Since then, India has gradually become one of the leaders in the global economy, and today, India has become one of the fastest-growing economies in the world. The aviation industry played an essential role in India's growing economy. My new job was in the field of military aircraft manufacturing and maintenance. A new job can be performed efficiently only after understanding many relevant things.

Recent globalisation, technological advancements, and job diversity have greatly influenced international business and multinational management activities. It was necessary to read and understand the skills supervisors needed to know to enable effective leadership performance in a diverse workplace. Everyone should know and follow these basic rules and instructions for any job. It is desirable to write them down below so that our future generations should know at least a little of them before joining any new job:-

1. Work as prescribed by the authority. Follow workplace rules and be punctual.
2. Be thorough, mature, and professional in work and related activities.
3. Dress appropriately for work.
4. Improve communication skills. Speak clearly.
5. Be willing to take on new projects and learn new skills to take the initiative and demonstrate leadership potential.
6. Never use alcohol or illegal drugs at work
7. Get along with others. Be willing to work in teams. And help colleagues with projects.
8. Be aware of political, religious, and cultural issues that may offend others.
9. Have a positive attitude and always be friendly to everyone.
10. Stay calm and focused under pressure. It shows that you can handle complicated or stressful situations.
11. When you realise you've done something wrong, immediately admit it and figure out how to fix it. Take responsibility for your decisions and actions.
12. Make the most of every opportunity to improve. It would be good to read and learn more.

We had the best neighbours in terms of security. On the back and sides were the high-ranking law enforcers themselves. The City Police Commissioner, the DGP, and the District Judge reside on three sides. Being elite does not mean we will receive special consideration or unique benefits. Aren't we proud of that situation beyond security, even if their friendship was not always received? City Police Commissioner Sridharan, who was nearby, played badminton with Tony. Several months later, when Tony was in the hospital, he often came to inquire about his well-being and help us by providing his car.

Have I got such a tiny house? Where would our relatives sleep if someone came over for a short stay? Aren't children growing up, too? There were many essential things, but I didn't think much of them when I got this house for a meagre monthly rent of Rs 200. I would console my children by telling them that the government would give us quarters to stay in when they grew up. Later on, that desire, too, became possible.

Kuriachan, who worked at Rail Bhavan, was familiar with concrete sleeper manufacturing technology and the companies. Kuriachan went to Germany to study the technology and helped to manufacture them in Indian companies. He took the lead in removing wooden sleepers from railway tracks and replacing them with concrete sleepers. One of the manufacturers agreed to hire Babu as a technical helper in a sleeper manufacturing unit in Bhopal. Achayan asked me to send Babu there, even though he would have a meagre income, and living alone in Bhopal was not a good idea. He only thought about a bright future for Babu. Babu happily agreed and went back home to get blessings from his parents, and from there, he went to Bhopal. Babu wrote that he joined to work there and lived with someone else. Raju came after his exams to Pune from home. When I was in Bangalore, he came to help Leelamma and the children.

A lot needed to be done before the family could be relocated to Bangalore. The rent paid in advance to the house owner could be deducted. Not only that, but adding up all the small sums of money that he has borrowed in between have been noted down, signed, and after adjustment, there may be little to pay back. I informed the house owner about our leaving the house. He has to take over the keys and give them to someone else to get his advance.

The registration for the cooking gas connection was returned, and a transfer certificate was obtained.

Tony Received a UKG Completion Certificate and Transfer Certificate from Vidya Bhavan. Leelamma went to Ruby Hall and saw the doctor, and the pregnancy was confirmed. After examining Leelamma's frequent headaches, the ENT doctor suggested a minor surgery for her nasal cartilage. The surgery was completed just two days before travelling to Bangalore.

Raju's presence was a big help to Chechi and the children when they were all preparing to relocate.

A large metal storage box was bought, and the utensils and small items were packed. The steel cot was folded and wrapped in a sack. The Cot and the metal box were sent to Bangalore by Railway Parcel Service. Suite cases and bags were packed with clothes, and a family of five left for Bangalore. The nasal wound was bandaged, the medicine was taken, Nitamol was on the shoulder, and the journey was difficult. Many friends had come to see him off at the railway station.

On April 19, 1981, We all came to Bangalore and lived at No. 208, Indiranagar Double Road. We cleaned the house together, bought the essentials, and started living in Bangalore.

The strike at the aircraft factory ended, and we could go to the office the next day.

The factory (HAL) bus used to come close to the house on the double road and pick up the employees, and it was a travel facility provided by HAL. Government officials working inside the factory would also be taken to the office by bus. Many such buses were running in the city. Therefore, when I started my job in Bangalore, I didn't think about an independent transportation facility.

Necessary items, food grains, and daily necessities were bought from the nearest provision shop. That was when the store was inaugurated and started working. All groceries were purchased from that shop until we moved from 208 to CV Raman Nagar.

All needed immediately was admission to Tony's first standard in a school. Nita also has to be admitted to the LKG class. The first search was at a new school that started in Indiranagar that year. Founder George Sir and Principal Teacher Saramma George admitted both children to the Bangalore Public School. Nearby was a Kerala Samajam-owned School; However, in the classes there, it was heard that the teachers often conducted classes in all three languages, so it did not prioritise that school.

When I went there and spoke, I met many friends who made Malayalam the only language of their living. No one there was highly educated. It was not out of indifference to or too much affection for their mother tongue. I have been an expatriate for fifteen years and have not handled my mother tongue easily or even learned it fluently. I did not work in Kerala. Even if my children grew up, I couldn't return and work in Kerala, and there was no guarantee they would be ready for it. Then, I kept my devotion to my mother tongue in my heart. I am not prepared to teach my children Malayalam and achieve virtue. I am not ready to decide without looking into the likely future.

When I went to pre-university, I left out Malayalam, thinking it would be difficult to score good marks, and opted for Hindi as the second language. Then, Malayalam was not needed for any activity during my work life. If required or necessary, I know how to use my mother tongue, especially in art, literature, and culture. It is enough to read a regular newspaper and enjoy the literature. No matter how much I studied, I could not have achieved a higher standard in Malayalam. Then why should I force my children to do so in their mother tongue? When they grow up, they will choose what they want. If they want to learn Malayalam, they are encouraged to do so. However, you can get a good job only after getting the necessary primary education. We communicated in the most common English language when they started speaking at a very young age.

There will be Malayalees (people born and brought up in Kerala) in any corner of the world outside Kerala. Still, with the Malayalam language alone, no one lives an official or work life. They may occasionally speak Malayalam with their parents, relatives, or peers. It is still possible at home to communicate with children without learning much. What other way of life should our children look forward to besides doing office work?

# 59

# Rehabilitation

Leelamma studied for a Bachelor of Arts degree in Malayalam for a job like teaching Malayalam in any school. After marriage and living with me outside Kerala, she had to live as a housewife, so she did not get the opportunity to work.

"Because I came with this man, I forgot even the Malayalam I had learned, and because I had to look after the children, I lost the opportunity to live by teaching Malayalam," says Leelamma. But sitting next to the mother, the children did not even get an opportunity to learn four letters in Malayalam. The practical truth was that Malayalam was not our priority in our expatriate life. It was a conscious decision. I must add here that things got better over time, and all our children could handle Malayalam personally. Sometimes for them, it was said that the rain (മഴ) was 'marra,' 'Anna.. pessaka' (അന്ന പെസഹാ) feast was sometimes stated as 'Anna Peshaka,' and the terrible rain is sometimes called a 'terrible marra' during the growing up days. No one blamed their mom for not teaching them Malayalam. What they learned was all learned by listening and imitating what others said.

Children were always eager to go to school. They liked their teachers. Nursery rhymes recited in the class would be sung again at home. The importance of learning and playing games in lower classes and cultivating enthusiasm was the most innovative, progressive, and contemporary in public schools.

For the pregnancy specialist care at Ruby Hall, Pune, if it was Dr. Sathe, after coming to Bangalore, it was Dr. (Mrs) Kamala

Unnikrishnan, renowned gynaecology specialist and consultant surgeon at the Chinmaya Mission Hospital. We met Kamala Unnikrishnan and had regular check-ups. Regular attention would suffice. We were sent back after advising for a regular check-up every two months.

We attended Resurrection Church at Indiranagar on Sundays. He met Mathews and his family, who lived nearby, and Mathews was a professor at St Joseph's College. His parents, after superannuation, came from their hometown and lived with their son's family. The intimacy and love shown by the retired officials at any level, especially older people, after getting acquainted were the unique characteristics of all, especially the Keralites. Mathews' uncle and family were so kind and loving to us.

The railway parcel to Pune did not reach in time, so we slept on a sheet spread on the floor for a month. In the early eighties, people used to say that all the old glory of Bangalore had gone, and a few years ago, Bangalore was said to be the 'paradise for retirees.' Summer heat, population growth in the city, the rise of concrete buildings, and climate change have made our lives more miserable. I bought a fa, so we could somehow sleep through the night. We searched furniture shops in Shivaji Nagar and purchased a pair of wooden cots. The kids and their parents could sleep together if the two cots and beds were parallel. The senior child, Tony, found happiness and comfort by keeping his head near our legs, on the cot, and sleeping close to the room wall.

My parents and brothers were happy that we moved from Pune to Bangalore for work, and their letters expressed their happiness. The places not far away made it easier for them to visit and go back occasionally. Babu was in Bhopal. Raju returned to Kerala to take his degree exam in May. After that, he, too, was ready to come to Bangalore, stay with me, and try to find a job.

The foldable steel cot and table were received at Bangalore City Railway Station after a month of transporting by the Railway Parcel

Service. Putting the folding cot in the front staircase room helped Raju to sleep on it at night.

When he was a little older, Tony slept with his Raju uncle, listening to bedtime stories. When Raju had free time, he also told stories during the holidays. He narrated short Bible stories and conducted quizzes based on knowledge gained from reading newspapers. Cricket was played in the yard, and Raju took them to the nearby park in the evenings.

I was assigned a responsible job in the public sector company where warplanes were being built. All defence services use aircraft. The usual practice was to purchase a small number of mission-specific aircraft directly from other countries for immediate use. Direct combat aircraft were bought for use along with the technology involved in their manufacture so that we could manufacture them within our country. With new technology, we could all work together to build enough planes in our factories. Design and manufacture of aircraft and allied equipment were done only in the PSU. Private companies in India have also developed the technology and started manufacturing aviation, space, and defence equipment with or without the collaboration of foreign private companies.

The responsibility of the Department of Defence is to ensure the quality of warplanes and equipment manufactured in India, thereby maintaining the non-hazardous condition and reliability of aircraft and providing full cooperation and support to our Armed Forces in the execution of military missions. A large team of technicians was working on this job.

They ignored the answer I gave to the UPSC board for the question during the interview, which said, "I didn't know anything about the aircraft." They selected me despite that, which meant they did not see in me the habit of neglecting or running away from the responsibility once it was given to me.

Therefore, my first responsibility was to know what type of machine an aeroplane was and how it worked. Then, I should know the science and technology used in the design and manufacturing stages of the aircraft. The test results should validate the intended quality when the design is approved. Then, the same quality should be ensured at the manufacturing stage of every aircraft.

I started studying.

At that time, the office had no basic training about what to do and how to do it as soon as and when a newcomer joined the team. Viswanathan was a colleague and my acquaintance of R&DE, Pune. Viswanathan took me to the final stage of aircraft assembly and inspection hangar.

A Gnat aeroplane known in India as Ajeet was ready to be released for flight. We climbed onto the top of the plane with the help of a step ladder. I stood looking forward like a mahout on the back of an elephant.

Vishwanathan said - "This is the left side; on aircraft, we say it is the Port."

Similarly, the name for the right side is Starboard. "

"Got it. Is it not enough to say left and right?"

"No, it is a vehicle that travels in the atmosphere like a ship at sea. Isn't the blue sky above like the sea? If you still have doubts, let me tell you something to remember. One R means PORT; two R means STARBOARD (Right)."

That's how it started—Parameswaran, a colleague, helped by giving me the notes written when he joined the workforce.

As Anantharaman said, books give more knowledge on any subject. Reading books can be supplemented by physical learning by coming to the hangar, looking, and touching with your hands. Sachin Tendulkar and Virat Kohli have been doing well in cricket. They have said that their bats speak their minds. That is the benefit of learning by touch.

Thus, I participated in the tiniest fighter aircraft, from Ajeet, which gained a reputation for involvement in the 1965 and 1971 conflicts, to the most modern aircraft still in service during its manufacturing phase and overhaul repairs and troubleshooting, defect detection, and design improvements. During my service, I participated with other experts and technicians to investigate the causes of the thirteen planes that crashed during service. I stayed near the sites of the accidents and conducted investigations. Modifications have been made to avoid similar accidents on such aircraft again, eliminate the cause of the accident, and make appropriate contributions to rectifying the technical defects and accidents.

I was in the service of the nation throughout these years. I was stationed in Bangalore from 1981 to 1993, in Koraput, Orissa, from 1993 to 2001, and in Bangalore from 2001 to February 28, 2006. I retired from DGAQA service on 28 Feb 2006.

I travelled from one place to other several places for work! I never got tired of working or did not do the work on purpose. I only thought about how to do the job better. All my colleagues at the workplace received full cooperation. I was friendly and cooperative while working with many officials in public sector institutions.

I did nothing against the general rules and did not participate in anything related to unlawful activities, violence, or misconduct. I shall describe my achievements and contributions to society and the country in terms of work. The ones that made me happy and satisfied and those that didn't make me happy.

I Learned and carried out my work. I learned more and worked harder. It was Mr Chhabra, my boss, who said once -

"Nobody gets tired by doing hard work!"

My interaction with Chhabra was like walking on a tightrope, always trying to make him happy. He quickly realised things that benefited the top echelons of the institutions where he grew up. His inclination and loyalty towards those institutions were his humble acknowledgement of the generosity he received. He was always in love with those who worked under constraints while maintaining good relations.

Once, I had to hear a critical comment from him. That was after our Head of the Department (HOD) listened to our grievances, including a lack of career prospects and opportunities. My data-based presentation about the common grievance was criticised as an unpleasant truth, pinpointing the lethargy and passive action on the part of the higher management. After the HOD left, he called me closer and responded:-

"You are a good orator. You could have sought a clarification instead of speaking the unpleasant truth and likely consequences." That was Chhabra, the local boss who did not want to embarrass the top boss.

I was happy because I worked regularly and earned a recurring income—no profit or loss. I had a monthly salary and lived on a meagre income. I was satisfied. It may not have been enough to cover all the expenses, but having been able to send money to Achayan every month was a relief to all at home. Money was shared when available—not shared when not available. I did not want anyone's money or property. Sometimes, it wasn't easy to make both ends meet - especially at the end of the month. The debt was repaid on payday. Mustafa and Parameswaran, my office colleagues, often helped. I did not regret what I did not get, and I did not regret not getting enough; I was satisfied with what I got - that was my life.

Raju arrived in Bangalore in May after completing his final Commerce degree examination. After getting the degree certificate, it was decided that applying for a company job was enough. He had previously written the Armed Forces Service exams, such as the NDA, but could not pass.

Babychan had completed SSLC and wanted to go to Alappuzha to study for a pre-degree like Raju. There, he did his pre-degree as well as the B.Com degree courses. Eager to explore further, he joined Edathwa St Alocious College and passed his M.Com degree there.

The Kannattumadom family grew into a big tree with many branches. Achayan was always proud to grow into a small tree branch of a big tree. Buds and fruits were formed on the small branches all over.

Only Achayan has provided all the children with primary education, promptly caring for everything they needed for growth and development.

That was something that no one else could claim from the other branches of the big tree, i.e., Achayan's brothers. It was rightly said that Achayan's family had received many blessings from God.

# 60

# In the Care of Parents

My mother came from home before Seema's birth. Ammachi and Raju were in Bangalore during Leelamma's delivery, which was a great help to the two young children.

Seema was born on November 12, 1981, at 9.50 pm. Dr. Kamala Unnikrishnan was in the hospital. Check-ups were done every month. There was not even the slightest difference in the estimated delivery date.

We arrived at the hospital in an auto-rickshaw that evening. It was just a km from the double road where we lived to the Chinmaya Mission Hospital, next to Sri Krishna Temple.

There were places of worship and prayer rooms in some specific locations in the hospital, as in some Christian mission hospitals. Prayers were also offered at particular times. I was waiting on a bench in the corridor opposite the hospital maternity ward from the previous evening. Sometimes, I walked up to the prayer room door and came back. The general calm and the stillness of the night had spread. Several times, I sat down and woke up dizzy. The silence of the night was long.

The door to the delivery room slowly opened, and a Malayalee nurse came looking for the father, who was anxiously waiting for the baby. The baby's father was delighted to see the baby wrapped in a white bandage and shed tears of joy. The nurse said the baby's mother was also well.

The nurse went inside with the baby after telling me the mother and child would move into the room in half an hour.

I ran home to tell my mother and Raju about the newborn. The distance was covered in ten minutes, and I got home. Knowing the news, the mother, as usual, offered sighs of relief, gratitude, and sighs with her hands clasped and her face raised to the heavens.

After having breakfast, I had just returned to the hospital room when I found the mother and child were being brought to the room.

A ten-month-long yajna started in Pune and was completed in Bangalore. For the successful completion, I congratulated the mother. When I kissed the forehead of the baby, tears of joy rolled down my cheeks. The baby sleeps soundly—the most beautiful girl in the world. Since I realised that a new life was springing up in the mother's womb, I believed that my family's gender equality had changed. This world has been waiting for us to prioritise, modify, or adapt to either knowledge-based male adventure or beautiful aesthetic femininity; there it is; even better was given to us by the birth of this child. We desire something, the universal force that generates and reserves for us and gives us the best, much beyond our desires!

Seema was the child we wanted. It never occurred to us that the third child would burden us. Until Nita was about two years old, we discussed gender equality and balance in our family. So, we have determined to love our children without any gender bias. Thinking that the girls must be married off, no one sees their daughters and sons as separate in this modern age. Since we have no responsibility to balance the genders, God's blessing on us will only increase if we give this world a partisan birth. Let the beauty of the world rise in a small way. Or, as our parents think, everything God gives us is for good. Let someone know that we lived in this world through these children. It is for them that we become the wheat grains that rot. Therefore, when they bear more fruits than we do, someone would say, "Whose children are these? They are of

Thomas and Leelamma, obviously!" That's enough. All that we need is to listen to those words. Through them, there will be some goodness in the world. They should light the lamp of goodness and mercy in people's minds and spread the light of mercy throughout.

Here in the hospital bed, absorbing the warmth of Leelamma is the girl who is not only to give more beauty to this world but is born to be valuable and worthy to the world, gaining knowledge. The girl is destined to find and explore the borders of the world. Therefore, the baby was named Seema, which means boundaries. She also set the boundaries of the family - crossing the wall, the thought that the Creator might not allow us to have more births in this generation. We talked about boundaries. The doctor also advised that it was good for us to be so.

The infant was baptised at Murphy Town Church. Mary - was Leelamma's mother's name, and the same name was given to the baby. Prof Mathews's Family were invited as God-parents. To our added delight, and with Mathews's consent, Mathews' aged parents volunteered to come to the church and happily accepted the responsibility of being the godparents. My parents and siblings from home sent warm greetings and prayers. The baptism was celebrated with money withdrawn from the General Provident Fund.

From Nashik, Kunjunju uncle and aunty came to celebrate Seema's baptism. They returned to Nashik after a week of magnificent celebrations in the tiny house on 'Double Road,' where we all lived happily together.

After Seema was born, Xavier and Thambichan congratulated me and gave me a virtual promotion. Thambichan congratulated his sister's husband, who got three stars like children, and called him Captain. He said the three stars have risen on my shoulder just like an army captain who wears three stars on his shoulder. No one in the current generation has three children in their family, till then. Thambichan and Leelamma had two daughters. The era of nuclear families has begun everywhere. Even years later, my captaincy, which my co-brother and brother-in-law placed on my shoulders, remained. Ottahaikal Babychan has one son and one daughter, and the same goes for each of the four sisters of Thambichan. Gracy has one boy and a girl, Kunjamma has a boy and a girl, and Mercy has the same.

Rosamma gave birth to her first baby boy. There was no difference in my family's number of children - the new generation population. Babu has two sons, Raju has a daughter and one son, and Babychan has one and two daughters. It was heard that the youngest Babychan would strive to attain a higher rank than the captain and constantly pray to God. Undoubtedly proud of his younger brother's rise in status, the senior captain prayed that the younger brother would become a major and that someone in the family would achieve even higher titles in time! I was happy to be called captain. Raising three children is a big responsibility. We never felt it was a burden. They probably wanted to call me Major. God might not grant us the favour even if we had desired it. Neither my siblings nor we regret it.

I was delighted to hear the call as captain. Raising three children was a big responsibility. It never felt like a burden to us. They probably wanted to call me Major. God did not allow their desire to do so. Neither they nor we regret it.

Tony and Nita were friendly with the eldest of Mathews' children, Sujith. Rajith (girl), the middle, and Ajith, the youngest. They were playmates. Tony and Nita would go to their house, take them together, and walk around the park and surroundings. In front of the house at 208, there was plenty of space to play, but they occasionally wanted to spend time with nearby friends. One day, Tony and Nita went out saying - "We're going to Ajeet, Sujeet." After an early breakfast, I went to the market and returned three or four hours later. My mother said -

"The children have not come back yet. They have not even eaten breakfast. Go and see mone; where are they."

The time was eleven o'clock. I looked out the door no sooner than I found them coming together.

"Where have you been for so long? Why didn't you eat your breakfast?"

"We ate from there."

My immature and unnecessary thoughts warmed my head. Wasn't that right if you said you went there and ate without eating here? - Breakfast is an important meal - it can either make or break your day. I jumped out of the way without thinking whether I would be right or just. I fetched a stick and gave a few beating strokes to both my children. The question was not whether the breakfast was shared with friends. Shouldn't parents and responsible persons look for and worry if they don't see each other long? Why such a failure or missed thought? He would have gone in search after that time had he been told. Even if they do not remember getting beaten up, they will remember what was said and understood. Was it always later, somewhere, even if it's a little late to get home, to say it early? Calling Mommy? Beating and being beaten are not correct. However, they should never forget that eating out with friends is not bad. Their parents 'hospitality is sometimes not acceptable. It is not right to go out with friends and spend time forgetting everything without obeying the elders' and mom-served home-cooked food. I feel happy that they always remembered it, subsequently in later life.

I realised the seriousness of giving beatings to kids only when my mother asked about it.

"Is this all matter to beat children? Haven't you learned anything after having three kids to look after ?"

"Everybody's a little kid. It doesn't matter, and I wouldn't beat anymore. They seem to understand."

"They may say it once that daddy beat us up that day and did not tell us why. So were you. "

My mother seldom advised me like that. There was something to think about.

"When dealing with children, it's not always easy for adults to feel right. It's not just adults who are right. Sometimes, kids, too, are correct.

It is better to cooperate with them than to command them. The best solution is to break your fears or problems into smaller steps. Spend time with them, talk to them, and evaluate the facts.

The older child should have pride. All behaviour is communicative. They also can consider the point of view of others. It is not good to impose anything. Beating is not good, either. "

After Seema's childcare, my mother returned home.

Colour television programs were telecasted in India on Independence Day 1982 for the first time. Subsequently, the Asian Games held in Delhi in November were telecasted in Bangalore. I took a personal loan from the Indian Overseas Bank and bought a black & white television set. Besides watching the Asian Games, we could watch popular serials. 'Sandokan,' starring Kabir Bedi, was the first English serial we watched with interest. When the film came on television, Tony, Nita, and Seema were lying in bed, watching keenly and intently, which was fascinating. There were no demands, no crying, no milk, and they cried if someone hid their view by walking in front of them. Subsequently, Door darshan Hindi serials such as Hum Log (1984) and Buniyaad (1986-87) and the daily news program Pranoy Roy's 'World This Week' made television a good source of knowledge and entertainment for the whole family.

Just before the end of the Asian Games, Achayan came to Bangalore to spend time with the children. My office then instructed me to go to Delhi for some official work.

Kuriachan's mother - my aunt - lived with Kuriachan in the railway quarters in Sadiq Nagar. I wrote a letter to Kuriachan and told him,

"This time, when I come to Delhi, Achayan will also be with me."

At native, Achayan rarely saw his sister - because she lived so close to the library that he hardly got any time to walk across to see her, and her whereabouts were known after going to Delhi.

For the first time, Achayan saw it as a great opportunity and blessing to go to Delhi, the capital and administrative centre of the country, where ministers and people's representatives were constantly going and coming. We went on a fast train that covered the distance in a shorter time.

**Achayan's visit to Kuriachan & family in Delhi (1981)**

Achayan was happy to go to Delhi, stay with Kuriachan, and tell jokes and pleasantries with his elder sister. We travelled by car and saw almost all the major tourist sites in Delhi in three to four days. We could pay our respects to Gandhi at the Raj Ghat by laying flowers. Shanti Van is a park with lovely greenery built around the place where the mortal remains of Nehru were buried, close to Raj Ghat. We could watch the Parliament proceedings from the balcony. Visiting the Parliament House and Gandhi Samadhi were unforgettable experiences for Achayan.

I do not remember taking any photos as we did not have a mobile phone or camera then. When Achayan returned home after the trip to Delhi, he explained the journey to Delhi and the attractions he saw to his friends in the library. I believe Achayan has written everything in his diary.

While Achayan planned to return to native, we thought everyone would go home together this time. The trip was planned to Kanyakumari as we intended to take the All India LTC and made necessary reservations. We arrived at Kanyakumari to see the southernmost tip of India, the confluence of three oceans - the Arabian Sea, the Indian Ocean, and the Bay of Bengal. He also visited the Vivekananda Rock Memorial. It was built in 1970 in honour of Swamy Vivekananda, who was said to have attained enlightenment on the rock. We arrived there by boarding a large sea ferry boat. The memorial has a prayer hall called the Meditation Hall, where visitors can meditate. We also meditated for some time there. There was always a strong wind in the vicinity of the meditation hall. Nita and my mother had to be given exceptional help to keep them from falling off with the wind. The design of the mandapam incorporated various styles of temple architecture from different parts of India. We visited the temples at Kanyakumari and the Gandhi Memorial there nearby.

The sunrise at Kanyakumari was a beautiful sight. Achayan and Ammachi were very happy. We returned without waiting for the sunset.

We visited the zoo in Thiruvananthapuram, the legislative assembly building, the Sri Padmanabhaswamy temple, and the Shankhumugham beach. 'Methan Mani' Clock Tower on the way to the temple - This clock, which is many years old, was one of the fascinating sights for the children. What makes this bell interesting is the shape of the face of a bearded man who opens his mouth every hour when two sheep come close and slam into the face from either side.

We continued our journey to Alappuzha by transport bus. While sitting before me during the bus journey, Nita saw something nearby disturbing her. When asked, she pointed to a passenger on the bus sitting nearby and frowned. She was almost crying. Achayan also saw Nita's face.

Achayan - "What's wrong with Nitamol? What's her difficulty?" he asked me.

I said - "No big issue; this is the problem (of apartheid) in South Africa. Nelson Mandela is continuing the struggle"!

Achayan understood. Together with other passengers sitting close to him, he chuckled heartily. Nita was a fair girl but silly. Can you tell why she changed her seat?

Raju was yet to return to Bangalore. Then, in the summer holidays of 1983, there was a Malayalam film festival in some cinema theatres in Bangalore. There was the desire to watch Malayalam movies, but how did the parents with three small children accompanying them enjoy the films? Nowadays, children say it is a Mallu movie, not a Malayalam movie.

It might be entertainment for the minor children. Still, the parents might not enjoy the movie, being busy looking after the needs of the children.

So, Leelamma discussed this plan with Subramanian Aunty. They did agree a hundred times to look after the children. There are no young children around them to look after. Their grandson, Arjun, was in Mumbai with his parents. So most days of the fortnight, we went to see the movies in the evening - all were good movies. I still long to watch those movies again. We, as parents, had left our three children with the neighbouring family to watch movies. Is it possible today? No matter how much we thank Subramanian aunty, it is not enough.

**Subramaniyan Aunty took care of the kids when we went to films**

Most days, Leelamma would go to Mrs. Sebastian's house in the neighbourhood to learn to tailor. Subramanian aunty looked after Seema. Seema had just started learning to speak. Aunty would ask -

"Cheema, where did your mommy go?"

Seema answered - "Mommy went to Thaikasi."

When Seema was three years old, Leelamma again complained and said she was in pain and needed to see a gynaecologist. Dr (Mrs) Kamala Unnikrishnan carried out the necessary investigations. I was sure that Seema was the boundary and the limit of a Captain wearing three stars on each of his shoulders. It was not a pain to become a Major!

"We need a minor surgery that requires anaesthesia - must be admitted. She has a slightly large ovarian cyst that needs to be removed. That'll be fine" - that was the doctor's conclusion.

Then it didn't take long. After the surgery, the sample was sent for a biopsy examination, revealing nothing wrong. Leelamma was sent home with advice to rest more. I came home and told the kids about Mommy's health - they embraced it with childish innocence. Tony and Nita confessed that they could help Mommy. Seema asked –

"Daddy, Can I touch Mommy with my little finger?"

That was what Seema learned from a film that she watched recently. We all went to the theatre and saw the movie "The Sound of Music"! Seema remembered a similar scene in that movie.

There were catechism classes at the church on Sundays. Tony and Nita both attended the classes. One day, there was a competition for children to present various art programmes, including fancy dress, at the church.

Raju has helped Nita to dress like Ammachi and to masquerade in a Chatta and Mundu Kerala Christian dress and Cavani (veil) like Ammachi and taught her to act with a monastic scapular and spectacles. Nita performed beautifully on the stage before the church and won prizes and accolades. She hummed a melodious Malayalam song on another occasion.

KJ Yesudas' song "Davidatmaja Mariame, Kanye Thanvangi ..." was sung well and won the prize. Raju prepared Nita for the performance.

Raju waited persistently for an interview call despite sending many applications and trying through his acquaintances. Raju doesn't remember much when I was home without work for over six months. It's a challenging period and a pathetic situation. Raju was often seen just thinking and feeling frustrated. Unless you start working on something useful, you will not gain confidence in doing any job or activity efficiently. He had learned Commerce, so I would sometimes jokingly say, 'Be prepared to open a pan shop,' but the tone of voice was harsh to take in the right spirit. That's how I once told him to use the newspaper, apply glue, and make carry bags or envelopes for the provision shops. It was just a matter of utilizing the time. Raju felt the pain. No more forcing him. When you think about what was being said, you will develop an attitude to do whatever you want, which was what was needed. Every job has its glory. The income earned is only proportional to intellectual and physical ability. Knowledge or ability - depends on education, experience, and training. Skill is the expression of that power of knowledge.

The advice that motivates anyone to apply his ability should be modest and comforting. If the same thing is said in the voice of harsh discipline, it may not be understood in the right spirit.

I then understood that studies in Commerce lead to excellent job opportunities in industry or Commerce. That's why I told him to go to different areas in the City- Majestic, Shivaji Nagar, etc. and try to get a salesperson job in any shop. After trying for a few days, he got a job in some shop in Majestic. Since it was just a temporary job, it only helped him to understand its challenges. Whatever job one does, that job has dignity. The first thing to look at is not what job you earned or what job you did but whether you can learn something from it, whether the training was valuable, whether you desired to do more, or have the scope to grow. If you did better, you must understand that any job would pay off.

Similarly, we should not stop working at any age. Still, we should think that whatever we do at any age is satisfying or beneficial to someone. You can do whatever you desire if you are healthy. Most people who work maintain their health. One should work, however. That is the secret of health.

On September 29, 1982, Raju got a job at the C&AG office in Bangalore. Central Govt job, a potential auditor job possible for relocation to Thiruvananthapuram. Raju was taken to CAG's office in Bangalore for employment, just as Tony was taken to Vidyabhavan School in Pune. Officials there received him at the CAG office in Vidhana Soudha. Thus, Raju became the second government official in the family.

# 61

# To Give Comfort

Thambichan's letter asked me to leave and go to Delhi in December. Meanwhile, Xavier and his family moved from Hospet to Delhi since Xavier was relocated to the MMTC office in Delhi.

Thambichan wrote that Xavier and Gracy had some disputes and marriage discord problems. Xavier had warned him to go there and talk to his sister so the conflicts would not worsen. He had also written that if Gracy did not relent, he could take Gracy back home. Thambichan told me I should go with him to give him additional courage and moral support while talking to the couple about the disputes.

The problem was the "seven-year itch." The seven-year itch is a psychological term that refers to the decline in happiness in a relationship after the seventh year of marriage. Applying the relevant ointment slowly - that is, talking out the reasons and helping to change misconceptions - could only be done, and that was the remedy. We went there and spoke to both of them, and they agreed to forget and forgive each other and be amicable.

To share the pleasure of talking about trivial things and solving to the satisfaction of everybody, we sat together. We played cards until the night was over, and it was almost dawn. You can calculate the blood alcohol concentration (BAC) for 40% abv, 80 proof x 1.5 litres, split into three, and we quenched our thirst. I slept until noon the next day and returned by train in the evening.

India won the last and final match of the Cricket World Cup against the West Indies, held in England from 9 to June 25, 1983. Kapil Deva was the captain. This was the first time India had won the World Cup. There was a live telecast of the semi-finals and finals. The victory was celebrated all over India and was the most significant in cricket.

Joji of Karumady was involved in an accident in Bangalore on March 24, 1984. Samuel of the Hindustan Academy sent a message. When I arrived at the Bowring Hospital, the doctors had pronounced the verdict that "the death had occurred when he was brought in." I have signed the statement that it was Alex (Joji), whom I knew and who was dead. The body was then taken for post-mortem.

Joji was on a bicycle at Ulsoor. An oncoming BTS bus (MEF 231, Route No. 136) came from behind and crashed into the bike, and Joji fell off, hitting a row of kerb stones for the road. Perhaps that was when he lost his life.

Joji was the eldest son of Leelamma's uncle's daughter. His parents and siblings lived in Karumady. He came to Bangalore to study electronics. Joji went on to study and work at Samuel's institute at Ulsoor.

He came home on a bicycle two days ago; he spoke well and had an endearing nature. He was adept at learning and worked day and night repairing electronic devices. He loved the kids and played cricket in our yard with them. I was told he would return in the next week before going. He was the only earning member of his family in Karumady. Joji's brothers and sister were small children. One of our post-wedding receptions was with his parents and siblings in Karumady.

Delivery of the body to the house in Karumady after the post-mortem was an unforeseen responsibility I had to undertake. Samuel placed the body of Joji, who had succumbed to his untimely death, in a coffin and arranged a tempo to go to Karumady. After preparing the certificates and agreeing to the tempo charges, along with Samuel's assistant, we travelled to Karumady. The body could be reached at the house in Karumady at about 11 a.m. When we reached Karumady, people in his hometown were gathered there to give him a tearful and respectful welcome. The weeping and wailing of the relatives in that small house were pathetic and heartbreaking.

The driver said he could return if the tempo rent was paid to him. The locals were watching me when I was looking for cash that was not there on my person, and at the same time, thinking and worried about how to pay the money to the driver!

The locals walked around for about ten minutes and collected the required cash. During those ten minutes, one of the natives approached me and asked arrogantly, as if I was the tempo owner-

"Can't you go soon if we pay the rent?"

What answer to give to that man! I looked at him in his eyes, and my look was like an angry frown; that was enough.

He stood around for some time.

Funeral services were held at Karumady Church in the afternoon. The local vicar, Fr. Sebastian Narakathra, who knew me, spent much time talking to me for information. After reassuring Chettan, Chechi, and Joji's siblings, I walked toward my house.

On the way home after Joji's funeral, I saw Leelamma Thomas's mother washing clothes on the ravine banks in front of their house. I introduced myself and told her the reason for coming this way. I sought the news of the daughters of that mother since they were my classmates.

"Where are Kunjamma and Leelamma, the sisters."

"Leelamma teaches at a Kendriya Vidyalaya in Kota, Rajasthan. Her husband also works there. She has two children, a boy and a girl."

After telling the mother to inform the sisters of my inquiry, I continued the journey.

On my return to Bangalore, Advocate SP Shankar was contacted on the advice of the Insurance man Thomas Sir, who lived on Double Road across from my residence. The Advocate filed a case in the MACT Court for compensation for Joji's motor accident. The necessary certificates, including Joji's appointment order with Samuel's signature, FIR, and post-mortem report, etc., were organized and obtained. The court case lasted nearly four years. I used to go to court for all the hearings. When I was taken to the witness stand to be questioned as a witness, the defendant's attorney said that I was a party interested in the case. And there were no further discussions.

The judge said that he already knew what I had to say. We're told to bring the deceased's next of kin, parents, or other interested persons on the day of the verdict.

On the day of the verdict, the elder brother came from Karumady. The court sanctioned a compensation of Rs one lakh. Chettan paid the advocate's fee after collecting the cheque and exchanging it for cash from the bank. The balance amount was handed over to Chettan.

After leaving behind the sadness that the lost life will not come back, Chettan and Chechi (the elder brother and sister) said several times that the amount granted from the court had helped the family generously. Chettan and his family always treated us with gratitude and love. Joji's siblings studied more and started working on their own. Their sister was married off.

In October 1984, when Thambichan and his family shifted to Madhuban, New Quarters in Paradip, we revisited them by going to Paradip on LTC, and we stayed there for a week.

In 1985, Achayan wrote letters asking for money for agricultural purposes. When I was reluctant to pay due to his continued recurring losses, Raju said he would pay me back if I took a loan of at least Rs 5,000 from my provident fund and sent it to Achayan. Half of my savings for the future until then could thus be used. While everyone else realised the loss in agricultural farming and switched to farming using modern technologies, Achayan indulged in traditional cultivation. The losses from agriculture continued to be mounting.

Tony bought a guitar and started training at school. The teachers at his school were sincere and good guides. They collaborated and participated in all school games and extracurricular activities. The students had the unconditional love of their classmates and teachers. The school authorities showed love and respect to the students and their parents.

I was annoyed by a harsh remark that the teacher once wrote about Nita's classwork. Children in a lower class can be told their works may be wrong and how to correct them if they write wrong. The teacher only wrote 'Rubbish,' without saying what was wrong or how it became unacceptable, without speaking or writing how to fix it. Many might call me a hot-tempered person, but I could not agree with such a comment. With love and respect, I wrote a letter to the principal the next day, informing him of my protest and disagreement with the comment.

"Rubbish is something that needs to be discarded. Sending children to school is not for collecting garbage. Teachers also do not need to separate waste. Good teachers teach children what is right and what is wrong. And if it is wrong, they teach how to correct it."

Principal George might have had discussions with many teachers for two or three days. Nita was lovingly called to his office and reassured, and he sent a reply letter to me. The letter contained an apology and the assurance that he would take care of such matters affecting all the children in the future.

Nita was reluctant to go to school for a few days. She was always encouraged by telling her many things; she was helped to wear her uniform for school, put her books in the bag, etc. Still, she had a stomach ache or a headache when she got ready! And she desired to skip her classes. She cooked up some weird scheme that she thought would earn her a reprieve. The disease was diagnosed after two or three days, and a remedy was given. After getting a minor blow to the painful part with a small stick, she got relief, smiled, and went to school!

Nita studied well and got above-average marks. When the marks fell short, she was encouraged to work harder. Mommy spent more time with Nita and helped her. At the end of the school year, the teacher said that Nita would barely pass the 4$^{th}$ standard. That didn't leave me very satisfied either. He went to the school and requested that Nita be allowed to continue there for one more year without promotion since she was in a small class.

I assessed that she could learn confidently, write the exam, and achieve unparalleled success when she studied more complex subjects in a higher class. Nita never knew she had missed an academic year when she went to the next school year with her new friends. It was then she studied better.

A good school has talented and inspiring teachers. They help students create opportunities for scrutiny, thinking, learning, and growing through hard work. Students improve their knowledge in various subjects and develop practical skills. They are disciplined citizens and good for society. Examination results for each year show the students' academic proficiency, the quality level of the school, and the teachers and the student's proficiency in extracurricular competitions and other eventful events.

**Together, we march into the world Tony, Seema, Nita (1983)**

# 62

# Siblings' Families

Babu continued his work in Bhopal for one or two years more. After that, the same company that won the railway construction contract in Iraq picked up Babu and the team that went there to Iraq. The contract work in Iraq was for fifteen or eighteen months. After that, Babu was informed that there was no work for him and that he needed not to return to Bhopal. They said they would inform him about the vacancy in other group companies.

Meanwhile, Babu got some marriage proposals. Achayan did not disappoint and sent them away but told them to wait until the construction work for our house was finished. By then, Achayan hoped that Babu's job would continue somewhere. Shortly afterward, Babu received instructions from the Indian Hume Pipe Company in Coimbatore on how to go and work there. So, he joined IHP Co on Avinashi Road.

Out of Babu's savings until then, a total of Rs. 6000/ after working in Iraq was handed over to Achayan to complete the rest of the unfinished house and make it comfortable. The realization that the work could not have been completed with that much money prompted Achayan to look for other means of raising more money. Everyone saw the goal of getting the house completed as urgent. However, the actual expenditure could not be met due to other necessities. After finding the resources and finishing the house construction work, Achayan realised it was impractical to have Babu's wedding. However, we compromised, stating that the facilities achieved so far were adequate and that the marriage should proceed.

As each of his children grew up, Achayan was determined to make timely decisions and fulfill his responsibilities at every crucial stage of his children's personal life. That was why Babu was advised to go ahead with his marriage proposal. When Babu returned from Iraq, Achayan spoke to Babu about the need to get married. The proposal came from Thresya, the youngest daughter in a long-time-familiar Kannamthara family, the daughter of Outhakutty; they called her name 'Kulantha.' Outhakutty and his family lived on the riverside, Paravur, and cultivated paddy in a nearby field. Outhakutty agreed with Achayan that the ten acres of agricultural land and some land would be earmarked for Thresiamma and her family to enjoy.

Achayan's letter came to me to take leave, go for the betrothal ceremony and wedding, and make it all successful.

We went home, taking leave for the holidays. The marriage ceremony went well. Babu and Thresyamma stayed at home for a year after their marriage. Outhakutty set up a house near their farm in the Poonthuram Padasekharam (collection of fields) in Paravur and told Thresyamma to go there and stay with Babu and look after the agricultural land. So Babu and Thresyamma moved from our unfinished family home to their house in Paravur.

I could see his happiness, peace of mind, and tranquillity in his letters from his workplace after he got the job at IHP Co in Coimbatore. The situation of staying home without work and after marriage can only be understood in depth if only one experiences it. I got the job when I was so frustrated. That was the relief and joy that comes to anyone's mind when he gets a job quickly after marriage.

Babu came home from Coimbatore every month and returned two days later. In the company, he had all the retail manual labour work. Occasionally, he would do the electrician's job when needed. The staff at the company were interested in him. Although he could save only a small amount from his salary, Babu was happy. He spoke friendly with everyone. He did not want any extra comfort or even good food. He did not tell anyone in detail about his job and the amount of income he earned. So, after the marriage, the parents at home thought that Babu had an environment where he got adequate income from work and farming, and the parents had high hopes for him.

Praga Industries, a Coimbatore-based company, manufactured and supplied pilots' helmets to Airforce. I went to witness the tests to ensure the quality of the helmets. Babu was called to the hotel where I stayed, and I talked to him in person. When I often visited Coimbatore for work, I always told Babu and asked him to come and meet me at the hotel where I was staying. Once, I went to IHP on Avinashi Road to meet Babu there. I wanted to see his work environment. I saw Babu running with a tester in his hand for some electrical repair work. His friends told me he had a meagre salary, though he worked hard and wanted to find a better-paying job elsewhere. We spent two or three hours discussing family matters every time we met. I tried to understand the hardships and sorrows of his day-to-day life. He did not complain to anyone. He never hurt anyone. Although his mother and father had some misunderstandings, it did not make him sad more than once. His love for others never diminished.

The DRDO Quarters Complex at CV Raman Nagar was completed in 1988, and allotment started soon after. We all knew that the accommodation at 208 on Indiranagar Double Road was inadequate for the growing needs of children. We have had no opportunity to stay in the quarters during my service life. So, when it was known that we would get DRDO quarters soon to wait until transfer or retirement, we attempted to get them. When I got the allotment of the new quarters, we thought there was no better happiness than staying there. We quickly moved to the flat DRDO Type IV D 9/4 and vacated the 208 house on Double Road. Everyone was so happy to come and live in the new big house with all the amenities.

The lack of adequate furniture in a house with five members and the lack of transportation from the residential quarters to the office were vivid examples of the absence of essential requirements. I took a loan from the Provident Fund and organized a few vital requirements. We bought a dining table. We purchased a refrigerator through the CSD canteen to keep the food items without perishing soon. We purchased two more cots and a wooden table. We bought a three-seater sofa set and two sofa chairs. We made a bookshelf with the plywood available from the packing cases. I purchased a small colour television set and a stand for entertainment to gather world information while relaxing.

We could bring enough water into the house without quarrelling with the neighbours, without obstacles, and without physical difficulty fetching.

Since we stayed at one level above, it can be said that there was no external interference or dust from the ground floor entering our dwelling place.

The transition from cave life in 208 to government quarters was a leap forward in modern living standards. We started living much more comfortably and availing of the convenience of modern living like many of our contemporaries.

A motor vehicle is meant to reach the intended destination quickly. It will help you to reduce the daily hassles of boarding a mode of public transport and save travelling time. I have been thinking about it for a long time. It was an essential requirement that got postponed indefinitely amidst financial constraints. The basic requirement became unavoidable, especially when relocating to the quarters. That's how I bought and used the Silver-plus Enfield Moped; it was a good relief.

Babu's children, Saju and Sony, were born between 1988 and 1991. We could not attend Saju's baptism ceremony as I had to fulfill some office responsibilities then. Achayan had written to express his displeasure towards me for that. When I went home during the next vacation, I went to Paravur and met everyone there. Whenever I went to Coimbatore or Paravur to see Babu or Thresyamma, I returned only after giving a small amount of money in their hands. That was to help the children with their studies, Babu's expenses, or other retail needs of the family.

This close cooperation between brothers was not known to many. I never tried to convince anyone.

I always thought that what was given might not be enough, and Babu was always grateful for what he got. I knew Thresyamma sometimes thought that what she got from me was too meagre. Isn't that why my Kochuppappan asked me - "Aren't you doing anything to help Babu's children and Thresyamma?" It became clear that it was because someone had misinformed Kochuppappan as such. Where should we move around and try to correct others' perceptions?

Whenever Ramachandran came to Bangalore, he would find time and run to Leelamma's fish curry prepared with Kuttanadan kudampuli (Garcinia gummi-gutta). I come for work in Bangalore every time, either before staying at the Star Hotel or returning from work in Bangalore.

Before returning home, Ramachandran gave us the order every time: "After my marriage, you, Nasrani, should come to Palakkad with your family and stay with me like a brother."

Ramachandran was married for four and a half years and had two children when, one day, he said, "Nasrani has not come home yet." Then I responded to him by saying that I had decided to land in Coimbatore by flight and take a taxi to Palakkad on my way home next time. Going by train, Palghat station comes too early before dawn, and it is a nuisance every time that dissuades us from getting down at Palghat.

That was how we boarded a flight to Coimbatore in December, along with Tony, Nita, and Seema. It was my first flight on Indian Airlines.

Ramachandran had arrived in Coimbatore in a taxi. We happily spent four or five hours with his family, a Singapore-born wife, and two small kids. When asked about his wife's indifferent attitude sometimes, Ramachandran changed the subject by hiding his innermost sorrows and saying, "Let's say that later." We said goodbye and continued our journey home.

Thankamma, the daughter of Peramma of Kainakari, who went to Thovalai near Kanyakumari, has lived in the hilly region of Nedumkandam (in the Idukki district) since her marriage. Thankamma's daughter Shiji was a schoolgirl when her mother brought her to my home at Vaishyambhagom for a stay and schooling. She attended school in Vaishyambhagom. When Shiji did not go to school, she stayed home with my mother and helped her. In March 1990, Shiji passed her Class X examination. My mother had written to me that she was waiting to return to Nedumkandam with her mother.

We went home during the summer vacation in April. Since the children were small, my parents had insisted that we go there and show the kids to them at least once a year during the school holidays. During the summer holidays, children also wanted a change from the boringly monotonous routine of continuously going to school for a year. They were also looking out for freedom from the restrictions of city life. They knew that if they chose the village, there would be no scarcity of places to run. Going to the village was a temporary relief to all. Apart from getting love and affection from the grandparents, children loved a change and vacation to the village home. Adults and children could play together if there is a lack of peers in the village. So, Babu and I went to play cricket with Tony. He made a folk bat out of coconut palm fronds and wicket stumps of bamboo or pegs. The ball is made of rubber; it does not injure the body, so the batting pads were unnecessary.

Adults who play with children often try to teach them the necessary skills. Is that why I hit the ball for a sixer and smashed the house window? Not once, but twice!

Then 'we' told the kids not to hit like that and break the glass!

Even a better-experienced lesson is to 'play with them, let them move on. It is not suitable to pretend to be superior to another person.

When we returned to Bangalore after our leave in 1991, we took my mother with us as we had started living in the new quarters. There were more rooms and amenities where my mother could be happy, too.

Raju handed over to Achayan the entire amount of Rs. 12000 /- that he could save from his salary till then to complete the unfinished house in Vaishyambhagom. Thus, the remaining work of the house was completed. The toilet was built elsewhere outside the home. The jetty to the ravine was paved with stone, making it convenient to wash and fetch water.

On 17, 1988, Raju's wedding was scheduled. He went home on leave before the betrothal. According to Achayan's instructions, I went to Pulimkunnu and saw the bride for Raju and their family. The ceremonies were concluded very well. After the wedding day reception, Raju and Tess went to Pulimkunnu. About two weeks later, they came to Raju's place of work in Bangalore, Kolar.

Everyone woke up in the morning to the sound of an autorickshaw coming and stopping in front of our quarters block in CV Raman Nagar.

Raju and Tess arrived in Bangalore after their wedding. Seema saw Raju's Uncle and could not recognise him immediately. His size, shape, dress, and hairstyle have slightly changed. She realised these changes could happen when the wedding ended, and the relatives' hosting parties for them were over. The kids saw the new fashion waves, even in his haircut and the style of dressing up. After thoroughly exchanging pleasantries and having Leelamma's special breakfast, I went to the office and took the children to their school.

Everyone needs not to be told every time, especially about how you raise a family and how to search for a rented house, etc. The usual step is to start taking advice from the elders and collaboratively consult with them about where to start, how to start, what to do, and when to start. Everybody does that, and nobody starts doing it on their own. What are the essentials to be arranged to start a family life? Don't the couple understand everything about each other as soon as they start living together?

Most couples talk to each other freely while planning with their elders. It was like that even when I moved eleven houses in Pune. There was no need to say anything with additional emphasis to each other for some of the moves.

Should the elders take the initiative for it, or did those who had reached maturity get married and take the vow to live happily ever after in happiness and sorrow?

I had Achayan's suggestion to do what was needed, but I was also waiting for Raju to take the initiative. If you take the initiative without waiting, some may wonder if I was in a hurry to leave or let them go. Or else -

Should I remind him that "Achayan has suggested that I should give him the support he needs and that he should tell his elder brother what he needs from him, and I should be taken along "?

"When are you moving to your new place? Should I buy everything you need and bring home milk (to boil on the stove) for the housewarming?"

From a young age, there was never a habit of asking for love, affection, and consideration. Then, thinking that Achayan had suggested it, I called him and asked. "What's your plan? When are you moving to Kolar and joining for the job? Why are you not talking about anything?" A hot rain of words was pouring out of my quick-tempered mouth. Even when it was raining, it seemed to be essential. Or else why all this neglect or contempt from you?

When the misunderstandings were talked out and over, and the voice and mind calmed down, the necessary cooperation came automatically, saying that we would never see such petty neglect again —we were not blaming or confessing. The relics of a bygone era, the generation, can only be seen retrospectively.

We had to spend an entire day in Kolar to turn the dilapidated company quarters into a liveable house, where all the previous occupants had left the rooms painted the 'patterns'(Kolangal). The electric bulbs, which provided only candlelight, were first replaced. Everywhere, washing and cleaning, including the overhead water tank, were done. The Sacred Heart was installed.

"Every family should be a beacon of faith," I remembered what Ammachi used to say every time I looked at the picture of Sacred Heart. Then, it became a lovely home for at least two people to live in, like the nest for the regenerated ones. Our attempts to go to Kolar town to buy furniture failed. Still, we purchased other essentials, kept them in the quarters, and later returned to our quarters.

We went out again to plant a family in Kolar. The priest came and blessed the house and boiled the milk, and Raju started living with Tess near his office in Kolar.

We bought the cot after a hot bargain, which I lost. That was due to a lack of planning earlier. I would have walked out if I had not remembered the couple's discomfort of sleeping on the floor.

From time to time, they visited us in Bangalore.

**Family on the occasion of the Wedding of Babu & Thresiamma**

**Raju and family**

**Top: Babichan and Family**
**Bottom: Enjoying the wedding meal: KT Antony (Babichan) & Tessy**

# 63

# Fire in the Chest

As Kuriachan had previously offered, Seema received a packet of the latest books published by the Children's Book Trust, a few bars of caramel chocolate, and a diary for me. The following was written with Kuriachan's signature on the Junior Encyclopedia of Science book.

"Dear Seema, try to overcome if your reading finds any 'Seema' (border).

Seema to reading is seema to learning; otherwise, there is no such seema.

So, keep reading. Indeed, not those who come on the road you walk by.

One who reads learns. One who understands teaches, and one who teaches understands better.

God be with you all the way. Yours Sd / - January 23, 1989.

Seema wrote below - Thank you, Uncle.

I have hardly any words to say – 'Seeing and remembering all this brings so much joy to mind.'

My colleague Bhaskaran wrote about it. Kuriachan met Bhaskaran in DGAQA office in Delhi. The packet containing the books, etc., was handed over. His wife brought the packet from Delhi to Bangalore via Mumbai.

Tony, Nita, and Seema were delighted, and so were we. Seema immediately began to write a reply, and four or five days later, she searched and found it and sent it to Kuriachan.

They were not old enough to understand Kuriachan's unconditional love. Sometimes, I used to say this to my children. "It is not money, but the will to share that makes a person rich." I cited Kuriachan as an example.

Books have always been a source of joy for my children. They found time and read more and grew up.

Seema started writing a reply to Kuryachan, addressing him as a loving and close paternal uncle. In the innocence of childhood, Seema wrote –

"I like the books and the caramels. I liked most the Jesus story books.

Mommy is making straw curtains; Daddy is washing clothes in the machine; Chachan is reading mystery books; Chechy is reading the Arabian Nights".

Seema wrote down her marks and explained that she had only gotten half a mark less in some subjects.

"We would get only 24.5 out of 25 for Hindi, English, Science etc. I got the full 25 for Maths only."

The light was in a child's mind who wanted to see the horizon, and Kuriachan could read her clean writing on the ruled pages using a pencil. She requested Kuriachan's uncle to come to Bangalore - What she wrote was -

"So sometimes we could go to your house and stay there for some time!"

February 11, 1989: When I woke up from a deep slumber that lasted forty-three years, as the transparent light of dawn passed through the window panes, she was standing there with a cup of tea and a hearty smile, wishing me many happy returns of the day.

After drinking tea, while I was looking through the newspaper that came in handy, I noted that Tony said, "Daddy, happy birthday and many happy returns of the day," and walked away quickly. Nita drew a picture and noted down the words of greetings. As I was getting ready for the office, I saw Seema drawing something on paper on the balcony. Seeing me, she was trying to hide it. And then she came soon after and said 'Many Happy Returns of the Day, with an underscored line and an innocent smile, and there I could see her Mom and Dad standing together in the picture -

"She drew me, and I look like a big mango fruit." Mommy reacted instantly when she saw it.

Mom was in a sari, and Dad was in pants. They have always painted us together.

It was another irrelevant birthday. I, too, wanted to say something like Nita, who sometimes said - 'Mommy, I forgot my birthday. At least this time, we will celebrate.' What a fantastic way the children and their Mom have celebrated my birthday. The children might have seen the roots of their existence on my birthday. Leelamma was at the fullness of femininity. How old are you? I guessed the difference between forty-six and eighty-nine. "Happy birthday". In a soft and close embrace, the calculations have all gone wrong! I was getting late to the office.

Babychan had arrived from Hubli for a short visit, the first after he got employment in the Railways. He came to the Resurrection church and then walked down to the quarters. Babychan got a job after writing an examination on the railways, and his first assignment was in Hubli. Less than a month has passed since joining there. It was no hard job. After a while, he could relocate to Bangalore or Kerala. Raju also encouraged him to write the examination when he got a suitable opportunity.

We ate the cutlets, specially prepared for the occasion, late in the evening after the rosary. Someone felt that Tony's forehead was warmer than usual. Then Mommy panicked. After giving him the fever pill, Mommy ate as much as the pill. Waiting for the heat to subside, she lay asleep with her hands on his forehead until morning.

Babychan went to Kolar in the morning to see Raju. Raju had arranged a party for his colleagues after he got married, and his brother was joining him. By evening, Tony's fever had increased a little. I went to the dispensary near the quarters and saw the doctor. He said monitoring at night and tests in the morning were required. If necessary, he would arrange medicine for typhoid from the polyclinic.

Even if we had been called to the party, at least among the hosts at Kolar, it would not have been possible to go. That was another matter.

Leelamma said something with expressions of sadness as she lay next to Tony, thinking of something.

"Babychan came here first after he got a job. He didn't even bring a toffee or bar of chocolates for the kids."

Achayan taught me many things, as well as he did my brothers. If they forgot it, how can I remind them about it? There is a limit to all that can be said.

Kuriakose, a friend at MES, showed more intimacy and love than a brother. What did he come up with? Without asking anything, I said, "Leelam, it is life. If you give, you will get in Kollam! You will never get it at home. No prophet has any dignity in his (country) home. Don't expect anything so that there will be no sorrows."

It was unacceptable for sreemathi to change the subject by telling some jokes.

"He didn't get the opportunity to buy chocolate on his way here; why don't you think like that."

Tony's blood sample laboratory tests showed he had an enteric fever. Medications were given. By 5 p.m., the fever had dropped by half a degree. Anxiety continued unabated.

He was breathing rapidly. Meanwhile, Tony reminded me of Xerox copies of the historical monuments and places he wanted for his class project. The weariness of things that were not moving as expected was reflected in some words. Later, I felt that it was not expressed at the right time. As my frustration and the untimely rain subsided, so did Tony's fever. It turned out that the last night was better than the previous four nights. Leelamma telephoned the next day and reminded me that I should get the reports and show them to the specialist on that day.

I had to face a more stressful strategy than usual in the office. I returned from the office with the satisfaction of having done a job well, firmly declaring that I could not override the suggestion of the engine designers in the interest of safety. A little love was poured out for the children. "If you're happy about a new success you've had, a little love will make your happiness even brighter," I remembered reading it somewhere.

I was pretty unclear about going to Shivajinagar and seeing a specialist. What if the doctor was on leave? It was necessary to go to the office. I went to the office. Even when I reached there, there was enough confusion prevailing that the quality of the aircraft was questionable.

Between the deliberations in the office, I could find time and quickly went to see a specialist at Shivajinagar. He remained on leave, with no one to replace him. By the time I got back to the office, the pressure from above was at its peak. The high-ranking officer took me with him to understand the technical issues. We went for lunch together, but I was not in the mood to have a fill; therefore, it was cut short.

When he returned home, the severity of Tony's illness could be read from Leelamma's eyes and face, and obviously, there was no relief!

It was immediately decided that reliance on CGHS was sufficient for my son's health care.

Before going to Amarjyoti, I spent moments of helplessness in solitary prayer before my beloved Sacred Heart. I did not know that tears flowed down my cheeks and fell onto the ground. I was determined to only return with Tony – 'this stranger, my son!

I am writing about a month when the fire in my chest was my food. No family will ever forget such struggles, conflicts, and worries. We will never forget it. Anyone can ever face such situations and anxieties. Then, we should not give up the courage and confidence of the mind, even for a moment. That would be the power and the motivation to live. Those are the lessons learned.

Dr Santhosh Kumar of Amarjyoti said – there was no need to panic. X-ray and screening were over. Dr Kumar calmly said - Pleurisy, i.e., fluid in right lungs.

"It would help if you admitted him so we could syringe the fluid. What do you say?"

Thoughts that suddenly ran through my mind were about the resource crunch. A lot of money would be needed. It could be arranged anyway. I must go ahead, and I agree to the suggestion immediately. Tony was hospitalised there. Early in the morning, I went to the office and asked my friend Janardhan to help by giving me a loan of a thousand rupees. And he gave a thousand, with conditions.

"March salary will be paid only on April 1, and the amount should be repaid on the salary day."

"Yes, I will."

Percy came with the car, and I returned to the hospital."

Janardhanan and Percy are my colleagues in the office.

Leelamma, by the side of Tony's bed, asked me, "Didn't Raju come?" Leelamma left the little girls alone at home and told Uncle Nath and Uncle Sood about her coming to the hospital. Their children were there to give them company.

"It's been two days only since we wrote to everyone. Not only that, nobody knew

that he had been hospitalised. It does not matter; we have many friends here to help."

In the morning rush, I forgot that today was Nitamol's birthday. There was no way to celebrate because of Tony's illness. Because there were no greetings from us, Nita said after a few days, "Mommy, I forgot my birthday. At least let Chachan come home; next week, we will celebrate. Nitinol was happy when she got a hug and a kiss on her forehead.

The doctor came late at night and wrote down the history and concerns about Tony's illness.

"Pleurisy is attributable to Pneumonia or Tuberculosis." When I opened my heart to the doctor and talked about the stress, my ignorance about the procedures in the hospital was apparent. I lay down beside Tony. The night was long. In silence, I heard the doctor saying the same thing repeatedly. "Hopefully, we will test it. We will syringe out tomorrow."

Dr Santosh Kumar performed a pleurisy tapping procedure to remove fluid from Tony's lungs the following afternoon. The doctor was confused; he only got air from the bag and nothing else!

The doctor said that the medication would continue, and another x-ray and another test to see if there was TB, so let us see tomorrow.

In the beginning, he said one week for all the necessary procedures. Several tests were performed. Three days more passed again.

Gave prescriptions for new drugs, which were purchased and provided. They were still doing the testing tomorrow!

I was going through fire and water.

In the evening, Tony was in more pain. He was frequently coughing.

The doctor came. "Perhaps you must take him to St John's.... No, you take him." He quickly wrote a letter. For a moment, I could not breathe in that cold environment. Then I phoned Percy to come with the car. The doctor took the phone from my hand and said, "Wait, let me screen him again."

Leelamma came and looked anxiously.

I could not hold out much longer and shared the concerns with Leelam after failing to hide them.

By then, the doctor had done the screening and came and spoke. "There is no need to rush. It is only the spasm, no leak, no dripping down". I did not know what he was trying to say. I had nothing else to say.

"I leave it to you, doctor."

The tension disappeared into the hot air. Tony's face also showed less difficulty. It was also reflected in Leelamma's face.

Pain and difficulty were seen on his face only when coughing. Because it was Sunday, Tony's friends, school teachers, my friends in my office, neighbours in the quarters, neighbours on 208 Double Road, and many others came to see Tony. Tony was happy. Eighth-standard girls came together. The "Get Well Soon Card" they gave Tony reflected their true love, affection, and concern. It read -

"You're sick? I can't believe it.

I've finally found something you do that I don't like.

Dearest Tony, we hope you will get well soon.

From the girls of VIII Std, with love. "

When the doctor came for the daily rounds the next day, Tony looked unusually happy. I realized he intended to attract the doctor and make him believe everything was normal. It was to think that everything was right. Still, the fever was more than usual, but the pain and cough were less. He had heard me tell the doctor about my worries and stress. The only way to go home and get more medicine and rest was to communicate with the doctor face to face, with eyes, and so on. The doctor gave hope.

"After I screen him again in the evening ...... let's decide."

Tony was happy. The doctor picked me up and went to the consulting room as I left. He calmly explained -

Between two days ago and today, I did not find any difference. We can only assure you that nothing got worse!

"Infection is there without fever but pain. I am giving the best Injection. Injection started today. After five days, if it does not improve, a year-long treatment for TB is needed. It must work. No other possibility."

The expert doctor defined the limitations that were best known to him. The situation was getting worse — a total confusion. I was almost tempted to inquire if you are trying different medications. I felt like dirt dripping from my feet. There is no possibility of even thinking about going home. How do we decide on the best treatment if the disease is undetected?

Raju and Tess came from Kolar. Well, they were done. The letter was received today only. They would have found something by themselves to cook and eat when they came home. Seema and Nita came with them to the hospital to see Tony. They must have felt lonely since their 'Chachan' was not there to play, eat, and laugh with them. The separation would help bring them closer together.

Tony was cheerful when the doctor came for the rounds in the morning. The doctor himself said the question and the answer.

"Do you want to go home? Yes, I will send you in the evening."

Then we waited for the evening to come. I returned to the office quickly with my pocket full of money and hoped to be home in the evening after discharge. When I arrived at the hospital, what I saw was not anticipated. The situation has changed!

Tony vomited, followed by shortness of breath. The doctor came quickly and checked up. He took out the letter he had written earlier. He said, "Go, Visit Dr Nityananda Shetty at St. John's Hospital at 9 a.m. "They have better facilities".

Suddenly, I came downstairs and arranged for the car to go to St. John's in the morning. On the way back to the hospital steps, two or three nurses who had just finished their day shift were going out after duty, and they told me –

"The doctor was looking for Tony's dad upstairs; see him now, hurry up. He said Tony should be taken to St John's immediately."

It was a terrible shock. What happened? Is the condition getting worse? I couldn't believe it—my head was getting frozen. I was running to the doctor. Leelamma was sitting next to Tony without saying anything. I was in great pain!

"Leelam, we can arrange a car to go to St. John's." She inquired which vehicle was now available. When I turned around, I saw Tony's teacher standing in front- Mrs Kurien. When I looked at her, she immediately responded, saying her car was available.

"Who will drive? "

"I can ride." Mrs Kurian volunteered.

Without expressing helplessness, the doctor absolved himself of responsibility for a moment, wrote off the discharge summary, and then comforted me by saying – "You come later. I can reduce the charges here."

I did not reply. I said in my mind – 'This could have been done a little earlier, Doctor,' I thanked him and left anxiously.

My prayers to the Sacred Heart and the determination in my mind were repeated.

As soon as we arrived at St. John's, Tony was admitted. St. John is a large hospital with many facilities, modern medical equipment, and expert doctors.

Mrs Kurian waited until after the doctor came, examined Tony, and left. Dr. Nityananda Shetty said –"Hello Tony, how are you? ...You are a smart boy, a big boy. Come on. Get up and walk. Good!"

Tony stood up and walked over. The sadness on his face changed, and pleasantness was visible. Immediately after, the doctor performed a pleural tap on him. The doctor concluded-

"There is no puss or fluid. It is only the Pneumonia remaining. Only a broad-spectrum antibiotic can work now- 4 hourly I.V. of Gentamicin injection and Benzyl Penicillin. Tony, eat well and have a sound sleep—good night" (23:50 Hrs).

We all ate well, and Tony slept. On the side bench, me too. It was a different night. Gone are the painful nights. A green light could be seen nearby. Mrs Kurian dropped off Leelamma and Raju at 12:30 after midnight at the quarters.

64

# The Green Light

The following day, Tony was very calm; he woke up early and strolled back and forth in the room. I thought Leelamma would make breakfast early and bring it to the hospital. Someone would be there to pick her up with their vehicle, as we had a few close friends ready to help.

I walked around the hospital and its surroundings, mainly to familiarise myself since I was coming there for the first time. On the second floor, I saw an impressive chapel.

I went upstairs and prayed there for a minute. The nun told me the schedule for the holy Mass and the way to the pharmacy. Tony ordered breakfast by himself and ate it when I returned to the room. There was a canteen. I saw Leelamma and Raju leaving the office car while I was looking out after drinking a coffee.

After that, there was a stream of visitors occasionally: Tony's friends, friends in my office, teachers at school, neighbours in the quarters, neighbours on 208 Double Road, and many more, until the evening. And it was the same in the following days. Friends arranged transportation for Leelamma and Raju to come and go every day. One day, Raju came to the hospital with Babychan, who had returned home.

Medication and care continued for Tony. Even though the initial medicines were changed to another, the fever and cough did not disappear. On the third day, he vomited and had some mucus.

"It's okay, daddy," Tony said.

When the doctor came, he said, "Good. The cough and fever will continue for another three days. Then, it will settle. He tapped Tony on the shoulder and said -

"You can read any book."

The doctor asked with a smile as he left the room-

"Has your mommy brought you a feeding bottle?"

"Hope she may not," Tony replied.

Among the books that Raju brought with him when he came on the following day was "The Seven-Per-Cent Solution- A Sherlock Holmes - Watson Story."

Tony opened the book, and he read out -

Holmes said - "All things come to those who wait, Watson."

There were more inquiries in the days that followed. Tony was taken for a CT scan and X-ray.

At ten o'clock at night, Dr Shetty came and said -

"All investigations show that pneumonia is confirmed by upper abdominal ultrasound. It may be a week before Tony can become all right. Since I will be away for two days, Dr Krishna will look after Tony."

The next day, Tony's hand was poked with several needles for the thirty-eighth injection while the nurse tried to find a vein. Tony was in tears and pain and got angry at the nurse. The nurse explained that this is the Injection of CP ten penicillin – the soldiers that fight the pneumonia virus. The needles had made a lump in his wrist. Tony commented - "They must be drunken soldiers going elsewhere instead of veins."

Leelamma came in the evening to stay with Tony through the whole night in the hospital. I used that opportunity to go to the quarters in the new car bought by Kuriakose.

Seema and Nita were happy. We ate together. Almost a month later, I was able to see their schoolwork. I wrote letters to relatives. Spending the night with the little ones on either side was tricky. The kids slept early. Sometimes, I told Tony, "I shall run away if you cough again." It was one of those moody times when I would endlessly monologue with myself. Today, Tony and his mommy spending the night together in the hospital bed would be a change for the better.

Office work sometimes had reached home and the hospital. My colleagues and officials in the office always cooperated with me.

Vinay was Tony's classmate and friend. Vinay could sometimes be heard calling Tony 'DD.' Usually, friends keep some secrets among themselves. When Vinay came to the hospital to see Tony, it made him even happier.

Tony woke up at one o'clock in the night and had some biscuits and coffee, and after that, he slept well. At six-thirty, the altar bell in the chapel rang, announcing that it was time to receive the Holy Eucharist. It was 01 March. With folded hands and prayerful thoughts, Tony also received the Holy Eucharist.

The doctor came and assessed the progress. He disclosed his analysis to us to avoid worrying about anything else. He intended to make us confident and indicate that our comfortable path was further away.

"It appears that some fluid is there. The fluid will get absorbed if he does not get a fever for another day. If not, we must remove it and send it for culture. Then, we can decide on the right antibiotic. The present one may not have been effective. Perhaps there might be a mistake. But there is nothing to worry about. It may take a little more time. I understand he has been ill for a month and has missed school, exams, etc. Anyway, he will be all right. Eat well, whatever, no restrictions, Okay."

They continued monitoring the fever for the next three days. Abraham spent a whole day in the hospital helping Tony. Another day,

Raju came and supported him. Leelamma visited and went back to look after the children. More books were brought. The bills for each week came in as routine. I have also spent some time reading books. Most of the time, I sought ways and means of financial sources to pay the weekly bills.

Tony's condition remained stable, but the fever was found to be high once a day, daily for the next four consecutive days, a baffling behaviour. The normal condition was restored for four to five hours. After about 20 hours, the fever started rising again. Thus, like a drunkard who was utterly addicted to alcohol, he had fallen asleep and calmed down; it was total discomfort if not drunk. What a test phase it was. Even the doctors were confused.

Tony's mommy started crying and groaning, saying, "Mother Mary, the fever is getting worse."

Tony said, "Mommy, fever is not a disease. It's an indication of disease."

The inquiry into whether any assistance could be obtained through CGHS continued. But it was only a proclamation that all the rules were obeyed literally, but there was no intense action. There were no humanitarian considerations beyond that. No one understands the plight of a junior government official. It was indeed a cruel bureaucracy with no mercy. It was a private hospital, so it appeared no help was to be given!

Isn't medical ethics the same for private doctors and government doctors? Didn't everyone make the same Hippocratic oath and accept the job? What is the use of such cruel laws without humanitarian considerations? What cruelty! Your dedication to service, or patriotism, will not get you anything in return. Is this called democracy?

The following Sunday, the doctor passed the needle three times and tried to exhale the pleurisy fluid from Tony's lungs. Even the best thoracic surgeon showed his frustration. After a few seconds, he withdrew, tired, and gave the instructions.

"I don't want to prick anymore, enough. Take out the I.V. of CP. Buy Sporidex 500mg Capsule."

All other medications were discontinued. On Sunday, all the pharmacies were closed. I had to go to a far-off place and buy the capsules. After wandering alone for two or three hours, I got the medicine. When Raju came, he had a share of my anxiety and frustration. I was not in the mood to say anything more.

I sat on the back of my friend's scooter and drove home. When the information was shared with Leelamma, I saw that Mother's eyes had turned red. I was helpless.

The next day, I waited long for the doctor to come. Widal test results to determine the onset of TB were negative. Until then, Tony's condition had been stable for the past 40 hours. The temperature remained normal, and there was no fever. Brightness was all around; the light on everyone's face slowly reappeared. When the doctor came, he saw a look of optimism on Tony's face.

"I thought we'd keep him for a day more."

He read the pathetic look on my face through the unshaven facial hair.

"Okay, you go today. But take care, have no relapse, rest, and eat good food. You may take a bath and go to school after a few days. No exertion for a few days. There is no TB, as we doubted. The fever should not have gone so suddenly if it was not so. Don't carry any notion such that, Tony, you were also afraid of it, weren't you? Even if so, it is curable. The fever could not have gone without anti-TB drugs.

So, no worry, eat good food; Tony should be like this, like a muscled man, he gestured. I will write it as Pneumonia with Pleurisy; that is it. Please come and meet me if he develops a fever. "

I called Leelamma and told her what the doctor had said. After 36 days of fighting, Tony returned home victorious. Upon hearing the discharge, friends came with the car. A six-month salary was paid at St John's. When I went to the pharmacy to buy medicine for another five days, they gave me 15 samples of Sporidex capsules for free.

A friend's (TS KANI) wife was admitted to another hospital for surgery and specialist treatment. As it was on our way home, we went there and saw them and later continued our journey.

Leelamma and I repeated what we usually do when we return home after travelling somewhere by looking at the Sacred Heart and whispering the word of thanks. We hugged with wet eyes. I remembered many friends who came to me with support and cooperation in overcoming a significant crisis in our lives and prayed for their well-being.

Nita and Seema had written a colour poster saying "Welcome Dear Chachan" at the entrance. Tony's room was decorated with flowers and colour pictures, and the study desk was decorated with a beautiful welcome, much to Tony's delight. They displayed a selection of decorative photo frames, books, and coloured pencils, perfect for displaying their favourite memories.

"**W**hen you

**E**nter this

**L**ittle room

**C**onsider yourself

**O**ne of the special

**M**embers of a group who

**E**njoys working and learning together."

Tony was thrilled and amazed at their expressions of love; in return, they could find the power to face the crises on Tony's face and hear the expression of Hurray!

Hoping for the end of an era when the mind was more troubled, we thanked God and men, slept, woke up, and began to pay more attention to official matters.

The year-end exams in Tony's class were already over. The class teacher and school authorities announced that Tony had been promoted to the next class. Their sublime expressions of love and care made everyone happy.

After a long time, Thambichan and Leelamma telephoned. They called Patro from Orissa, who is staying in our neighbourhood, and introduced themselves in the Oriya language.

Purely personal interests, self-loathing, or sadness from mutual dissatisfaction have long disturbed us and kept our relationship apart. We sat quietly without seeing each other at the two ends of a telephone line as if a storm had calmed down and the storm of family relationships and minds had subsided. The mind and earth cooled like the first rain of summer. Satisfied with swallowing grains of wet sand, the snakes returned to their dens.

As Tony's illness changed, the relationships returned to normal. Thus, Tony's condition helped revive the privileged couple's family relations in both families without expiring. It created an excellent opportunity to forget and forgive everything of the tasteless past.

It was a testing time of hard work in the office, like family responsibilities, and utilizing one's ability to fulfill them satisfactorily within one's limitations.

Efforts to ensure the aircraft's quality were seen as creating more obstacles by some in their easy path for those working towards completing production. They can be left astray and lose the right direction if left unmanaged. I have learned that the right and safest way was to follow the rules freely and in order. We needed more working hours, and we knew we would face difficulties. However, the only way to achieve the goal was to understand the problems, analyse them, and find suitable solutions for ensuring the safety and quality of the aircraft. It was acceptable for the bosses to understand and take responsibility for themselves. They always stood by and supported our efforts. I was proud and happy to have AV Ramaswamy as my boss.

Raju and Tess went home for Easter. The Babychan was transferred to a place near Kolhapur by railway service. Babychan wrote that he started living in a house with colleagues, cooking, and eating. He was starting to live alone in other places away from home. How many more places does he have to travel and live in? That was the way many people learn and move forward in life.

Promotions in government jobs were more dependent on the higher officials' efficiency rather than the individuals' capabilities. It does not depend on the employee's efficiency or key performance indicators. Most existing rules promote working individuals' incompetence, indifference, and laziness. Even if someone initiates periodic changes in the law, the bureaucracy will thwart such attempts by injecting their selfish interests. Maintaining a sense of relentless justice is not desirable for those who thrive in positions of power. The general impression is that the law has no eyes, but law enforcers may have. The lack of compassion in the officials' sense of justice often makes some people fall prey to the ruthless. The tendency to react to injustice must be innate; therefore, sometimes, I have responded inadvertently. Eventually, it was all stopped. The policy was adopted in the later years.

Knowledge will give you power, but the character only gives you respect. Respect authority. When you gain knowledge, you get more respect and authority.

When I did not get the growth or promotion I deserved promptly, I accepted the above policy and continued to work sincerely. Realising my responsibilities would be faithfully executed, the superiors entrusted me with several more responsibilities. I got a promotion more than seven years after entering the service. I have been doing my superior's job regularly. So, for promotion, I did not have to change the location. I did not change the chair I was sitting on when I got the promotion, except that I cleaned it thoroughly.

As I feared, my name was not on the officers' annual relocation list this time. But it has been widely discussed that the relocation lists would come again, and my name would appear there. I was told that if I let the authorities know where I wanted to get transferred, they might consider it seriously.

Tony wanted us to move to a dry land area as the doctor who treated him prescribed. He agreed to leave Bangalore because he knew one of his favourite teachers was leaving. Leelamma wanted us to return to Pune because it was a place where we could get a good education, get the weather favourable, get quarters, and make many good friends.

When Pune and Nashik were suggested as priority places to relocate, Ramaswamy reassured me - "Such a change of place may not come this year. I might get it changed if it comes."

Trade unions are the medium of communication between workers and management worldwide. The main objective of the unions was to examine and unify the workers' grievances and present the needs to the management together and collectively. Managers who understand things and work for the ordinary good try to move forward by reaching a compromise through negotiations. In most places, a 'union' is voluntarily formed to benefit the workers and the common good.

That was how a petition and subsequent peace talks happened in my house. The three children met Mommy with a petition. Putting everything into action, the executive and the secretary of Management set a time for peace talks and informed every stakeholder. Everyone arrived on time.

The conference started as per the schedule. The senior student leader introduced the resolution. The Secretary explained things and invited suggestions. The resolution was passed unanimously without much discussion. 'All students receive a fixed amount of pocket money at the beginning of each month, which they can spend. The Secretary will sanction if more money is required for any particular purpose.'

It was great to see that our children have learned a good way of presenting union, leadership, and collective needs.

**Students at Bangalore Public School (1986)**

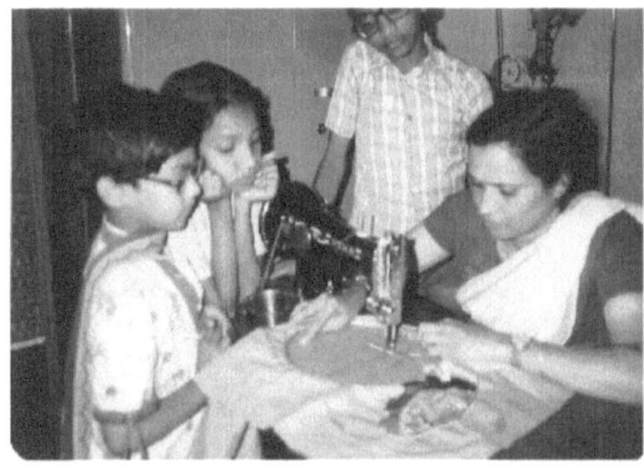

HARDWORKING MUMMY WATCHED BY HER CHILDREN

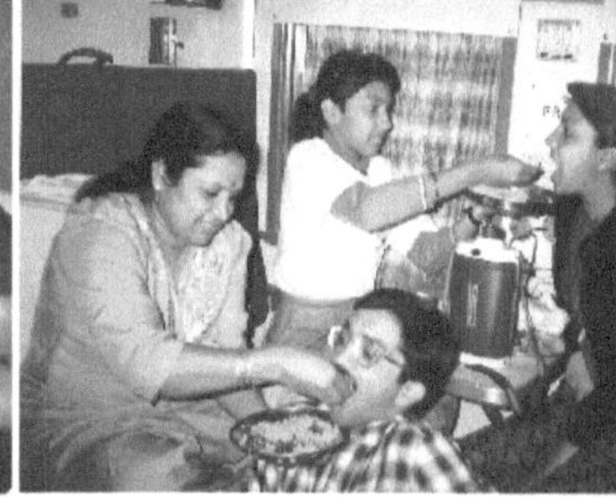

FEEDING SESSION AT SUNABEDA

FOURTH BIRDAY OF SEEMA @ D-9/4 QUARTERS

FRIENDS ASSEMBLED AT D- 9/4 SITTING FIRST ARE MATHEWS ACHAYAN, SARAMMA AMMACHI

**Leelamma was kept busy by her children and friends**

65

# The Ice Melts

Thambichan arrived in Madras on an official visit from Paradip and informed me by phone that he would like to go to Bangalore and Kolar. Krishnan of 'Roll Well' later called and said that Thambichan would arrive the next day.

Raju and Tess arrived on Sunday at 6 p.m. Raju told me three things in three minutes –

a) "He was going to Madras for training,

b) Tess was applying for a job at a school in Vaishyambhagom, and that

c) He was trying to relocate to HMT Kalamassery".

Being busy, he returned quickly! Saturday and Sunday were holidays. Three minutes later, they returned after seeing their elder brother and family on a Sunday evening. Great! It was enough to upset my mind's balance at that time. Then I thought - everyone may have their matters needing attention on priority. Why should one be concerned about it and spoil the peace of mind? There is nothing to do for me on all three matters he mentioned, either for the matter or against it!

Thambichan came on Monday morning. After a long time, we sat together and spoke at length. In Paradip, Leelamma was preparing to give birth to a baby again, and she was in the $16^{th}$ week of her pregnancy. Thambichan said the sign of pregnancy, the size of a pear, was now more visible to everyone. Two weeks back only, she had recovered from chickenpox.

The next day, Thambichan went to visit BEML in Kolar. Tony accompanied him. After visiting the factory, they visited Raju at his Kolar residence. They came back in the evening.

Managing Director of 'Roll Well' Krishnan had invited Thambichan and me for an evening dinner at a restaurant on MG Road. While having food there, Thambichan recommended hiring a person in Krishnan's company. He agreed to do so from May 15$^{th}$. In my mind, It was the request Ammini made to help Sunnichan while I was talking to Thambichan to recommend a job through Krishnan.

Eventually, Sunnichan, the eldest son of Ammini, who lived in Thovala, later shifted to Nedumkandam, and the daughter of Kainakari Peramma came to Bangalore.

I submitted a summary of one-year activities to the authorities as part of the annual evaluation of office work activity - as a yearly report of everyone was to be submitted every year in April. There was an extensive list of achievements and valuable contributions to describe during the last year.

An attempt was made to see if the government would reimburse the cost of the drugs used for Tony at St. John's Hospital. The health care of the persons and their families is included in the benefits to government employees. I went through many stages with a reasonable request for reimbursement of the medical expenses because of the declared benefits in mind. The bureaucracy, as inhuman as before, finally had the last laugh. It was for me to tolerate the humiliation and suffering; what else to do?

The children's examination results came as scheduled. I was happy. As usual, I checked the reports, like every year, chewing the chocolates with everyone at home.

— Tony was promoted to standard IX.

— Nita Progressed in regular study and was promoted to VI standard.

— Seema climbed to II standards with commendable success (rank 2). Seema's classmate ranked 1, got only four more marks.

They all showed their interest in learning. In limited facilities, they played and participated in extracurricular activities when convenient. Upon arriving at the quarters, they found more toys, equipment, playgrounds, and a garden nearby and used them.

Tony's final year at Bangalore Public School was in Std X. Due to the teachers' constant efforts and the student's hard work, the children achieved great success.

Nothing bothered Tony more than that of his parents. Tony always kept his head on his shoulders. He was intelligent and good at making appropriate decisions. Instead of acting on emotions or ideals, he was happy to see the situation with wisdom and realism.

Even before Tony's Std X (ICSE) examination, the National Talent Search Examination was announced every year by NCERT. At first, it was at the regional level. His confidence increased when he could make it to the top ten. Tony also participated in the All-India NCERT Final Examination held at the Indian Institute of Science Examination Center. He came after the exam and got behind the Silver Plus (Royal Enfield 50cc) Moped, and said -

"Daddy, I am hungry. Let us go home and have food."

"Okay. We are going now. How was your exam? Hope you wrote well."

"I did well. Let us wait and see."

Examination results came from NCERT, along with a letter and detailed terms and conditions. NTSE granted the scholarship to Tony and several other students all over India. Upon acceptance of the scholarship, a complete study in the plus two classes, any degree after that, and up to post-graduate studies, including the total fees, would be awarded as a scholarship.

Tony desired to study for Std XI & XII (Plus 2) in the National Public School; therefore, I bought the application form, filled it out, and gave it to their office along with a copy of the Std X Certificate. As a result of his respectable marks and the interview results, Tony got admission to Gopalakrishnan's school for the next two years.

Nita remained in Bangalore Public School till Std VII. She continued her Std VIII and IX at the St Ann's School, Ulsoor. The state syllabus was thought to be much easier for std X for Nita. She used to commute in the school bus run by the DRDO.

If the DRDO school bus was missed, she had to travel on the BTS bus to reach the destination and usually became late. Nita realised that living like that caused unnecessary psychological stress for her parents - sometimes even after getting a beating with a tiny stick.

At Std X (1993), Nita was placed in a hostel adjacent to the same school when I was transferred to Koraput. Nita remained in Bangalore for only one more year. Realizing the hardships of hostel accommodation and enduring a lot, completing the year was a great relief to Nita. When she succeeded in Std X, Nita earned a transfer certificate. She moved to Koraput and enrolled in Std XI at Sunabeda Public School.

Seema studied at Bangalore Public School till Std III. Seema also switched schools when Tony joined the National Public School. Seema studied at Sacred Heart Girls School for Std IV & V. When he moved to Koraput, she took a Transfer Certificate and joined Std VI at Vyomayana Samastha Vidyalaya, at Sunabeda.

# 66

# Children's Skills and Strategies

Tony's overall performance during both years at National Public Schools was satisfactory. Continuous reading, hard work, determination to achieve notable success, and time management efficiency helped him gain the desired result.

Simultaneously, he was preparing for the IIT entrance examination from Std XI onwards with the desire to study Computer Engineering. The notes for Brilliants' IIT Entrance exam were reviewed regularly. The entrance exam was also done well.

Every day was hopeful, but the kids spent most of the holidays reading books. We went home for two or three weeks and spent the time with my parents. The closeness and efficiency of the children made everyone at home very happy. We returned with many blessings for the children from my parents.

It was an ordinary day, and as per routine, I looked through the newspaper before going to the office. I saw an advertisement- "Applications are invited from students who expected a creditable pass in their plus two for the SIA-NOL Scholarship to study for a four-year degree course at Singapore University. A monthly allowance of $ 600 / -would be provided for food expenses and accommodation, and the course fees would be free.

After reading and learning the details, Tony desired to send the application. Copies of the certificates to be attached were made ready, and the application was sent within two to three days. He was waiting for the interview. All of us prayed and wished that if he got the scholarship, it would be a great blessing. There were many concerns to address, but our only thought was to let an attempt be made without further thinking about them and complicating the matters.

When a senior colleague, CP Anthony, went to Delhi and returned, he brought my transfer order to move out. It had been signed some six or seven days earlier.

"You have been transferred to Sunabeda, Koraput."

Will it be necessary to continue the children's education in a place known as the 'Onam Kera Moola' (the corner where the Onam festival will not reach) in Orissa? It would be a new school, new circumstances, and unfamiliar weather. Everyone who reaches there would like to go away from there. That was history. I must gladly accept the transfer and return it as soon as possible. That was the initial reaction, I thought. After seeing my nearest top official AV, Ramaswamy, I decided that all further deliberations would be fine.

It was the 'Vishu day'. I gave my transfer order received from Delhi to Ramaswamy, like a 'Vishu Kaineettam' (gift). After reading it carefully, he picked up the phone and called the top boss in Delhi without saying anything to me.He got the line after calling almost ten times in an hour and repeatedly tried without moving away from his seat during the hour. I could not believe Ramaswamy's patience and words to the highest official authority.

"Hello, Sir. Did you forget what I told you? There must be some distinction between donkeys and horses- one who does normal duties and one who applies his heart and soul. You transfer anybody from Bangalore. It is a personal request; Defer it for a year. Meanwhile, let me train someone on Jaguar. You are the boss... Okay... will write."

It was not enough to praise Ramaswamy's personality, humanitarian and merciful! After drinking Aunty's tea and saying thank you, I thought, 'Let it be as it would come; let the office decide.'

I reported the position to all my friends and colleagues. Janardhanan was the only one who reminded me about replacing the broken washbasin, which Seema had accidentally knocked down, before saying anything else on my transfer. Some friends are like that, but some are not so. If you like to call them friends, you must accept their positive and negative attitudes with coolness and a calm mental state, especially after a shock or disappointment or in a difficult situation.

The next day, the proposal to postpone my transfer was sent to the higher-ups with explanations and justification. Ramaswamy said to me "Keep working calmly. I will not fire you even if the boss says so."

Ramaswamy said he received a phone message from his boss while attending the annual dinner with the officials of the cooperating institutions in the evening. "There was a confirmation from HQs that there was no need to move this year."

The annual activity report was submitted the next evening and forwarded to the superiors regarding outstanding achievements.

On the following day, while laughing with friends in the office, the cold aromatic wind of praise, an unusual telephone call came in for me. It was Leelamma, and I listened intently.

"Seema went out of the house to play at 8:15 in the morning. It's 11:00 now, and she's not back yet. We looked everywhere in the complex but could not find her. I am scared."

The poor girl forgot everything, including breakfast, while playing with friends. We ran back and forth in search of her. "She didn't even come for breakfast." "Maybe playing with friends somewhere. Don't be afraid, and I'm coming there right away."

I quickly got home with my colleague Percy. Seema has not yet been located. Lots of friends were looking for her. Security instructions were sent to all the gates of the residential complex. Some fear and apprehension shook my mind. I prayed that nothing would happen.

When we decided to leave the information with the local police, we saw Seema in the same park where she first went to play. After playing with other friends, she went inside a nearby house and came out now.

The anguish turned into joy and the fear to great relief. Our minds are like the sky almost daily; sometimes clouds gather in with mixed emotions running, staying there for some time, and disappearing with time and wind. Sometimes, happiness, sadness, fear, contentment, emptiness, relief, anger, humour, warmth, love, helplessness, and despair. All tastes and expressions were contextualised. It's just that there are fluctuations in quantity.

I went to the school with Seema and collected books for the following year. On the way back, we visited Col. Subramanian and Aunty, who stayed in the house at 208 Binnamangala. It was a visit after nearly three months, and Aunty was thrilled. When Aunty asked, "Where did mommy go?" Aunty repeated the answer that Seema used to say in the younger days. "Mommy went to Thycassil."

She came out and hugged Seema and took her inside the house. While living there, Leelamma used to go to another neighbour's house nearby to learn to tailor. While doing so, it was Subramanian Aunty who always looked after Seema. Aunty has not forgotten it, and even Seema. She would take Seema and Nita with her, sit on the floor, and tell stories to them. Occasionally, Auntie would care for the children we left behind while going to a movie. Aunty had given them good food and comics to read—their closeness, humorous conversations, and caring and sharing disappeared when they went to the quarters. Col. Subramanian used to teach the French language to children. After retiring from military service, he would translate French writings and articles into English for those in need of them. After almost two years, the elderly couple moved out of 208 to an apartment in Jalavayuvihar, where their daughter Prema lived nearby in another flat.

Raju came and took Seema and Nita to Kolar during vacation time. We in the house felt a void when all the noise, rhythm, and chirping sounds suddenly stopped, though temporarily. That was why I called Raju two days later and asked him to return them; I did not know whether Raju misunderstood that. In 1988, Raju moved from Kolar to the C&AG office in Thiruvananthapuram. When Raju started going to the office in Thiruvananthapuram, Tess stayed with her mother in Pulinkunnu.

Tony grew up, and his delicate, light moustache that had first grown when he was thirteen was suddenly missing from his face one morning. He shaved. Clean upper lip raised suspicion. He was seen as embarrassed when asked. It could have stopped there. But with the help of some lies, he tried to justify what he did. I could not stand telling lies. I could not comprehend that he had not been sincere with me. I was always his friend, so I wanted him not to lie. He has the right to shape his face according to his will, but did he consider the consequences of doing it so early? Shaving a delicate moustache at a young age will become a thick black moustache and a more significant embarrassment during adolescence.

But my most important concern was something else. If you cannot say that you did this confidently, then what you did may not be appropriate. Whatever you do in secret and being reluctant to tell others is often a mistake. Therefore, stay away from doing such things. He admitted his mistake, and Tony considered what he heard was a lesson.

Tony chose a film for all of us to go together, and the film was - "Who Framed Roger Rabbit." We walked around the Vidhana Soudha in the morning and visited St.Mary's Basilica in Shivajinagar. We prayed in the church. In the afternoon, we came to Cubbon Park, sat around and ate the mommy's packed lunch from home, and again walked around the park until it was time to see the movie in a theatre. We all liked the film; it was a tremendous technological revolution combining cartoons and real actors.

When the school re-opened, the girls started going to school on the DRDO bus and Tony on the BTS bus.

67

# Transfer for All

I prepared a paper on 'Sealants for Aircraft Integral Fuel Tanks' to be presented at a national seminar in Bangalore and co-authored with Lokanatha, a scientist at Cemilac. What I learned from the aircraft industry, my work experience, and other publications I read from the library helped me write the paper. It resulted from some months of tireless efforts to present such a technical paper in the presence of eminent personalities. It has been included and published in my first book, Safety Follows Where Quality Leads. Congratulations were raised from the audience for presenting the topic well - especially the review of inappropriate material debris recovered from the fuel tanks. It was the forerunner of many authoritative papers presented during my service.

More challenging tasks came to me when everything in the office moved smoothly. A Jaguar crashed in Dharmapuri near Bangalore. I was nominated to be part of the team to investigate the accident. I was entirely behind on that task for about three months.

I went to the Naval Unit in Goa for aircraft-related work. I went to HMT, Kalamassery, to inspect a machine tool purchased by the Air Force. When I went to HMT, I remembered looking for a job with Thambichan 23 years ago. I went home one day after work in Kalamassery. Babychan had come home. He was supposed to go to Bangalore to pick up his sister-in-law. It didn't happen because of my trip to Goa. I went along with my mother to see Mercy's firstborn son not too many days after she gave birth. Thambichan, Xavier, Josekutty, and their families were all there. They were there occasionally together. Gracy and others came to help Mercy. The thought of moving out of the house in the middle of the paddy field and living near the ravine, the desire to move to another place after Babychan got married, and the shortfalls in agricultural farming income all seemed to cause minor problems in the interpersonal relationships there. Thambichan only said he was looking for a place for his parents to stay on the ravine shorefront. The comment that Ottathyckal Achayan shared with me was criticising his younger son. - "That 'bad guy' went to the field and sowed it on the day of the 'curse'- (moolam star) (The meaning of Moolam is root or the base. As we know, no plant can flourish without its roots; similarly, every event or happening in the world is associated with some reason at its very root. As the roots of the plants are not visible, this nakshatra indicates the deeply buried or hidden facets of one's life. Hence, Moolam nakshatra is associated with the end of life or events and a precursor to the new beginning. According to Hindu philosophy, he was an ardent follower.)

"He does not have the 'nature' to obey anyone!"

Within a month or two, the Ottathyckal family was re-planted to a new plot they found on the ravine shorefront and built a small house there. Leelamma never forgot that I brought her from the middle of the paddy field (island) to the ravine shore stretch of land to facilitate easy travel for her to the outside world! Occasionally, it was a joke we shared, but it was not wrong to say so.

Leelamma's brother Babychan and his family started living in a house built at Thundiyil Thommikutty's place.

Then, the whole vacation was spent waiting for the Std 12 (CBSE) exam, the school, and the students. The results came. The National Public School and its Std 12 students achieved notable success. All students passed with more than 90% marks in all subjects. What could be happier for teachers and parents than that? Tony was invited to participate in an interview conducted by the team sponsoring the SIA-NOL Scholarship immediately afterward.

No one needs to say that life combines peace, happiness, fear, anger, disgust, distress, interest, surprise, joy, occasional pain and rejuvenation, small suffering, despair, and hope. The taste and aroma of everything have been known, at least to a small extent, since childhood. It is a great power, and it is the capital. The strength to face whatever comes in large quantities is being rewarded daily by the one who controls everything. As Achayan wished and blessed me, the glorious words 'His son will be his helper' were fulfilled. This was the beginning, the foundation stones.

Everyone congratulated Tony on his outstanding achievement. The next day, he went to Chennai (by the time Madras was renamed) to attend an interview for the SIA-NOL Scholarship. I waited in the lobby of the Star Hotel in anticipation of good results. I saw a smile and optimism on Tony's face as he came down after the interview. He knew I would be eager to understand how the interview ended.

"It was lovely. It was very cheerful and encouraging.

Most of the interview questions were from the initial application's answer: to write a paragraph on the subject "What do you want to study, why, and where?".

(My fascination with computers, a career in this field, knowledge, and application with the ultimate aim of achieving a better standard of living for all humans....... Studies set me on the right track towards a career of challenge and excitement where my talents and aptitude are fully utilised.)

"They also asked me what agitation was happening in Gujarat nowadays."

"Narmada Bachao Andolan by Medha Patkar and group?"

"Yes, daddy. The General Public benefits from irrigation and electricity. But the large Dams cause damage to the environment and tribals.

(This was due to the close and long-term interactions between two communities (Adivasis & other indigenous peoples).

"What is the name you call for that relationship between two groups of people or communities? They asked, and I said – "symbiotic relationship."

One word was enough, and they must have rightly assessed Tony's reading and knowledge depth.

By the time Tony returned from Chennai to Bangalore, the courier had arrived. Tony opened the cover, read the letter, and shouted! "Yes. Got it! Hurray!"

The result of the IIT entrance examination also came within two or three days. Tony was offered a seat, a rank of 250. It would be best if you came to Madras IIT to choose the subject and study institution. Double sweet!

Tony gave the application for a passport on the first of June. City Police Commissioner Sreedharan, who lived in the neighbourhood, wrote a letter to the Assistant Commissioner of Police - "I have known Tony since he was young, and now, he is going to Singapore to study to get a scholarship. They sent the police verification report to the passport office. The passport arrived within ten days.

The medical test was completed on June 14 in Chennai.

In addition to cultivating a general awareness of all subjects, Tony's focus and dedicated effort were solely on the learning path leading to a computer-based career.

Therefore, we have reached a critical stage of making a decision. Children learn well and grow with their parents' interest. In such a situation, the courage and hope that the children give to their parents are invaluable. They enjoy it. Thanks to the blessings from the ancestors.

Achayan has said - "When children do their duty to their parents, those earthly deeds are always blessed by God."

Both are good ways of future growth, and we must choose one. Such a choice is always pleasing to any parent or guardian.

Should Tony be sent to a university in Singapore about which we have not heard much? None of the known people have experience with higher studies there. However, there is a scholarship available. Is it, not an honour to be able to study in one of the best IITs in India, which can be described as a rare privilege? Which one to choose?

Tony's clear answer was- "I asked for Computer Engineering at NTU University, Singapore, and they have agreed to give it. That's enough for me."

Even if you attend an interview at IIT, you may not get Computer Engineering. All the institutes have only 200 seats. The rank list will close at 250. "

Even if you get a merit seat at IIT Chennai, you must find a job after studying and searching for it. Soon after completing his studies at NTU, he may not be searching for a job elsewhere as he has to fulfill the condition that he must work in Singapore for six years.

The exact answers to the questions have been found. Doubts and doubts have no place anymore.

When Dr. Shetty at St John's Hospital asked Tony, "Has your mommy brought a feeding bottle?" In a similar situation, Leelamma's trembling voice came out -

"Should we leave our baby in another country, at this young age and far away?"

"My dear Leelam, Tony has grown up as an intelligent college student. He has the discernment to make decisions, give him good guidance, let him make decisions about his future, and decide what to study and where to study, etc." That was my reaction to the trembling voice.

Leelamma's fears, anxieties, and doubts are perfectly justified, and that's the feeling of a mother '. I made more inquiries; I had to.

Wise and informed friends will always make acceptable comments. Their comments were heard and pondered. He was working as a general manager in the HAL Aircraft Division, a well-read person who has travelled extensively, and he was there- Dr. Char. I went straight to him, saw him, and talked for half an hour with him. He removed all our fears and instilled a good deal of confidence in me. Good friends should be like that.

When you come home, share new information, and instill confidence, fears, and expectations, change everyone's minds. Tony wished to study in a reputed institution anywhere in the world, and let us wish him all the best. We thanked Sacred Heart for being able to decide. Those were the defining moments of my family's future.

Tony met Mommy alone and confidently asked about Mommy's opinion - "What do you say, Mommy ?"

Mommy said. - "Even if you study at IIT, you will have to look for a job after graduation, so don't you think that if you had studied in Singapore, you would have got a job without looking elsewhere? Mon studied everywhere, and Daddy and Mommy just wanted you to have a good job and be comfortable and happy. If you decide, it is acceptable to us. Our Jesus is with us. "

Then, it was the thought of fulfilling my desires. I firmly believed everything would happen as routine because my passion and determination were resolute and undaunted. Tony must go within a short period; he needs adequate money for the essentials and food. My savings are meagre. It was while sharing concerns that my colleague Benjamin suggested a way out.

He said- "Some friends would buy the shares and pay at the market rate within two days. If there is anything to sell, I will fix the money for you".

It was another great moment that God sent for me. When Reliance first allotted shares to new owners two years ago, I bought 30 shares at Rs 50 / - for Rs 1,500. Two days later, Benjamin gave me a small bag of currency notes. When I brought it home and opened the bag, the sight of the notes lined up on the bed was unprecedented and extraordinary. Leelamma also stared in amazement for a while.

It was thirty thousand rupees. For the half amount, we bought a dress and a suitcase. When the other half was converted into Singapore dollars, which was considered enough to carry with Tony for his essentials, I received only 300 SD to pay Tony 15 days' expenses in Singapore.

April 1993. I returned from the office with mixed feelings. As expected, I was transferred from Bangalore to Koraput. I must go within a month.

There were a lot of essential things to do within a month -

- Tony has to go to study in Singapore
- Nita was in standard ten and could stay in a hostel near St Ann's School. After completing standard ten, she would continue in Koraput for her plus two.
- Seema can get a Transfer Certificate and continue her education at a school in Koraput.

I wrote letters to parents and informed them. Achayan wrote back, comforting me -

"A change of place must be experienced by all those who receive government salaries."

Only my colleague Jagannathan had expressed concern. "Working in Koraput will allow you to study and work a lot. It will be difficult for you to travel to your hometown, visit relatives, and spend money on that."

With nothing else to choose from, I was ready to go to Koraput, confident of seeing things as they came to me, as it was part of the routine life.

When I came home, I had my dad's letter. When I opened and read it, I was shocked to know that Kunjachan Chettan, the eldest son of Thathampally Ammayi, had died in Bilaspur. Achayan writes that he had jaundice for a week. Kuriachan and Thommachan might go and attend the funeral. Kunjachan Chettan was able to do small contract work there. Lilly has been the only one there supporting him for more than ten years. What else could one do if one cannot do anything or go there? I prayed that Chettan's soul might rest in peace.

# 68

# Life's Lessons

Leelamma told me she had a small lump that was not painful in one of her breasts. We went to Kidwai Hospital for a detailed examination. We met Dr Gopinath there on the advice of Gp Capt Varkey. When I returned with the test report, I was told that fibro oedema is a benign (non-cancerous) tumour and that it is better to remove it. Leelamma endured the pain and did not know how much tearing she would undergo. Subramanian Aunty was always with Leelamma to care for her in the hospital. Colleagues arranged transportation. Balakrishnan's and Abraham's wives prepared food, gave it to the children, and cared for them. It was a simple procedure, in a way. At the same time, I was confident there would be no trouble, so no one was explicitly informed or called to share the information. The biopsy report also confirmed things were satisfactory. We were relieved.

Meanwhile, one day, Thambichan called from Paradip. They had a third daughter. Even before congratulating him, Thambichan said, "That baby didn't live for long." She was hospitalised in Paradip. I had no words to comfort him at a time of disappointment. Despite the caesarean section, I was relieved to hear that there was nothing to worry about regarding Leelamma's health.

Tess, the wife of Raju, gave birth to their first child, a girl, Nithyamol, in January 1990. That, too, was a caesarean. Achayan had written that Thambichan and Leelamma would be coming for the child's baptism in April and that the date would be announced soon. Achayan also congratulated and complimented Tony and Seema for getting into their respective classes with rank/distinction and Nitamol for passing her exams with good marks.

When Nithyamol was two months old, Tess got a teaching job in a high school in Changanassery.

At the end of the school year, Achayan wrote: "I am glad to know that Tony Mon brought many presents. Praise be to God. Bouquets of my heartfelt congratulations to Tony Mon. Heartfelt prayers that the gifts may continue to be collected. Arrange to show all these gifts to me as the joy of seeing them with the winner would prolong my life."

My parents prayed for their grandchildren. Achayan wrote to each of them individually - "God bless you. Be sure to believe and pray to God with an open heart."

In April, I was in Goa for work on the Naval Project. Due to that, I could not attend the baptism ceremony of Nithyamol.

The newly built St Antony's Church in Vaishambhagom fulfilled the locals' lifelong aspirations. Kavalakkal Kurunnappan and their family had donated some land. More land was reclaimed from the adjoining paddy field. The locals collected money, reclaimed the land, and built the church there. From the beginning, Achayan was an active member of the church construction committee and later in the church committees, but not always as the leader. Sacraments and prayers began even before the church was completed.

Nitamol's First Holy Communion was held at St Antony's Church. A Christmas vacation was set aside for that.

Vaishyambhagom Church was under the administrative control of St Mary's Forane Church Champakulam. The ancient tradition of Champakulam Church was one of the celebrations held by the parishioners at the diocesan level and in the parish. Achayan wrote - "Our ward won the speech competition, and I got second place in the final round at the diocesan level. In general, everyone said that I spoke well. Your mother won the first prize for Bible reading."

April 1990. Fifteen years ago, Achayan borrowed about Rs 15,000/- from the Thakazhi Society to build a house. We repaid about Rs 40,000/- including principal, interest, and penalty interest in over thirty instalments. Though I had sent the required amount to Achayan several times, he could not pay the total amount to society. Over a while, with delays and lapses in repayment, the interest and penalty interest payable there increased.

I sent all the receipts to Achayan as he desired because the mortgaged property will be returned after the loan payment receipts are produced. Satisfied that one of my significant duties has been fulfilled, I wrote jokingly that -

"I'm happy with the end of the loan repayment sacrifice. I do not know if there will be another sacrifice."

Achayan's response made it clear that such an innocent but prejudiced statement was unnecessary. From Achayan's writing, I realised that together with other misconceptions, there started a controversy, which saddened Achayan and, through him, my mother.

From a young age, my mother told me I was inclined to be misunderstood by others - it was right there even now, and Achayan reiterated it. I replied by explaining the positions and quoting figures to change the misconceptions. It was written without any disrespect or using any of the wrong words. But it reverberated as if it was a story of long-standing pain in my mind. I had fulfilled part of my responsibilities to bear the burden of the family running and the household expenses, especially when all my siblings were much younger and in school. However, I had never claimed any priority among the brothers for being the eldest. Unnecessarily, lining up the facts hit the sharp edge of the argument and scratched Achayan's mind.

I was saddened and thought I had aroused feelings of tenderness, sadness, or nostalgia in an exaggerated and self-indulgent way. Mothers are always kind-hearted, and it was on my mother's insistence that Achayan wrote to me again - that these were some misconceptions brought about by ignorance and that the property and the individual shares would be determined by him on a reasonable basis and sent soon. "This grief is due to Achayan's pure heart." Achayan explained- "without blaming anyone, calmly giving all the blessings to the children and grandchildren without claiming any achievement, humbly, and without being proud of anything, with the utmost humility." He reiterated that he could not establish a rich legacy to leave behind for our benefit.

I was delayed in further commenting on the days ahead. The conditional 'wealth commitment document' is supported by the statement that it was the fulfillment of duty, which was received subsequently. Then, I did not reply for some time because I firmly believed it was not the time to think about it, as no sibling wanted the prop, the house, or any share of it to progress their own life! Everyone was concerned about the parents' health. All that was essential was having someone to stay with the parents at home to care for their welfare and health!

I did not like anyone to doubt my sincerity or integrity. It was always like that. Even if someone criticized me, I knew reacting too quickly would be wrong. When you think calmly, you can respond adequately.

Whatever Achayan considers or bears in mind, I will not decide his right or wrong.

My mistake was that my sincere love for my family, parents, and siblings was not highlighted or exclusively expressed to anyone. A vision of my life ahead was not shared with anyone, and I kept it to myself, or I was unclear. At least I could have told Achayan where I plan to settle down after retirement to avoid his unwanted concerns!

“No matter how much he has grown up, he is still the mischievous old boy and a sulky character; he kept a hard grip on everything,” If someone had thought about me as such, no one could be blamed for that.

Ideally, love and affection should be expressed and highlighted in a particular way.

Don’t the elders say it? Keeping one’s love inside is not enough. It should be expressed. Why did I not do so? Everyone else is their own; My parents, siblings, and I are not separate but one. That was my sincerity, so can I be misunderstood if I did not show, express, or highlight my love? Isn’t it wrong to misunderstand like that?

It is good to express love to each other, but why do they not understand that what was not represented was due to some different external pressure? Why did they not inquire about it? Lovers do not demand love explicitly. Or does he not pay attention when you tell him something to do?

Or was it not preferable to express interest once again, humbly, without blaming others before doing something by misunderstanding?

What could I say except that it was wisdom that blossomed late? Factually, the influence of external pressures caused such indifference; not writing the reply or the unnecessary reply written earlier hurt Achayan. It can be written later.

Achayan’s wish and prophecy - ‘your son would help you like this’- were fulfilled later.

Achayan had said - “Children do their duty to their parents. Parents are satisfied with it. Children’s earthly support towards their parents and others will be blessed before God.”

It was one of the biggest lessons of life that Achayan taught me – “No matter how right you are, never argue with your parents or elders about anything. You should be able to respectfully submit your information without arguing".

Great life lessons that you can't get from any university!

Some people plan and execute everything according to the plan. They are known as great people. They are doing great things in the world. Such things happen in the lives of even ordinary people. Nothing is ever pre-determined and executed by anyone. Here are some of the things in my life as an ordinary person.

The following are two or three personal thoughts that I had in my mind before reading Achayan's misunderstandings and my reactions to it, but I never shared with anyone: -

- Land, house, and property will never be acquired by borrowing money.

- After retirement, if I live and maintain health, I must do something, work or serve and earn an income. Kochuppappan is a role model in this regard. Doing exciting work is taking rest itself. Work is complementary to life and health. Hard work, especially an exciting job, does not tire us.

- After retirement, if I need to work, I do not desire farming/ agriculture. I need appropriate training in the job, and if I must travel, I must stay at a suitable place convenient for traveling quickly. Therefore, staying in the countryside is not a priority, especially in the Vyshyambhagom district. Living should be according to the children's best interest, prioritising their comfort and convenience in the future.

None of my children wants to live in Kuttanad. Tony said, "Daddy, Alappuzha, and Kuttanad are all good places. What do we do next after two weeks of touring and recognising the local delicacies? It will take us a day to get to Vaishyambhagom from the airport."

Achayan took a loan and built a house for everyone to live in. When my brothers have their accommodation, I will only look for a place and accommodation.

When read altogether, relationships, interactions, and involvement in family affairs were soon reduced to the abbreviated form of fulfilling the duties of an elder son as a solution to the lingering issues and responsibilities towards home.

# 69

# The Pain of Separation

**Ottathyckal Achayan ND Thomas and Ammachi Marykutty (1950)**

On the morning of September 04, 1990, Thambichan's phone call came. Ottathyckal Achayan died of a heart attack. He said they would leave Paradip and reach home on the following day. If you want to glimpse Ottathyckal Achayan's body before the funeral, you must take the morning bus. If you wait for the evening train to leave, it will be noon the next day by the time you get there. My friend AK Nath & Mrs Nath live downstairs in the quarters opposite my house where the telephone call came for me. The children were left with their peers in AK Nath's house, and we were allowed to go. AK Nath took us to the KSRTC Bus stand and saw us boarding the bus. The bus travelled via Mysore, Bathery, and Palakkad, reaching Alappuzha at night. After midnight, we walked from Pallathuruthy to Ottathaikkal via Thaicherry Church.

Achayan's children were outside Kerala except for Babychan, who was nearby. Joy was working in a merchant cargo ship. Joy could not even be notified, as it would take time for the ship to reach the shore. Everyone else arrived in the morning.

The end of Ottathyckal Achayan was sudden. We did not know of any illness he had before his departure. He used to go to Pulickal market every morning, drink tea there, meet the locals and greet them, and return home before lunch at noon. Achayan was always cheerful. The hard work of adolescence and the family's hardships were old stories. Performing the mundane responsibilities one by one, the time has passed. The days of rest and more joy were near. On one of the days of contentment, when the whole state was getting ready for the Onam celebration, it was past noon on the Thiruvonam of that year; he went down to see the various Onam games in the countryside. A regular village volleyball match was in progress on a nearby stretch of land. The youngest son, Babychan, went there and told him: - "Ammachi has a fever, so Achayan may go home now."

Achayan went home in the evening.

The following was what Ammachi narrated to me -

"At seven-thirty, I was served hot rice porridge – It was the first time he did that - and I finished. Then he said -

"I'll give you medicine again after midnight so you may sleep now ." I laid down.

At about nine o'clock, Achayan felt sharp chest pain. He woke me up, called me, and then went to the toilet. He returned to the bed and told me to put on the fan as he was sweating profusely. When I put the fan on and looked at Achayan, I saw his chest rising in agony.

I was frightened, and I screamed. There was no one nearby. Achayan saw me crying loudly, and he slowly raised his hand and said, "Don't cry." Then Achayan did not speak anything. It was half past nine... People came running from the neighbourhood, hearing my cries. " She wept.

Achayan's departure was a shock for Kannattumadom Achayan. It was a unique and ideal relationship that they had. Collaboration since childhood, having done the same work together for a long time, working in the same team, forever friends, the status of rare relatives who have exchanged their daughters for their bright future in the life journey, the relationship of two people as fathers of two sons-in-law. It was very unusual. Achayan's heartfelt sorrows were visible on his face as he retreated after placing a wreath on the frozen body of his close friend.

I am forever indebted to him for the love and trust he has shown me and the dedicated partnership he has demonstrated to Ottathyckal Ammachi, who together held the hands of their dearest daughter and gave to me in marriage for life.

In the afternoon, the funeral occurred at the cemetery burial ground in St Mary's Church, Champakulam, in the presence of the locals, relatives, friends, and well-wishers, who formed a large crowd.

There was a heavy downpour as soon as we started to fill the pit after burial.

Ramachandran wrote to me that he was sharing our grief. Ramachandran was my colleague and best friend at CME who convalesced at Palghat after his open heart surgery.

Parents need constant attention and care in their old age, especially for the essential routine daily needs with the help of a paramedic. When Raju and Tess were home, Ammachi received the care and service she needed. Later, Tess went to her mother's place at Pulinkunnu for childbirth.

Babychan was in Gulbarga, Karnataka, for work. Babu was in Coimbatore working on a meagre salary. Babu's family continued to live in their own house in Paravur. Sometimes, I thought of asking Babu – "what if you quit your job and stay at home for two or three years or permanently so that you could stay home and take care of things at home"?

In the present situation, I asked Achayan for his opinion on whether this would be better for Achayan and Ammachi's permanent care, if possible.

Achayan's response was emotional and prejudicial. Simultaneously, some suggestions were given, which challenged me to implement them.-

- "Now, we can pull on without support; let it go as long as possible. Come back often and keep in touch in writing."
- "If he (Babu) is brought and left to look after his mother, the poor man loses the property of his wife's share and the house already given to her.
- Take Babu's share, give him money, and let him do some work. If his mother and wife are together here without any harmony, I am afraid it may not work as it happened before....

How do you tell others things you can't do on your own? Things went so badly for me. Family priorities changed. Life's stresses had to be redefined in the light of changing circumstances, their needs, qualifications, safety, and quality. I also tried to correct the mistakes.

Anjiliparambil Varkichan - Achayan called him Kochuppappan - died at the age of 104 in January 1991. He was the caretaker of the family for three generations. He was the head of the family when the family reunion was held at Anjiliparambil.

The book 'Family History of Anjiliparambil (1730-2012) records prehistory and written history. The names and details of all the family members are registered in it. The book was published on April 08, 2012, at Kudumbayogam, held in Punnapra.

# 70

# Babychan's Marriage

Mother is the sweetest, the most profound word. The word 'Mother' combines love, mercy, and sacrifice and is synonymous with goodness.

Mother is the only person who can give selfless love. My mother was like that.

"Who can describe the pain my mother suffered during her childbirth?"

Ammachi will sometimes remember those days when I was in her womb; her whole body was tired, her food lost its taste, she vomited, and she pushed away all her troubles and worries.

Which son or daughter can repay that debt to their mother who has made so many sacrifices, suffered the pain of caring for the baby, the sleepless care, the mother who feeds the baby even when she is starving?

Mom! No matter how old a son becomes, his obligations cannot be fulfilled in one life.

My mother knows how to love only. I don't remember receiving any bashing to correct my mischiefs, even with a small, slender stick. Ammachi's literacy was limited to only reading newspapers and writing in Malayalam. Before the end of class five or six, she finished her studies and was given full training in household work. She married off from Arackal house and was sent to Kannattumadom home. Ammachi could forgive as much as the earth, bear all the sufferings, and take everything smoothly without complaining. Ammachi did not even comment on any subject she was unfamiliar with. She bravely faced financial pressures. The guests who came to the house were happily provided with food and amenities. Though no exact time was fixed, he would sit in one place and pray attentively whenever the rush of work was over. When I was young, she used to teach me to sing little songs and pray. Ammachi never did the usual rigmarole in some other places, got up between prayers, and attended to cooking. Ammachi was very happy with her children's various engagements and achievements, and she was delighted with their growth and the achievements of the head of the family. She always folded her hands, looked up, and thanked God for every happening in the family. Ammachi comforted her children without understanding their failures. Ammachi never knew to analyze the reasons behind domestic difficulties.

My mother sent me a special letter when I had some failures on my part during my lonely life. "Mone, I gave birth to you when I was 21." The notes ended with, "Do not do anything that will upset your father." She abundantly poured out blessings on her grandchildren.

Achayan wrote to me after he came and stayed in Bangalore with his grandchildren for Christmas and returned home –

"My Travels, trips to Delhi and Kanyakumari were like never before, green as a garden that spread fragrance in my heart,"

"When I ate with the kids there, my stomach was not only full, but my mind too was full,"

"At such times, especially when the children have come and gone back, the house was like an empty nest, and I cling to it like a slaughtered shrub. I can only look back at the healthy, energetic shrub that I was. I thank God and adore Him for the joy he has given me with the good seeds that sprout beneath that shrub."

"Live as pure children of Christ, with a pure heart, offering both gifts of joy and sorrow to God."

Although Achayan had little knowledge of English, he had a good command of Malayalam. He read many newspapers and magazines and wrote and preached in his sober and straightforward style. He had a lot of worldly knowledge. His excellent faith in politics and democracy has always been intensely expressed, along with nationalism and patriotism. Integrity was held equal importance in interpersonal relationships and the community. Therefore, in Society and all public affairs, people respected Achayan and wanted to be their leader. We, children, are reflected in that love and affection from individuals and society. The children were always proud of their father's position in the community and society.

Achayan often wrote news, 'fenced' special news, and newspaper feature articles. Achayan was happy to see everything he wrote was printed in the newspapers. Achayan has been directly involved in social activities ever since I remember. He was responsible at various levels of the Indian National Congress. The children were not forced to pursue any of his political interests. Other than loving them, I don't remember reprimanding or punishing his children harshly. Once, at a general meeting of the library, Achayan had to face sharp criticism. And that too from people who should have received so much love and gratitude from him. The allegations were not that serious. Achayan also gave proper replies to the criticisms in good, mild language. The only thing that hurt Achayan more was that his brother harshly criticised him. He chased me outside the reading room near the window since I was in a public meeting and listening to all these allegations and harsh words. He glared at me and said, "I say you go home quickly." After hearing his harsh criticism, Achayan thought my love or respect for his brother should not be diminished.

Achayan has rebuked me for many of my misdeeds. Playing cards with stakes (money), angry outbursts, and bad words while quarrelling with someone - I have been punished for not correcting such unnecessary habits. I remember not repeating those bad habits after I was punished.

Needless to reiterate, I had a lot of gratitude, love, and respect for my parents and other elders for guiding me in the right direction. No matter how comforting my mother told me at a young age, 'It is my bane or birthmark to be misunderstood by others after the effects of the misunderstanding have been felt, everyone has calmed down and regained peace because I was short-tempered and quick-tempered. Not only because I was born on Ashtami Rohini day, as Ammachi said, and being such a sensitive person, but I could also often react wrongly without even realizing the mature situation. Attempts have been made to change such behaviour, but it has frequently failed. Those who accept me with these flaws do not quarrel with me. Because quick temper never resulted in violence, taking up a weapon, or causing physical harm after stabbing a man in the leg with a thali, never again. Didn't my back hurt so much that I lost my temper and stabbed him in the leg with a thali? Enemies might have said that the earthen pot fell from his hand instead of being hit with a stone thrown by me!

Babychan went home at the end of December. Achayan said that with the help of Babychan, he could repay the arrears of the loan he had borrowed from the Society for Agriculture and dumped gravel in the fields. Twenty-four years after I got a job, I was glad to hear that my siblings had also started helping my parents.

Babychan saw a girl from a not-far-away house as part of the marriage proposal. She worked as a teacher in a school, and Babychan liked her. Babychan liked that girl's name from an early age, i.e., when he was in school! Just the name, but I had never met the girl before. There was a reason why it was only the name. Our daughter Nita was born to us when he was studying in school. Babychan wrote to me while considering many names for the girl child; he suggested that 'Tessy' would be the best name, rhyming as Tessy after Tony, names that rhyme well. Babychan's wish to give that name to his niece was considered, but it was not given for another reason. If it had been accepted, what would have been Seema's name rhyming with Tessy, such as - Tully (Irish, devoted to the will of God or quiet, peaceful) or Turku (a seaport in southwestern Finland) or Tuas (Malaysia–Singapore Link)?!

I went for an interview for the Scientist post at ADE (DRDO). Mr Radhakrishnan Nair also accompanied me to the DRDO Recruitment Office in Delhi. I was called for an interview one month after my sending application there. We travelled together on the train, went a day earlier, and stayed with Kuriachan. My director, Hussainy, was also a member of the interview board. Although all the questions were answered satisfactorily, the person working temporarily in the same position in ADE was selected. I went to our HQ office to take advantage of the opportunity to meet Director Hussainy. During a friendly conversation, I asked what class his son was studying. Like Tony, his son was a Plus 2 first-year student. On behalf of his son, he requested that I share Tony's notes from the Brilliants course while he was studying for the IIT entrance exam.

I have agreed to that. Until Tony's Std 12 was over, I requested that he help us without distracting Tony by changing our place of work. He looked straight ahead and said with a laugh.

"Let us see; continue your good work on Aircraft."

When I returned home and told Tony and Leelamma that I was not sad about not getting the Scientist D post, everyone was relieved that there would be no change of place that year, which was seen as a matter of celebration.

During the conversation with Thambichan a month back, I told him there would likely be a transfer for me to Koraput in Orissa. Thambichan later asked -

"I know the boxes are packed, but you should inform us before you leave."

Ammachi had occasional intermittent asthma problems— with an increase in blood pressure. Since Babychan was at home, he took Ammachi to the doctor for tests and treatment.

Even in an emergency, my mother had to be taken to see the doctor in Kanjipadam, organizing a boat trip. It was found to be an arduous task practically. Travel and care were complicated when the mother became ill, and Raju or Babychan were not home.

The most challenging journey for Raju was going to work in Thiruvananthapuram every morning and returning home in the evening. The journey of changing boats, buses, and trains in any weather completely erased Raju's joy of doing a job in the native state.

Although Raju's job was in Thiruvananthapuram, he mainly worked in Palakkad, Thrissur, Alappuzha, Kozhikode, Idukki, and other places for audit work. So, it was a great blessing to be home at least once a week to look after our parents' well-being, overcome difficulties, and move on for days and months.

Babychan quit the railway service and joined the C&AG office in Bangalore in May 1991. Raju also first started working in that office. Subsequently, Babychan moved to AG's office in Thiruvananthapuram in 1994.

Babychan's wedding took place in November 1991. Since it was my youngest brother's wedding, every far-away relative came together at home, and the wedding ceremony and the subsequent receptions got over smoothly.

It was the last ceremony in the Vaishyambhagom house, attended by Achayan's brothers and brothers-in-law - Chittappan, Perappan, Kochuppappan, Kunchacko, Kunjommachayan and most of their family members. The other uncles and their families were in Delhi and could not come.

After the reception, everyone returned to their homes. We had to return to Bangalore as there was school and office work the next day.

# 71

# No More Bus Journey

It seemed necessary to discuss the matter with Achayan, believing that a temporary solution to the difficulties at home and a permanent solution over time could be found. These were the topics of discussion -

- If the mother and father have health problems, children have difficulty caring for them due to the lack of transport facilities.

- Raju and Babychan have difficulty getting to and from the office and waste time using various modes of transport apart from walking a long distance. It was also due to the lack of travel facilities.

We must relocate to nearby areas where major roads and facilities are available for transportation. You can rent a house in Alappuzha, Punnapra area, for the time being, buy land as time allows, and build your own home there. I presented the topic to Achayan in the evening -

Achayan's response came soon before he could hear the whole thing.

"What, do you want us to move out from here today?"

I have never experienced Achayan reacting to me like this under pressure. I didn't even say that Achayan's reaction hurt me. I felt it was better to keep certain things in mind and not express it spontaneously. Achayan had no heart to listen to my explanation, and we never spoke on the subject again. Given the opportunity to discuss issues, was it a mistake that Babychan's wedding day was chosen after all the functions? If so, we could agree to discuss it later and could have postponed it. To whose benefit did I present the topics? What would I say if it was my congenital disability that caused a long-standing misunderstanding of 'presenting a topic' to remain as such for longer? Did I have any selfish motives?

Early the following day, we left back to Bangalore.

I used to come home for the holidays without remembering the misery of returning. All the savings and reserves for the expenses must have been exhausted. Unless thrown away before departure, some heartburns might linger on during the return journey. When we arrived, we attended the ceremonies at home, shared all the joys and sorrows, inquired with the natives, and cooperated with the neighbors. The intensity of the participants might have decreased in the later years, though, due to the growth of the family and the complexities associated with it.

Return travel – by bus from Alappuzha to Ernakulam and train to Bangalore. Since the children accompanied us, we always took the train reservation.

The bus journeys from Alappuzha to Ernakulam have been unforgettable at least twice, with someone in need picking up my pocket, making it much more difficult for me on the trip by the pickpocketer taking away what was in my purse.

Both were on our return journey from Alleppey to Ernakulam after a vacation at home. The KSRTC bus from Alappuzha to Ernakulam was available, even though there was a heavy rush of passengers. The suitcase in hand, the bag on my shoulder, and the walk-in front should have been Nita. Leelamma boarded the bus ahead of me with Seema. Tony and I picked up the small baggage box and followed.

I remember taking the cash for the bus ticket and putting my wallet in the back pocket of my pants while travelling to Ernakulam. The conductor of the Ernakulam bus came and gave me the ticket by the time we reached Cherthala. I realised my wallet was lost while reaching into my pocket to keep the balance. When the bus stopped at Cherthala, I told the conductor about the matter. An announcement was made on the bus immediately.

"If anyone has taken it, you can drop it off and get off the bus."

Everyone cooperated. I knew that if my government identity card was lost, a complaint should be lodged with the police.

Then - "I didn't have much money in my purse. I lost my Govt of India identity card and a few postage stamps, so I don't have to go to the police station." I told the conductor. Travel time from home to Bangalore does not take 24 hours. The money for essentials, starting with lunch and dinner, was always kept in my pants' front watch pocket, about a hundred rupees.

The wallet was nowhere to be found on the bus.

'Someone must have taken the money and thrown out the wallet, 'I thought.

That's when someone said -

"It was hectic in Alappuzha, and another bus came after it. It would also come to a halt at Cherthala. If someone pickpocketed and got on to the bus, he could be on the bus just at the back; please get out and ask there on that bus, and maybe you get it. Especially since there was not much money in the wallet." That seemed like a good suggestion. "Let me try that." I got out and got on to the bus behind our bus.

I addressed the locals and passengers. No one responded. A young man sitting in the front seat lifted my purse, stood up, and asked-

"Is this yours? "

I took it and looked, and I saw my identity card in it.

"Thank you, thank you very much. There were some unused stamps in it, did you see?"

"I took the stamp."

"Okay, take it. Thank you very much, everyone."

I got off the bus, took the first bus, and continued my journey to Ernakulam.

The second incident was also similar, so I am not repeating it. I realised that the wallet was lost at a stop just after Cherthala. The conductor requested that the driver turn the vehicle to the nearest police station. The procedure was repeated. This time, the police controlled it.

The wallet was nowhere to be found on the bus. The hundred rupees I got from Achayan for travel expenses were accidentally kept in that purse. It was lost along with the identity card, which caused me to worry about what to do next. It was visible in my mind that -

- 'You can borrow from the police inspector, get the address and send it back to him next week!'

And that was done. The inspector helped me by giving me money for the travel expenses. He wrote the complaint, I got a receipt and continued my journey.

Police may not have pursued the investigation, thinking that the pickpocket might have thrown away the wallet, which contained no money.

While these old events are irrelevant today, credit/debit cards remind us of what the past was and the challenges we faced. Besides, these challenges teach us some suitable lessons!

Within five years after the bus journeys mentioned above, the dream of forty years of coastal rail travel for the natives became a reality, and the rail services via Alappuzha commenced. The long-distance train service began by completing the Ernakulam-Kayamkulam railway line.

We never traveled by bus from Alappuzha to Ernakulam. We did not face the unpleasant experience of losing my wallet during bus travel.

# 72

# Defining Moments

Babychan got a house in Banaswadi in Bangalore, where he lived with his family. Achayan suggested taking the newlyweds to their rented home and arranging a comfortable stay. Accordingly, they started living independently in a small house.

"Loving parents see their children through the letters they get." If Achayan was late in receiving the letter, he would write again immediately, saying that it reminded the children to promptly reply.

"When we love and raise our children, they will love us in return. We always want to know the welfare of our children."

Most of the writing was about my mother's illness and that none of their children was with them.

"One night, Ammachi had more intense asthma and nausea. I woke up the neighbours, grabbed a canoe, and had to go to the doctor at night. She took the injection. By dawn, the illness had subsided."

"My elder brother is not well. He is being treated at the medical college. He has regularly been given injectable medicine, but no big change has occurred. The disease will go away in a few days, and then it will reappear. That was the routine." He has left us, leaving all the treatments up to that point in vain. Funeral services were held at St Antony's Church Cemetery in the presence of his brothers, children, and the locals."

"Babu came and took Ammachi's cow to Paravur. Ammachi was sad because she could not manage the cattle due to ill health.

"Raju rented a house in Thuruthi and moved there. Tess got a job in a school in Changanassery. It is convenient for her to come and go from Thuruthi."

"Frequent floods in Kuttanad happen every year. Ammachi went to Chethipuzha Hospital with Raju and is undergoing treatment there."

"I got your letter and money. Everyone went to the wedding in Punnapra, and Babu also came there. For the return journey from Punnapra, we were brought here in a car and left."

The above was the standard text of many letters from Achayan. Life moved slowly along the usual path. Everyone must fulfill their responsibilities and obligations. With as much mutual support as possible, life on the regular track can get a little livelier and more energetic.

No one has time to set aside entirely for others. But it would help to make time for your family's needs. That's how often some get into a dilemma.

Sometimes, it was not possible to distinguish between right and wrong.

No one could sit idly by saying they were in a dilemma. It was enough for someone to take the initiative to bring a little energy to life's journey by minimizing the difficulties.

Leelamma and I left the children under the care of Babychan and Tessy and went home to attend Rosamma's wedding. It was at that time in Bangalore that Tessy suddenly became ill. Babychan called after admitting Tessy to St. Martha's Hospital due to some bleeding and pain. Tests were performed quickly. The operation was carried out immediately.

She was brought to the room after the operation when he went to see her in the hospital. It was a great relief to have survived the challenging moments. The final diagnosis was an ectopic pregnancy. Doctors advised her to take two weeks of rest and medication. She was also advised not to lift weights and observe abstinence for at least three months.

Babychan began to experience the realities and hassles of life. It was hard for him to care for his wife, work in the office, and quickly bring Tessy back to his routine everyday life.

He asked for a transfer to the Thiruvananthapuram office, and he got it soon.

If Tessy gets a job at any school and stays at home, life will be much better, and she can give our parents the care they need. It is not difficult to get a job as a teacher in a school because of her education. If Tessy receives a job, she can mentally prepare Achayan to move near the road where she can travel from the Kuttanad, which is surrounded by water and without transportation. Thus, the workplace was changed, and Babychan was anticipating various blessings. Then, Babychan left Bangalore.

Raju and Babychan worked in different offices in the same department in Thiruvananthapuram. Most of the time, they stayed in Thiruvananthapuram together and came home every Friday evening. They travelled to Thiruvananthapuram earlier in the week and reached the office. That was regular.

Babychan wrote the departmental examination for the section officer. He said that he passed the exam in the first rank and got an award of Rs.500/- from the office.

Xavier, Gracy, their children, and Kunjamma, who stayed with them, moved from Delhi to Madras. When they came to Madras, we decided to meet them and go on a pilgrimage to Velankanni.

We went to Madras by train, and one day, we travelled by car to Velankanni. Xavier made all the arrangements for the trip, accommodation, and meals. In the evening, we visited Sri Aurobindo Ashram in Pondicherry. We had dinner at Pondicherry with the special drink 'Piranthi,' stayed overnight at the hotel, and went to Velankanni church. We walked around the temple, its surroundings, and the beach. A Christian pilgrimage centre has been developed as a good tourist destination that attracts everyone.

Less than six months later, a departmental inquiry was launched against Xavier, and he was suspended from their office in Madras. These events left the family devastated. Unable to cope with the pressure, Xavier fell into some bad associations and indulged in bad habits, such as gambling and drinking. Most days, he would go out in the mornings and come back when it was very dark in the evening, and that was it. Sometimes, it took two or three days to return. Gracy sadly endured a bit. Xavier went without even saying where he was going. He was tired and disfigured three or four days later when he returned without changing his clothes. However, Gracy said she was lovingly behaving with her husband. The children were also distressed. They decreased focus on the study as well. He just went to Pondicherry once and came back four days later. When she could not hold back, Gracy informed her brothers. Some came, and they had to return without making much change.

It was the second or third time such an emergency had occurred. At Gracy's insistence, Josekutty and I were called to 'Come quickly' and help her bring Xavier back to normal. We arrived in Madras from Bangalore and Vishakhapatnam, respectively. We could not trace Xavier after several attempts. Josekutty returned on the second day without seeing or talking to Xavier.

Gracy refused to file a complaint with the police. Since then, Kunjamma and I have set out every day in the vast city of Chennai in search of Xavier. It's been a week since Xavier returned home. On the third day, Kunjamma and I went to a club in T Nagar, where a friend told us that Xavier was playing cards. We carried a photo of Xavier.

We searched at four or five clubs and bars near T Nagar.

We were asking people at a place with the help of a photograph of Xavier, whom we were looking for.

The man looked at me carefully and said, cautioning me -

"Beware, it's like regular police looking for criminals with photos. Criminals do not spare anybody looking for them."

He (Anbu) himself went inside and searched the club - at the Dhana Lakshmi Recreation Center in Mambalam - and came back and said to us -

"Sir, Savariar was here and went to Pondicherry half an hour ago. He will be back tomorrow."

So, our second-day attempt also failed.

The next day, we went to the same place, and someone said that Xavier was on another card-playing team in the same building. When we went upstairs and inquired, we found a vacancy in the card-playing area. Xavier must have seen us and walked out through the front door.

Failing again, we retreated. We resolved that it was not a suitable job for us.

I went back to Bangalore. Gracy announced that Xavier had come home a day later, to our great relief.

Xavier's work and family problems were resolved over some time. Xavier never went to work again. Everyone believed he remained submissive, responsible, and family-oriented despite losing his job.

A few years later, after participating in the All India' Quality Quiz' competition, I went to their house one evening with the second prize - Shield, written 'Quality' on my shelf- that my team received, thinking I could spend the night with Xavier. Gracy said he went to Dindigul to see his mother. Gracy and Joe talked to me warmly for a couple of hours. Only once did they ask me to help them, and they insisted.

"We need to separate, .. the children do agree," Gracy said, "I want to be free from the domestic abuse that Xavier gives me!" The children will look after her for the rest of their lives ". Gracy said.

"Remember the love of Xavier, who gave you his children, the care he gave you for so long; please don't do that. I cannot help you do so. That is not right."

I told them I loved them without a doubt. "Love Xavier more. Stay with him. It's good for the future. It's acceptable to all adults, even to heaven itself."

Then, nothing happened. They must have thought that I was not ready to help them. It does not matter. When we got to see Xavier, everything was lovingly spoken. Xavier had obstacles when talking to us on the phone. They lived in love. The children, Joe and Jay, were well-educated and got jobs. Joe got a job in Madras, and Jay got one in the United States of America. Xavier and his family were later seen at Jay's wedding. Jay and her husband came from America, got married, and returned to America.

We also attended Joe's wedding. Xavier and Gracy could be seen walking together lovingly. Joe and his family protected them and took care of them in Chennai. Xavier and Gracy lived with their daughter in the United States twice, six months each, and returned.

# 73

# The Transfer

Within a month of issuing the transfer order for me to move to Koraput, every preparation was to be completed, packed, and loaded onto a truck. We decided to move by train before the luggage reached there. Before that, we must get the quarters there; the goods can be unloaded from the truck. It was necessary to go early, take a month off, come back, pack, and ship. Do what is needed, go quickly, and report to the new place. That was the plan. You can stay alone at the guest house there for a week.

It was suggested that the transfer trip be postponed to facilitate Tony's departure to Singapore. The appeal was not allowed by authorities.

When I was ordered to leave immediately, I got a train reservation and set off alone.

Our office in Koraput was inside the HAL (Sunabeda) factory. It had a spacious township, fully staffed quarters, a guest house, a hill, and a forest nearby known as 'Bhalu Pahad' on one side. The township has all the amenities, such as a market, theatre, playgrounds, garden, hospital, and School Std up to 12—a small church nearby at Semliguda, where the Christian community prayed together every Sunday. There were no colleges for higher education.

The nearest town was Koraput, which was 20 km away.

The most difficult was the travel facility. Vijayanagaram was the nearest railway station, 120 km from the township. The Orissa and Andhra Pradesh border had hills, gorges, and uphill roads. The closest city was Visakhapatnam, another 70 km after Vijayanagaram. Buses ran in the morning, afternoon, and evening as the only mode of transport going out from Sunabeda. Private taxis were available. Telephone facilities were scarce.

After understanding the situation at that place for a week, I took leave and returned to Bangalore.

I went to Nita's hostel and encouraged Nita to live alone, study amid difficulties, and succeed well in Standard Ten. I also met and talked to the hostel authorities.

The cooking gas connection was shifted to Sunabeda.

I went to Seema's school and bought the transfer certificate. Seema got the T.C. but was too sad and too lazy to leave the school. Not only were they unaware of my transferable job in government, but many teachers at the school loved Seema so much. Her school activities, studies, religious learning, and extra-curricular activities were commendable to the school authorities.

After Nita started classes in June, we planned to go to Vijayanagaram, and from there, we would go by taxi to Sunabeda and book tickets accordingly.

A truck was arranged to transport the luggage. Having learned to do the work independently, I thought I could make the packing good if I could get more packing materials such as sacks, cardboard, etc. The carpenter at MES came, measured, cut, and nailed the wooden packing for the refrigerator. My local trips were on Silver Plus, so the bus travel and waiting time could be avoided.

I went to the bank, took the advance money received for the change of place, put it safely in my watch pocket, and went towards the KR Market. I bought five or six sacks from the market and some cardboard and put them all in a small bundle in the carrier of my moped.

I remember driving from the market, waiting for the signal, and stopping at the junction, but I do not remember further what happened.

When I opened my eyes, I saw unfamiliar faces gathered around the bed where I was lying, not knowing where I was. I tried to get up. Someone grabbed me, and I asked in Malayalam, "Where am I?"

They understood and said, "Marthas Hospital."

Then I remembered that I was driving the moped; I reached for my hands and feet and looked at the whole body. There were no problems. It seemed that I was safe and had no significant injuries. Someone asked for my name and home phone number. I gave AK Nath's phone number, which I had kept with the identity card.

"What's the matter?" How did I fall?"

Someone came from behind and hit the vehicle, waiting for a signal at the junction, my moped. I fell, and my helmet and moped were thrown away. The traffic policeman has seen that. The auto-rickshaw man brought me here. Someone explained.

"The autorickshaw driver who brought you here is waiting. If you give him something, he will go away."

I remembered the money I had kept in my watch pocket and looked for it. There it was, and I was relieved. I took a note and gave it to the autorickshaw driver. He thanked me and left happy.

"Where is my helmet? Where is the moped?" Someone said that everything was taken by the police and taken to the police station. You can find out the station tomorrow.

I felt like lying down again, so I leaned over, laid down again, and fell asleep. I woke up to a call -

"Daddy, ... Daddy ..". Seema, I looked up. There was Leelamma, Tony, Nita, and AK Nath. Yes, Nath brought them all driving in his car.

Seema was scared and crying. I held her close and said - "It is okay; nothing happened to me; I am all right." I could see the fear and relief on everyone's faces. No one said anything. After a while, everyone started talking - what's up? How did you fall?

The wounds on my forehead and hands were then seen, and there was no pain. After two to three hours of observation, I was discharged in the evening at six o'clock. The doctor at Martha's Hospital gave me a note about the tests I had to do the next day. I came home in the car with Nath.

Tests were conducted the next day at Martha's Hospital and NIMHANS Hospital - for 'the signs of a concussion after a blow. Test reports stated that there was nothing unusual.

Leelamma and Babychan searched for the police station and found my Silver Plus. It was serviced and brought home, packed in sacks, and made ready to be loaded onto the truck, which carried my luggage to Sunabeda.

The packing was completed within the next two days, the luggage was loaded on the truck, and we boarded the train to Vijayanagaram before all the wounds had healed. After a strenuous journey, we finally reached Sunabeda, the unique township known to friends as 'Vana vasa.'

Tony was curious about his mother's age during the train journey.

"Mommy, how old are you?"

Mommy said - "I am 39."

"No, you are not. You don't look like that much."

We arrived in Sunabeda and stayed at the guest house for the first day. I had got the quarters allotted in the township. Mammachan from the Maintenance department of HAL did the whitewashing and distempering of the house and made it ready for our stay. When the truck with our luggage arrived, we unpacked all the furniture and belongings and started living there.

Baby and Vijaya Chandran fed us supper on the first day of our stay in Sunabeda township. They were the first friends to meet in Sunabeda.

More than 200 Malayalee families were living in Sunabeda township itself. All were HAL factory employees and members of the management team. Many people came to see and get to know the newcomers in the township. Johnson, Suma, P.J Nair & Savithri, all belonging to Thiruvananthapuram, Anthonichan from Alappuzha, wife Manichechi, Baby, Raghavan, Sankaran Kutty, Valson, Pillai, Vasu, KG Nair, Zachariah, Thomas John, Kuriakose, Alice & Jose, Satish Kumar, Paulose, Radhakrishnan, Thankamani & Mohan .... ..., and all their family members. Kerala Samajam was functioning, and every year, it organised cultural events and national festivals. The Malayalee community worked together with great unity and contributed to the factory and township. Everyone cooperated with their participation in all the activities. Some Malayalee friends who have lived in Sunabeda for a long time said it was here like a paradise on earth. It is here. People living in their native places said this was our lost paradise. The best thing that can be learned from the strong family ties of Sunabeda Malayalees is to help others through cooperation, help, and prayers for each other. We had a great fellowship there with some good hearts, both known and unknown.

The Samajam convened a public meeting to get everyone together. They were introduced to a Malayalee family who had just arrived in the township. Thanking them, I replied-

"I come from Kuttanad, the paddy barn of Kerala. Kuttanad is like a painting of a beautiful art'.

'പാരം കരിമ്പ് പനസം മുളക് ഏലം ഇഞ്ചി, തളിർ വെറ്റില ഏത്തവാഴ ഇവയൊന്നും ധാരാളമായി ഇല്ലെങ്കിലും തെങ്ങ്, കേരം തിങ്ങും കേരളനാടാണ് കുട്ടനാട്. പാടത്തു മുഴുവൻ കൃഷി നെല്ലാണ്.

തെങ്ങു കല്പവൃക്ഷമാണ്. മനുഷ്യോപകാരപ്രദമാണ് തെങ്ങിൽ നിന്നും കിട്ടുന്നതെല്ലാം. അതുപോലെ കുട്ടനാട്ടിൽ നിന്നും, കേരളനാട്ടിൽ നിന്നും വരുന്നവരും.

I introduced my family and said I was working in a government department looking into the quality of products they make in the factory. Let us be here on this journey, cooperate, and celebrate life. Thank you for the love and consideration you continue to give.

Seema was admitted to Vyomayana Samastha Vidyalaya in Standard VI. She had to learn the Oriya language as an additional subject.

It was time for Tony to go to Singapore. The flight was from Chennai. He received the tickets sent by his sponsors.

All matters communicated to the home included Tony's successes, my transfer to Koraput, Nita's hostel admission, and life in Bangalore. Everyone came and started staying in Koraput; Seema was admitted to a new school at Sunabeda, Tony's trip to Singapore, etc., were also informed to Achayan.

Babychan occasionally went to the hostel in Bangalore, met Nita, and inquired about her welfare.

Achayan and Babychan prepared to arrive in Chennai and send Tony to Singapore. My mother had to be rushed to Thathampally Hospital due to her illness. Achayan conveyed the blessings of Achayan and Ammachi and a thousand praises to God for the blessings granted to Tony. Raju had come to Madras from home to represent Tony's grandparents. Leelamma and I went with Tony to Chennai via Visakhapatnam, where we rested with Josekutty and Mercy at the MES quarters. We took the early morning train to Chennai. We arrived in Chennai and stayed with Xavier until we all went to the Airport to see Tony off.

We took a taxi and arrived at the airport three hours before the flight departed. Xavier and Raju were with us.

None of us knows anything about boarding flights on an international airline. You need a passport, and you need a visa; you need a ticket. Why go to the airport three hours early? Wasn't it enough to go straight to board the flight directly like you board a train or a bus?

At the airport, I was able to get acquainted with two or three of Tony's co-passengers, who were also selected for college studies as Tony—Ajith Mohan from Aluva, Nitin Pai from Mangalore, and Maya from Chennai. Everyone said goodbye and headed inside the airport. After checking in, Tony looked up at us as we headed up the elevator for the emigration check - the Thumbs Up sign, which was a victory sign - everything was going well, and bye - showing up and laughing. Then, I felt Tony had the confidence and courage to conquer this world.

"I know that Civil aircraft is huge. How can such a big plane fly? Can a manoeuvre like a 'dogfight' on a warplane happen on a passenger plane? How long does it take to get to Singapore on a warplane?"

Xavier's questions and doubts were appropriate and timely, or how to wait until the aircraft was airborne. When Raju heard this, he also stood up. Tony's flight will take at least an hour more to take off. Until then, Tony's mommy waited, saying, "I'll see my baby go flying."

"Passenger planes take four hours to reach Singapore and fly at about 800 KM/hr. Modern fighter planes fly at double the speeds, so it only takes about two hours. Warplanes usually carry only one pilot. Large passenger planes can carry 150 to 525 passengers. On regular fighter jets, you only see the fuel to fly for two or three hours. However, because they are so big, passenger planes have 12 to 18 hours of flying capability and sufficient fuel to keep the power plant running. "Because of the size, speed, and a large number of people as passengers in it, manoeuvres like a 'dogfight' are not done; it is not safe to do so, and it is unnecessary."

Xavier asked again –

"There were various modes of transport. Ships in the sea, vehicles on the road, and aircraft. Which method of transportation is the safest, I mean having the least number of accidents?"

"It is with confidence, and we understand the technology and quality of aircraft, we can say that the aircraft is safer than any other vehicle. The number of accidents per hour of operation can measure even safety."

According to the International Civil Aviation Organization (ICAO), the number of passenger plane crashes worldwide was forty in 1960, the number of accidents per million departures. Last year, it dropped to just three. Since there has been a fivefold increase in air traffic, air transport is still the best for safety.

It does not mean we are satisfied with fewer than three accidents per million departures. Thousands of engineers worldwide are working tirelessly to achieve zero accidents for flights.

"Beyond the differences in how aircraft are used and their mission, what are the significant differences in design and construction between warplanes and passenger aircraft?"

"While ensuring the technology and quality of warplanes, I can see a lot of similarities in the technology and quality of large passenger aircraft but understand that the technology and quality of warplanes are more complex and rigorous.

For example, while the force of gravity on safe-flying military warplanes can be 10 to 12 times, the gravitational load on passenger aircraft does not increase beyond three times. That's why aerobatics like 'dog fights' are not performed on passenger aeroplanes. I will tell you more when I have time. Tony's flight is about to take off."

Let him have a safe flight!

We stared blankly at the plane until it took off and flew away. We could conspicuously see a set of lights on the aeroplane, indicating its position and direction of motion. It consisted of a red and green light on the port and starboard wing tips, respectively, and a white light at the tail. The plane carried away our dreams of life!

Although I could not see the water in Leelamma's eyes in the darkness, I could hear those heartbeats in the stillness of the night!

There was an enormous delay in getting a telephone connection at Sunabeda, and mobile phones were not widely used. Friends helped us. By the time we got back to Sunabeda, we had received a phone call at a friend's house (Krishnan) at Sunabeda - Tony had gone to NTU College, joined, and got reasonable hostel accommodation. He began to taste and like the Chinese or the food of the Southeast Asian countries available locally there.

Tony established good friendships with 32 students selected in the same batch from India. The best science and technology experts led the studies at the University, and the college facilities were the most modern.

Tony validated his decision to go and study there. We waited and talked for Tony's regular phone calls at a friend's house at the same time every week. We also received his weekly letters regularly.

# 74

# End of Achayan's Public Services

Achayan used to write regularly from home. Sometimes, mother wrote, and sometimes both shared an inland letter. If I were late for writing, Achayan would write again. The critical information in every letter was about the mother's frequent illness. Inadequate travel facilities and some canoes were available for boarding on it. Going to Kanjippadam to get the injection, bring her back home, and get the regular medicines were helpful, and there was no big problem. If the illness were severe, the doctor in Kanjippadam would tell you that it was better to take her to the Hospital at Thathampalli; Achayan would arrange to take her on the road journey, stay in bed for two or three days in the hospital and return home after the illness subsided.

Achayan also sometimes had minor ailments. Achayan was not interested in regular checkups or buying medicines unless essential. So, he wrote to me -

"I believe my diabetes is under control. It was at 325 (mg/dL), now down to 145, because the doctor advised me to eat not more than a cup of rice in the afternoon. Two chapatis in the morning and one in the evening are my routines."

With no grandchildren nearby, even when someone is around, they cannot spend happy time with them, and with so many health issues, parents struggled to spend time. But they did not tell anyone about their grief.

This condition continued for two to three years, from 1992-95. Information was known through various letters of siblings. When I got the latest letter, Achayan wrote, "Thomas Kutty from Arakkaparambil is working in Alappuzha Telephone Exchange. We have given the number you provided to Thomas Kutty. It is often possible to get information by phone through Thomas Kutty."

This situation changed after Raju relocated from Bangalore. At the end of the week, Raju went home, took his mother to buy medicines, and helped her do the household chores. A maid was permanently hired, and before even completing three months, the woman left the place without accepting payment terms and not even taking leave. When the children were away during the school holidays, Lillykutty from the neighbourhood sometimes came to help my mother.

After Raju started living in a rented house in Changanassery, Babychan moved back to the native from Bangalore. Babychan and Tessy provided the care and assistance the parents needed from then on. Babychan and Raju tried to help their parents as much as they could, even amid the hardships of their own lives. Babychan took his mother to a doctor in Muhamma who was practicing a different treatment for asthma. That was what Achayan wrote-

"Ammachi is relieved by the medicine of the doctor at Muhamma." Babu had recently written that he did not have a job and that most company employees had been told to go on unpaid leave due to a lack of orders for the company.

'Raju - Tess couple's second child - Nitin - was born at Kottayam Medical Center and had to have her uterus removed after a caesarean section due to bleeding.' - Achayan wrote: "After seeing the new generation in the hospital, Raju went to Kochi to attend Sheeba's wedding."

Although he knew he could not write in Malayalam, he read Tony's letter from Singapore - "I'm going to listen to it by getting someone to read it." Achayan wrote a reply to Tony for sending an envelope to his grandfather and mother as a Christmas and New Year gift -

"I got Tony's cover. There was enough in the envelope for us to be happy that we could prolong our life -the letter and gift of money. I believe in myself and that I have no discomfort. I thank God. My body is submissive to my mind." Achayan always felt comfortable and considered himself satisfactory in favourable conditions or difficulties.

Achayan also wrote a story for the children to read, as below.

"A hen sat on top of the duck's eggs and gave them enough warmth to hatch. The eggs hatched, and the chicks came out. The hen rejoiced. The hen rejoiced even when the ducklings found their way to the nearby stream and found an attractive place to swim and play.

The story was about their grief about not having children and grandchildren with them during Christmas. Achayan also did not show grief in his mind.

Achayan wrote about the dates for commemorating the death anniversary of Appan, Amma, and Perappan (22-23 Feb) forthcoming soon:

"Remember and pray."

Raju and Babychan were teachers in the catechism classes at church on Sundays. In addition to the office work, they taught the parish's children religious subjects. Descendants of Anjiliparambil continued the tradition of grandfather Varkey. He was always alert and sincere in his dealings with the church. They pray more fervently than anyone else in the family. Therefore, it was evident to them that 'the heavenly Father gave abundant goodness to those who ask of it.' Everyone in the family was getting the benefits one after another. The greatest gift of God was the first.

The Babychan-Tessy couple gave birth to their firstborn child on 17 May 1994, shortening their father's name Thomas to 'Tom' and calling the given name Tom Antony. Two years after the ' ectopic pregnancy,' everyone was delighted by the gift.

Tom was ready for baptism; I took leave from the office to be present there but was caught up in some other official duty. Apart from that, I had planned to return from Koraput after two days and could not go to the function.

At each stage of Tom's growth, his grandparents would write about their experiences to us. Seema called Tom' Undappakru,' and he liked that. He was waiting for Seema Chechi to reach home - why? To call Seema Chechi 'Undappakri'!

The second child was born to Babychan - Tessy couple before Tom was two years old - Teena was born on Republic Day, 26 Jan 1996.

I attended Teena's baptism along with Babychan.

Several days went by for Achayan and Ammachi without the presence of at least one of their grandsons nearby, without hearing a laugh or cry or playing with them. It was difficult for them to pass the days. Babychan fetched Tom from his mother's house after several persuasions by his parents.

"Seema's Undappakru is running all over the place." That's what Babychan wrote.

After giving birth in January, the baby and mother were not brought back home until three months later. At the end of April, when we went on vacation to see the parents, we all came from Koraput, and then Tessy and the baby were not brought home from their house. When asked why it was so, Babychan said something and did not reply directly, and he left. I heard Leelamma say -

'I don't know if there was a misunderstanding between the mothers about the baptism or the fact that they did not return home after fifty-six days, or about the ritual that was practiced in the old Travancore Christian homes, about those sweetie pie, which were brought home by those responsible for the solemn celebration."

Babychan did not say anything; he did not answer, did not blame anyone, and walked away empty-handed. One day, Babychan said "They are going to baptize my baby. None participated from here due to the ill feeling. It was all because they didn't come here to inform or invite my parents to the function!"

"Didn't you go for our baby's baptism? Why didn't you go?" I asked my mother. My mother ignored my inquiry silently and without saying anything.

I decided to go alone to the function in the church. I asked Babychan, who explained how to get to the church and the scheduled time. Tessy's house was near the church.

I wanted to participate in the function at the church, and I walked down that distance in the sun and reached the church on time. There were only a few people who came to the church. Of those who came, I could recognise only Tessy and her mother as familiar faces. I went to their home from church.

I asked Tessy's mother - what's the problem? Why were they not sending Bavichan's baby and the mother, to his home?

Tessy's mother said, "Your mother told me something" that she did not like at all. After that, she remained isolated with chagrin, and nobody ever tried to remove their misunderstandings. So far, no one has sent in a perfect solution, which is not strange.

I said to Tessy's mother: "I apologise for what my mother has done or said. Beyond that, what can Babychan or I do? Isn't she our beloved mother? How can I tell Mom that she was wrong? Do not hold the baby and its mother for that; they have a life. You allow them to go. I'll take them to Babychan's house. "

Tessy's mother could not answer anything. They quickly dressed up the baby and sent Tessy and the baby along with me.

Tina was sleeping on my shoulder, and I was holding the umbrella upright and walking the distance to get home in the afternoon sun. Tessy grabbed a small bag and walked behind.

How can I find happiness if my brother's mind does not find peace and tranquillity in daily life? It does not require hard work or significant investment to make them happy and peaceful.

75

# Beginning of Silence

The village library and reading room have been in operation since 1950. Since the appointment of Kochuppappan (KTAntony alias Anthonichan) as a journalist in Alappuzha in 1960, the post of secretary of the library has been entrusted to Achayan.

It was unlikely that there were people who had served as library secretaries for 34 consecutive years in the nearby villages. He was the Kerala library movement leader. Achayan has been a secretary for a long time since Kochuppappan got a job in Alappuzha.

Just as PN Panicker sir, who was the leader of the Kerala library movement, had to give up social work almost after 50 years due to political influences, KT Thomas, who was a sincere friend and great disciple of PN Panicker, sir, also had to give up the post of secretary of the library in 1994. Achayan was saddened when the only means of his social interaction and reformation activities of public service were blocked, and the task was to be discontinued. Implementing a selfish political agenda and prejudicial behaviour of a few young people caused the breakdown. If some thought that the decline of the library started with the local panchayat's takeover, then there was no mistake in it. Achayan felt completely lonely when he left the library's secretary position and stayed indoors without going out, reading Manorama, and listening to the news on TV.

The library, founded by Kochuppappan, was renamed CYMA by his friends after some time. Eventually, it became The United Public Library & Reading Room after about ten years. During Achayan's reign, the library acquired its land and own building. It increased its collection of books and periodicals, gaining substantial grants yearly from the government. Achayan was the secretary who made the library venture successful and gained popularity. Like the locals, Achayan's library activities made Kochuppappan very proud.

The reading habits, organisational training, and leadership skills the library has personally imparted have been an excellent beginning for me. As a boy, I stood and preached in front of P.N. Panicker Sir, and his support preceded future teaching-speech training. At that time, the secretary of the children's library was the son of the library secretary. The secretary of the children's club had all the freedom in the library. The first lessons of public service were learned from the library. No special permission was required to read any number of books each time. Most of the time, the secretary of the children's club would write in the issue register and bring back the books taken for reading. No defect was found in the periodic stock verifications.

Those who read the book became acquainted with knowledge and proficient in studying among my siblings and peers. Local children organized other children, focused on the library, and formed children's alliances and associations that have benefitted the library.

Achayan, who used to go to the library daily, and his friends could find time to work full-time from the forefront of building the local church, which was great.

It had been a while since we had started thinking about stopping the newspaper distribution by then. It was a job he loved so much that he did not want to give up. It was not just a job; it was a passion. What started with 25 newspapers has grown to over a thousand subscribers. Whatever the role of newspapers in human civilisation and growth, Achayan was happy to pass it on to an entire village for a generation, for 35 years. That is why Achayan's name was added to the number of local social reformers, and everyone happily said so and remembered.

All his children were very proud of him; that was the great wealth and heritage that Achayan had given to his children.

Achayan's 35 years of self-sacrificing family life were his only reliance, and the means of his daily work were the agency and the distribution of newspapers. He has been running for 35 years. It was still the primary source of income and breadwinner for our family. The family grew up, the number of newspapers increased, and the business quality improved. The situation was becoming increasingly disruptive for the newspaper agency to continue and sustain itself as a profitable business. Times have changed. Debt to the newspaper owners can be repaid only if the agents receive the total amount from their subscribers and sub-agents. But lousy credit always became predominant. No matter how many failed attempts, the country's economic security and people's attitude remained the same.

When the newspaper agency and distribution responsibilities were handed over to someone else, there were more than two hundred names of those who did not pay the due amount in the accounts book. The average amount to be recovered from individuals was over two hundred rupees each. They continued subscribing to Manorama, Deepika, and Kerala Kaumudi without paying the dues, paving the way for the agency and distribution to stop. Gratuity and other benefits due to the agent were denied to the agent by the newspaper owners while settling the business accounts. Mathamma acquired the small boat of Anjili wood used by Achayan until then and kept it as a possession. On a concluding day, he did not tie the canoe to our shore but took it to Mathamma's house directly.

He only said, "I am taking the boat." Mathamma. Achayan did not give any reply.

Manorama owners agreed to ease some of the debt, as did other newspapers- Deepika and Kerala Kaumudi. The newspaper owners decided to reduce the arrears by combining the amount owed and the amount they were encouraged to pay when they left. At the end of 35 years of hard work, Achayan knew that business policy and commercial considerations were the basis for their decisions, but he did not take them seriously. "It simply came to our notice then. Enough, let's stop here. Didn't the losses together for a long period? Didn't we live happily so far, and even after this? Grown-up and growing up are the benefits we possess !"

"Jehovah has helped me so much, and God has led me.

Jehovah has lifted me out of nothing and helped me so much. "

"ഇത്രത്തോളം യഹോവ സഹായിച്ചു, ഇത്രത്തോളം ദൈവം എന്നെ നടത്തി..

ഒന്നുമില്ലായ്മയില് നിന്നെന്നെ ഉയര്ത്തി, ഇത്രത്തോളം യഹോവ സഹായിച്ചു..."

(Lyrics & Music: D.J. Ajith Kumar, Vox: M.G.Sreekumar, https: // www.facebook.com / Top Tunes Official)

Always believing that He had "done so much for Achayan and his whole family," Achayan lived that faith and made it a part of his daily life, singing and walking silently. It was decided that the agency and distribution of the newspapers should be stopped, and the responsibility was transferred to others.

Seeing something unique to read in Manorama's Sunday special supplement is common. Babychan would collect weekend magazines that come on every Sunday. I would love to read the extraordinary language resources I get on the holidays away from a remote village in Orissa.

Achayan would reserve a unique Manorama calendar for me every year in December. I once wrote to him when I was the Kerala Samajam president that I would need more copies of the calendar, thinking that the society could distribute them to the members. Achayan's reply came.

"I have kept a copy for you . It is better to write directly to Kottayam for more copies if you need them, as I have stopped paper distribution".

Leelamma and I were always happy to have my mother come and stay with us and the togetherness of my parents. Mom would ask us from time to time.

"What is Achayan doing at home? Is he eating anything?" Sometimes, my mother would share such thoughts with a deep sigh. Her concerns would disappear if I reassured Ammachi that Achayan was fine there. Achayan disagreed when I requested both of them to come and stay together with us. He would say that there was no need for the concern. Apart from managing the distribution of daily newspapers, participating in social services kept Achayan healthy and happy every day. He had set aside the whole time for it.

**Nita's First Holy Communion, and Nita at a Fancy Dress Competition where she won first prize; both while at 208, Binnamangala (1983)**

# 76

# Loathsome

Experiences and knowledge change our attitudes and behaviours. Achayan was very much aware of where and how to react in such situations. That is one of the essential lessons that Achayan has taught us.

An incident that hurt me badly haunted me for two years and upset me. I could not contain it and could not forget, forgive, and erase it like a deadly foreign object debris in my mind. The psychological conflicts that followed since learning of the incident led to tensions that made it impossible to cooperate with some and even look at each other and laugh at individuals—deliberately avoiding many situations where we needed to get together. You can be more cooperative if you realize you are wrong and find a way to correct yourself, whether with relatives or friends!

Plane crash investigation and searching for truth are similar, the difference being that the first is primarily physical and in public service, and the second is purely personal and psychological.

I was searching for the truth. Halfway through, I found that reality has a lot of colours. When we repeatedly look at a puddle of rainwater, there might be many colours, while everywhere else, it might be awash with blue, silver, green, and oyster colours. Isn't it the same thing to motivate and be unresponsive? Doesn't knowing and not responding sometimes seem like an incentive? In my personal but utterly unnecessary interest, I felt it appropriate to do so for my peace of mind, and I did two things-

a) If I must defend myself and fight for justice, I must share it with someone who can mitigate the risk to my life, or the truth will remain an exception. I did this to reduce my mental burden. Before listening, he did not say - I'm not willing to listen to your worries. I am not interested; spare me.' But what he said after listening was – "You should not have told me this."

How is that possible? Will it be practical? I can admit that I was wrong, perhaps.

b) I must share this matter with someone who understands and comforts me about the cause of my recent mental disturbance. I tried.

I had warned that this matter would hurt him as it had hurt me, so first, kindly express your willingness to hear me. When I started, the listener paused me and refused to listen subsequently. In reply, he said -

"I'm not ready to worry about any matter like that. I refuse to carry the burden on my mind" (Maybe because I have a loving and tender heart!)

Great lesson! That is discretion. Only someone with intelligence and self-control can respond that way. That's right.

I got the light. The following expert advice helped me to find it -

"Don't forget that everyone has the right to live their way. Interfering in their lives, be it relatives or friends, is trespassing. It is an unnecessary interest."

Whatever the colour of the truth, if it was a weakness or thoughtless or reckless action, it would be unpleasant and might hurt anyone involved or nearby. That's normal. But it is not polite to highlight it with colours, show excessive interest to know, and thereby upset one's balance.

There is ignorance that arises from the misconception that one is self-righteous. If we examine ourselves, we will see that we do not have the right to blame or reprimand others.

We can advise our friends or near ones to live wisely. Beyond that, interfere in their matters only when necessary."

It was too late for me to realise that the hatred was towards the weakness and ignorance shown and not the weak and the ignorant. They apologized to God in my presence when they realised their shortcomings and ignorance. That is how the hatred changed, and I gained the knowledge and awareness to forgive the weak and the ignorant.

I realised that I had no right to interfere in the lives of others. If you love, look from a distance and watch them. That is the desirable thing.

The stains that clung to the mind were erased and washed. Then, everything could be forgotten and forgiven. Two years later, I became a new man.

Everyone's life must go on. So, I took the bundle of problems to the beach together, added the salty wetness of apology, and threw everything into the sea.!

It must be assumed that Achayan was still unsatisfied and felt inadequate with his daily work and life struggles until he was seventy-five. By then, losing some of the most valuable things in life, the idea of being alienated had made Achayan sad and nostalgic. However, Achayan later actively participated in the church's prayers and charitable activities (of St Antony's Church at Vaishyambhagom), which he built with his efforts out of love for the village community and its progress.

He was a farmer, artist, and freedom fighter for thirty years. Over the past five decades, he has enlightened the masses and inspired them on secular and socialist political thought through his involvement in library activities, journalism, and the construction and reconstruction of churches. Achayan cooperated in the high school and hospital constructions, contributing his time, effort, and finances. He never wanted any position in society or politics till the end of his life. He never asked for anyone's help except to help others. The self-respecting, pure-hearted, and humble man, Vavachi, was described by the loving natives as the social reformer of the time. Still, he was also the family's father who set an example of a self-sacrificing family life for our family members.

How invaluable was the legacy mentioned above and the tradition that Achayan had set? He always said, 'I have not earned anything for my children. He left a legacy that was unique and acquired by his selfless activities! It highlights Achayan's impeccable attitude.

Tessy got a job as a high school teacher at an aided school in Thathampally in the diocese of Changanacherry. It was inconvenient to cross the river by ferry, get on the bus from Kanjipadam to Alappuzha, and get to the school. Babychan can take a direct bus to Thiruvananthapuram or a train from Ambalapuzha. Considering all these possibilities, Babychan found a rented house in Punnapra and paid in advance. He had decided to move to a roadside house, and all that followed was sudden.

Achayan and Ammachi agreed to move from the house in Vaishyambhagom to Babychan's rented home in Punnapra. Achayan was not initially interested in moving from his house to a rented one. Babychan and Tessy found the most comfortable place to stay and go to work after leaving the kids at home by renting a house in Punnapra. Achayan and Ammachi had to accompany them after finding no alternative.

When they decided to move to the rented house at Punnapra, they asked permission from their parents. They said they would move out for convenience only if the parents accompanied them. Even if the consent was given without the parents accompanying them, they said they would not change and would continue to face the difficulties. Having no other choice, Achayan and Ammachi agreed and had to go with their son. The furniture and other belongings were packed and moved only after that consent.

At Punnapra, Achayan's dearest younger brother - Anthonichan - stayed close to the rented house, and the church was nearby. It did not take more than ten minutes to reach a well-equipped hospital. All this motivated Achayan to remove the objections and prepare silently for the move. He did not particularly mention his consent and was hiding his enthusiasm.

"Well, let everything be as you wish. What can I say at this age!" That was the maximum he could say.

Achayan was a father with a vision, knew his children's difficulties, and was willing to give up whatever his likings and desires and make any sacrifice if it benefited his children's happiness. That's why he has agreed.

I had previously failed to influence Achayan by presenting the same thing carefully and diplomatically. However, what I could not do, my brother did. That was my happiness. Babychan's mission to bring a lot of energy into the lives of everyone in the family was commendable. This change of place must have helped prolong the parents' lives without ending prematurely. That proved that plenty of benefits were still to be derived from the family.

My Kochuppappan wrote, "It was a great pleasure for Vavachi and Chedathi to come and stay in Punnapra with Babychan. We could almost always meet, and sometimes you walk up and down."

Achayan reluctantly moved house to Punnapra to be with Babychan. That's how he wrote it 18 days later to me -

"Nobody lives in the house in Vaishyambhagom now. Let's think about renting it out. The house is priced up to Rs 2.25 lakh each.

Do you want to sell it? I go there once in two weeks. Illnesses are low here. I was taken to the hospital, tests were done, and medicines were taken. "That's it. No reply was written about the movement from the water-hole to the shore. So far, so good, well, happy. It was reasonably hoped that both parents would have an increased life expectancy.

I took on new responsibilities in the new office. The main work done in Bangalore was the final tests, which ensured the combined safety of the aircraft. Sunabeda had no aircraft and only made engines to power the aircraft. The engine is a complex system with thousands of parts. The flight of an airplane depends entirely on the performance of the motor integrated into it.

Manufacturing and assembly of engine parts designed in Russia occur in a factory section. Another category is repairing engine parts - repairs and periodic overhauls and servicing. Hundreds of engines are assembled, tested, and shipped to Defence Department facilities annually. Engines are integrated into the aircraft, and they fly the plane.

My main job was ensuring technical standards and acceptable results when the aircraft was tested and integrated with an engine to ensure the aircraft's quality during construction.

Koraput was home to the busiest engine factory. All kinds of workers lived in the township. Shift work also took place at night. Since people lived in the nearest township, everyone went to their homes for lunch. They returned after meals and rest. Most of the employees were locals, and they spoke Oriya. Most people understood Hindi. Many Malayalees also worked in various posts. Workers were allowed to work in the factory wearing a uniform. Since my office was part of the government office, we could work inside the factory wearing plain clothes.

Office work in Sunabeda was full of challenges. So, every day, learning something and finding a technical solution always make the job exciting. My work has enabled me to gain the best possible engineering experience in specific technical excellence and study engine defects and problem-solving apart from personality development. Important lessons learned were presented as essays in the book 'Safety Follows Where Quality Leads.' Here is an experience that was not written in that book.

Some industry personnel are too loyal to their organization and occasionally work to intimidate high-ranking government officials into gaining praise from their superiors. If officials clarify the reasons, issues that could be narrowed down could sometimes become personal encounters. Such an encounter happened to me once. The message was not to harass government officials for their selfish interests; unfortunately, it was a clash of two personalities. The matter was like this –

Run the engine on the testbed at night and make the government officials witness the same until midnight, or one o'clock, to ensure quality while the engines were tested. Witnessing was part of duty, and it was essential. Similarly, the public sector company manager called me at night and told me I had to give him regulatory assistance immediately.

"You must come to the office in the vehicle being dispatched to you, and an urgent matter needs to be decided in a meeting as well."

"No matter what it is, discussing when sleep and fatigue are at the forefront may not be the right and good decision. So, we can discuss this with priority in the office in the morning."

It did not seem satisfactory to the gentleman on the other end of the phone. He raised his voice and responded commandingly.

"No, you have to come."

"Sorry, I cannot come now."

"No, you have to come. You are paid for it ."

"Your father-in-law is not paying me! I am keeping the phone now."

The cold wind that blew through the 'Bhalu Pahad' forest cooled the heat near the telephone.

I do not know if he complained to my boss. Anyway, the following day, when he answered my morning greetings, he asked unusually, looking straight ahead and laughing -

"Hope you had a nice sleep last night."

My boss was also present when things were discussed in the morning. The decision arrived at was not in their favour. One can only guess why there was so much pressure at night!

Some time ago, he tended to scare a government official for temporary gain by putting off doing his mandatory work. He scolded me when I did not allow anything detrimental to the quality standards -

"I keep meeting your boss on various occasions."

"Welcome, Sir; you can be very friendly with my boss."

That was my answer.

The irony is that, years later, that gentleman who was the manager of the public sector company came to be my boss in my government department. He did not have hatred towards me then, but he also had love and respect for me that he did not show anyone else. Unexpected and unfortunate situations may arise in the government service as well. You can always succeed if you are true to your conscience and dedicated to your duty.

Once, a Bengali boss called us to his residence, and such visits would help ensure more cooperation as people work in the same office and are familiar with family relations. After friendly conversations, he invited me to learn about his prowess in gardening. He had a good garden. Curiously enough, he cut eight to ten twigs from a stem and planted them at one end of the garden, each two feet apart. Kappa (cassava) thrived in fertile soil, becoming large, tall, and flowering. No flower was found to be turning to fruit. That is what made him skeptical. He asked me curiously - how long does it take for the Kappa tree to bear fruit?

I did not laugh when I told him that if the soil was removed from the bottom, there was a chance to see the fruit - it was evening time, and he agreed to do so the next day and bid us a good evening.

Two days later, we met at the workshop. I was called closer to him, and he whispered, “I dug into the bottom of the Kappa tree and found the fruits with every distinct root, like a small log of wood. Next time, indeed, we will harvest good cassava yams!”

SITTING: VARGHESE PULLAD, SELF, VIJAYACHANDRAN, RAGHAVAN, PJ NAIR (THEIR BETTER HALVES RESPECTIVELY ARE STANDING BEHIND)

SELF, GOPINATH, JOHNNY THOMAS, JOHNSON NARAYANAN, RADHAKRISHNAN, POOKKUNU, NARAYANAN, SAKHARIA, LEELAMMA, RUGMANI,THANKAMANI & Mrs POOKKUNJU

**Friends at Sunabeda Township**

# 77

# The Tableaux

Tony saved his scholarship money to go to Sunabeda on vacation. He spoke in detail about the study and living conditions in Singapore. There were very few days off when Tony's first year was over. He came to Chennai taking a flight Ticket. It was possible to alleviate the boredom of eating Chinese Malaysian food. He was ready for a difficult journey, even though the holidays were short and costly, as he thought he could eat the mommy-made food at home for at least a week. The beautiful Pomeranian puppy doll that he brought always remained a curiosity for the guests in our house. Mommy provided a pedestal that was relevant to it as a seat. When I saw the Pomeranian, people were reluctant to go inside, and I told them it was just a doll! Even in the award-winning tableau "Manishada" in Sunabeda, the Pomeranian, which sat next to Bhardwaj, was inappropriate there but attractive, like the architectural flaw of the Taj Mahal.

During his first year, the university encouraged Tony to pursue some extracurricular activities.

One of his assignments was to start a chapter on the International Red Cross and Red Crescent Movement at NTU. Within a year, they inquired about the Red Cross movement at their Singapore branch, talked to the authorities, and organized several charitable activities, including a chapter at NTU. In the years that followed, that chapter grew and expanded.

Tony was shy and generally introverted in school and was more or less a bookworm. When he studied in Singapore, he tried to overcome these traits, which was how he joined the NTU Debating Club.

Twice a week, he learned to analyse numerous statistics, distinguish critical arguments, and develop innovative policymaking that would benefit the debating team through intensive training classes. Tony was specially trained to lead the team in different situations and gained more experience responding quickly to the dynamics of the debate while maintaining the team's overall strategy. Discussions on various issues also aroused his curiosity about the factors influencing economic and social development.

By joining the NTU Debating Society, he participated in international debating competitions and led the NTU team.

A debate he participated on the then British Prime Minister Margaret Thatcher was recorded, brought home, and made public.

His newfound success in debating has inspired him to participate in and lead many other activities on campus. It enabled Tony to interact better with his classmates and adapt to Singaporean culture.

Tony has been a member of the International Debating Championship team at NTU since 1991. As part of the NTU team, he travelled to neighbouring countries like Malaysia and the Philippines to compete with local university teams. Tony sent me a video recording of some of the debates that he participated. It was fascinating to hear the preaching. For two consecutive years, in 1993 and 1994, the team consisting of Tony won the championship trophy in debating. Those gold-coloured trophies, which are well-designed and carefully crafted, still rest in our showcase without losing their novelty.

When I joined the college in my first year, some friends in the same batch made fun of things like ragging but not hurting each other. On one similar occasion, Mommy saw a photo brought by Tony of his friends carrying Tony and throwing him into a pool. When asked about it, Tony said that it was when he fell into the water and could not swim and breathe; his friends jumped into the pool, grabbed Tony, pulled him ashore, and persuaded him to learn to swim.

After a few days of preparation, friends and classmates who knew Carnatic music performed a "musical evening" of classical, simple, and film music on the college campus. Thus, they grew with great pride among the students of Southeast Asian countries.

Comprehensive growth of students was possible when they were prepared internationally for an excellent professional career through leadership training, academic excellence, ability to apply technology, and extracurricular activities. With the right decisions and the blessing of more adults, Tony wanted this and tried to achieve it to some extent.

Tony explained the study facilities, the skilled teachers in the domain, and the diet he got. Maybe that should have inspired Seema as well. That was when she also began to see Singapore as an opportunity for higher education. Nita had similarly started thinking that life after study should be done with something satisfying to her. Isn't that what I saw in her: she studied more enthusiastically, came with a tenth pass, and showed interest in joining Plus 2?

Tony went to Bangalore and brought Nita with him. For Nita, hostel life was satisfying, too. Everyone celebrated Christmas and New Year in Sunabeda. For Christmas, all the friends in the office shared a cake. For the New Year, the Malayalee friends in the township prepared a meal together, sang songs, made jokes, and made the time very happy. Malayalee friends gave hints about the upcoming picnics and cultural fairs. They hoped that the coming Sunabeda times would be more enjoyable and satisfying.

Tony and Nita returned to their study area in the first week of the new year.

In a short time in Sunabeda, we built a community of good friends. The closeness and cooperation that followed made it seem like they had long waited for us. Since we met, Johnson, Baby, Raghavan, Antony, Mammachan, PJ Nair, Thomas John, Zachariah, and Gopi have become family friends who visit almost daily. Zachariah, PB Pillai, Johnny Thomas, Radhakrishnan, Narayanan, Soman, and many other friends who were active members of the Samajam came forward ready to organise any function.

Various languages and cultural clubs regularly held annual conferences and cultural fairs. The Kerala Samaj regularly organised Onam celebrations, Onasadya, one or two cultural evenings, including social drama, one or two picnics with the Samajam's family members, and a trip to another township.

The table exhibition was regularly held at the Sunabeda Parade Ground during the Republic Day celebrations, like the one seen on the Rajghat on Republic Day in Delhi.

In preparation, the Samajam office bearers gathered at the Samajam office for a discussion. I also attended as an invited special guest. What emerged from the debate was that our tableau had been good in the previous years in which the community had participated but had not received the prize and that the awards essentially favour the Oriya Club.

"They attracted more people every year and made fairs like the chariot festival in Puri as the subject of tableaux. It was hard to put together a festival, boat race, or tableau with so many people participating, so we may decide not to attend this year," some commented. The opinion was raised that non-participation would be misinterpreted and affect the popularity and prestige of the Samajam. I also commented.

"It was not good for Samajam to display a tableau just to get the prize. If you wish to participate, you can present a meaningful topic without too many people participating. Just be satisfied with a good theme or message, and do not prepare anything for getting the prize."

The Sunabeda Malayalee community had good artists, sincere workers, people willing to go to great lengths, and good intentions. Some of them asked -

"Let us listen to the theme or topic. If possible, we can do it".

Making use of the opportunity, I presented the topic.

In short, it was based on the slogan "Live and Let Live." In detail, you know the first hymn in the Ramayana - Adi Kavi's song of sad unrest -

'Ma Nishada Pratistham Tvamagamaah sasvati Samaa

Yat Kraunchamithunaadekam Avadhi Kaamamohitam ".

There are many meanings, yes, many meanings, for one verse. This is one -

"Oh, hunter, because you killed one of the crows you loved, may you not survive. Or "O Nishada (hunter), because you killed one of the Kraunca couples who was engaged in love, may you never obtain peace.!"

"Design this context as a tableau- The Ashramam of Rishi Valmiki, woods and the hunter. The hunter shoots one of the birds in the tree, and a depressed Valmiki takes care of the fallen bird. Rebuke the hunter! What else can he do?"

'Manishada'. Don't be a savage! Mahamuni told the hunter who shot one of the innocent parrots enjoying the culmination of his love affair. 'Manishada'.

The message of Ramayana is 'Manishada'. Saying no is to a savage, no to all men who commit evils and atrocities."

Sunabeda had several good artists in the Malayalee community. I was sure everyone would support me.

A badly worn-out old and abandoned lorry was allotted to prepare a tableau for the Kerala Samajam. Many have said that this was a deliberate ploy by someone to thwart our efforts. "Instead of accepting this, we must react, and we have to protest. Can we do anything on this lorry?" someone said.

Raghavan, who always respected the workers' feelings, said, "The idea of 'live and let live' is good, and the plan to build is also good. But it is doubtful that anything can be done right on this wretched lorry. Do you want to waste your efforts?"

All I had to say was - "Wise people do not look at the shape and condition of the lorry. They will only evaluate the tableau for its theme. If we can present our idea well, that will be a success. We should be satisfied with good work, and we do not want to do just anything. We will not clamour or argue for a prize."

Everyone agreed with that position.

Zechariah cut down a branch of a tree, removed all the green leaves, cut paper into the shape of leaves pasted on the branch, and made it look like a big tree. The Ashramam was built by covering the lorry's cabin with a coloured tarpaulin. 'Speed' Gangadharan, a sincere executive and always walking speedily, went somewhere on the hillside, picked up a giant anthill (valmeekam), brought it in a handcart, and placed it near Rishi Valmiki. During the night, Abraham caught hold of two pigeons from the attic space of an empty house, where the pigeons nested. One pigeon was tied to a tree, and the other pigeon's wing was covered with red ink, creating a look like bloodstains. GJ Nair played the role of a hunter. Anthony became Valmiki, holding a wounded pigeon in his left hand and with his right hand signalling "no" to the hunter. KG Nair had the role of a disciple of Valmiki, Bhardwaj, who performed penance in front of the Ashramam. Thomas John, Gopi, and the others came ready to do anything. They worked tirelessly all day.

'Manishada' also won the first prize for being one of the best Republic Day tableaux on display at Sunabeda.

At the next general meeting of the Kerala Samajam, they elected me as the President of the Samajam. I said we could do a lot together and nominated Johnny Thomas as the secretary, who was elected.

The community participated in Republic Day tableaux for the next five years and won prizes. Featured themes were presented, and I had a part to play in designing them. The following is a brief description of them -

(1996) Heaven of Freedom: The Red Fort symbolises our great nation's past glory and sovereignty, where the national tricolour was hoisted for the first time since independence. Rajghat is the tomb of Mahatma Gandhi. The Temple of Non-Violence is a place of worship where people of different religions pray. Rajghat, with its Red Fort background, was summarised in Tagore's lines: -

"Where the mind is without fear, and the head is held high,

The world has not been broken into fragments by narrow domestic walls,

Where knowledge is free,

Into that heaven of freedom, my father, let my country awake" (second prize)

(1997) Onam Celebration - Traditional Culture, Colours and Rituals. (Second Prize)

(1998) The Task of Nation Building: The Tableau and Nation Building Tasks Presented by the Kerala Samajam on the 50th Republic Day of India symbolically depicted the role of each one of us in it. The efforts of engineers, scientists, agro-industrial workers, athletes, soldiers, and politicians could be seen. To continue this unfinished mission, we must each do our best. We aim to build a secular nation based on free democracy and socialism that is economically strong. (Second Prize)

(1999) "Chalo Milkar Hum Dharm Ko Jod Den": "All religions aim to achieve peace and tranquillity and to unite with God." Although we are all Hindus, Muslims, Christians, and Sikhs, we are all children of God. So, we are spiritual siblings. Our Constitution gives freedom of worship. Secularism shows respect for all religions. Religious tolerance is a sacred duty of every citizen. This year, the tableau of Kerala Samajam expressed the essence of secularism. This means that no matter what religion we follow, it will not be an obstacle to the well-being of others. Secularism must find a place in our hearts. Let us work together for mutual respect and national unity." (First Prize)

The 1999 tableau was presented to protest and offer condolences on the murder of Australian Christian missionary Graham Staines and his two children while asleep in their vehicle three days ago (January 23, 1999) in a village in Orissa.

CL Jose's 'Manalkaadu' was a play performed by the Kerala Samajam, which attracted the attention and admiration of all Malayalees around Sunabeda.

It was the story of a great judge who possessed sacred ideals and wanted to lead a family life on the path of Dharma. It was the story of a good man who overcame temptations and trials by overcoming the influence of love and relationships even when his home was on the ridge of a dune.

Community Hall in Sunabeda Township – Bhanjamandap- was full of Malayalees when the play was staged by the Samajam members viz- Antony (Alappuzha Kuttappan), Khadeeja Kunju Muhammad, Johnny Thomas, Reji Varghese, Sneha, GJ Nair, Johnson and Thomas John. Artists behind the stage were CR Narayanan, Radhakrishnan, and Zachariah. Costume: Balakrishnan, Background music: Mohan, Indirani Sound and Light: Unnikrishnan, Kuriakose. There were a lot of friends to help.

In Sunabeda, Kerala, Samaj's plays were usually directed by the participating leading actors. This time, they honoured me by leading the team of directors. There was nothing to do except that I co-ordinated activities with the excellent cooperation of all. The play was a great success and a source of pride for the community. The dignitaries of the factory were also present to witness the event.

'Maa Nishada Pratistham Tvamagamahsāsvati Samaa
Yat Kraunchamithunaadekam Avadhi Kaamamohitam' KERALA SAMAJAM TABLEAU (1994)

"Chalo Milkar Hum Dharm Ko Jod Den"
KERALA SAMAJAM TABLEAU (1999)

**Tableau designed for Kerala Samajam in Sunabeda**

# 78

# Onam and Neighbours

The Onam celebrations in 1997 were an unforgettable cultural fair in Sunabeda. Onam was traditionally celebrated by Malayalees every year. Soman Pillai always stood in front of the Onam celebrations and worked. The community members came together to organise the ceremonies, prepare and serve the dishes, and present the occasional entertainment, an inseparable part of the celebrations. Everyone was dressed in the traditional Kerala style. Onasadya was attended by all the Malayalees from the surrounding areas, especially from the NALCO, Daman Jodi township. Due to the absence of modern communication amenities, transportation, and entertainment at Sunabeda, popularly known as the 'Onamkeramoola,' perfectly reflected the Onam culture of the expatriate Malayalees of Kerala while residing at Sunabeda.

Good artists, actors, organisers, and the women and children of almost every Malayalee family showcased their talents during the cultural feast that followed the Onasadya.

At the cultural festival in the evening, they performed (solo and group) dances (classical & cinematic), songs in different languages, and satirical shows for only entertainment. According to various religions, dance forms were the most notable event - the homemakers performed the Thiruvathirakkali, Oppana, and Margamkali dances. As part of their unique cultural heritage, each dance was performed by different faiths and was performed by ladies of all religions, thus celebrating religious harmony. Before the national flag, all the artists performed the tableau 'Bharat Mata.' Mrs Savitri Nair directed the musical dances.

In 1998, the HAL Employees Welfare Committee organised a drama competition for various language clubs in the township. The competition was announced a month ago. Bengali, Oriya, Tamil, Hindi, Malayalam, Telugu, Marathi, and Kannada dramas should be performed. Duration should not exceed one hour for the presentation. Excellence will be rewarded. The organizers provided the stage and auditorium. Almost the entire township population will be in attendance, and the judges will be eminent persons nominated by the institution. The Kerala Samajam also consulted and decided to participate in the drama competition. The task was in hand - select the play and start the training - for the President of the Samajam.

There was a sudden inspiration - 'If you write a short play of one hour in length and give it to the blessed artists of Sunabeda, they will perform it and make it a success.' I heard it loud and clear. A step was taken for the courageous move forward, thinking 'all is for good!

A national award-winning Oriya film, which I happened to see recently on TV, came to my mind. Although I did not understand the language, I remembered the story and the context. I thought of it and found time to write the play. The play was written in three or four days. Johnny Thomas, the then secretary of the Kerala Samajam, helped me to read, evaluate critically, correct the mistakes, and make them suitable for presentation on the stage.

It was named 'Neighbours'. Overall, it seemed flawless. The cast was decided, and the rehearsal started within a week. After ten days of training, the technicians, artists, and actors gained the confidence to perform the play on the stage.

We presented the drama on the stage in precisely sixty minutes. Most Malayalees and other township residents who spoke different languages came to see the play. Excellent responses, encouragement, and compliments were received from the audience. We were delighted with the presentation.

'Neighbours' is the play that stars Johnson, Pookunju, Rukmini, Thankamani, and two children. Behind the stage were CR Narayanan, Zacharia, Thomas John Costume by Balakrishnan, Background music by Indirani, Sound, and Light managed by Unnikrishnan, and again there were many friends to help. I wrote and directed the script, and the presentation was by the Kerala Samajam, Sunabeda.

Outside the township, in the small town of Semiliguda, there was a Christian church, the congregation of which met only on Sundays. There was a Malayalee priest in the church and three or four Malayalee nuns/sisters in the nearby ashram. There was also a primary school attached to the (Madam) Ashram. Nuns taught children in school. On weekdays, the priest would go to the Ashram and offer the holy Mass there.

After completing a half-century in this worldly life, Leelamma and the girls invited the priest and the nuns to our house for a banquet. Raghavan, PJ Nair, Antony, Baby, Johnson, etc., who were very close to our family, were occasionally invited home for a treat. They were also hospitable in reply. Foreign liquor in small quantities was also an unavoidable attraction at such get-togethers. None of the Malayalees was alcoholic. And everybody considered it as only a small pleasure, a nourishing substance that energised the unity of the diaspora!

Even before Tony completed his two years of study in Singapore, Nita completed her SSLC studies at Ann's School. She came to Sunabeda after taking her exam. The holidays were celebrated with Seema. Nita met friends in Sunabeda. Nita passed the SSLC exam with good marks. Her further studies were determined to be in the nearest English medium school in Koraput – the Sunabeda Public School. I bought TC from her school in Bangalore and enrolled her in the Sunabeda Public School.

I got the telephone connection after two months of applying it. The grocery store owner had a phone near Bavichan's rented house in Punnapra. If I could call there, someone would tell my father or Babychan to come near and talk on the phone after ten minutes. Then, if you inform them early that someone will be standing close to the phone, I could contact them and communicate that way.

Nita and Seema took Library Kuriakose's daughter's (Tittee) bicycle and rode around the township. Nita had not practiced cycling much. That was why she fell once. That's when Titee came over and told me. No significant cuts or bruises were seen on her body. It appeared that it was difficult for her to lift her left hand. A closer look revealed that the bone of her left hand (Radius or Ulna or both) had slipped from the elbow. It looked like a chapati rolling pin had been put into a cloth bag, ready to penetrate the skin and come out.

I put her hand in a sling and tied it around her neck; that was the first aid, and I took her to the Sunabeda hospital. Since it was Sunday, there were no doctors at the township hospital. I had the freedom to go directly into the CMO's room. Neither CMO Dr Mishra nor Ortho Surgeon Parida was present in the hospital. They were also not in their residence and had gone to Visakhapatnam. They would return in the evening only. I was disturbed that I had to wait until the evening since no medical help could be obtained nearby. Sometimes, there was no pain, but her hand had a slight swelling that would worsen if it remained longer.

I thought for a while about what to do. As I learned in school, the elbow joint I remembered was the ends of bones encased in a smooth cartilage similar to just a ball and socket joint. When the upper end of the lower bone is inserted into a cartilage ligament, it acts as the joint. There would be pain and fluid flow if there were any scratches or breakages in the cartilage. Those symptoms were not shown here. Then, what I thought could be done safely.

The hand was removed from the sling and stretched out, pointing down as usual. I grabbed the wrist and pulled it gently down without

Nita noticing it. The bone appeared to have entered the cartilage and was in the correct joint. It relieved her of the pain, and she could move the hand freely up and down. When I felt at her knee joint, I could realise that the bone had fallen into the casing! There was no pain, and it was not difficult for Nita to raise her hand. Nita did not understand what had happened. I took a deep breath, closed my eyes, and meditated, remembering the faces of my elders. I went home and took a rest. I got a message when CMO Mishraji returned home in the evening. I went there with Nita and showed him her hand; he said she was fine, which was a great relief for all of us.

A week later, Achayan wrote, "I think Nita's hand is fine."

It was learned through Babychan's writing in May 1995 that Achayan was admitted to Cherthala KEM Hospital. He tried to inform me over the phone through Thomas Kutty but did not get through. Urinary tests and investigations were done on Achayan. An operation was done earlier to remove the urinary obstruction. Hence, he was retaken to the same hospital due to the pain and related discomfort.

Achayan underwent bladder tests and other blood tests in the hospital. An operation was performed earlier to remove the urinary obstruction, and there it was. He went there because of a recurrence of pain and urinary incontinence.

I took leave because I was told that his prostate gland needed surgery. The doctor put in a tube to help Achayan to urinate after the operation. When in pain, Achayan said that this was not necessary. Understandably, Achayan's thoughts and fear about the bill had driven him to say that. Babychan, on leave, was in the hospital every day. Within a week, the pain subsided, and the obstruction disappeared. I came back after Achayan was discharged from the hospital. Babychan passed the departmental examination after he had studied and spent time at the hospital.

Babu had gone to work temporarily with a wiring contractor. If he got a call from Coimbatore, you would go there.

Achayan wrote letters about the Independence Day celebrations in Punnapra and the information that Narakathra Kuttappan had gone to see Achayan. The happy father announced that his son Benson got a job in a fishing boat. When I was in Pune and residing at Range Hills, Kuttappan and his wife had come and lived in my house before the delivery of their firstborn. Benson grew up, and when he was four years old, his father brought him to me to begin his writing auspiciously. Happily, I made that baby write sitting on my lap that day. That boy had grown up and was working now. Later, whenever we could see Kuttappan, the feelings and memories of the great sorrow permanently silenced our conversations. To this day, no one knows what happened. Within a year or two of starting his work in a fishing boat, Kuttappan learned that a fishing vessel had wrecked in a cyclone or tornado off the coast of Gujarat. What he would do after leaving the post in the Army Medical Core was unknown. The investigation has been going on for many years. Pakistan had arrested a fishing vessel and its crew for violating maritime boundaries. During the question-and-answer session, the people's representatives also discussed the issue in our Parliament. The minister said there were no such prisoners in Pakistan. The grief of Kuttappan and his family over their son's separation is still remembered with pain.

# 79

# The Great Sage

Raju bought a 15-cent plot of land in Illimoodu at Changanassery. In his rush to run around for finance, he wrote to me to some extent.

I was willing to give, as always. But it was tough to find that much money together at hand. Saying no might have resulted in unfair thoughts, and it felt like that from a no-brainer. That was more difficult.

My thoughts apply only to me. If I use the same thing to my brother, it may be construed as interfering in his matters. "Do you have the money to send for an essential thing for him? If not, is it possible to get a loan? The exploration is over. No reason could be found for taking a provident fund loan, even illegally. There was no other way to explore. After replying to him that it was impossible without assigning any reason, the afterthought came to me. I could have written more gently while writing, and the harsh nature seemed unnecessary to my brother. I didn't even learn from the experience! 'One of the elder brothers was having a 'Musetta Subavam' (stubborn character), and the comments had no answers!

A month later, I was told – "I could buy the land because my wife and her family had helped me." As always, things have happened for good, which relieved me adequately.

Achayan wrote to me while resting in Punnapra after his treatment at the Chethipuzha Hospital - "Should I sell my house in Vaishyambhagom? What price should I get? Should I get the proceeds and put them in the bank? Or should I send it directly there?"

Raju's writing came earlier when I kept my mind calm by thinking about the precise meanings of Achayan's writings. I wrote primarily to inform you about the health conditions of Achayan and Ammachi. Both were treated at the Changanassery Chethipuzha Hospital for a week. Achayan went to Punnapra after recovering from his illness. My mother stayed back with Raju for about two weeks. It was also written that Nitin was enrolled in a Montessori school. Raju must have talked to Achayan about selling the house. That's what his comment mentioned to me in writing -

"I think it should not be sold until Kochayan retires."

I wrote to Achayan, "Sell it when we can get more. "

I had a clear sense that it would be best to allow time, at least until retirement, for the private thoughts of my mind to come to fruition.

The workload in the office increased. It is common practice in the Department of Defence to inquire into the causes of fighter plane crashes. If the aircraft were fitted with an engine manufactured at Sunabeda, several interested party representatives would undoubtedly have been included in the investigation team. I was included in a few investigation teams and was nominated as an aero engine expert. Once the investigators went to the accident scene, it was impossible to return for thirty to forty days, i.e., until it was completed. Over time, I have been able to work as part of several investigative teams that have made significant contributions to technical studies and safety. The quality problems we saw in our daily work and the technical solutions found were precious. The most important of these were discussed in a book I published after retirement. It is appropriate to state an experience not mentioned in the book and involving an extraordinary person.

In the wake of the frequent loss of many fighter jets belonging to the Indian Air Force, The Ministry of Defence has appointed a COFA Committee headed by Dr APJ Abdul Kalam, the then Scientific Adviser to the Minister of Defence. I was fortunate to join that committee, which included many eminent scientific and technical persons and experts. We visited all warplane manufacturing facilities and studied aircraft quality problems and their solutions. That was how the committee reached Sunabeda. I was tasked with presenting the findings of the accident investigations, in which I participated to the committee for deliberations. After explaining the results and the corrective measures taken during the manufacturing phase, many people asked questions, and I answered them. Everyone left for lunch. That was when Dr Kalam called me and took me to the factory.

I was taken to the workplace. Dr Kalam told me -

"Come, let us go and see the shop where the gear was manufactured, and let me understand how the problem happened."

I took him to the workplace, where the hobbing process was done while manufacturing the gear on the hobbing machine. I explained the process in about ten minutes. -

"After completing one stage of the hobbing process, the gear was sent to the process shop for carburising. After proper processing, it was brought back here for the next stage of the hobbing process. When all the machining processes were completed, the gear was inspected and accepted for assembly. It was the gear used in the engine gearbox; the teeth had fallen off, damaged, and lost functionality. "

The investigation found that the error (error of omission) was accidentally made here at the workstation, where more material was machined off after carburising."

I looked at his face curiously to see if any more explanation was required to convince him after emphasizing that all the engineering solutions had been implemented so that the omission error would never happen again.

He approached closer to me, put his left hand on my shoulder, smiled, and pointed his right-hand finger to the factory workers returning after lunch. He said-

"Thomas, they are all the 'Vishwakarma's and... you are the 'Viswaamithra' .....He paused momentarily and continued, "Thank you, come, let us go for lunch."

Suddenly, I was astonished- 'Here is a Muslim, speaking Hindu philosophy to a Christian!'

Suddenly, I was astonished- 'Here is a Muslim, speaking Hindu philosophy to a Christian!'

I did not understand what the philosophy was. I felt what the great man said must have some significant meaning.

Although I did not understand the meaning, his words remained in my mind like quotes inspired by a prophet. I tried to understand the meaning from my Hindu friends. My respect for Dr Kalam turned into adoration only when I understood the meaning.

Here is a brief of what I understood-

Viswamithra: Vishwamitra Mahamuni, overcoming temptations, controlling emotions - Manager. Vishwamitra was the complete friend of the universe. Vishwamitra, who attained the Brahmarshipada by karma, proved that one could reach the heights of knowledge through diligent and meticulous practice.

Vishwakarma: Vishwakarma is the sculptor, the carver, the sculptor (Worker, Machine Operator), the craftsman god, and the divine sculptor of the gods.

All workers perform their duties only in a manner controlled by the Manager. (All workers will only do their work as directed by the Manager.) Since you are the responsible Manager, you must exercise proper controls and reach the level of knowledge to avoid quality problems since "You are the responsible Manager."

This is only understood when read in conjunction with the basic process control principle - "Prevention is the best way to control quality."

A worker, a machine operator, or an inspector may become distracted or forget to complete a task (Omission). That is how errors occur. Procedures, regulations, and managers need to be established to avoid mistakes.

(Preventive measures, including process controls established by the Manager, can prevent the error from happening.)

To learn how faults occur in industrial equipment and products and how to prevent defects. That is the true meaning of burning up bad psychic imprints. As some people usually believe, it is not the fault of individuals when mistakes are made.

Such universal truths can only be found in mythology or religious scriptures. Only an Acharya Maharishi/ Mahatma equal to the Prophet can give such a word of wisdom!

With a multi-faceted personality, that extraordinary man shone as the President of the People, the Missile Man of India, Dr APJ Abdul Kalam. A practical philosophy that the great man often spoke of,

I like this philosophy - here I quote it.

“A large part of your life will be filled with your work. One way to get absolute satisfaction is to believe that you are doing a good job, and the only way to do a good job is to love your job. If you have not yet found what you want, keep looking. And, as you can see, like any good relationship, it’s getting better and better over the years, so keep looking and do not relax until you find satisfaction.”

# 80

# On the Lap of Nature

Koraput was known as the 'Lap of Nature due to its natural beauty. But India's Koraput district was the most backward before the HAL factory came to Sunabeda, Koraput, in 1964. Most of the people living in and around Sunabeda were tribals and Adivasis. The roads were broken, and there were no suitable communication, education, and transportation facilities. It took a long time for development to reach these areas.

In Koraput, roads and roads were once avoided by travellers. But over time, that was likely to change. You can find wide streets in Koraput, roadside restaurants, petrol pumps, and beautiful tribal homestays. Modern mass media and ideological communication facilities came all over the area.

In the early days of Sunabeda, tribal women came to the houses for domestic work without adequately covering their breasts. So were the many women who sold vegetables on the streets at the Simliguda market. Within a few years, we could see a change in their dress code.

By the 1990s, more facilities, including smaller restaurants, petrol pumps, an ATM, a Tribal Museum, and Tarred Roads. Ten kilometers from HAL, the National Aluminum Company (NALCO) set up a bauxite (aluminium ore) mining and refining plant at Daman Jodi, where many workers settled. The Koraput-Sunabeda-Daman Jodi area was rich in scenic locations, hills, mountains, valleys, and picnic spots like a wildlife sanctuary, Colab Falls, Tribal Museum, Chilika Lake, and Bhalu Pahad. It was typical for family picnics with children for a full day and to return to the township in the evening after enjoying the scenery, cooking lunch, relaxing, and playing tiny games outside the house. Organisations like Kerala Samajam organised excursions, trekking trips, and extensive group trips for the community more than once a year. The main pastime was preparing, serving, and eating food together. Some used to carry utensils and find a place to eat and cook food at the destination while the rest engaged in various games and sports. Such picnics and excursions that children and adults enjoy were the unique entertainment of the residents of Sunabeda Township. Many picnics and trekking camps at Bhalu Pahad in Sunabeda continually refresh the mind and body during the holidays.

If you want to catch a flight, dine at a good hotel, or go to the beach to enjoy the breeze, you must travel at least 200 km from Sunabeda. The first choice was to travel by state bus, which only arrived twice daily for a one-way six-hour journey, including climbing up and down the hilly terrain. Essential parts of the body needed to be protected from much damage. These hurdles must be resolved to enjoy a luxury trip, delicious food, or celebrations. Then, there was no pastime other than short trips or picnics mentioned above. Or maybe it was just an easy way to meet faraway relatives. That was Sunabeda.

Daman Jodi township had many of our native friends - Mathukutty, Narayanan, and Prasad - so we occasionally went there and returned in the evening. Friends from Damanjodi and their families attended every event in the Samajam.

This kind of continual cooperation of people who were not available in everyday routine in the city or even the village was a unique feature while living in a factory township like Sunabeda.

Tony completed a three-year BASc (Computer Engineering) degree course at Nanyang Technological University and joined the (Honors) class during the fourth year in 1995-96. That was the case in some universities. Essay-based honours degrees prepare students for research-based postgraduate study, which may sometimes allow them direct access to doctoral programmes.

Tony only had a few days to come home and return before the start of the new year's studies. So he came unannounced and without any prior notice.

That day, I was getting ready to go to the office early. Seema was also getting prepared to go to school. Somebody came from outside and pressed the calling bell so that the ringing was heard suddenly and unexpectedly. Leelamma went and opened the door. She was momentarily frightened and blinded by a flash of lightning.

I looked when I heard a voice calling out enthusiastically, "Wow!" or something like that. Tony also appeared, holding a camera, looking at Mommy, and laughing. Tony was ready to give us a surprise. To our surprise, he filmed his frightened mommy's face on camera. He got the results he intended.

After a minute, Mommy got convinced, or she improved her face from fear, laughed in surprise, and hugged him, calling him "Mone." Seema came after that and was surprised to see her Chachan.

Tony landed in Calcutta, reached Vijayanagaram by train, and reached Sunabeda by the first bus at 6 a.m. Tony himself narrated the sad state of his journey throughout. During the fourteen-hour trip to Sunabeda, he ate only a packet of biscuits and a bottle of water he had bought when he landed in Calcutta without even getting a little sleep; why all these troubles, I did not dare to ask?

While taking out the laundry from his suitcase in the evening, Tony hid something in his hand and handed it over to his mommy. When Mommy opened her hand, it slipped from her hand and fell. As something dropped out of her hand, Mommy yelled "Aww" again as if frightened by a small green reptile!

I saw a green snake lying down when I looked there, but it was not moving! It was a toy made of rubber. Believing that size, colour, and shape were like a live reptile. Then everyone laughed and joked, and Mommy's fear was removed. Mommy warned Tony after being so scared of dogs and snakes -

"Don't bring anything scary things like this again, Mone!" Tony obeyed.

1996 Tony joined the Hewlett Packard Software Company for a six-month industrial attachment following his fourth-year annual examination. At the end of the training, the project manager and marketing manager gave Tony a letter of commendation, praising Tony for the skills and contributions he made to the job.

Tony wanted his parents to visit Singapore to participate in the convocation - the university's graduation ceremony in 1997. Although we wished to go, we could not attend the same because the situation was not conducive to meeting the travel expenses. The ceremonies were viewed through video, which Tony shared. Then he brought photos to show and make us understand everyone. A large group of Tony's friends and classmates filmed their victory celebrations, partying, and merriment could be seen among the photos. Most of his friends were from India. Tony's junior batch also had a girl named Joysy John from Kanpur who studied Computer Engineering (included in the fourth batch selected from India for the SIA - NOL Scholarship).

Before joining the job, Tony said goodbye to NTU University and its Hostel by purchasing an air ticket to return to India as per the SIA - NOL Scholarship and an air ticket to return to Singapore. He subsequently moved into a residential flat in Singapore with some friends.

Six years of compulsory employment in Singapore was a condition for Tony to be awarded a scholarship for studying BASc (Hons) degree courses at NTU. Therefore, the authorities did not allow him to pursue postgraduate studies there after graduation. Bond had prescribed that he return to work immediately and stay in Singapore for at least six years.

On August 04, 1997, Tony joined Hewlett Packard Company. He worked as an IT Solutions Specialist at Hewlett Packard Far East from Aug 1997 to May 2000. Subsequently, he worked for seven months at Lante Singapore. Tony found it convenient to pursue further studies, even part-time Post Graduate Studies, and joined the National University of Singapore (NUS) for that.

As soon as he joined the Hewlett Packard Company, Tony decided to attend evening classes for graduate school. The National University of Singapore is another university in Singapore. Tony chose M.A. (Southeast Asian Studies) as a general subject for his undergraduate studies. Postgraduate degree in an Arts subject after graduation in Computer Engineering!

By the time the post-graduate studies at NUS were over, the requirement to work in Singapore for six years had also been completed. What next?

His parents had almost decided that Tony would settle down peacefully in Singapore with a promising career and look for a happy married life. However, he would have liked at least one of his sisters to get married first. He seldom shared his plans with his parents.

Even though he did not mention the target he was aiming for, he had a clear sense of purpose since Plus Two – ".. Job opportunities where the knowledge can be applied to achieve a better standard of living for all humans". He stated that goal while applying for a scholarship in Singapore and during the interview when the University selectors asked him to spell out his vision for the future.

Nita passed Plus Two from Sunabeda Public School in 1996. While looking for admission at St Joseph's College for Women in Alappuzha for further studies, she said she would like a hotel management degree course at Christ College. Tony agreed with Nita.

At that time, Tomichan, the younger brother of Checkkidikadu James, was studying to become a priest at Dharmaram College. I wrote to Tomichan and applied for her admission to the BHM course at Christ College. I went to Christ College with Nita when she was called for an interview. Fr Thomas Chathamparambil interviewed Nita for admission.

Father asked her -

"Who told you to go for a Hotel Management Course?"

"It is my wish. Parents support me."

"Where are your parents from?"

"Father, they are from Kerala, Alleppey, Kuttanadu region. Now my father is working in Koraput, Orissa."

"Some look upon the Hospitality Industry as dealing with restaurant chores, extra working hours, more suitable for men, etc. Still, do your parents allow you to go for a Hotel Management Course?"

"Father, those are false perceptions. I want to learn more about the hospitality industry. I am looking for an evolving career and profession."

"What profession do you want to pursue?"

"Father, I want to be an air hostess."

She must have heard her father talk about aeroplanes and air travel Or her friends. She might have heard she could grow fast and reach greater heights if she studied well.

Nita replied to the father, thinking she would grow a little taller by the time she completed her degree course. Nita loved to fly in planes over land and sea like colourful butterflies. Nita had replied to the principal's father that she would get the required height to become an 'air hostess' after completing her degree.

"Didn't hesitate to skip. Then Daddy, why am I not growing taller? I was not so fat, too," Nita once asked me after passing her degree.

"Sometimes, regarding height (and intelligence), it may be due to your mother's genes, even though Mommy might not have agreed."

"I have sufficient height, and it is enough for a mother," Mommy replied. "Didn't Mommy say earlier that adding drumstick to your curry makes it for a good height?"

True, Mommy used to tell Nita that she would eat well with such curries to grow taller at her younger age. It would help if you had a good height to be an air hostess. "

All you can do is calm her down by saying, "Where in the hostel is curry with a drumstick served? You have stayed in hostels all the time during your studies."

Nita was not short, but she was not tall enough. The height to become an air host was 162 cm. She did not apply for the job after passing the degree. She also realised no point in blaming the food at home or outside the house for maintaining her height.

Nita got admission to the first year of the BHM course. Fees were paid. The arrangement was made for her stay in a lady's hostel near the college. BHM was a three-year degree course. She was taken to Sunabeda after the examination at the end of the first year. Brother Tomichan looked after Nita as a local guardian until he was ordained as a priest in 1997 and left Dharmaram.

Nita was able to stay in the hostel without much difficulty. The food at the hostel did not always have to be good. Nita's dilemma was that she had to do all the study, project work, and allied work independently. Over time, with patience and cooperation, Nita completed her three-year degree in 1998-99.

(1996) Nita talked about her college friends when she came to Sunabeda for summer vacation after her first year of BHM exams. Four siblings from a family from Tatanagar, Jamshedpur, were studying in various degree classes at Christ College, two of whom were in BHM - Hannah and Samuel. Two were for the BBM course. One John was for a computer engineering course. It was reported that Samuel's sister's wedding was planned in Tatanagar during the summer holidays. Samuel was coming to Sunabeda to invite Nita and her family to attend the ceremony.

'Hannah and Samuel will come to Sunabeda to invite me to the Tatanagar wedding of Samuel's sister ?" – Nita said.

"I do not think so. Come on, let's think about it only when somebody comes here with such a request," I said, adjourning the discussion.

Who knows when and what is there in our lives? What the Almighty has planned for us! How many people would we have to get acquainted with before we reach the final goal?

Time will answer all our issues.

That faith has always been there. Steps should be taken cautiously, and I had no interest in taking high risks there. All other risks must be carefully handled.

Nita was a thoughtless moron with no blemishes on her mind. No matter what anyone says convincingly, Nita is mesmerized by the eloquence. If she had thought about another aspect or felt that something else was better, she would have considered that and been able to choose the most suitable one for her. I did not believe that Nita had such intelligence at that age.

Is it possible to teach children every responsibility without having some amount of trust in them? So, it was decided to do each step carefully.

Samuel came to Sunabeda from Bangalore and told me he was going to Bhubaneswar to visit his relatives there. Instead of inviting Nita alone, Samuel explained the details of the wedding ceremony. He asked Nita and her parents to attend the wedding at Tatanagar. When I tried to avoid it, I said it was challenging to participate in the function at such a distant place. I saw no other escape than to admit that at least Nita and her Mommy had to be permitted to go on the plea that Samuel's parents had also explicitly requested that we participate. I also reserved train tickets for Nita and her Mommy on the same train that Samuel's brothers, whom Nita knew, were going to Tatanagar via Vijayanagaram. That was how Leelamma and Nita travelled to Tatanagar and attended the wedding of Samuel's sister. They got to know everyone in the family and participated in the related celebrations. After the wedding at that house and the receptions, they returned safely to Sunabeda.

# 81

# Milestones

Seema's studies and extracurricular activities at the Vyomayana Samastha Vidyalaya from Std VI to Std IX were generally good. In her early years, she had to learn the native language, Oriya, quickly afresh. A few tuition classes and her teachers helped her to do her language studies well. The excellent foundation from the Sacred Heart School in Bangalore benefited her in the higher classes.

The Malayalam coaching class was started to introduce the mother tongue to the Malayalee children of Kerala Samajam members in the Township. It did not progress beyond preliminary studies. However, very few were interested in the mother tongue and tried to read the words in the books. Seema also knew her mother tongue apart from learning the local language (Oriya). The Malayalam language was not used much by the children at their home. Children were burdened with studying different languages in primary classes in modern education. However, it is essential to remember that learning multiple local languages depends on the children's interests and the school's syllabus.

Seema reached Std X in 1997, a significant milestone in her school education. No special attention was necessary for Seema's study matters; she understood everything and would do everything with her mommy's blessings.

I was getting at least one letter every month from home. Most of the time, Achayan and Ammachi wrote in the same inland letter as they shared everything else, and Achayan himself wrote rarely. When

I opened the letter from Achayan alone, I understood that my mother was not well enough to sit quietly and write. Chronic maternal illness was sometimes exacerbated by asthma and breathlessness, often necessitating long-term treatment. Weather changes and cold winds made everyday life more difficult for my mother; she could not get vigorously involved in everyday activities and sometimes required emergency or urgent care to breathe correctly.

Babychan or Thomas Kutty would call if there was anything special to report. Or I would reach out and arrange to tell the information at home.

Relevant passages of letters from home often stay in mind for a few days. A snapshot of the complexities of life at that time – thus, at one time, it was the state of affairs- just to be aware of -

In a letter last month, Achayan wrote, "Your mother was in the medical college hospital for a few days."

Since Raju and Babychan were in their home state, they went home every week to look after their parents and care for their health conditions.

1/97 "Tom was left to study in a nursery class. Babychan bought a site to build a house in Punnapra itself. He bought it for Rs 2 lakhs."

Raju moved from his first rented house to another one. Both Raju and his wife were going to work.

3/97 Achayan wrote, together with other information - "Kuriackose (uncle) sold his site and our ancestral house in Kannattumadom and went away to live with his youngest son Sunnychan in Mannanchery. I heard that Kuriakose bought a house and land there. But he did not tell me anything about the purchases or any information that he changed his residence to Mannanchery!" He did not want to express his emotional feelings and was conspicuously silent in the letter.

4/97 "Our old house at Vaishyambhagom was rented out sometime back. The occupant vacated the house, and we again rented it to someone else. I got three months' rent in advance."

6/97 "Tessy started teaching in the high school class at Thathampally School. At first, it was challenging. Preparations for the next day's class were not going on. It's difficult to even at night because of the power cut." Babychan wrote - "Students' misfortune." "Even in hospitals, there was no electricity, no surgeries, and sometimes no oxygen available. No rain. It isn't easy to get water, even to drink. There is not going to be much progress in this state soon! "

"Tessy had to endure many hurdles to receive her salary, which took months."

I thought to myself. Even a wild thought of going and living in Vaishyambhagom or somewhere else in Kerala was misplaced!

When thoughts go wild, it leads us to a state of mental disorientation, like a situation of being trapped in a forest in the dark. Issues become complicated when thoughts wander wildly and restlessly, like the movement of a wild animal in a cage. I remember reading somewhere. "We need to watch our emotions as if we were watching the flow of a river to have peace. Never try to run away from our thoughts. It will never happen. Thoughts stay within the past. It will never fade."

7/97 Achayan wrote - "Rs. 25/- - from Tony's first salary should be given for the requiem mass homily for your father."

10/97 Raju came with 'Onakkodi' for his parents. Achayan was very interested in knowing Tony's welfare and information. Babychan was promoted to Senior Auditor. It has been announced that Tomichan's priestly ordination will be on December 27.

I took leave for the Christmas holidays in 1997 and reached home. Nita also came from Bangalore. We went to Checkkidikadu church with Achayan and Ammachi. There, we witnessed Tomichan's priestly ordination and his first holy mass.

During those days, Thambichan-Leelamma's children, Saji and Ansa (Siji), studied in degree classes at Christ College, Bangalore. Nita maintained good relations and friendships with them. The younger Ansa was staying at Nita's Besania Hostel. Whenever I went to Bangalore those days, I met them and cared for their welfare.

Ottathyckal Ammachi wrote: "Joychan bought a house and land on the riverside in Nedumudi." The plan was to move there for a permanent stay. The school and the church were close by, adding to the conveniences.

As his mother had written, Joy bought a house and land on the riverside in Nedumudi and moved there soon after.

Achayan wrote that he got Tony Mon's letter and money - "I received it as if it was the fruit of my life and mission, and thanked God for the same."

"Oommacha, Tonymon will give you ten times more help than you have helped me. That is the will of God... Here, Tom is going to the nursery class adjacent to the church. Ammini will take him there and bring him back."

Family friends PJ Nair-Savitri, Johnson-Suma, and KG Nair left Sunabeda after retiring from their jobs in December and returned to their hometown, Thiruvananthapuram.

Savitri wrote, "PJ Nair is gardening, focusing on farming, and preparing for Sangeetha's wedding. Our son Satheesh has returned to the Gulf. We regularly meet everyone who has returned from Sunabeda. KG Nair and his family are frequently going on pilgrimages. When is the next picnic of the Samajam being organized? We wish you all the best."

I was in Chandigarh for two weeks because of my work. On the way back, I stayed in Delhi for a day. I reached the RK Puram Quarters at night, where James was staying. Early in the morning, I met and informed my superiors in the department of the technical findings in Chandigarh. I flew back to Visakhapatnam in the evening and reached Sunabeda in the morning by taxi. A lot of letters from home received me -

1/98 Achayan wrote - "Your mother was in the hospital for three days." My mother wrote - "I was sick but went to see Chedathi (elder sister) for the last time. Though I had to walk up to the church, I could pay her my last respects. She was in the Medical College Hospital. Chedathi died on 23rd January. She had a blood clot in her brain."

2/98 Achayan writes - "Kuriachan, his wife, son Dias, and Thommachan were present. Davis' manasammatham (consent for his marriage) was on January 17. More than 100 people attended. A necklace of twelve sovereigns was placed around the girl's neck!"

3/98 I was feeling really like a political leader! When I woke up in the morning, the world around my body seemed to revolve slowly on the axis of my body. I did not walk forward since I thought I might fall. I sat on the bed for a while. After a few minutes, everything seemed fine.

I went to the township hospital instead of going to the office. Dr Das and Dr Mishra advised me to rest in the hospital for a whole day after doing some tests. The doctors assured me there was no need to go to a big hospital for further tests. My blood pressure was a little high. Medications were given. And I went home in the evening. My blood pressure was not high in any tests conducted since then, but no doctor allowed me to stop the medication.

3/98 Achayan's letter came. "Your desire to come to the native place and purchase ten cents of land is good. I also desire that. There are 20 cents of land to sell near Molamma's house here ..... I am also happy to learn that Nitamol has reached the marriageable age. We must understand our responsibilities."

Tony's postgraduate examinations were held in April 1999. Even before the examinations, Tony had written to give my opinion and plan an extensive tour outside Sunabeda, either to Mumbai, Nashik, or Ooty, Alappuzha, and many such places, including visiting his relatives when he came for the summer vacation before the examinations. Tony was still keen to use his time to have fun visiting unknown and unseen territories. I told him that planning extensive trips from Sunabeda and getting the reservations were difficult.

Nita and Seema also considered going to Singapore after their exams. In the meantime, the trip had to be postponed due to project pressure and the office not permitting long absences. Tony's writings have always been very detailed, with instructions on learning to his sisters and our welfare issues. Tony wrote about Nita's attempt to get a job after graduation and Seema's preparations for the Plus 2 final exam. Who else could say such things well, especially about hard work and time management?

After graduation or post-graduation, when you look for free time to take a vacation, more and more work comes - Parkinson's law: "Work expands to fill the time available for its completion." More work comes to you before you finish your important work," that is, "More work makes you more productive," says Tony. Tony always looked for time to meet everyone and travel extensively despite his busy schedule. I have never seen any relative show such a deep personal relationship.

Leelamma and I applied for our passports at the Bhubaneswar office and got them within a month. We have developed an interest ever since Tony travelled abroad. We thought that if it was the will of God, we could also go somewhere abroad sometime in the future!

# 82

# The Departure of My Father

In Sunabeda, within the HAL compound, a newly constructed building for our office - the government regulatory authority for military aircraft - was inaugurated in the last week of June 1999.

As requested by Kuriachan in a rare letter, we went to the wedding of Kuriachan's son Davis in Delhi in November. Seema could also go to the function because it was her school holiday. I also saw some of our relatives who had not been visiting for a long time. Seema had never seen them before. This visit to Delhi also helped Seema to get acquainted with Dennis and Dias, Kuriachan's other sons. We got a letter a few days later from Thommachan and Rosamma, who came to Delhi from Nagpur. They had written that they were happy to meet us in Delhi and that their daughter Greety was in regular touch with Seema. The members of the new generation should get to know each other and the blood relationships they share!

An essential chapter in my published book is a paper on 'Quality problems and their solutions,' including failure analysis of aero-engine mechanical parts.

Technological advances in this way are invaluable regarding the safety of military aircraft. They were written to present at the National Conference on Quality Engineering in Aerospace Technologies, held from Aug 20-21, 1999, in Bangalore. Its preparations lasted for two to three months. Permission was also obtained to present the same during the conference. My colleague Achutha and I were nominated to attend the meeting, and we departed for Visakhapatnam on August 18.

We slept at the HAL guest house in Visakhapatnam and planned to board the morning flight to Bangalore.

Achutha woke me early in the morning and told me the saddest news - 'Leelamma's phone came to the guest house. ' Your father passed away'. Call her, and you will get more information."

I felt like I had lost everything. I stood there without any movement, as if I had nothing to do, and was numbed momentarily. I lost consciousness of the environment, stunned by the will of God's decision. Darkness entered my eyes. Slowly, I tried to regain the balance. I have telephoned Leelamma.

At the time of Achayan's death, Babychan had gone to Chennai for training. Only my mother and Tessy were nearby. Babychan called Sunabeda and told Chechi the sad news. "Our Achayan has gone." In the night, Achayan had some breathlessness, and he called Tessy. After getting up and walking to the bathroom,

"If I should die, let me lie down," said Achayan.

Achayan might have remembered the Bible: "Jacob laid his feet on the bed and died and joined his people" (Ref. Genesis 49:33).

The doctor was called. Kochupapan was called, and he came. The doctor examined and confirmed that Achayan had left us. Then they informed everyone.

I informed Babychan and Raju that we would reach home only by noon the next day. The body was being shifted to the Thathampally hospital mortuary, Babychan said. Babychan and Raju have also agreed to make the necessary arrangements.

After Seema had left Johnson's house, Leelamma arrived at the Visakhapatnam airport in a taxi arranged by Johnson and Antony. We flew to Madras and boarded the evening train to Alappuzha. We could reach home in the afternoon the next day.

Achayan kept telling me throughout the journey, “Even if you cannot see me, I can see you from wherever I go. You will remember what I have been telling you. God bless you! ....”

On Achayan’s bed was a white sheet spread with Achayan’s photo at one end, a cross, and a candle behind the head side of the cot. Ammachi was nearby. I looked at the picture, stood there still, and prayed silently. I could not believe that Achayan was not at home.

Babu, Raju, Leelamma, and Babychan were there, all in great grief. Kochuppappan came and evaluated different arrangements and asked for my opinion.

“We were waiting for you to come.”

I said that Achayan desired his last rites to be performed in the church built by the team, including himself, at Vaishyambhagom and that the cemetery there should be his last resting place. Kochupapan informed me that he has another desire and interest in that regard. He said-

“I thought I could think it over with you, and I was waiting for you to come. If I bury my brother in our present parish, St Gregorios, Punnapra, I can walk up to something from time to time as it is nearby.

“Kochuppappa, Without disrespecting Achayan’s wishes, I feel it’s better to do what you said. Visiting the cemetery, praying, and obsequies will be more convenient for everyone. Moreover, it will be convenient for you to come too because none of you are living in Vaishyambhagom now.”

Respecting the wishes of the living is always the priority over the desires of the departed. Thus, the decision was made. Everyone agreed. Grandpa said -

“That’s fine. When you visit Achayan’s grave, I’ll be there nearby. I’ll have a share of your prayers, too!”

The following day, Achayan's body was brought home from the mortuary. The uncontrollable sadness made me fall upon my father's body, wept upon him, and kiss him on the lips of the frozen face. We read that son Joseph did this to his father Jacob's corpse. (Ref. Genesis Gen 50: 1) Last time I returned from vacation, I remembered touching my father's feet and seeking his blessings. That was the first time I touched my father's feet. It was a confession I made to my father that I was sorry for the distress I had caused him, and it was an expression of remorse after a confession. A thought arose that if the result were 'not to meet again like in this instance,' I would never touch anyone's feet again.

As you read and learn more, you realize this attitude is wrong. The scientific analysis of bowing down and touching the feet of elders in Indian culture is as follows- When saluting the feet, the ego is offered there, and knowledge and power are sought as blessings. As the energy of touch is received through the sensation of nerves, mutual love grows, and misconceptions are corrected.

Relatives, locals, and many other dignitaries came to pay homage, especially from places like Ambalapuzha, Champakulam, Nedumudi, Chempumpuram, and Vaishyambhagom. Special vehicle facilities were provided to fetch the locals from Vaishyambhagom. Many priests, nuns, and local people's elected representatives came. All the newspapers that Achayan had associated with for four decades published the news of Achayan's passing away with photographs.

Achayan's embalmed body was externally wiped clean by Joychan, Thathampalli Thommachan, and other brothers at Kannattumadom, dressed in Achayan's favourite khadar dhoti and juba - adorned with spices and flowers and laid out in a coffin. Funeral services were conducted by Chalangadi Achen and attended by Tomichan and other parish priests, and the procession began from home. We carried the cross and the coffin on our shoulders during the mourning procession from home to church, followed by a large crowd of brothers and relatives with prayers and mourning silence.

Before the funeral, in the cemetery, when I said goodbye with a final kiss, I could do nothing but burst into tears and see nothing but Achayan's face, to be remembered with respect and love forever. I took Achayan's black-framed spectacles and put them in my pocket. Or it could be preserved for memory. When I returned from the cemetery after throwing a pinch of frankincense and soil (This tradition symbolises the deceased's return to nature of the life cycle - meaning that the body turns to dust when the soul is released. People participate in this ritual to pay respect and bid a final goodbye to their loved ones). I felt sad that I could not love or care for my father a little more! God did not allow Achayan to wait for that. He was called earlier because of the reason given in the memoir on the seventh-day obsequies of Achayan's death: "I have fought the good fight, I have finished the race, I have kept the faith. Now there is in store the crown of righteousness, which the Lord, the righteous Judge, will award to me on that day—not only to me but to all who have longed for his appearing. (2 Timothy 4: 7-8)

We all slept at home at night, and I rested in my father's bed. When I heard someone shouting in fear, I woke up half-asleep. "Aaraada," I asked, not realising what had happened. Knowing that it was Raju who made the noise, then we slept peacefully. Raju was overseeing the work done by the gravedigger at the place allotted in the cemetery by the church for the tomb until very late last night.

Together, we bore the expenses for the funeral.

We returned to Sunabeda and engaged in our routine work. My colleague Achutha attended the All-India Conference in Bangalore. He presented my paper on my behalf and spoke. The paper was well received. Achutha brought gifts, souvenirs, and a collection of all the papers presented at the conference.

Seema was working hard in preparation for the Class XII exam and appearing for the entrance exams.

Tony was on vacation but could not travel to India as he had to do the final project work for the part-time postgraduate course.

Achayan loved and blessed his children and grandchildren as much as possible and always prayed for them by participating in the Holy Mass. He was not on his sick bed, not even for a day, and he wanted his departure without causing any inconvenience to anyone. So, during his last days, he ate what he got without saying any word of hesitation to my mother, without worrying or complaining to anyone. He read the newspaper all day, listened to the TV news, prayed, communicated directly with his children and grandchildren through letters, rested, and lived a simple life filled with joy and compassion. He was always ready to return to eternity.

Achayan, for all of us children, was 'Valyachan' for his grandchildren.

Achayan will always be there in the loving memories in the hearts of all of them. All the children attach the family name to their names, and they love and worship the family head, Kuruvila Thomma, the saintly soul, as the family deity of Kannattumadom.

The children and grandchildren saw and loved the noble son of the saintly head of their family. He was always seen as a guide, knowledge source, and the family's lifeline. Achayan was the eternal light of our entire lives. He shall remain the true light in our hearts until we return to everlasting life.

"They believe that by the forefathers' blessing, good intelligent children are born into the family, wealth increases, and that is the basis of all prosperity." That was written by Achayan in August 1998, precisely a year before his departure. It has come to happen accordingly. Achayan had seen his death and burial without any concerns!

"Ammachi regularly goes to the hospital and receives medication and injections. I'm over 82 years old. Though I have appropriate physical stress, I consider it as usual. I need to go to get my eyes checked. Let the rush of attending to the dead and their funeral be over. Arackapparambil Joseph Sir, who died on Thursday, was cremated the following Monday, and his body was lying in the mortuary of Thatthampally Hospital until yesterday."

Babychan also went to Thiruvananthapuram on the third of this month and took charge as an officer of Gazetted rank. Raju has been an officer for years.

By blessing my children and son-in-law, God has blessed me. God honoured me even though I did not deserve it and never desired it. I am proud of that. Praise be to God. In this state, I feel happy to die. To all of you, including my grandson, God bless you all. It is the only gift I can give you.

"Babychan sold the land he had purchased earlier and purchased another 12 cents in Punnapra for Rs 24500. More sites and places with good facilities are available here.. (if you desire)."

"Thanking God once again for all the blessings He bestowed on us," he concluded as "yours satisfied and complacent father." Ammachi also wrote the same things below his signature-

"...I will serve rice to Achayan at noon. I will also eat a little rice twice a day. Despite this, my body will always tremble. Let me conclude by praying specifically for everyone. Your loving mother."

As a continuation of the letter that Achayan had written earlier, he wrote to me again in October. I could read that his self-confidence had diminished. It should be seen as his last words in writing (swan song) as the head of the family. My brothers may not have seen this letter. It reminds us of the virtues that Achayan gained in this worldly life and the heritage he left behind for the good of others. So, I copy that text here. -

"I have high blood sugar (350 mg / dL) and a lot of medication. I have more difficulty walking, and my eyesight is weak. Nowadays I read no newspaper. I cannot attend church daily, so I go for the second Mass on Sunday with incredible difficulty. Someone helps me while crossing the road. My hearing is reduced, and my handwriting is causing partial damage to the letters, as you can see.

I will have to leave the world soon, and I am preparing for it. Although I lived in poverty as a young man, I worked hard to earn a living. I started handling 25 news dailies when called upon by a good brother and when there was no work for me. I shouldered the responsibility until I could distribute more than a thousand newspapers daily. I managed the family to make ends meet despite much deception by the support staff. All the children were taught. The family property earmarked by my father for me was donated to another brother who lost his share over time. Yet the Lord my God has not forsaken me. I have been leading a leisurely life for a long time, having been provided with everything, having supplied to me through my loving children. I did only good. God gave me all the excellent things. I am ready to say goodbye happily whenever He calls me. I owe immense gratitude and obligation to God and my brother Anthonichan for helping me and my loving children. I have done many social services in the community and neighbourhood to make you proud and remember even after I go. Chempumpuram Health Center, Library, CMS Church, Vaishyambhagom High School, and St. Anthony's Church are all parts of my blood and sweat.

I remembered something and wrote it down. Now the domestic affairs..... I am praying for everyone, Achayan (signature) ".

**With Antony Kaduvaparambil & Mani Chechi, at Sunabeda**

# 83

# After the Vanavasam

Most of my colleagues in the department had applied for a transfer to another location within a year of moving to Sunabeda. Most of them had left their families in their hometowns and lived alone, hoping they would return to their chosen station soon.

Having no complaints, I did not even apply once, with the hope of getting a transfer to another place for work. I had spent seven happy years in Sunabeda. Then, once my boss visited Sunabeda and asked me -

"Are you in love with Sunabeda? Would you not like to go somewhere else?"

The question was expected, so I answered him with a smile -

"Yes, sir. I want to move to Bangalore. It is the right time for my daughter to complete her degree. I have thoughts of her marriage."

"You see, a huge task must be completed here by the end of the year. You know that. Therefore, even if you go, can I request you to come back here for some time to help them clear the year's task?"

"Sure, Sir, I can do that."

The boss, who visited Sunabeda, returned to Delhi and issued me a transfer order within two weeks.

"Go to Bangalore and report there within a month."

I was ready to leave for Bangalore in two weeks. Logistics were planned. I left the Sunabeda office on 30 November 1998. Leelamma and Seema continued to stay in Sunabeda in the quarters.

If I go to Bangalore, I can find a place to stay for the time being as I will be alone. It would be nice to return to work here shortly after leaving, as my boss had indicated, taking one or two months of temporary duty. I could do the finer logistics here, and getting quarters in the DRDO township in Bangalore could be explored. I can take my family to Bangalore and send the household items to Bangalore; by then, Seema's 12th exam will be over. If you go to Bangalore, the rest of the family affairs could be easy. The Almighty, who manages everything well, is always with us.

Nita's BHM degree exam will also be completed. She could end her hostel stay.

One era is getting over, and let's welcome another era. Thank you, God, for the twentieth century. Let's welcome the twenty-first century. Everything will happen as planned.

I arrived in Bangalore in the evening as I flew in from Visakhapatnam. I went straight to Nita's place of residence. She had moved from the hostel to another place near where her friends stayed. Nita joined a group where four siblings from a Christian family in Tatanagar, Jamshedpur, stayed together. They rented a house with four or five rooms, where they could cook all the food and eat at home. Nita said, "Since you will return to Sunabeda in two weeks, Daddy, you don't have to look for another place to stay." I agreed with Nita on that plan.

I joined the Bangalore office on December 2. I was posted to the Aero Engines group since many groups were in Bangalore. I have experience working at Sunabeda, which specializes in Aero Engines. That's how I started working in the engine group in Bangalore.

An untrue allegation erupted in Bangalore offices: ' I had moved from Koraput after asking for a specific transfer.' In place of that vacancy, the Delhi boss asked one of the favorites of the then-Bangalore boss to go to Koraput.

'Many offices have such creepers (loranthus) that live off the mercy of the more robust trees. Because of this, it will be difficult for those who dedicatedly work and pursue the common good to segregate for each. They only look at their conscience and the rule of law. Minor controversies that arise when one does selfish work without concurrence from the top may affect the public good.

A directive had come from HQs without mentioning the production objective at the Sunabeda office and highlighting the need for the services of an experienced officer there until the end of the financial year (March 31). One officer should be sent there.

I learned that the then-boss in Bangalore had decided not to oblige the boss at HQs. I replied that he was not ready to let anyone go to Sunabeda and (further refused to talk to the boss who gave the directive.

When I informed the boss in HQs - he detached himself from the matter and tried to soothe me by opening up his mind on the phone -

"You are perched on a loop where your excellence is no goodness to me! "

The boss in an organization looks to fulfill his responsibilities with the same policy and goal. When decisions are made in favour of any personal interest, it may harm the very best interests of the institution, no matter whose interest they desire to fulfill.

I did not comment because I did not want to get involved in a controversy. My going to Sunabeda did not materialise and was not a crucial issue for me. The local boss must have thought I would go and pray to him to do the favour, but it was too late to amend since he had already written and signed the letter. I had no reason to postpone my travel to Sunabeda, especially since the family was there and Christmas was fast approaching.

I took a month's leave from December 20 and went to Sunabeda. The Christmas celebrations were magnificent. Many friends gathered, and art shows, food, etc., followed in return for their love. Everyone was happy; it was the last Christmas in Sunabeda, the last of this era.

Then, it was time for send-offs from Sunabeda accompanied by parties of family and friends. Most friends will soon relinquish their jobs and return to their hometowns. No one was preparing for permanent residence in or around Sunabeda. Another major problem was that the number of Malayalee families in Koraput declined every month, and no new ones were arriving. There were 300 families in Kerala Samajam in the early days, but it has reduced to ten or fifteen in the last five or six years. That, too, will be gone in another four to five years. I said goodbye to all my friends and hoped to see them in their native place next.

Tony came on a vacation at the beginning of the millennium (2000) after I returned to Sunabeda from Bangalore. He did not stay for long. We knew the hardships of travelling in India. The itinerary was to Visakhapatnam - then to Madras - to Kuttanad - to Bangalore - then to Madras. No matter how much he travelled, he was not bothered whether he had enough food on the journey. He decided to visit his grandparents and other relatives at our native place; he was determined to return with great satisfaction after undertaking great effort.

Tony had lunch on the train before arriving in Madras. By the time the Coromandel train reached Madras, the train from Madras to Alappuzha had left. Then Tony learned and boarded the special train for the pilgrims – Ayyappas - to reach Ernakulam town. After arriving at the junction from Ernakulam town and catching the local train to Alappuzha, he saw Babychan and Appachi waiting for Tony to come there. Babychan went to work in Ernakulam. It was late afternoon when Tony arrived home at Vaishyambhagom with his uncle. He had reservations for the train journeys, and his relatives waited to pick him up. Still, every trip and opportunity came to the forefront without warning or preplanning.

Tony wrote that he ate 'Ferrero Rocher chocolates, which he carried for relatives at his native place, and drank bottled mineral water until he reached home. He was hungry. "Twenty-four hours later, when I got home, Ammachi served me, and I ate rice, fish curry, and fried fish, my favourite dishes." Tony wrote - "First proper meal after lunch on the train yesterday."

Undoubtedly, the Almighty, who has insight beyond time, has always worked behind Tony's determination to meet his 'Ammachi' and everyone else, undergoing all the hardships. I remember reading somewhere- "No one needs to tell their children to love their parents. Instead, we must love our parents, and our children will learn from us; and love our parents and relatives." It is valid at all times in any level of growth or decline. As it is said, there can be variations such as "far from sight, far from mind." However, under the influence of modern technology, even the most intimate contact and sharing are possible, even from a distance. Elderly parents need to touch and feel the love of their grandchildren and insight as much as in their physical proximity. Then only they have the satisfaction.

The next day, he took photos of all the growing cousins - Saju, Sony, Nitya, Nitin, Tom, and Tina - standing before the Christmas tree. His uncles and aunts had arrived. He went to church after seeing his English Valyachan.

He received all the blessings from Achayan, studied for six years in Singapore, and came after he was employed and met Achayan last year. This time, he could not meet Achayan. Achayan's grandson prayed for the departed soul's peace during church Mass. He went to the cemetery, remembered his grandfather, attended the obsequies at the graveyard, and prayed. An inscription of the name was carved over the slab at the top of the tomb.

Tony went to Bangalore by bus. He gave a sumptuous banquet - 'spending' to Nita and all her friends, including Hannah, Subhash, John, and Sam, who had helped during her college days. Most of Tony's schoolmates came together in the evening one day, and Tony gave them good hospitality. After wandering around during vacation in 1999, he finally reached Madras and returned to Singapore with a handful of memories.

Seema's Standard 12 examination was held in March. Seema was ready to join the entrance examination coaching centers, confident she had written well for every subject. The desire and effort were to enter a degree course related to medicine. The decision to join any entrance coaching class was because the study of medical subjects and the related entrance examination were rigorous.

Knowing that there was a good coaching centre in Thiruvananthapuram, Seema was taken to Thiruvananthapuram for admission there. She stayed in a hostel and attended classes at the Tandem Coaching Center. The college and hostel arrangements were all done by Raju and Babychan, who visited and worked at Thiruvananthapuram then. She wrote all the possible entrance exams and returned to Sunabeda, hoping to get a selection in any of them.

She has written the entrance examinations for Medicine for Karnataka CET, Vellore, St John's Medical, and Kerala CET. Knowing that I lacked the confidence to get a seat on merit for Medicine somewhere, I persuaded Seema to write for any engineering degree entrance examination as a standby choice. That is how she wrote for the Engineering Entrance Examination in the Kerala CET.

Seema has achieved great success in the CBSE 12$^{th}$ examination. She also won the "Dear, You are the Best Outgoing Student of VSV" trophy. The award was presented by Mrs. KP Puri (wife of the Managing

Director (MiG), HAL), the then First Lady of Sunabeda township, at a colourful ceremony at the school. She had scored good marks in all subjects. Seema also received a CBSE Merit Scholarship that year. Although she applied for re-evaluation on suspicion of missing five marks each in two papers, the authorities concluded that the CBSE determination was correct.

Long before she wrote the entrance exams, Seema was aware of her parents' financial ability to support her for a degree course in medicine. Seema was told only a small message as an additional. –

"The greatness of a noble profession is likely to be compromised by the eagerness to earn money or repay loans, and that you should not do. If Seema is willing to execute the profession, it should be done with its nobility. If one does not want to succumb to temptations or compromise, one should get a Medical seat on merit. One should study well and pursue success. We cannot afford to pay donations or capitation fees for admission to a Medical seat in private colleges. Get a seat on merit anywhere, and you can go, stay, study, and pay college and hostel fees."

Seema did her best, aiming for a conscious and self-sacrificing healthcare profession. The results of the entrance exams came in. The rank obtained for the Medicine seat was much higher than the number of Merit seats everywhere. Therefore, her chance of getting a merit seat was meager. Her rank in Kerala CET was good enough for a merit seat in an engineering subject. So far, so good. Seema reconciled with the situation and did not hesitate to study engineering. Then, she searched for an engineering discipline more closely related to a general medical treatment-related department. The subject of Electronics & Biomedical Engineering was taught in only one college in Kerala. Admission to the Model Engineering College, Cochin University of Science and Technology (CUSAT, KOCHI), (Model Engineering College, Thrikkakara, Kochi) was, in a way, the desired merit seat. She got it. After mastering the technology, Seema was fortunate to do the noble healthcare service. Biomedical engineering subjects were included in the technology that ensured the smooth functions of the machines used in the hospital and the healthcare services.

There was also a hostel near Thrikkakara College. Seema enjoyed excellent local food and native and incredible friends at the hostel. In four years, how fast the girls grow up, and the time passes so quickly that parents will experience the four years as four months!

Seema could meet her relatives in Kochi occasionally when she wanted; if she needed anything, she could reach them immediately, ensuring safety and security. Seema desired to be a medical professional from childhood, even though she did not explicitly pronounce it. 'Doctor Seema' was a cool gaming name, which Manoj or Vinod of Nashik used to call her. The desire remained a dream. Seema has learned more, and she has gained more. Who knows, she will one day be a PhD doctor!

Nita did not have to look for a job for long, and soon after finishing college, she got a job at Hotel Central Park on Sankey Road in Bangalore. She searched for the job and found it herself. She rented a house together with her friends. Most classmates who studied and passed in the same batch got jobs soon after passing out; some were in star hotels in Bangalore, some were in airlines, some were in the facility management field, etc. Six months later, Nita became a concierge at Le Meridien. My job was to help guests by booking tours and making theatre and restaurant reservations. She commuted to and fro in a scooty with a learner's license.

We packed domestic items for the relocation to Bangalore without much difficulty. There were a total of 45 packs, excluding portable suitcases. A truck was arranged at Semiliguda. The telephone was transferred. The vehicle I used in Sunabeda was a Silver Plus moped, which was inadequate for city travel and, therefore, was sold in Sunabeda itself for good.

The furniture and luggage were loaded on a lorry and sent to Bangalore on March 20, 2000. Thus ended 'the vanavasa'- our stay at Sunabeda. Another change of house. As the flight from Visakhapatnam to Bangalore was scheduled to depart in the afternoon on March 23, we took a morning taxi from Sunabeda. Many friends had come to see us off and give us farewells and greetings.

Josekutty, Mercy, and the children had already moved from Visakhapatnam to Chennai.

Visakhapatnam was hesitant to send us to Bangalore! Waiting for a long time at the airport was rather inconvenient. The announcement came around 6 p.m. when we were ready to fly to our destination. "Your flight was indefinitely delayed; hence, the flight is cancelled for the day." Without a doubt, we were disappointed at first -

Then, the further announcement came. "The airlines have arranged the night accommodation at a Star Hotel in Visakhapatnam. You will be taken there by bus; you can rest until tomorrow's flight, and food is provided. All passengers will be taken to Bangalore by the next day's flight."

Until then, relax at a hotel in Visakhapatnam. Travel and hotel accommodations were arranged by the airlines! That was a welcome message. We had nothing to do soon after reaching Bangalore on that day!

The flight was delayed due to a 'knock-on effect'. One of the reasons for the delay in the flight's arrival was that the flight was delayed on its previous route. It was nice that the airline did not run away from the obligation to compensate for the delay and protect the passengers' rights.

Thus, we were able to spend more time in Visakhapatnam. The hotel's accommodations and meals were comfortable.

We travelled 200 kilometres up and down the hills. For the first time in six years, we got compensation for the hard work that saved our body parts by bearing the hardships - we slept peacefully, without any moans or groans in our minds.

WITH SEBASTIAN (BROTHER) AND THARAMMA (2010

PAUL MATHEW AND SHANTAMMA

**With my friends and college mates: Sebastian (Brother) & Tharamma; Paul Mathew & Shantamma**

# 84

# Purification Process

The flight departed the next day as per schedule. We arrived in Bangalore.

When we arrived in Bangalore, we wondered where to stay until we got to the quarters and where to unload the truck when it came with the luggage. For now, we may go to the same place where Nita was staying. We also thought that when the truck arrived, we would seek the help of someone in the office.

The truck arrived, and we unloaded the goods temporarily in the quarters of a colleague named Kodandaraman, who was staying in the DRDO Quarters. He agreed to do so by taking advantage of his family not staying with him.

DRDO Phase II - Quarters including car garage, E-34/5 was allotted to me a week later. Before anyone else could stay there, we could remain the first occupants in the newly completed quarters.

After cleaning up the quarters, I brought our luggage and furniture from Kodandaraman's quarters, furnished them, and made them habitable. Some of the furniture was also stored in the empty car garage. Block E-34 (12 quarters/flats) was allotted exclusively to our office, so my colleagues stayed in the nearby apartments. I was delighted that the neighbours were all known friends. As in Sunabeda, a Malayalee-only community culture was not found elsewhere. Having the same language-speaking communities in townships like Sunabeda was a unique feature. Not only in DRDO in Bangalore but also in other residential complexes, no such special language groups could be found because Bangalore is a big city with many offices and commercial establishments where people from all over the country come to live and work. People of various languages and religions inhabit together. In the city alone, Kannada, the state language, ironically is not spoken by more than 30 percent of the population.

When we started living in the new quarters E-34/5, Nita's friends came and cooperated.

Telephone and cooking gas connections were soon established.

I bought a Hero Honda Splendour Motorcycle for transportation and started using it for all travel. I purchased the motorbike with a loan. I have to use a motorbike until I retire from service. I bought a technologically better vehicle for half a lakh rupees. The lightweight helmet (helmet) received as complementary from Praga helped protect my body's most critical part. When using a motorbike, you should wear a helmet. You know why, not because someone is forcing you to do it, but as an example, I often gave it as an example of risk management in the management classes.

"If you are injured by a fall, you can return from the hospital in three days, but if the injury is to your most important part of the body, returning from the hospital is very uncertain!" Wearing a helmet while riding a motorcycle dramatically reduces the 'operational risk.'

The new motorcycle was driven regularly to the aero-engine section in the morning. No special training was required as there was not much distance to the destination.

Everyday work in the field of experience was done well and accurately. Timely overhauls and maintenance of various aero engines were controlled precisely to ensure quality. Unexpected problems were minimal as the machines were widely used. So, I got a lot of time to do ancillary work.

An in-depth study was made of the 'quality assurance methods' used by the world's major aircraft manufacturers, which have evolved. A comparative study using our quality assurance method was conducted. A thesis was written and submitted to the Ministry of Defence outlining specific proposals for additional changes required to align with world-class standards. The title was "Change the Way We Assure Quality".

Like Kumaran Asan's "Change the rules yourself, or the rules will change you..." the lines aroused people against some rituals they traditionally followed and brought social reforms. I did not expect revolutionary changes. Still, I hoped efficient and effective changes would be possible and improve our work. If that happens, it would positively contribute to the country and the industry. In the prevailing bureaucracy, it was impossible to predict what would be the priority there.

When I later asked the boss who visited us about the progress of my suggestions, the cryptic remark was, "One swallow does not make a summer!" I noted that the usual bureaucratic response meant, "Even if something good happens, the situation will not be good, and you will not be able to overcome it. There has been some discussion and follow-up, and that was good news. It remained to be seen whether this growth could be sustained in the coming days." I could not do anything further for the following two years.

The swallow is a type of bird that we know of. This refers to the arrival of migratory birds in Europe at the beginning of summer after spending the entire winter in the south (e.g., South Africa).

I was glad to know that my suggestions were not completely ignored. In more detail, it can be said that the reference to the swallow (in the allegory) helped to learn and re-write a 'quality management system' later that was acceptable to all.

I submitted another paper written in 2005 incorporating the complete Quality Management System (AS 9100) for aerospace and defence organisations, approved by the International Aerospace Quality Group (2000). Subsequent articles I presented attracted the special attention of the Ministry and the Department. It was a matter of pride that I could cause the changes. Books published in 2012 and 2017 provided examples of implementing the 'International Quality Management System' in an organisation, citing the experiences as examples in simple language and comprehensively. It is a matter of great satisfaction that these books are being used by many industries and individuals worldwide.

Nita's close friends, who studied together in the same college, passed the hotel management degrees. Everyone worked in various places in Bangalore itself. Nita's close friends called and addressed Nita as "Nita Didi" (elder sister); They called us Nita Deedee's Daddy and Nita Deedee's Mommy. Samuel would visit Nita with friends and inquire about her parents' well-being from time to time.

Samuel and five friends came to our house with an older gentleman one evening. Samuel introduced the gentleman - "This is Thomas Uncle, my father Peter's younger brother. The rest are my cousins John, Hannah, and Mintu; friends - Amit from Tatanagar, Raj, Subhash, and Dada ........." All Residents of Kolkata, Bhubaneswar, and Jamshedpur came to study in Bangalore, stayed together, finished their studies, and got to work here. Everyone was pleased and joked, cracking while eating the snacks and tea served hastily by Leelamma. Dada said -

"Auntie, we've all got together today; we need a party."

"I'll give the party, but it is not possible today. You came without any prior intimation. Let's do it some other time."

The smirk was there on everyone's face. They changed the subject by telling another joke to cover up the confusion. They inquired about Tony and Seema.

After a while, Thomas mumbled something mysteriously about Samuel - (naming him 'Tinku')

"Brother, You do not know Tinku; he has obsessional behaviour."

I had nothing to do with it, and I had heard nothing, and a few moments of silence followed.

"Tinku wants to marry Nita. Uncle and Auntie must agree to that."

I was silent without saying anything, as I had not considered the subject before. I was thinking about what to reply to. It was not at all unexpected. However, the methodology and approach were puzzling. Is this how relatives initiate a proposal important for changes in one's life? If Tinku is compelled, will I send my daughter along with him as he desires? Is the common courtesy different in other parts of the country? This is not the time to argue about anything. I said - "Let the time come. I'll think about it then."

"Okay, brother, if we get an answer, we can move further."

"Let's think about it. Many people in my family love us very much and cooperate; we can only answer after we discuss and decide together."

No one else spoke a word. Everyone was hiding something in their minds.

"The decision must be positive. We believe that it is positive. Let us leave now."

"I didn't say anything, did I?"

"Okay, we are getting down."

"That's good. Glad you have come".

We were preparing to discuss the subject with others. No one talked about it at home for two or three days. It was the mundane routine every day. Nita said nothing. She didn't even say anything to her Mom. No one asked for her comment. One evening, three days later, Samuel's friend Amit came home alone.

Continuing what Thomas of Jamshedpur had said, it was understood that Amit had come to talk about Samuel's marriage. Amit was Samuel's childhood friend and classmate, like Thambichan and myself. Amit's parents lived nearby in Tatanagar. Amit was married with one child and has moved to Bangalore to run a small dry cleaning business. Amit described Samuel's parents, their family, and relatives. Peter had a job at Tata Steel Company. He brought up his children and sent them to Bangalore for higher education. Other relatives' children also came with Samuel and were admitted to Christ College. Peter's brother, Thomas, worked at XLRI - Xavier School of Management. Amit also narrated the family tradition, their connection with Cuttack, Samuel studying there for a while, and so on.

Finally, he came to the crux of the matter. Amit inquired about Samuel-Nita's marriage and the results of my consultations with my relatives.

I said, "Discussions have just begun, and I have to go home and discuss. Only then could I say something."

During the conversations, Amit, while resting, casually said something, looking blankly at my face -

"Uncle, Samuel, and Nita registered their marriage three days ago."

"Amit, I did not understand what you said!"

"Sorry, Uncle, we came here last time after returning from the Registrar's office"!

I was blinded, speechless, and shell-shocked. I did not know what to say or how to respond to the thunderstorm. It affected my senses.

I was unable to get up from where I was sitting. I lost all the wetness in my mouth and did not know how long I was sitting with my eyes closed, not even looking at Leelamma. My heart was pounding; I heard it well. A jet flew away over my ears.

I said something to Amit. Amit looked at me. He looked unfamiliar and then said so sympathetically -

"Uncle, I'm leaving. Take rest, uncle, and I'll come later."

Can't I believe I have to say something to Amit or ask?

"Amit, tell Sam to see me and come with the marriage certificate from the registrar's office." It was a pathetic cry of a defeated and helpless man.

"Okay, Uncle". Amit went outside, and I got up and slammed the door behind him.

Looking back, Leelamma was before me - my breathing was interrupted. I burst into tears, suddenly sighing and unable to breathe deeply.

Leelamma asked me - "What, what, Oommacha?" I could not answer anything.

Nita came down from the inner room.

I got up, took Nita's hands, and thrust them into my left hand. I don't know what I got in my right hand, but I raised that hand to hit her with burning anger -

Leelamma stopped me, roaring, "No," and "Do not hit her."

My strength and energy got drained out. It's not right to beat up girls. I called Nita and asked her - "Did I hear right?"

Nita stopped crying and said nothing.

"Why did you do that, Molay? Couldn't you tell me?"

"No, Daddy, I did not know. I got it wrong." She was crying.

"I won't go anywhere without telling you, Daddy!"

I stretched my legs and approached Achayan's photo on the bookshelf's top. My eyes were full of tears; my head was heavy, and I begged for a way out. Even before I could look at Achayan's image, I burst into tears. When I got exhausted and calmed down, I told Leelamma and wished Achayan had heard the same.

"Leelam, our Nitamol's wedding is over…... It was told to all but not to us. What answer can I say to all in the family? That is what Amit came and spoke. It must be true. I told him to bring the certificate and show me."

Leelamma stood in shock, not understanding anything, unable to respond or say anything. It was very challenging to suppress the emotions without speaking or crying due to grief or strong feelings! She felt ignored and disrespected by her daughter.

Not knowing what to do next, I apologised to my father, and when I looked at the photo, I heard it clearly as if my father had told me in silence.

"Don't worry. You see Ramaswamy, and he will tell you what to do."

Then, Leelamma's concerns came out - "But what was wrong with our baby? Did they all together seduce her to this end? Were we not waiting for good proposals to come soon? Can we file a case? She's too innocent and trusts anyone! What wrong did we do to reach this situation?"

After the marriage registration and getting the certificate, his uncle came to perform the dramatic scene here! Without getting carried away, I should ask him calmly, why was that third-rate farce enacted here?

Then why did our daughter go to the registrar's office? Have we lost sincerity and love from our daughter? Is there a greater shame than this? It is said that Biharis (Jharkhand) is a race that does not look forward or backwards when fighting a case in a court or combat wrestling. Who knows what is going to happen to us?

The new generation has lost their sense of responsibility, no respect for their parents, and no social commitment. This is their time. I never thought any of our children would be like this. It's normal for friends, boys and girls, to walk together, work together and collaborate. We never felt, nor did someone warn us that it would happen like this, without our knowledge!

"Anyway, I have decided one thing. Whether Nitamol loves us or not, we will not end our lives with this setback. There are still two more children left. We have to live for them too!"

Can we do like some people say, 'We don't have such a daughter'? Can we leave this girl and live without any intimacy and cooperation for the rest of our lives? What is there to gain by living like that?

Are we not simply the melting candles? Let it burn as long as it can. When a grain of wheat falls into the earth and dies, it bears much fruit.

The grains of wheat that we are must get rotten for them so that they would become more fruitful than us.

"Let's go to Ramaswamy; he will tell us better things."

Aunty and Ramaswamy received us most cordially, as usual.

# 85

# Another Shore of Consolation

The question from Ramaswamy was, in Vadakkancherry slang, "What's up, Thomas, the news?"

After listening intently, he responded with a loving pat on my shoulder and a smile.

"So what? Let it be. You conduct it, and everything will come for good! It is nothing, Thomas, don't give trouble to the children. You conduct everything. It is all due to none of our mistakes. There is no mistake, and nobody is at fault. It is the change that happened in our times. We must move with the times."

It would be best if you calmed down, and you must contain it. There is no other way. Do your duty best; the future will come just as it would. Let us pray for their goodness and bless them.

For one thing, Thomas, you are fortunate. The boy is educated, working, and almost in your community, so why bother? Everything will be fine. "

When we left after thanking Ramaswamy Sir and Aunty, my mind became moist with indescribable peace. Most of the disturbances in my mind have vanished. Do good, and everything will become good.

I wrote something with emotions in a letter to Tony from the office. Everything changed in a day. How quickly the wisdom from experiences and knowledge changes our attitudes and behaviours! The information was again written warmly to Tony. It will take a week for the letter to reach there, and even if he replies immediately, I will receive it a week later. By then, things would have moved. Tony was regularly calling, then every week. The information was quickly given and communicated.

I do not remember Tony having written any reply. When he called, he said, "Don't worry, I will also talk to Nita and Sam."

Samuel came home one evening. No rudeness was shown. When he arrived, he made a hundred apologies and apologised. When I sat down and started talking, the first thing I asked was -

"Let's see the marriage certificate."

Sam handed me the scrolled paper -

"Uncle, I am sorry for this too. It is a stupid thing that I did without getting your permission. I have also said sorry to my father."

I unscrolled the paper and read it. It was the appropriate certificate. I have kept it for a long time since then. I have not shown it to anyone, nor did I tell anyone.

The impasse could not be continued. I had to start talking calmly to Sam. Leelamma also came and sat with me on the sofa and listened to what we were discussing. Nita was in the inner room. She must have noticed that Sam had come, and we talked. I thought peaceful cooperation was the best policy forward. I told Sam: -

"Sam, what you said was the most foolish thing to do. It was even more foolish that you all came here together with your Thomas uncle. Because Sam was so persuasive, he requested that I agree with the marriage proposal. Is it the way you people initiate a marriage proposal? Are your parents not alive? Is this what happens in your community? I am disgusted."

"I am asking your pardon for that, too, uncle."

We were silent for a while. I liked Sam's attitude toward achieving his goal through patience and perseverance, without using his wounds for prowess and heroism. Achieving goals is always based on a willing attitude. This young man knows how to do things strategically. That is why he chose the path of reconciliation.

I was wondering how to take a few positive steps forward. I prayed in my mind that let it begin well. I believe that it is always desirable, at least, to meditate and pray in mind where God lives before I start a journey or do anything.

I wanted to ensure he had the basic requirements for an alliance with our family. That must be understood before he receives any sacraments. The best way to get started was to ask like the priest asking the aspirants for baptism or marriage before entering the church -

"Okay, now forget all that has happened so far. Let us start afresh. ....

What do you desire?"

"Uncle, I wish to have a family life with Nita."

"Are you a Christian? "

"Yes, uncle, right from my great grandparents' time, I know we are Christians."

"Do you believe in God Almighty?"

"Yes, uncle."

"Do you believe in Jesus Christ? "

"Yes, uncle."

"Are you a Catholic?"

"Uncle, we go to the Indiranagar Methodist Church on 100 ft road. All my parents and relatives in Tatanagar go to the Beldih Baptist Church, Jamshedpur."

"You will have to receive the baptism in our church. Are you willing?

"Yes, uncle, I will do."

"I will have to talk to the Parish Priest and let you know. What next? How will you proceed? "

"As you say it, uncle. I will do anything as per your directions."

"Okay. I will also discuss it with my elders and family and tell you. In the meantime, ask your parents to come and tell me what they wish and how to proceed. I shall wait."

"Thank you, Uncle. I assure you that I will earn your goodwill and prove myself worthy of deserving the hand of Nita. Even though I have no plan to go abroad, I will continue to work in Bangalore and prove myself economically sound like anyone else serving abroad. "

All answers were recorded in mind and on the journalist's voice recorder. I did so for Tony. These conversations may be the cornerstones of a historical event, foundations, or the beginning of a new Christian family.

It doesn't matter, even if the distance is still there. It did not take much research to realise that this young man could give Nita a family life and that he had the mind and determination to do so. From his speech and demeanour, you can tell he was honest and sincere in his approach. As someone responsible for the future, he knows his desire to grow. What else can parents expect from their daughter's fiancee? I am willing to give Sam a pass mark when evaluating the expectations from the fiancee according to traditional needs such as family background, health, education, employment, and wealth.

There are strengths, weaknesses, and opportunities; nothing can be judged as excellent or good enough, but marks can only be given to pass the exam. I analysed SWOT (Strengths, Weaknesses, Opportunities, and Threats). Threats can only come if the event is not likely, does not happen, or we oppose it.

I think they can have a better life if they use the opportunities. College-educated students will find that success in anything depends on their discipline and willpower. The first steps of resolve are apparent quickly, and little is known about his discipline. Then, take the risk. Parents are not the only ones responsible for this. He also has parents. I don't know much about them either. Let's wait for the good to come.

Tony was informed of the incident. He might have talked more with his sister and others, but he didn't respond. As Tony rushed to get a better job, he realised that family problems could be more thought-provoking.

The events of the week echoed in my mind again and again. Leelamma's grief was more from Nitamol's 'senseless act.' She did not care to ask her mother to understand things and move on with her life. Forgetting one's duties and responsibilities, under the impression that they are good friends, doing everything as they say, forgetting one's parents, and entrusting one's friends to control one's life, can it be said that it is ignorance? Is it because of not thinking correctly? Shouldn't you at least discuss things with Mommy? Did you not boast that your brother (Chachan) was being everything and communicated these things to him, or did you not ask him for his opinion? I do not know.

Moreover, wrong tendencies arise in the blessed 'family institution' we have built, which was always happy and peaceful.

No one here has a misconception about love. If it was love and presented peacefully in the right way, if it hinted that nothing was needed, a well-thought-out decision could have been made. Now it is decided, and let the rest come as it may.

The ups and downs and obstacles in the journey of love between young men and women are not unknown. So far, such a risk has not even been carefully considered.

Isn't love the strongest emotion in this world? Is emotion the only way to a better life? Love is always a complex concept. It is difficult to explain precisely what love is. Famous psychologists define love in many ways. One popular definition is: "Love is the intense attraction of having sex, idealising one's partner, and intending to continue." (Jankowiak, W. R. Fischer, E. F.)

The Christian definition is no different. "Love is forgiveness, love is kindness, always hopeful, always enduring. Love never fails "(1 Corinthians 13: 4-8). "God is love" (1 John 4: 8).

Love is an intense love for another person. Love also means feeling passionate affection for others.

In the scientific analysis of eminent scientists, the three essential elements of love in a relationship between men and women are unity, contentment in life, and commitment -

a) Emotions such as the intensity of the 'union' relationship, the intimacy between minds, unity, and solidarity;

b) The goal of raising children for the good of the world, as good human beings (in the Christian spirit), is the sexual desire, ability, and resourcefulness to raise children through reproduction to achieve 'life satisfaction.'

c) 'Commitment' refers to the determination that a man and a woman love each other and intend to maintain this relationship throughout their life forever.

Like some of our campuses, love that gives no importance to commitment or a relationship that decides to stay together solely based on sexual orientation without consideration of the harmony of minds is unlikely to last long. Harmony refers to a positive state of inner peace, calmness, balance, and the feeling of being in tune with the world.

Unwise actions should not have occurred on the part of our daughter. It has been a completely immature, all-forgetting act. What more can I say about it? Was it something that could be corrected, an incident that could be forgotten, erased, washed away, something that could be left behind? Is everything not over when you have a legal certificate? That has closed all possible escape routes!

There was a need for better attention from our side. We believed them unthinkingly. They have proved they will go to any extent by sticking to their hidden objective and wounding others. We could have thought about the possibilities and consequences well in advance. But it all happened so soon without any symptoms or indications. It may be the will of God. It has to be accepted.

"If this registration was to take place, it could only happen if it was booked at least a month in advance and advertised on the local notice board. Rugmini Balakrishnan had mentioned once that the name of 'Nita, daughter of Thomas' was seen on the notice board! Neither of us bothered to probe further and ignored it, saying it was just trickery or information about someone else."

We experienced everything; what else would we have done? Shouldn't we have suffered the consequences if we had left common decency and behaved inhumanely? They have done this with the preconceived notion that we may not allow it if they had told us. We were not responsible for it, so we should not punish ourselves. That was how it was decided.

Nita was oblivious to everything, which may not be because she was selfish. She was driving from home to work and returning. We practiced a few minutes of prayer before leaving home for any job or journey. For us, prayer was like taking an 'insurance coverage' for satisfactory completion of work or journey. Nita's mother regularly reminded her to pray for a few minutes before leaving home.

Adolescence is a stage of growth when children are concerned solely with their desires, needs, or interests. Naturally, some elders see this as selfishness or think the children are oblivious to their surroundings.

Leelamma tried to recall the day we were thrown out into the fire, unknowingly –

"That day, Nita got ready as usual, took her helmet, and went downstairs....

I did not notice anything unusual. That was when I reminded Nita to pray as usual."

"Why don't you pray in front of the image of Jesus for a minute?"

"Never before has she been so egotistic and arrogant. She turned around and rudely retaliated to me -

"This mommy will call me back no matter where I go."

"Yes, if you pray and go, you will fulfill your desires. That is why you are told to pray and go, do you understand?"

"She did pray, and afterward, she hurried downstairs as if someone was waiting for her. She still didn't say it was for this reason she went out."

We have been imprisoned and tied up, and then they politely came in disguise to ask for her hand. Was it not a farce showing the treacherous force of challenge? A group of people come together, but did they speak a word of truth? Did Nita say a word? So all this was cleverly planned to deceive us; it was not their intelligence. It was pure malice!

However, My conscience consoled me and controlled me.

I thanked Jesus that none of my negative personality traits dominated me during the trial period.

It was our Nita who deceived us—no one else.

There is nothing more to ask and nothing to say, so forgive everything. That is all we can do. The weak can never forgive. We are not weak. Forgive them all, and we'll have peace of mind. Anxiety robs us of energy. By forgiving, our anxieties go away.

Achayan said it to us through Ramaswami - "Do your duty by organising everything. Find solutions to problems yourself. Most problems are easy to solve if you react calmly and don't get angry. But remember one thing. Never make decisions or think of solutions when you are angry. After your mind becomes calm, think of what happened. Analyse them why it happened and solve the problem."

We decided on one more thing. We only need to know our grief and sorrow. None of our relatives or friends should know it soon. Let no one blame or insult us, especially when they learn of our daughter's irrational actions. We strive for the good. If our children are living well, let others see it and understand. The humiliation we have suffered will be changed. Our embarrassment or disgrace will become honour and glorification when the world ends for us.

# 86

# What do You Desire?

Sam's parents had told him they would come to Bangalore from Tatanagar during the Dussehra holidays. They came home one Sunday afternoon. They were warmly received. I realised that they were calm and did things with mutual respect. I could get into the matter and talk more, and I started with essential hospitality etiquette.

I spoke about our thanks and loving regards for them travelling more than two thousand kilometres from Jamshedpur to Bangalore and coming to see us.

After a pause, I politely inquired -

"Aap kya chahate ho?" (What do you desire?)

Peter replied - "Brother, I want to consider your daughter as my daughter and make her a wife for my son."

Peter was soft and sincere, and he had no aura of pride in his words. Neither of us felt the need, hence, for a formal discussion after that. They did not put forth any demand. I discussed Sam getting baptised and conducting the marriage in our church, to which they agreed. The wedding will be held in Bangalore, and the wedding date will be one day during the following summer holidays. Peter spoke in detail about his family and work. He worked for the Tata Steel Company in Jamshedpur. Peter lived in Tatanagar until Peter started small animal husbandry and dairy farming, where milch breeds of buffaloes are reared for sustained milk production. He explained about his brothers, including Thomas, his married daughter, and how his brothers' children decided to come and study in Bangalore together. He also requested that we go to Bhatia Basti in Tatanagar and receive their hospitality.

It was agreed that the Betrothal (also known as 'declaration of intention') would occur in September and the wedding in May. Sam's parents lovingly shared a friendship and took leave of us to see each other again.

There were no significant difficulties with the engagement ceremony and meal arrangements. No outdoor arrangements were required as the number of guests was limited to the rooms in our quarters. Fr. Norman Bernard provided very loving and compassionate services. After a few Bible lessons, Sam was baptised when he was ready. We attended the baptismal rituals as godparents. Nita and Samuel participated in a counselling class at the Sacred Heart Church and received a certificate. Nita's baptism certificate was obtained from the Aundh Village, Pune church. Fr. Norman Bernard came home, and the betrothal ceremony was held on September 14, 2000, at E-34/5 DRDO Quarters. It was conducted and blessed beautifully in the presence of all relatives.

All the relatives and a few friends of Sam and Nita came home to attend the ceremony. Tony could not come from Singapore since the wedding; the more critical celebration was scheduled for May. Coming and attending both functions, one after another from Singapore, was strenuous in his student days. All the close relatives from Alappuzha and Chennai were very loving and cooperative in their presence, wished Sam-Nita all the best in her family life, and gave her gifts.

Samuel was always 'Tinku' to his parents and relatives. I did not inquire about the young man's life before I met him. We have called him 'Sam' all the time since we met. Our relatives also called him Sam. After getting acquainted, I was convinced that Sam's conversations and actions were all that of a well-disciplined, well-mannered, well-meaning young man with ambitions and desires. I firmly believed that it would help my daughter's bright future.

Sam and his family were introduced to my relatives. In a family where love marriages have happened rarely, my relatives saw a novelty because Nita loved her classmate and brought him into her marriage and life. No one knew anything about the mental conflicts that had taken place before this meaningful ceremony and the storm that had raged through our minds.

The privilege of getting purified comes to only a few parents willing to endure the heat and stress.

Good human beings need to see it philosophically as similar to refining gold. (One of the methods of refining gold is to melt it in a crucible with a heat of about 1100 degrees C).

Josekutty surmised a few other relatives' veiled thoughts and commented as follows -

"When we were told to come and join for Nita's engagement function, we were thinking something else to happen like - You might have been in trouble here since the groom's party was from North India!"

I answered confidently – "Josekutty, the influence of the Almighty over our matters was marvellous, as always."

(Did he think it would be something like what happened in Chennai sometime back?)

## Immovable

On April 6, 2001, Tony sent me the following text through one of his friends in Singapore.

"Dear Daddy, Mommy, Nita & Seema,

I hope you all are having a good time in Bangalore and that Seema has enough time to relax and enjoy after returning from Kerala. Here, I give you a warning - The content of this letter may surprise you all. I suggest reading this with a nice hot cup of coffee and when not in a hurry. There are many surprises, but not all are uncomfortable. This story, like most memorable ones, has a happy ending.

Exactly four months ago, I lost my job! I am writing this to explain - what happened later on.- now, what is happening and - to understand why I decided not to tell you.

On Wednesday, December 6, well began; I got up early, put on a formal dress, and packed a tie because I was planning to see a client related to the company business. I was calm as I had made all the preparations the previous night. I arrived at the office around 8:30.

The first sign that something had gone wrong was that the office seemed busy. Usually, only a few people came at this time. My two elders were standing by the big window. Walking to my desk, I saw a few people sitting in suits inside our conference room. My Technology Director stopped me and showed me a printed page, saying, "I do not know any better way to say this." I read it: "Lante Reorganization is closing offices in Singapore and Delhi to take over for a charge of $ 17 million.

I was shocked, blank, and dumbstruck due to surprise or confusion. I didn't feel anything! My office has vanished from today.

My boss came and asked me softly, "Did you know?" I nodded silently.

We invited everyone into the conference room.

The corporate head stood up and briefly said the company had closed its Singapore operations. "We have arranged a compensation package for each of you to sign. We have also arranged for PricewaterhouseCoopers to better support other job seekers."

Other elders also tried to say they did not know anything about this before and were equally shocked. But he said they would do everything possible to help everyone find another job.

It was harrowing to see that our dreams were shattered so mercilessly. The corporate head did not allow the local authority to explore other options, such as disbanding a team or maintaining at least a small presence.

We went to clear our office desk. Some were busy replacing the locks on the front doors. None of us should go back and open the door! Security guards were ordinarily detailed to stand by to deal with any untoward violence. But in our case, it was avoided at the last minute.

I could not believe that anything of this was real. At first, I didn't pack anything. I called some friends, and we ate breakfast at my favourite 'Bread-Prata' stall at the nearby food court.

We returned to pack our things in the office. Luckily, I had a full backup of all my files a few days ago. I finished the rest. All my files have been deleted from the system. I handed over my notebook, staff pass, and keys to the conference room. They gave me the final termination letter and a one-month salary severance package. That was the minimum the company decided as compensation- a month's salary. We had nothing to say about it. Singapore corporate law generally favours companies and does not support employees.

Then I walked around the office building, where I was until yesterday, which was now owned by someone else. I remember the long hours I spent designing the layout to maximize light and shared space while in charge of the project. I saw a photocopier, a table tennis table, a printer, and some wires scattered when I looked around. The fridge was also stocked, and I opened a beer can as I thought this was an unusual situation. Many of my colleagues quickly joined me.

We were all hungry by then, so we went out for lunch. We have time until 3 pm.

After lunch, we returned to the office and, with the help of a friend, took all my boxes and bags home in a taxi.

Because of the shock of this event, what I was doing, without a doubt, was the best job I had ever done! I felt like I had found something good and liked to do it, and my productivity was at its highest.

They hired me as a senior project analyst responsible for project management. After the initial dissatisfaction, I got involved in a small research activity in a real estate business. We were sure it would succeed, and the research was just a general reflection on the state of the real estate industry in Singapore.

I increased the scope of the research. In addition to Singapore, the situation in Hong Kong was also studied concerning the real estate market. I prepared a comprehensive white paper, which was an instant success. My boss was very supportive of this and asked me to lead the presentation to the client. The fact remained that I had never attended a client meeting before.

My presentation incidentally made a good impression on the client. When we returned, my boss asked me to give a model presentation to standardise such meetings.

Within a week, I presented another business proposal to another large corporate client.

I had three birthdays to celebrate in the office on December 1, including my birthday. We organized a short wine appreciation course. It was so much fun- we sampled many wines and learned the right way to spin the wine with our tongues, the right way to hold the glass, and so on. We came from different countries and were finally becoming a team and company.

On December 7, the weather outside was nice and bright. Since I woke up today after losing my job, I felt the weather was unfair.

Our team intended to meet at a Starbucks coffee shop near our office. We discussed some of the possibilities of staying together as a team. We had valuable resources, people, and projects worth several million dollars. We got a new workplace to think about and plan our Internet banking project a week later. We thought we could start a new venture by the end of December. Discussions and meetings continued uninterrupted.

We planned partnerships with a new internet consulting firm, but they said their funding would take three months. We lost that hope, too. It was likely to take even longer.

I did not write any of this earlier because after having said all this and nothing was specific, it could have led to more frustration when nothing happened. Not only that but considering the various activities required to coordinate Nita's wedding arrangements, I felt that it would be better for the situation to remain the same and then apologize later than to place more on your plate.

I moved from my living room to another room just before Christmas. I went to Malaysia after Christmas to attend a friend's wedding. I returned and resumed meetings and job search from January 5.

Although things seemed very dim, I clung to my dream of being able to find something like what I had done in the last office. Initially, I applied for all kinds of IT jobs. I have seen that the IT industry did not perform well. I changed my applications and approach to certain institutions, bringing more clarity.

The year-end holidays, the Chinese holidays, and the 'Hari Raya' and Eid festivals came one after the other, which worsened the scrutiny of applications and candidate interviews. It lasted until February.

Chinese New Year celebrations moved on to traditional family reunions and dinners. I was thrilled to be invited by one of my lecturers this year. She, her son, and I met at a Chinese restaurant. We started the dinner with the traditional "throw away the fish," -, which included various crispy snacks, vegetables, noodles, and many small pieces of uncooked fish. The main species was fish. The raw fish was so delicious after pouring a lot of sauce. Chopsticks were used to stir the mixture. Several courses were available after the start. First, we had shark fin soup, finished with fried chicken, steamed fish, and fried rice — a Filipino band was in attendance dressed as cooks, and they sang Western pop songs.

My job search continued. I used to spend the day in the office space. I did not have a computer at home, so I went there to access my mail and apply for jobs. I could not describe this period adequately - you must wake up every day knowing you do not have a job and sleep with the same despair. When I started counting the months, weeks, and days I remained unemployed, the time stretched ahead of me, and everything else lost importance. Maybe, in my case, it took too long because I started applying seriously only in mid-January. By the end of February, I had abandoned the previous approach. I looked for general project management and various technical jobs. Although I wouldn't say I liked any of these, I decided to reconcile.

One Friday in March, I met the Director of Pre-Sales at SAP Market, and on Monday, they offered me a job. The package was 10% better than the previous job and a 20% bonus based on performance.

Other interviews took a week or so to complete. They needed some time to sort things out administratively. I finally started working for the new company, SAP Market, on March 23. I was so excited to begin my work on a Friday!

All my other colleagues got jobs in many companies as well. I was planning a few exciting new ventures, such as consulting and solution development. So, I had hope for the future. Sometimes, hope is essential!

I look forward to seeing you all in May.

Sincerely, Tony"

I read Tony's long letter, and he came home before I could reply. Tony's letter illustrated the sincerity with which he did his job. It summarised the difficulties he faced when he lost his job.

You may have been trying for a job after working hard and getting an educational qualification. Often, you get worried about not succeeding in getting a job. It is not because you have yet to put forward the best efforts. When you read this, you get a message that you are motivated to keep trying. It also sends the message that you should keep believing in yourself and your abilities without giving up hope. The mental conflicts you may experience as an average young person in trying situations are also indicated.

I was unemployed for more than six months after college and while with my parents years ago. In contrast, Tony was abroad, alone, unable to share the hardships and having no source of income to survive. Undeterred and confident in his abilities, he made constant efforts and got a new job. Tony has now shared that joy with us. He did not share his trying time after he lost his job.

"Without being ecstatic when getting honours,

Regrets not, even when humiliated

Tranquil as the depth of the Ganges,

He who saves dharma remains wise! "

Shallow rivers and oceans always make noise due to the current or the waves' force. The deep ones are silent and still. Men of little knowledge continue to make great commotions, quarrels, and arguments. When a pot is dipped in water, the water getting in makes a loud noise. The sound will stop when the pot is full. Wise or intelligent are seen as calm, soft-spoken, and sometimes quiet because of the depth of their wisdom. Even the silence of such will be sweet and eloquent.

"Tranquil is the depth of the Ganges. He is the one who saves dharma..."

I was happy to see that as Tony's character. Although it is impossible to say he is 'a chip of the old block', at least it can be said that 'he keeps his good head on his shoulders' and his feet on the ground.' These attributes were due to the blessings of God and the good deeds of older generations that vanished from sight.

It was the same in Achayan's writing, which he asked his grandchildren a few months ago.

We can similarly judge all our children, Tony, Nita, and Seema. However, our love for them and their love for us cannot be compared at all.

87

# As Daughter to Us

Nita's wedding preparations were paramount in the matters that followed.

First, the goal was to raise the necessary funds. I can withdraw more than half of my provident fund. When it was given as a loan, I could ask back since it was an absolute necessity. Even then, after requesting Appachi repeatedly, Appachi returned it only after several months. When he said he was ready to return it, the wedding date had already approached.

It was imperative to avoid unpleasant remarks and situations such as "gave away the daughter because she had made her own choice'. It did not first obtain the happy consent of her parents, 'leaving her without giving any asset, "what was given was not appropriate,' or 'that it was not according to her dignity.' Relatives may make comments that may refer to her parents. Seeing that it was advantageous for us since they do not know the complicated social evils, I am not prepared to imprison my conscience. Whether the people of North know the Travancore Christian tradition or not, even if the family did not ask for anything, everyone desires that Nita be the happiest and take care of the family life according to the family tradition. We owe it to ourselves to make it so.

We all knew that we were the tools for it. Division of property can be done when the time becomes right. Suppose there was property, savings, or valuable property to be divided. In that case, it can be given on that day, or an appropriate will can be written. I want to break the traditional notion of "give everything (due assets) and send your daughter away" forever. I do not wish to send my children away as such anywhere, anytime.

'Sending away daughters married' is an outdated idea. No one sends them anywhere. Parents do the duty of making them capable of leading a good family life. Parents have a responsibility to make their families happy. Children choose their lives, whether studying, professional work, or marriage! Parents are responsible for being the facilitators.

Even after marriage, children will always be children. Even if children grow up and become parents themselves, their relationships as children of their parents will continue throughout life. Married daughters are also responsible for caring for and protecting their parents according to their needs. That is human nature and natural justice. No law of humanity is against it.

Sam-Nita opened an account together at the post office, and we deposited a reasonable amount. The passbook was handed over to Nita. They were also beginning an independent family. We thought that let it be used as a reserve fund for the present. Necessary gold jewellery and wedding dresses were bought at the discretion of Nita and her parents.

The wedding ceremony was at the Resurrection Church, in English, their language of study and profession. It was convenient for everyone who came from Jamshedpur. The reception and dinner were held at the DRDO Community Hall, CV Raman Nagar. The wedding and reception of the Sam-Nita couple were attended by about 600 people, including all family members, relatives, friends, and office colleagues.

My job for a month or so was to prepare an Informative Data Bank for the invitees. It later became a good collection. Necessary letters were written to those far away, who were advised to make travel arrangements well in advance. Invitations have been sent by phone and by posting wedding invitation cards. The invitation was given in person to office colleagues a month in advance.

Tony arrived from Singapore. He met Sam and his relatives, renewed their acquaintance, and prepared for a new relationship. He undertook the administration and other duties for the ceremonies. All arrangements were made for the wedding ceremony and reception.

The Christian Church believes marriage is as sacred as all other sacraments and the mission of Christ in the world and in the Church, which man and woman undertake through the marriage contract and try to fulfill through themselves.

Not only were the ceremonies local, but because Sam's parents belonged to a different Christian denomination, their ceremonies were likely slightly different. That was why I spoke to Peter to have a mutual understanding of the ceremonies to be performed. Peter entrusted me with complete responsibility, saying everything should be as I like, without complacency or coercion from anyone.

Marriage is a ceremony for an adult man and woman to live together with the permission of society, religion, and their relatives. The Catholic Church has included marriage as one of the holy sacraments. The Catholic Church also has a ceremony called consent (Manasammatham) before marriage. Thali (mangal sutra), mantrakoti (wedding sari), and the ring are commonly seen in Christian weddings. After the wedding, the church-controlled ceremony ends when the bride, the groom, and the witnesses sign the church register.

There are various local ceremonies before and after the wedding reception. Lighting the brass pedestal lamp before the special ceremony and inauguration of the reception is believed to be auspicious. Some rituals are praying, giving sweets, cutting the cake, the bride and groom sharing and tasting the cake and wine, feeding each other, and distributing wine and cake to all those present at the festivities.

All the relatives and friends involved in the consent rejoined at the wedding. In addition to all the other relatives, especially the Ammachi of Kannattumadom, the Ammachi of Ottathyckal, Kunjommachayan, and Aunty from Kochi, and Kunjunju and family from Nashik had come earlier for the wedding. Kuriachan and Chechi came from Delhi at E 34/5 Quarters the previous evening. They returned after blessing and giving gifts to Nita. Appachi and James had come. Joy from Kochi was expected, but he did not come. James and his wife from Arakkaparambil had come from Hyderabad.

Going home after the reception, the mother makes the sign of the cross on the foreheads of the bride and groom before entering the house. Sometimes, they are garlanded. They are taken home and to their private room. The bride steps into the house with her right foot first, followed by the groom. In some communities, the bride's brother seeks permission from the elders present to lead the couple and escort the bride and groom to a room decorated for the bride and groom (Manavara).

Sam had arranged for a team from Jamshedpur to prepare the dinner for his wedding day reception. They arrived two days earlier. Arrangements were made for them to stay at the JCO Mess itself. The team planned, prepared, presented, and distributed the food. For distribution only, some college students trained in the subject were hired. The dinner was a little late because they were late in reporting.

Everyone loved the food and the associated ceremonies. Everyone ate and drank to their heart's content. Congratulations to Thomas and the team members who led the team.

Relatives went to take the Sam-Nita couple to their own home in Bangalore - (sasural). Traditionally, Leelamma took her daughter's hand and handed her over to Sam's mother. As a reflection, I shook hands with Peter, the head of the family. I realised for the first time that handing over my daughter to another family was not a smooth arrangement. Although it was satisfying, it was rather heart-breaking!

Peter realised it as he had done the same a year ago after his daughter's wedding. It was due to that wealth of experience that Peter held me close and comforted me.

"भाईजान, आप बिलकुल चिंता मत कीजिये। यह मेरा ही बेटी हे, हम इनको अपनी बेटी की तरह पालेंगे।"

("Brother, don't worry. This, too, is my daughter; we will take care of her as our daughter.")

When Kunjommachayan and Aunty returned to Kochi, I took a ticket for Ottathyckal Ammachi to go with them on the plane. Thus, the difficulty of train travel was avoided for all the older people. Kunjunju and family returned to Nashik. Similarly, all the other relatives who had come from our native place and Madras also returned. My mother remained in Bangalore.

**Wedding of Samuel and Nita**

Sam-Nita went to Tatanagar with relatives from Jamshedpur. As a representative of our family, the couples Raju-Tess, Thambichan-Leelamma, Tony, and Seema went to Jamshedpur for the reception and got to know Nita's parents-in-law's surroundings and relatives. The Sam-Nita couple returned to Bangalore after a month's leave and returned to work. Sam rented a house and started living there in Kaggadasapura. The two came home together most of the weekends and were very cooperative. Since we stayed close by, we also went to them often, always cooperating and lovingly spending the days.

After the busy schedules, trips, and visits, Tony returned to Singapore and continued his work at SAP Marketing.

As the college re-opened, Seema returned to the hostel in Kochi for her second year of study. Boiled rice and traditional local cuisines, the cohabitation of local shy girls, the wayfarer girls carrying backpacks, and the wayside mischiefs were all things that made Seema happy.

Seema's first year of college and hostel experience did not disappoint her. Seema had earned a good reputation and respect among her friends for her excellence in the English language and for doing project work in the class at the college. Some Malayalam words like 'adipoli,' 'chethinadakkuka,' etc., came out in the conversation with Seema because there was no need to look for any other proof that she was acquainted with the astute girls of 'God's own country.' Seema also had the opportunity to work with the World Catholic Youth Organization, the Jesus Youth.

Seema became a more mature student after learning about the irritating situations faced before Nita's wedding and the subsequent ceremonies. Tony's post-graduate work experience with Seema enhanced the excellent qualities, thoughts, natural aptitude, and capabilities that time does to the youth. The expertise and knowledge changed Seema's attitude and behaviour for the better. I was glad to see it. That is how our reputation grows in our society and culture.

# 88

# A Place for Us to Dwell

Once the children leave home to study and work, the chances of all the children and parents getting together will generally decrease. Before Nita's wedding, everyone had a rare opportunity to get together without any particular purpose at home. The primary references in Achayan's recent letter were the subject.

It would be less than five years for me to retire. I can stay in the quarters if I have work. What do I have to do after retirement?

What changes would happen in our lives in the next five years?

After the marriage of two more people in the alternate years, retiring from work and giving back the quarters, where will Mommy and Daddy go? There are plenty of options, and one of them should be chosen quickly. Only then will a smooth transition be possible.

Everyone agreed that the transition to post-retirement life should be planned at the earliest.

Then, we can decide which option to choose from. Any decision must be considered with proper foresight.

a) Achayan's instructions were as follows.

   - The existing house should be repaired, made habitable, go and live there, or
   - In Punnapra, near other relatives, you can get a decent plot of land, buy it, and build a home to stay there.

"Daddy, it's good to go and live in Alleppey for a fortnight or a month, like a happy picnic, and we, the children, can come and return. Moreover, there is no air-road travel facility, which causes great difficulty for the children. Didn't you say - "Even after you retire from your current job, you should still be doing something"? Wouldn't it be difficult if the job required air-road travel to do so? And in the socio-political climate of the state, with no peer friends - to those under sixty, daddy and mommy would be strangers - wouldn't it be difficult to continue daddy's agreeable lifestyle?"

- If you want to do something even after retiring from work, and if you want to continue your happy lifestyle, then Bangalore is the best place to live because it has the facility of air and road travel, which takes a shorter time for children to come and go. It would be best if you had a home here.

You can buy a flat or buy a house. It will be possible in the next five years.

Even though Achayan has gone, Achayan and other relatives will forgive us. We can reach them overnight to meet all their needs in the native world.

Although this has been thought about many times, let's not delay it further. I had in my mind a well-thought-out private plan. All that I thought of as the Panchatantra or resolutions were -

- Shall not acquire property by borrowing,
- After retiring, continue to work on something and be engaged.
- If you must travel, you must stay in a suitable place.
- Living wherever should be in the best interest of the children
- My siblings will have a house to live in, and only then I will have one.

These are strategies - a decision must be made to accomplish that. That was how we decided to stay in Bangalore when I would retire after five years. The first step was to find and buy a suitable place nearby. Building a house is to be decided after that. If necessary, I can take a repayable housing loan from the government with a slight change in the strategies, and the rest will be fine by that time.

Hearing that a 60x40 site was for sale in B Narayanapura and the owner Ajay Vohra, who worked at ADA, I called him and enquired. The price of 5 lakhs seemed reasonable. I saw the place, purchased and completed the registration without further detailed checks.

First, I sketched according to how the house should be constructed, the directions of the place, the positions of various rooms, the road, etc. I visited the place and inspected it in detail, thinking that I could make a detailed estimate. There was a small road and tiny houses on all three sides of the site, looking like a narrow enclosure, and on one side of the site, I saw a small anthill, in front of which someone had lighted an earthen lamp. Leelamma expressed her displeasure, thinking it was a small ancient traditional anthill worship place. If it was demolished, it might be a controversial issue.

Moreover, no acquaintances or Malayalis were seen in the neighbourhood. I stopped my sketching there. After finding a better site and doing more detailed checks, we decided to sell out this one and buy a better site. Our search continued.

It was always with me like a birth sin that some essential things in life must be done not once but at least twice. My Certificate of School Education, i.e., SSLC book, had to be obtained twice; the original was lost, and a certified copy was later. I broke the mangalsutra (thali) tied in the church on the neck of Leelamma. When we came home, I got a new one again so I would not marry again. Having earned my dwelling place, I had to change it and search for another one - you don't need to know why, but that's how things happen for me. If it happens like that, it will be correct and the best! Scribbling over some skull is like that!

Tony bought a Hyundai Santro car for us to travel with my Ammachi to church. Tony revealed the happy news to us just before the showroom. Then, it took two or three months to learn to drive and get a driving license. The Santro was beneficial for going together to the Resurrection Church. It was a combined reward of joy to get the new car and the pleasure of a long drive to the tourist destination - the Nandi Hills, just beyond the new Devanahalli Airport in Bangalore, about 100 km.

I felt happy and comfortable since Sam, who had much driving experience, and Tony were with us. We went in the morning and came back in the evening. We walked up the hill and down.

Our search continued for a better site for us to dwell.

We could see a lovely landscape from the terrace of the four-story E-34 block of the DRDO quarters. There were signs of a distant metropolis on one side, arranged layouts of two or three rows of houses next, and scattered random houses on the third side. Occasionally, there were uninhabited small and large sites on both sides. The rest were empty land or vineyards and coconut groves.

We went up to see which overhead water tank we got the water from, and some water overflowed. While coming down, I felt like telling a joke to Leelamma.

"If we climb to the terrace and look around, there are a lot of vacant sites; we'll go and buy it. We've got vineyards too to live in !"

I just wanted to help Leelamma, who was always looking to buy a site, find an uninhabited area.

Leelamma regularly walked two to three kilometres a day in the evenings. When I was lazy, I read something or watched something on the TV. If cricket was being telecasted, then that was my time pass.

After the evening walk one day, Leelamma insisted that we take the car and see a site. "It's very near here, come on..."

"There is one MEG layout just outside the DRDO Phase II quarters. Govindankutty, who lived next door, was a man who retired recently from CDA and came to walk with us regularly. In that layout, his colleague in CDA was selling a site he knew and told us. This is the place that the Almighty has brought for us. Let's go and see. "

We went, saw it, and we conquered!

Adjacent to the DRDO phase II compound wall, the vacant site 60x40 was at one corner of the layout. It looked like a planned reasonable layout, with about 100 nice houses and excellent wide roads within the layout. The only way to get inside the design was narrower as if they were starting to cut the way to heaven and then not finished for some reason. The road may be widened over time.

The Defence Accounts Department Employees Cooperative Housing Society was a cooperative layout for them. They all lived in this layout after retiring from work. One did not construct a house here as he had another one in the city, Sadasivanagar.

"This place was waiting for Thomas."

A church was about to be built nearby, at a walking distance of five minutes.

This site was not far from the site at B Narayanapura, but it was better and more convenient. The fact remained that the price was a little higher but fair and transparent. This site was visible accurately from the terrace of the E-34 block. We went to Sadasivanagar with the agent. We met Pushpa Sekharaiah, talked to her, and gave her a token advance. The registration was done the following week (March 5, 2003). He came with the local councillor Nagaraj and was ready to buy the site at B Narayanapura. Negotiating quickly without much bargaining on the profit and loss, selling the site without further delay, and receiving the cash was possible. Tony also sent the extra money needed to buy the site at the MEG layout.

Being a government employee, I needed permission from the government to acquire the property. It was the office rule, and I sent an application. The characteristic question of bureaucracy arose - where did the money come from? I replied that after paying income tax on my 35 years of government service, meeting the family's requirements, the amount raised to pay the five-and-a-half-cent piece of land for the residential house was the savings of a lifetime. The additional amount came from the amount paid to the parents by their son, who worked in Singapore. A receipt of the provident fund and a photocopy of Tony's cheque were sent as proof. It is the natural bureaucratic delay that permission from the government to buy the land and build a house there has not yet been given to me. When I inquired, a reply came that it would be sent soon. The crazy routines of a bureaucracy do not add any value at all!

One Sunday, when we returned from the church with my mother, our desire to show the family property recently acquired to Ammachi became obvious. When Ammachi set foot on the site, I told her -

"Mom, this is where we will construct our house."

"I have blessed you," Ammachi blessed us and permanently resided with her son's family on this earth! (I solemnly remember and pray as such), I firmly believe so.

## 89

# Pilgrimage to the Holy Land

A proposal had gone to DRDO Headquarters to send a scientist from GTRE named Sathya Keerthy and Thomas from DGAQA to a company called 'Chrome Alloy' in Israel to inspect and report on the GTRE work going on there. The decision was made to send us for three days of work. Keerthi said he had organised the official passport and visa for both of us and purchased a ticket from Mumbai to Tel Aviv on a Saturday morning.

Travelling abroad was not so exciting for me. I had an attitude that if the authorities decided that I go abroad someday, I could go. Nobody needed to expect any crazy and tireless effort from me for a foreign trip. As CJ, the playwright and literary critic of Malayalam literature, said, "If there were black monkeys in India, it would be white there. That's all the difference."

Humans, science, technology, and quality will be almost the same everywhere. By understanding the differences, improvements could be made in our defence equipment. That was the assigned job.

Another thought went through my mind. Israel is where any Christian desires to go at least once, as it is the Holy Land of Jesus. If possible, I could visit the holy places. If you take two days off in addition to the three working days, you can see all the important places around. Taking Leelamma along with the tour was unaffordable, and it could be challenging for her to sit alone in a hotel room while I went to work. My mother was also at home, and it would not be right to leave my mother alone and go on a trip abroad.

When we got home and shared the news, in two minutes, the smiles on the faces of Leelamma and my mother turned to excitement and joy. They silently shouted - 'Someone from home is going to the Holy Land! I saw so much light in their eyes.

"Wow! Great!" Seema, Nita, and Tony were screaming in chorus. Leelamma wished very much to accompany me if they were in the station. However, she knew it was a short trip and would cost extra, and she could not leave my mother alone at home. That is why Leelamma did not show her displeasure.

I also kept a few dollars in hand. Tony had warned that the expenses would be higher in Israel.

"Don't you take the suit? Or a sweater. What's the weather like there in Israel?"

Brushing aside Leelamma's worries with a winking smile, I asked her-

"Is there a Bermuda for me? Or something like that?"

"Ayye!"

My friend Vishwanath had mentioned that July and August would be scorching hot in Tel Aviv.

"Even if you are walking outside in normal pants & shirt, people will look at you strangely and think you are a foreigner. Therefore, it would be better to take a pair of bermudas and wear them while walking on the beaches of Tel Aviv!"

I had time to look through the information provided by Tony through e-mail. He gave me instructions on using the international calling card and sent his best wishes.

My mother wanted to return to Alappuzha. I could read it from her face. I told my mother I would do so when I returned from Israel. My mother could only smile when I said that -

"Okay - on the way - get ready. I'll leave Ammachi in Punnapra."

I remembered my classmate and friend Paulos telling me pilgrims prayed at the Wailing Wall according to Jewish custom. I remembered that Vishwanath further reiterated that the scraps of paper with thanks and prayers written to God were being deposited there. Vishwanath also mentioned taking a hat from the basket placed there, wearing it before going near the wall, and returning it after use. When told about this, everyone in the family sat down to write letters to God. Nita, Sam, Ammachi, and Leelamma quickly wrote each page without wasting time! Since it was letters God would read directly, everyone could have written more for more blessings!

"What are you writing, Oommacha?" Leelamma wanted to know why I am writing a complaint. "What I have to write, I can say directly."

I put all the letters in an envelope and closed it. No one else knew what each one had written to God. In their excitement, pilgrims visiting Wailing Wall have very little time to write on a small piece of paper, but for those sitting at home, a page full of things could be written!

My mother was eager to write the address outside the envelope, she asked me! She was mainly asking me to affix the required postage stamps. I consoled her by saying that I would give it directly by hand.

All the preparations were done in one day. I flew to Mumbai with Keerthi and stayed at a hotel near Santa Cruz Airport for the night. I boarded the Royal Jordanian Airlines aircraft Airbus A-310 in the morning. After landing in Amman, we took another flight to reach Tel Aviv.

Mr. George, his wife, and his son occupied the seats to my left. It was nice to see a Kerala Christian family on the plane. On asking whether they were going to the holy land, George told me they were going to the USA via Amman. They were going to settle down in the USA. He went to Kerala to settle down with his savings from Saudi Arabia. But finding

Kerala's social changes and political environment were different from his liking, they left Kerala. For a long time since then, we had nothing to talk about.

The man sitting on the right spoke to me.

He was also going to the USA. He had no relatives staying in India. He had two sons, and both were living with their families in the United States.

"It would be better for us to go to the States and stay with our sons and their families than ask them to come to India and stay with us."

He asked me for permission, put a towel on my head, and closed his eyes. Both hands were raised and held opposite his face as if going to touch the nose and cheeks with the same effort. He turned to me and said -

"It doesn't matter how one sits or to which direction the eyes and face are pointing. Prayer is what one needs to do."

He was absorbed in silent prayer. He moved his lips, closed his eyes, moved his head to the left and right, joined his hands, held it like a mirror before his face, and concentrated on prayer.

We landed in Amman. There, George and his family left me. I greeted them and wished them all the goodness in life. After moving a few steps forward, Mrs George returned to me. She introduced me to Lily, the girl filling out the form at the transit counter, and then asked, "Can you help this Malayalee girl who came with us to Tel Aviv?" "Sure".

"Lily got a nursing job at an Israeli hospital where Lily's sister Shirley works. Shirley will be coming to the airport."

The journey continued to the holy land in another small plane. We arrived at Ben Gurion International Airport in Tel Aviv an hour after taking off from Amman. The eastern approach and landing of the aircraft from the Mediterranean Sea were smooth. Stepping into the Holy Land of Israel was a significant and joyous event.

When Keerthi and I completed the entry formalities, we could see an immigration officer taking Lily from the counter to his office for questioning. Lily came up to me and said -

"Uncle, this is what I was afraid of. My photo in the passport does not exactly match my face. It was taken about two years ago. I do not know how to convince this officer."

True, a photo taken two years ago would likely differ from its current shape. There was no doubt about how fast young girls grow and how nature changes their faces.

I politely told the officer. I reassured Lily that the officer would oblige and allow Lily to enter Israel. We will tell Shirley, standing outside, that it would take a little more time for the customs authorities to check and allow Lily.

As we walked outside, Kirti asked how I could find Lily's sister in the small crowd. I told him that it was not difficult to identify a Malayalee girl in any dress anywhere by the features on her face.

There she was! I asked her in Malayalam, "Are you Shirley?"

"Yes, Uncle". She was so happy that she ran up to me from the other side of the barricade, accompanied by another girl, Nisha.

I told them about Lily's situation and consoled them. Shirley was reassured that the immigration officer would recognise Lily in the photo of her two years ago and that Lily would be out soon, and we went outside and walked towards the taxi stand.

Rooms were allotted to us at the Carlton Hotel. Keerthi and I were given separate rooms. I tried to identify the method to unlock the electronic door. The room had all the necessary amenities.

I used an international calling card following Tony's instructions to talk to Leelamma. The time was 16.30 hrs local and 19:00 hrs (IST) at Bangalore. I spoke to Tony, too. If only we had the iPhone and WhatsApp then!

# 90

# The Holy Places

We devoted the first three days to the assigned work in the industrial unit. The Israeli industry was renowned for welding and repairing aero-engine turbine blades using modern technology. I published an article on technology in my first book, Safety Follows Where Quality Leads.

The company representative took us to their industrial establishment, which was seventy kilometres from the hotel. Farmland and industrial centres could be seen throughout the journey. The most prominent feature I have seen was farming on dry land where all the rivers and lakes had dried up.

Electric Power is generated using nuclear energy. Desalination is the process by which the dissolved minerals and salts in seawater are removed. This is one of the most used processes in Israel to obtain fresh water for human consumption and agricultural purposes. Water is supplied to the base of each plant through drip irrigation.

We had two days left after work when we used to take the tourist bus and travel around the historical sites and holy places in Israel.

The first day was spent wandering through the holy places. There was no holier place in Israel than Jerusalem. Jews, Muslims, and Christians consider Jerusalem sacred, the promised land of the Jews. For Christians, it was the holy land of the life, death, and resurrection of Jesus. For Muslims, Jerusalem is the site of Muhammad's ascension. God also commanded Abraham to sacrifice his son Isaac at the Dome of the Rock, a mosque in Jerusalem.

Mount Zion is where the 'Last Supper' took place. "Love one another. If you call me Lord and Master, and I have washed your feet, go and do the same to others." There, Jesus gave his disciples the basic tenets of the Christian faith.

As we approached the place known as the West Wall or the Wailing Wall, Israeli police stopped us. We were moved to a closed glass room in a corner. We were instructed to stand there and observe the Wailing Wall. Just then, a police van pulled up near the mourning wall. Police said they found an unidentified object - a suspicious bomb-like explosive device - near the high wall and that a police van had arrived to remove it. We watched it with bated breath as a robotic man came down from the van, picked up the object, and left it in the van. Soon, we heard two pistol shots, a clearance signal that allowed us to go closer to the wall.

The Western Wall, often known as the Wailing Wall, is an ancient limestone wall in the Old City of Jerusalem that forms part of the more oversized defensive wall of the hill known to Jews and Christians as the Temple Mount. The Wall is the holiest place where Jews can pray outside the former Temple Mount platform. The most sacred site in the Jewish faith is right behind it.

According to Jewish custom, everyone must wear a hat before approaching the Wailing Wall. There was a basket full of white caps kept at the entrance. There were also small pedestals for use as desks for writing.

Everyone can write their prayers on a piece of paper. Letters can also be deposited in the crevices of the stones of the Great Wall. As I was carrying the envelope containing the letters written by my family members, Keerthy wanted to write one as well. He asked me –

"What did you write, Thomas, to give directly to God?"

I responded with faith and humility, like the Roman centurion, by misquoting the original ("Lord, I am not worthy to receive You, but only say the Word and I shall be healed-Mathew 8:8") for fun to Keerthy-

"Answer the prayers of everyone in my family, and my soul shall be healed. That is what I wrote. What more could I ask for? "

We approached the Wailing Wall, and there were already many pieces of paper in the gaps between the exposed stones on the wall. While placing the larger envelope, some pieces of paper fell from the gap between the rocks. It was not intentional. An adherent Hasidic Jew standing nearby looked at me and smiled softly. Shaking his head back and forth, keeping up the pace of his curled, long, swinging sidelocks, he continued chanting Hebrew mantras with his lips.

Perhaps he looked at me strangely in the white hat and wondered who this new Jew in town was!

After the Wailing Wall, we visited the Church of the Holy Sepulchre. Everyone will reach the church by walking the way Jesus carried his cross. Although the exact route has varied over the centuries and remains a matter of debate, the original Way of the Cross was accepted by tradition as the Via Dolorosa in Jerusalem. We first saw the sixth station of the Way of the Cross. The door panel was inscribed VI STATION, where Veronica wipes the face of Jesus. Jesus's face was left printed on the cloth that Veronica used. Named after the words 'Vera' and 'Icon,' meaning 'fixed seal,' Veronica, the feminine gem, became part of biblical history.

The Way of the Cross to Calvary, although known by other names, Calvary or Golgotha, was the place where Christ was crucified outside Jerusalem.

Before entering the church, we could see the STN X and STN XI plaques on the wall. The Church of the Holy Sepulchre is every Christian's holiest place on earth. It is the central temple of Christianity.

The last five stations on the Way of the Cross were inside the church of Holy Sepulchre. In the middle of the shrine, walking near the altar, there was a large cross. On the left side of the cross, we saw the statues of Mother Mary, and on the right side, that of Mary Magdalene, adorning the altar.

The altar was surrounded by large candle stands, hanging lamps, artistically decorated flowers, and carvings. The proximity of the altar increased the peace of mind. I knew my mind was filled with concentration, peace, respect, and adoration when I stood in the solemn, peaceful environment. We spent a few minutes there in silent prayer and took photos. People walked around and observed the details with great reverence and silence. There was no restriction on wearing footwear or for taking photographs. Although a few candles were burning on a candle stand near the altar, I did not see anyone offering candles or flowers at the altar.

A 2 m x 1 m marble slab was found on the floor before the altar, and many decorated lamps were hanging in different rows. People knelt there, prayed, touched, and venerated the slab. This was where the incense and spices were preserved, and preparations were made before the body of Jesus was taken down from the cross, wrapped in linens, and eventually buried in the tomb.

The Holy Sepulchre (the tomb in which the body of Christ was laid) was below the high dome. Its entrance opened to a circular hall. A structure built like a high tower was in the middle of the hall. Architecture, carvings, sculptures of angels, tall large candle stands, ornate lanterns, and marble flowers surrounded it. It was modelled on the monuments built for the Roman emperors.

This high-domed house is called the 'Chapel of the Resurrection.'

A small part of Jesus' tombstone was almost in its middle. It was permanently fixed to the floor, and all sides were covered with marble carvings. The top was also covered with a thick glass in a frame. The old limestone, which was light brown in colour, was visible through the glass pane.

On the right, the entrance to the tomb was wide and shallow. The visible tomb is carved out of one large rock. It was the temporary resting place of Jesus' body until he was resurrected on the third day- from the first Good Friday to Easter. The whole environment was calm, totally peaceful, venerable, and serene. Indeed, I felt it was heaven, the abode of the Supreme. I received the holy spirit by holding my breath, and the few seconds I could stay there were heavenly. It was God's presence - I felt while entering the tomb, like looking within my soul; as Babu Paul wrote, "One must bend the waist, bow the head, be humble enough to crawl on one's knees, a thing that is not impossible for the wise and the ignorant, only then, it is possible."

The most blessed thing was that I remembered my family, relatives, friends, and co-workers while I was there.

From the bottom of my heart, I prayed fervently for the peace and prosperity of all. With folded hands, I thanked my God Jesus.

Words of gratitude got stuck in my throat, my breath choked, and my eyes filled with the inner fountain of my mind. I reluctantly left the place to make way for others to enter.

I desired to sit on the lap of the most holy Son of God, experience divine love, and fill my heart with peace. If I could take home those three minutes and keep them for the rest of my life, that would be the best souvenir I've ever acquired. Or the three minutes spent there should be repeated at home or church. Life will be blessed.

There is a great historical monument on the west side of Jerusalem—Yad Vashem. We went there. It is a Jewish memorial that moves human minds and disturbs tender hearts.

The word Holocaust means 'massacre'. The Holocaust was the name given by Nazi Germany to the persecution and extermination of European Jews and their collaborators between 1933 and 1945. Sixty million Jews were systematically murdered, including 1.5 million children. It was central to the Nazis' broader plans to create a new world order based on their ideology. Thus, a creative society was destroyed.

'Yad Vashem' is Israel's official memorial to the victims of the Holocaust. The literal meaning is 'memorial and name.' It was dedicated to the memory of the dead. The monument was erected to honour the Jews who fought against the Nazi oppressors and the Gentiles who selflessly helped them; The Institute researches the phenomenon of the Holocaust and genocide, in particular, to avoid such incidents in the future.

The 'Hall of Remembrance' of the deceased children is a large circular hall with a high dome. Entering it carefully, I saw that it was pitch dark inside, and looking up was like looking up in the clear sky on a moonless night. Above the sky, we see countless thousand stars twinkling, representing the souls of 1.5 million children. That is the children's monument, and there was total silence.

Photography was not allowed. If you pay close attention, you can hear the giggling sound of an innocent child coming from a distance, like a soothing breeze in the hall. When hearing it, the human heart will be melted, making one compassionate and tender-hearted.

Yard Washem is the second most visited Israeli tourist destination after the Western Wall, with about one million visitors annually.

Again, a tourist bus took us to see the Dead Sea. The Dead Sea has been a tourist attraction for thousands of years. Summer desert conditions prevailed all around. The Dead Sea attracted thousands of visitors. They came here to enjoy the hot mineral springs and to float and swim above the surface of the ocean water. Now, it was our turn. The lake's surface was 1,412 feet below sea level, making it the deepest salt lake in the world. The water in this lake was 9.6 times more saltier than in the ocean. This saltwater created a harsh environment for plants and animals to grow, hence the name Dead Sea.

It was not because of swimming in turbulent waters in the White Sea but because of the concentration of saltwater in the Dead Sea at 1.240 kg /l, which means it was denser than fresh water. The extremely high concentration of dissolved mineral salts in the water causes the water to be denser than plain fresh water. Since our body is less dense than the density of the water, it becomes buoyant in the Dead Sea, making it easy to float. I was able to float in the water like a canvas armchair. Keerthi, who does not know how to swim, found it a little tricky—supported by a finger protruding from the back. It was a relaxing experience, relieving the stress and allowing the whole body to rest. I could remember floating in the sea for the first time and enjoying the experience for a lifetime.

The water was crystal clear and appeared like pure water. If a droplet gets into the eye, it irritates you so much that you cry and sweat simultaneously. A sharp, sour taste can cause rapid vomiting, too.

The surface area of the Dead Sea is rapidly diminishing. Salt crystals filled the jetty's pillars, planks, and beach sands.

We had time only to visit a few places. Whatever we had seen was entirely satisfying. We hoped to see what was left out, like the church in Bethlehem, during the next trip. When we returned to the hotel and woke up after sleep, it was time to pack and start our return journey home.

A taxi drove us through the deserted roads to the Ben Gurion Airport on the Sabbath day. We arrived early for the flight to Amman, but the customs clearance took a long time. They took out everything from the suitcase and handbag and checked thoroughly. They repeated the questions like who packed the bags, and what are the things you carry?

I was able to sleep on the trip. It was early morning when we landed in Mumbai. A new dawn in our own country. So, we forgot the fatigue -

Thus, we arrived home at noon by Mumbai-Bangalore-flight.

Travelling to Israel was the only overseas trip by flight during my nearly forty years of government service. It can be described as a coincidence that it happened to be a Christian pilgrimage to the Holy Land, in addition to professional work.

## 91

# Value of The Unity

During Ammachi's days in Bangalore after Nita's marriage, we continued the usual way of life. On some days, Ammachi was having health problems like asthma. It was controlled by administering her routine medicines. Ammachi was not known to have any other lifestyle diseases; diabetics and cholesterol levels were not alarming. That was when we noticed the symptoms of memory loss and inconsistency in her behaviour. One day, after taking a bath, while standing in front of the mirror, she started talking to her image in the mirror - she asked the image her name. She wondered where she came from and where she was going and laughed at her. Another day, she packed some of the clothes, took them in her hand, and walked towards the door, saying, "I will go to our house." She opened the door and prepared to leave. Even though she was stopped by saying, "Let's go later," the insistence to leave occurred again. Initially, she was brought back to normal with small jokes, but such incidents were repeated, and our concerns increased.

When I consulted a doctor, he told me that dementia was a symptom of Alzheimer's, no special treatment could be prescribed, the patients should be cared for like children, and there was no life-threatening condition. I anticipated that the future would go smoothly without any accidents. Ammachi had to be provided with routine care amid our busy city life, work, and children's schooling. We feared that some difficulties might always be caused. We decided to take Ammachi back to Vaisyambhagom and get closer to Babychan and his family. I requested Babychan and Raju to pay more attention to Ammachi's health, similar to when Babu was there, what he had done.

My parents had not prayed like others that "they had the desire to go away without bothering or burdening anyone!" They did not blame anyone. They knew that when their children grew up, they would study, work, get married, care for themselves, and fly away. They never interfered with their children's needs or comforts. They did not impose their own opinions or decisions. They always prayed for their children, family, and grandchildren. Even as they slowly moved towards the helplessness of old age with diseased bodies and drained or exhausted minds, in pain and suffering, without even caring about their health and well-being, they tried for the welfare of their children and grandchildren, inquired about their extraordinary achievements, gave encouragements and incentives for further learning and moral and spiritual growth.

Every parent longs for their children's presence, often in old age and sickness. However, because of their children's work, travel, and distance, they do not even see it as an imminent need, tolerate everything without questioning, and run through old age. Our parents showed us such a life of sacrifice.

Achayan never taught us any theology, never used any quotable quotes, and never directed us to live on the right path. But as a perfect example, his way of life was everything to us. The value of brotherhood, the value of taking care of older people, the value of educating children, and the value of sharing and social service, all through his lifestyle, all he showed. He showed everything to his children through his own life. We always thought that his way of life was the most valuable legacy he could leave on earth." Such a legacy cannot be written down in any document. It was the investment of the head of a family to be kept in the memory of his children, imitated day by day, and passed on to all the generations to come.

Achayan's legacy, spiritual advice/lessons, experience, and traditions passed on to his children were innumerable. Achayan did not think it was 'for his spiritual satisfaction.' A father lived and showed his children how to learn and imitate. A father sets an excellent example for his children, knowingly or unknowingly. It is derived from the family's traditional culture and passed on to the generations.

The 'heritage' left for the children to experience materially has been put together by many years of effort, starting from nothing.

The children all did what they could in their circumstances and cared for their parents in the hardships of old age as best they could, sincerely.

There was only one sadness left for me, as they did not wait to experience the blessings of modern life, albeit much less. Earlier, even before that, they moved over to eternal happiness.

Babychan's letter came. "Everyone, including Appayi's son Sibichan, has quoted up to four lakh rupees for our house and land in Vaysyambhagom. It is the current fair price here. It may not fetch a better price if we continue to hold it as it is. The longer we hold, the cost of maintenance will also increase. If we give it to Sibichan, we will get cash immediately."

I wrote back to do so after getting Babu and Raju's opinions. We agreed to sell the property, including the house, to Sibichan soon. It was mentioned that we could execute the sale deed whenever we joined during the holidays.

I took out the financial determination statement or testament of legal declaration (Will) prepared by Achayan on December 08, 1991. I sent it to his children, and I reread it. What seemed to me as a more valuable legacy was another letter that contained, in that thought-provoking letter – the reason perhaps was that he did not fully understand my preferences – he wrote to me particularly this -

Dear Ummacha, I am preparing a financial arrangement for all of you for our site and sending it to everyone. I know that Ummachan does not get as much as he deserves. You can imagine the state of mind that I, as a father, and you, as my children, would have if my children did not get their due share. I did this by understanding that situation and considering Ummachan for my position. I know that it is inadequate, but I am sorry. God, who knows everything, will provide you with good things. I need to be more competent and educated. But, I praise the Father for the immeasurable blessings that I have received to do this. Thanks, thanks, and Praise be to Jesus.

You know that this property is only for one person to live in. If that is possible, Ummachan would take it yourself. Please give it to the rest at their convenience for their site needs and own this one entirely. The estimated price is Rs.175000/-. Prices may increase or decrease with time. Please keep in mind and do what you wish after talking with everyone. I want you to know that I have given you that responsibility.

I want to inform you one thing in particular. Accept it by changing your mind due to resentment towards me or not cooperating with your younger ones. Because if you pain the mind of a father nearing the end of a human life, know the consequences would be terrible.

How long will I be with you, my children? My conscience tells me that although I have not been able to do much good to you, I have done nothing to harm you. Therefore, there should be no quarrel, confusion, or other sentiments towards me. Act from my position by accepting this financial determination of mine wholeheartedly and share it with everyone according to what has been mentioned. With this, I transfer all authority over this property to Ummachan.

Forgive me for all the wrongs I have done to you due to my ignorance, and continue to stand as the head of this family. With best wishes to all, Your affectionate father (Signed).

I have accepted the contents of the accompanying letter entirely. Despite the delay, Achayan's financial determination statement was implemented with two minor differences.

I requested permission to keep aside Achayan's desire to "take it if you can." I have apologized to Achayan and decided to stay in Bangalore for other reasons and in the interest of my children as well. He has accepted my request.

Two - The share of Achayan's financial determination has been revised to be more beneficial to all than what Achayan desired. The price received by selling the property was higher than the amount previously estimated. Another list was drawn up for the proportion of the proceeds to be shared, with my discretional freedom to decide the particular case and more, but with an equal share for all the siblings.

Kochuppappan distributed the share of Rs. 4.0 lakhs as follows:-

| Sl No | Names | Achayan determined the Shares Percentage as per his will (%) | Kochuppappan distributed the Shares in (%) |
|---|---|---|---|
| 1 | Oommachan | 40 | 21.25% |
| 2 | Babu | 15.5 | 21.25% |
| 3 | Raju | 20 | 21.25% |
| 4 | Babychan | 15 | 21.25% |
| 5 | Ammachi | 3.25 | 6.25% |
| 6 | Leelamma | 6.25 | 8.75% |
|  | Total | 100% | 100% |

Babu and Babychan were requested to pick up the furniture for their use. The small coins under Achayan's pillow were handed over to Babychan for offertory at the church.

Kochuppappan came home, sat in a chair like Achayan, and called each of us by name. Wrapped in the Manorama newspaper handled by Achayan, Achayan's legacy was handed over to his children. I gave the Kochuppappan a paper coin for everyone as a token of gratitude.

The tears in our eyes reminded us of the excellent example of mutual love that Achayan taught us, which went beyond the inherited shares.

The wind of loving comfort blew from nature, from the environment to wipe away the drops of tears, and passed by caressing everyone. Kochuppappan said the reason for the family's happiness -

"It is always a pleasure to be a judge where there is no dispute among the parties!"

Even though no one's opinion or suggestion was asked, the close relatives, including Kochuppappan, praised the decision to share the financial resources. Obedient children have implemented it as an example.

Thus, when children and grandchildren are growing up in a family, the unique interests of the children and grandchildren take precedence over the interests of the head of the family. It is the change of time; metamorphosis is the change that comes under the situation. It is not merely human interest that governs it. It is the nature. Nature is God. No one should see it as a refutation of family ties or mutual love. Parents who do not have much time to live should show a favourable attitude towards the interests of their children, who may have a longer time to live. I believe that favouring and prioritizing the interests of children should not be seen as a lack of love or respect for their parents. However, children should handle such situations sensibly and diplomatically and in a manner that does not hurt the sentiments of the elders. It will always be commendable if more positive decisions could be implemented to satisfy parents and children alike.

Not only did Achayan himself teach, but It has also been practically shown, and there are many examples, not just one. We can only see it when we slow down the pace of life. Do not insist on rushing and deciding immediately; think slowly about who will benefit from the decision. That decision would be correct if we could decide with the interest of 'let's get together' without having any ego or self-interest. Thus, when the decision is implemented, no one's eyes will be wet; the minds will not hurt.

Until such a decision emerges, think over it, let the time pass, tolerate, forgive and forget. Good decisions expect good participation from us. The more views we gather when deciding, the more likely our final choice will meet the most needs, address the most concerns, and increase mutual understanding.

What the inheritance Achayan gave me, as he has given to his other children, I saved it in the bank to spend on the house being built for my family in Bangalore. I believe my siblings, too, did the same.

# 92

# Tours to South-East Asia

We could not visit NTU at the University Convocation in 1997 when Tony received his degree, so no tour of Singapore was possible. Since then, Tony has searched for the most suitable time and convenience. He reassured Mommy by telling her that Daddy had gone to Israel alone but planned to take us to Singapore soon.

We renewed our Passport. Tony got us the visa necessary for our month-long visit to Singapore and sent it along with the ticket. April 2002 was a time when the office was not so busy. The weather in Singapore was similar to that of Chennai and Bangalore. So, for the first time, Leelamma and I went on a tour of Singapore.

We started seeing interesting sights right from Changi Airport itself. It was a groundbreaking design that included aesthetic elements such as theme gardens. The best airport in the world, with its scenic beauty and modern facilities, welcomed us warmly.

A room was prepared for us in the well-equipped Toa Payoh flat where Tony stayed with his friends. Then, the trips to Toa Payoh church, tourist attractions, the university campus where Tony studied, large audio-visual lecture halls, the library, hostels, and the beautiful natural surroundings of NTU were completed in one day. Tony arranged all the facilities and travel for our comfort. Metro rail cards could also be used for daily buses, journeys by metro, then by taxi, and buses to parks, malls, and more sights. The most impressive sightings were at the tourist spots. Sentosa Island was a world of wonders. The world-renowned Singapore Zoo, Night Safari, bird sanctuary, aquarium, dolphin circus, and Light and Sound Show at Waterfront in Marina Bay Sands were seen. Tony's many friends, office complex, posh areas like Orchard Road, and Chinese, Malaysian, and Singaporean restaurants with various cuisines and food were all integral to our sightseeing tours.

Among Tony's friends from India, we met a girl named Joysy John. Tony introduced Joysy at the Sacred Heart Church. She came from Kanpur and studied Computer Engineering at NTU with a scholarship in the junior batch.

Having left to see more than we already saw, we returned after a satisfactory tour, hoping that we would come again. If you saw more than 500 photographs we have in Singapore, you could understand at least how cool a month of excursion was for us.

In 2002, Tony continued working at SAP Marketing. To continue his education, Tony prepared to send applications to top-ranked business schools such as Harvard University, INSEAD, London Business School, MIT, and Stanford. The application should be sent with great care and attention, along with resumes, copies of certificates, and essays were also to be sent. Since INSEAD is in Paris, French translation of English certificates was also required. You must have studied French. Colonel Subramanian, our neighbour in Indiranagar, did all the translations. The preparations itself took about a year.

Tony was always interested in travelling worldwide, visiting unfamiliar places and tourist attractions, and participating in life's little adventures. It was Tony's interest that, before he left Singapore for higher studies, his parents should go there once again for a trip and that we would travel somewhere together from there.

Many tourist destinations in Thailand, Indonesia, Phi Phi Islands, and Phuket were selected. We returned to Bangalore after a two-week tour of Singapore and a one-week tour of Thailand. Phi Phi Islands - One of the most beautiful islands in the world is in Thailand. With the incredible scenery of the tropics, the voyage to the island was on a large cruise ship. A thousand people enjoyed the beautiful view of the islands in the Andaman Sea and the spectacular colours. The island was full of coconut trees, and the beach was full of fallen dried coconuts.

We went to Phuket a year before the tsunami. At the Floating Market in Phuket, we saw hundreds of small boats carrying vegetables, fruits, fish, meats, handicrafts, groceries, figurines, paintings, and handicrafts made from coconut. Only the Aluminium utensils on the boats of the floating egg traders in Kuttanad were not found, but everything else was there. We could have started a small business there if we had taken the small boat in, which I went to college. We could have profited at least 500 Thai Baht daily (i.e., Rs.1170/ -approx). All the goods were so expensive there.

AT FLOATING MARKET IN PHUKET

COCONUT BEACH IN PHI PHI ISLAND

FLOATING MARKET PHUKET

FEAR NO MORE@ SENTOSA

INDONESIAN TEMPLES

**Our tour to Southeast Asia: Singapore, Thailand, Indonesia**

Sam-Nita lived happily after marriage. Sam joined a facility management services company called Updater Services. Nita moved from Hotel Le Meridien, Bangalore, to The Leela Palace, Bengaluru, a five-star hotel on the old airport road. Although there were shift jobs, she moved there as a Concierge (Resident Care Taker) because she got better job opportunities, facilities, and benefits. In addition, it was best to work with world-class hotels, which would help her get better experience in the various departments of the hotel industry.

Seema continued her studies for the third year at the Engineering College. She was writing letters, and we got the information regularly. Occasionally, she would go to Kunjommachayan's house at Kumbalangi. Seema loved the hostel accommodation and food there. She had a lot of friends, and her vernacular conversations in Malayalam continued. Seema had a good sense of purpose, discipline, and her own rules, not because of the teachers in the study or because her parents were rigorous at home.

Seema had acquired a good sense of realising that some of her compulsions were on the rough, arduous paths of practicality, and when they hit the stones and scattered, she chose the smoothest path as the best path. Seema did well in her professional engineering subjects and project practicals. Seema enjoyed attending the International Jesus Youth Movement and holiday prayer meetings. Despite the lack of excellence and efforts in the arts and cultural fields, Jesus Youth's Christian ways and leadership training helped her to change her introverted characteristics. Only after Tony joined college did he start showing leadership skills and extroversion.

Aero-India is a biannual air show and aviation exhibition held at the Yelahanka Air Force Station in Bangalore. The Defence Exhibition Organization of the Ministry of Defence organized it. Our office, DGAQA, also set up a particular stall at the request of the Ministry to attend the 4th Aero India Exhibition held from 5th to February 09, 2003. The fair, which was participated in by 176 companies from 22 countries, was inaugurated by then-Defence Minister Jorge Fernandez.

I was assigned to explain information from the stall to dignitaries and visitors on essential days. When any officer came to replace me, I visited other stalls during my leisure time and understood the modern technologies displayed there.

It was exciting to see up close the aerobatic displays of the planes that took place daily. Later in the years, when the air show took place, I took the family members to Aero India.

After Achayan returned to his heavenly home, the arrival of letters was reduced from home. Ammachi had the mind and interest to write, but her body did not allow her adequately. And even if it were occasional, Babychan wrote a few lines. Raju was busy with work, travelling, and overseeing household chores. Raju and Babychan did not even get time on Sundays, as they took charge of the catechism classes in the parish. Babu, by then, had forgotten his writing habit. If I had seen him occasionally at the native or in Coimbatore, we could have spent some time together. Above all, people in cities and villages have embraced the new communication technology - the mobile phone, which can always be carried in hand and used for receiving or calling directly. Phones are from the smallest to the most expensive, according to the convenience and features available. Like most revolutions, they started small and spread like wildfire. The essential interaction was the feature that allowed everyone to buy and use a mobile phone. The revolution began in 1995, and soon, the mobile phone became the permanent companion of all. For most, writing has been reduced to a subject of study associated with ancient cultures.

Every technology that offers modern amenities comes with some negative consequences. Used properly, it can streamline commerce and make the world smaller. The impact of mobile phones on youth and society is enormous. Today, everyone, in general, knows how cell phones affect teenagers and others who have no specific jobs.

- Excessive cell phone use can lead to arthritis, affecting bones, muscles, tendons, ligaments, and soft tissues.

- Studies show that adolescents are more prone to stress, anxiety, depression, insomnia, and carelessness when they use cell phones excessively and incorrectly.
- Video games and inappropriate images for teenagers can seriously affect their mental state and future.

Sam was the first person to buy me a Nokia mobile phone. Then Tony purchased an iPhone, each with more features, for his parents. With that, I stopped writing to anyone. Office writing was occasionally done on the desktop computer after the computer was installed. With the advent of the Internet in India, text and telegrams declined, leading to the closure of the Telegraph Department. We started sending e-mail messages to e-mail addresses. It's been years since I wrote a letter on paper with a pen, and I can't even remember when it stopped writing.

Before the second wedding anniversary, the Sam-Nita couple wanted a place to live independently. When asked to look for availability, I was reminded of the flats built and sold by my friend Kurian. We immediately negotiated with Kurian and agreed to buy one at a discount. Receiving a sum of money as a blessing from her parents was a timely help to Nita, who was ready to buy her own house.

As the first step towards moving into their own furnished and decorated home, housewarming is a joyous, auspicious ritual for any couple.

At the end of July 2003, Nita gave the good news to her mother. It was confirmed after a medical checkup. Nita was on her family- way. The happiest news for a mother is that her daughter is pregnant. For parents, as a continuation of their own life, to be a tool to recreate proof of their existence is the first encouragement and recognition of their life's purpose. The news was happily accepted. Mommy served Samiyapayasam and entertained Sam and Nita! Mother said, 'You must handle it carefully; more gifts are coming later.'

# 93

# The Dream of Owning A House

It was Tony's routine to make a telephone call from Singapore on Saturdays or Sundays. The talk continued to Daddy and Mommy for a long time until the money marked on the International Calling Card ran out. Then you can use the new card next time. The International Calling Card in Singapore featured various designs, pictures, and tourist attractions. Until Tony completed six years in Singapore or until he bought his new mobile phone, this exercise of limited talk continued. I had lined up a hundred calling cards he used to call India and placed them under a teapoy glass, like a photo frame. It is so attractive that I'm not particularly eager to throw it away.

The call came as usual on a Sunday. Tony spoke. Mommy had gone down to walk somewhere outside. Having said all that, Tony gave a special message that did not seem out of the ordinary -

"Daddy, I am in love with a girl here."

"Good ...... Who is the girl? "Amazing experience!

"You know her. You have seen her here, Daddy; Joysy John, my Junior in NTU, got the same SIA - NOL scholarship for studies. She is in her final year now."

"Hope you have thought about it and told her."

"We are going on a sightseeing trip to Bali tomorrow. Perhaps I will propose to her." I wanted to tell you and mommy before that...."

"Where is Bali?"

"It is an island in Indonesia. It is nearly a two-and-a-half-hour flight from Singapore ".

"Okay, the tour is good, but please ensure you don't make any mischief."

"Yes, Daddy, I will."

"All the best for your trip. I will convey this to Mommy.

"Thank you, Daddy. I will call from Bali."

Bali is one of Indonesia's most popular tourist destinations, and it is an island. Bali is world-famous for its stunning beaches, beautiful terrace paddy fields, fragrant cuisine, and rich culture and heritage. With its vast temples, endless beaches, and some of the finest coral reefs and waterfalls globally, Bali offers travellers a combination of relaxation and adventure. Bali is a popular destination for people worldwide with various spiritual awakenings and hard work. It is the perfect place for young couples who want to get married to share their minds. The children are coming of age. The happiest thing about parents is that they start to think about family life. The ability of children to make their own choices is a sure step for parents to achieve their purpose in life. The marriage of children is the biggest dream of parents.

I shared the information with Leelamma that Tony had called when her outside walk was over. Leelamma also did not see it as surprising news. I was waiting to be informed that Tony would contact me from Bali for more information.

I found a site to build a house in Bangalore, bought it, and my mother blessed me. The first step was to prepare a plan and estimate for building a house. The house at Vaisyambhagom was based on a plan I had drawn up from a magazine. Without an accurate estimate, the walls and roof were put together when the project was built on the ground. All the changes that could be made to reduce the costs were made with the main help of the construction workers. The work was not finished, and the result was unsatisfactory. Those walls also did not want a family to live there for long. Since the toilets and bathrooms were not inside, time had determined to relocate us from there before we were subjected to the difficulties of going outside and being affected by the wind and rain in our old age!

Wouldn't it be better to fix the defects of the first attempt, to plan a house with amenities as much as possible, with suitable light and ventilation, and ideal for the times when all members of the family can relax together, taking into account each one's personal needs,? Tony suggested that we seek the help of an architect-engineer who knows house construction techniques. It is adequate to draw up a plan, estimate the cost as a complete house within our budget, and do the work again as necessary without increasing the price. Is it not better to see everything, including the layout, in advance and begin the work only if we are satisfied? With modern technology, a 3-D model of the house can be created on the computer, and a run-through can be made in image and mind to create an impression of walking inside the home. That's the first thing to do. It will help to arrange better facilities without extra cost.

As Tony suggested, I called Aparna (Aparna Krishnakumar), his schoolmate, and invited her for a preliminary discussion. They discussed the approximate size, shape, and requirements. In about four or five visits during the planning stage, they came and saw the place and understood everything in detail. Aparna was only told not to deliberately give up the advantages of architecture. During the last discussion, they brought a walk-through 3D model of the house and showed it to us. It was sent to Tony, Nita, and Seema for their comments. They all liked it. The plan and estimate were prepared and given to me a month later. A good strategy for all was to have a 4BHK house of about 2300 sqft, at an estimated cost of around Rs. 25 lakhs in 2003.

For a government employee, whether a Gazetted Officer or a Non-Gazetted employee, I knew that the terminal benefits received after employment would not be sufficient for all the routine needs, especially before the Sixth Pay Commission.

The terminal benefits will not be sufficient for even the basic needs of building a house on your land and living as a family for the rest of your life. Even if the terminal benefits that can be received after three years are summed up, it will not be more than 20 lakhs. The calculation was made to accumulate at least 20 lakhs, and the monthly subscription payment to the provident fund was increased yearly. Responsibilities keep growing. How dare you give an order to draw the house plan and request an estimate? That is planning and confidence. It was not suffering; it was the enjoyment of life. Everything in life is an arrangement! According to priority and importance in life. The thoughts that there is always the Almighty, someone who takes care of you, the blessings of your parents are abundant, and the courage to live to face all kinds of challenges push you forward.

Ten years later, when the children and grandchildren are together, they should all be able to sleep under the roof for at least one night. That is the importance, the hope, and the prayer! Considering it ten years later, you may regret it was too late.

Tony also encouraged me. "Lay the foundation, start the work, and we will see the rest; everything will be fine." Plan approval was obtained from the Mahadevapura BBMP office in August. That month, a Malayali contractor called Scaria came, discussed the contract, and undertook the work. The work for another friend's house he had undertaken was almost finished then.

That was how we started the house construction.

Tony came on vacation next in October. The primary purpose was to go to Kanpur during the Dussehra holidays, meet Joysy's parents, and get their marriage fixed. So, train reservations were made for the journey to and return from Kanpur. Tony and his parents announced that they would come to Kanpur. Joysy had also arrived in Kanpur. Tony himself handled all communications between the two households.

Even before the foundation was laid for the house, the location of the tube well was pointed out, and Scaria himself marked the location of the tube well by showing some gestures, such as doing some pooja. A tube well was dug up to 450 feet, and it took about twelve hours until water was obtained using a borewell machine in the site's northeast corner. I have been waiting for it with expectant eyes since early morning. They stopped digging further when the water source was sighted in the evening. They all went away after covering the borewell mouth at the top end of an 8-inch pipe.

Scaria's team measured and marked the foundation of the building on the site. After excavating the soil for the foundation, the family members laid the foundation stone of the house together.

Each one did his part well in the laying of the foundation stone. Leelamma and Tony took the granite prepared by the builders, scooped the cement mix with a spoon, and deposited it on the stone. A specially prepared packet was buried with the cement mix so archaeologists could find the immortal treasures, maybe years later. The non-degradable packet was prepared symbolically, containing a Christian symbol, a gram of gold, an Indian coin, and a Singaporean coin, all covered in words of prayer. It was placed on the stone and covered with cement to form the foundation stone. The stone-laying ceremony was completed with one more stone kept on top and cemented together. The ceremony became optimistic with the presence of Sam and Nita.

After that, the excavated soil was removed, and concrete was spread on the ground. The floor was divided with granite walls at the base of the rooms. The foundation was completed in about a week. The whole floor ground was levelled with soil. Scaria maintained it as such for 21 days.

The trip to Kanpur was meant to be during the house construction interval. The onward journey was by train to Delhi, with a connection train to Kanpur, and the return was vice versa. At Kanpur, we laid the foundation for a new family.

Scaria gave the bill, including all the soil excavation and filling for the foundation and the foundation built with granite. Aparna Krishnakumar agreed to verify the bill and pass the amount on to the contractor. Accordingly, when the bill was passed, Scaria was paid. I said I had sufficient money left in the bank to pay another bill. Tony handed me a cheque he had prepared before coming from Singapore. A comfortable sum of money, praying it would result in finishing the house - It was more than a government employee would have earned in 35 years. Tony saved up the amount in about 35 months of employment- 25 lakhs to build a house for the family. I remembered Achayan's words and Achayan's foresight. Dispersed from the eyes, what fell out on the cheque in my hand was the gratitude and love for Achayan in the form of tears of joy!

John and his family welcomed us in Kanpur and took us to a hotel room. After breakfast, we gathered in a small space for friendly conversations.

John started with a prayer -

"Thomas Chetta, thank God you had the opportunity to meet us and talk here. What do we have to talk about and decide?"

"John, we're here to get John's daughter to be my son's wife."

John struggled to express his joy and gratitude to a loving God. He covered his face, raised his eyes, and said only a few words-

"I am Happy, Joysy, and we all love Tony. Thank you, Thomas Chetta."

It was decided that the consent and marriage would occur in Bangalore, and the date could be fixed per mutual convenience.

Friendly conversations with other relatives continued. Joysy and her mother spoke affectionately.

While getting ready for lunch, Leelamma accepted Joysy as her daughter and symbolically wore a gold necklace on Joysy. Everyone congratulated Tony and Joysy.

In the afternoon, we were taken to John's house in Kanpur. John and his family lived in a duplex flat where two houses on the same floor were joined together. He was planning to move to Chennai soon. John had three children: Joysy was the first girl, and Jency was the second. Son, Jacob was the youngest. Jency was studying in the degree class, and Jacob was in the pre-degree class. John's family was Chorikavungal in Nedumkunnam, and his mother and siblings stayed there. Joysy's mother was a native of Mala, Thrissur, and her relatives were also in Mala. John worked for a private company in Kanpur. He wanted to quit his job in two years and move to Chennai. Chennai was more convenient for Jency and Jacob to study and work in. John participated in the Potta meditation, other Christian activities, and liturgical worship services at the local Christian church.

We went to the school where Joysy studied and to the local church. Joysy was an outstanding student in that school, which helped her get an SIA-NOL scholarship, go to Singapore for higher studies, and get to know Tony.

Seema focused on her final year of engineering studies. Manoj's wedding was in Nashik in October itself. When Tony came from Singapore in October, Seema also came since the time must have been the semester break. At the end of October, they all went to Nashik to attend Manoj's wedding. At Nashik, almost every relative of Manoj, especially the children, came and participated in the ceremony, which lasted two or three days.

Tony's baptism certificate was obtained from the church in Champakulam.

When he returned to Singapore, it was time for Tony's further studies. He was admitted for a one-year MBA study at INSEAD in France. Tony happily set off for the course, which started in January and ended in December. He returned in December and planned to get married in early January 2005. By then, the house construction would be completed, and we would start living in the new house.

# 94

# Natasha

One of the consequences of changing workplaces is having a gap in friendships. Out of sight can mean out of mind. There can also be close friends who have met and were sometimes in a deep love relationship. Transfer of workstations is an undesirable factor that breaks the continuity of close interpersonal contact, especially when communication resources are limited. Ramachandran knew nothing about my going to Koraput in 1993 and returning after seven years.

After my move to Bangalore in 1981, Kainakari Kadamattuthara George has been out of touch for a long time. So many friends could not be informed when we moved away from the place we lived together. Some of them were friends who gave me much comfort, joy, and cooperation when needed. I haven't forgotten any of them, but the changing circumstances, changing the place of work, and busy schedule at the new station might have diverted my attention from being in touch with them. Being in touch with them is necessary to maintain friendships when a particular event occurs in one's life or family. Thus, I tried to establish contact with old friends like Ramachandran, George, Babu, Thankachi, and others from Pune. After sharing all the details, Babu, who used to stay at Shirin Lodge in Pune, told me the shocking news-

"Thomas, our Ramachandran died in a road accident!". I was the one who palpitated and froze. Two minutes later, I regained my composure and could hear more from Babu.

"Our friend was killed when a lorry hit him from behind while riding his motorbike with someone on a major road in Chennai. It has been six months. He died instantly and did not have to suffer any more pain. He was not wearing a helmet. The family was in Chennai itself. The relatives brought his body to Palakkad and conducted the funeral. The children and his wife went to Singapore to stay with their relatives. It had been less than six months since he got a job as a Sales Manager in a company in Chennai."

I have never felt so sad when my relatives or other friends departed.

Last time, Nasrani need not remember again the few words of isolation spoken in private when Chandran came to the quarters to taste the 'Kuttanadan Nasrani' fish curry from Leelamma. Even those children have been taken somewhere far away from Palakkad!

When I called Babu after four or five months, Babu said -

"Ramachandran's Mumbai friend, who used to come to Pune from time to time, Sreekumar alias Asha Menon, who worked in an advertising company - a great writer, he is in Kerala and - has written about Ramachandran in his recently published book "Adarunna Kakkakal." I remember they both came to meet you in Khadki Bazar."

I bought and read the book 'Adarunna Kakkakal.' Asha Menon remembers and writes touchingly about Ramachandran, a close friend who left prematurely! I, along with Asha Menon, wish the excellent friend peace! When we meet in the green valley on the other side of 'Chitalimaala,' if we remember, we can share the anxieties and losses of human life!

An air crash in Ambala created a nationwide sensation. After completing the accident investigation into the Jaguar plane crash in Ambala, when I returned, I had to present the investigation reports at multiple venues. It was an excellent opportunity for me to play a crucial role in finding the exact technical reasons for the accident.

I have included the technical matters in the book "Safety Follows Where Quality Leads." After that, significant improvements were instituted in manufacturing and using the Jaguar aircraft. It was an excellent opportunity for me, and I am proud to have contributed towards the future safety and security of the plane.

Higher officials recommended my name to the Aeronautical Society of India for considering my name for presenting the Biren Roy Trust Award 2003. Justification included my contributions during the accident investigation and other outstanding contributions made by me in the department to ensure the quality and safety of aircraft and recognise outstanding contributions to the aviation field during that year. No one sought any favour or influenced the officials to grant the award, and I did not get any award. When selected from about forty candidates, I learned my name was one of the three in the final round. Therefore, I felt great satisfaction because at least four or five people considered me eligible for such a prize that generally only great people get.

Seema passed the May 2004 Electronics and Bio-Medical Engineering final examination at Cochin University. The result came in July. Since then, she has been preparing for the TOEFL, GRE, and GMAT exams to pursue Masters / Post-graduate studies. She sent applications to various universities. NTU, where Tony studied, was a university of particular interest to Seema.

Ammachi's memory almost started to 'go south' when she reached Punnapra from Bangalore. When she started to go outside the house without anyone watching, Babychan closed the door and locked it. Though she had thin, bony hands, she resisted him forcefully. Her food intake was reduced. He ate a little if something was fed with a spoon or by hand, and often she slept for more time.

Her adamant insistence on doing things her way became more predominant. She sometimes even forgot essential things.

Strange are the ways people behave when affected by Alzheimer's disease or another form of dementia.

Doctors advised there, too - her Dementia (Alzheimer's) was advancing. There was no particular medicine, and symptomatic drugs for cognitive impairment in dementia are not beneficial for people of advanced age. As she had no lifestyle diseases, the fact of old age is to take care of like a baby, so much care should be given.

Childhood memories learned facts and knowledge of daily activities were mostly remembered, but in the recent past, recalling what was learned yesterday was seen as a difficulty in such patients.

Natasha was born on April 21, 2004, at a private hospital in Ulsoor. Natasha's grandparents were waiting in the hospital hallway. A small golden star covered in white opened her eyes and looked at them as a former acquaintance. Their minds were filled with joy.

Natasha was baptized in May at St. Jude Church. Most of the relatives were present.

# 95

# Contractor Strategies

The house construction progressed further. The builders lived in a small shack along the road in front of the house - site. The water in the borewell was adequate for their daily use and house construction. The ground floor superstructure – brickwork – was completed. For the upper floor, the pillars were concreted. The roof for the ground floor was also moulded. Cement, metal, and sand were prepared in a concrete mixer, and the workers lined up and finished the roof casting in about four hours. I don't know if it was due to carelessness or intentional deception. Still, Scaria was seen to be less sincere in his work. I suspected he had reduced the cement in the concrete mixture. I left it for further verification. To progress the job faster, however, they piled the bricks on top of the wet concrete, according to Scaria's instructions, on the same day.

I asked, "After the concrete is cast, don't you need to consecutively soak it for 21 days?" Scaria, though he was a civil engineer, declined to give an exact answer to the question, which cast doubt on his engineering knowledge or his deceptive ways.

When the work was done, the 21-day concrete curing requirement did not impact him, and he was prepared to continue his work without the due interval.

He continued to pick up the bricks from the ground and laid them on the terrace. I said-

"Scaria, this is not going to happen here. If you want to continue working here, sufficient curing is necessary for the concrete. How is it okay to pick up all the bricks and put them on the wet concrete before curing the concrete? Shouldn't we water it all the time?"

"Oh, it doesn't matter. The work must be completed for the workers to start another job."

"You can start another job. Enough curing should be completed before continuing the work here."

Eight o'clock at night.

When he also realised that he would be unable to continue the brickwork on top of the wet concrete from the next day as he had intended, he realised that his strategies were futile.

Skaria left without replying and did not return the next day. The work was continued only after three weeks. When the brickwork on the second floor was finished, the scaffoldings were done for concreting on the roof, and the reinforcing work was completed by tying steel bars.

Scaria was also told that we would use ready-mix concrete this time, and the roof would be concreted without much labour and effort. Scaria didn't expect that much action from me.

The following day, he came, collected the bricks, and started working on the staircase and the parapet walls on the terrace without wetting the concrete.

"If the work continues on the terrace without curing, roof leakage is possible," I said. You may not take the responsibility for that damage.

Is it not enough to continue the work after finishing the curing? I didn't ask you to complete the work by next week."

Scaria disagreed with me.

I said, "Scaria, we should not just fight for the technical requirements. Could you give the bill up to this point and continue the rest of the work later? That too if I ask you only. Under any circumstances, I do not want to compromise the quality of construction."

He did not expect me to be so persuasive. He had no choice but to obey.

Scaria gave the bill, and I passed it on to Aparna Krishnakumar for verification. A week later, Krishnakumar said, "The bill is not correct. Scaria came for the discussion. We returned the bill to him to rectify the mistakes and re-resubmit."

Krishnakumar said - "In the revised bill, the quantity and the calculations were written in excess, and there is an error of more than three lakh rupees. In the corrected bill, more than two and a half lakhs were wrongly added. I don't know what to do, Uncle; please do what you need."

I requested Scaria to come and talk to me in person.

Scaria refused to amend the wrongly inserted amount and bill again. I said - "It's been a month since the concrete was finished; why is the work still not ongoing?"

He maintained silence.

"If the bill is corrected, I will give you the money. Start the work."

Scaria said after a while.

"There is nothing to correct. Krishnakumar must have made a mistake. I went and explained everything. Pay the amount as per the bill; I will do the rest of the work."

"Scaria, that's not right. Both are qualified and experienced architects. They came here, checked the completed works as per the drawing, verified the calculations, and said that you had asked for three lakh rupees more. You were given a chance to correct it. You have corrected it once, but two and a half lakhs are still more. “

Scaria sat up without saying anything.

“Come back after three days; I am not a person to quarrel with you. Somehow, you only need money anyway. I will give you the money, but before that, the workers, the work materials, and the hut they live in should be dismantled and the area cleaned thoroughly. I will do the rest of the work.”

Scaria then did not stay to say or hear anything. He went away. Three days later, he came and collected the cheque and left. He did not even come this way when invited to the housewarming ceremony.

The lover of money will not be satisfied with money, nor the lover of wealth with gain. This also is vanity. (Ecclesiastes 5:10)

How many people like Scaria and those who pretend to be Christian have heard these scriptures? At least some people in this world are like that; what is the use of telling them more? No matter what anyone says, none are willing to be corrected.

When I informed Aparna that Scaria had been excluded from the construction contract, Aparna told me that Scaria had offered a bribe of Rs 25,000 to close her eyes and clear the bills!

“When we refused to accept his gift, we expected him to cause some trouble.”

The uniqueness of the construction sector is that almost all construction contractors earn a lot more than their reasonable profit. It is prudent to admit it, and things will progress. In addition to the contractor›s negligence, the work being done without following the prescribed layout and proportions, the contractor›s delays, and the rectifications required due to changes made by someone in the first plan are usually additional costs. The first plan, decided by an experienced architect in consultation with the householder, need not be changed later, which is the advantage of a plan prepared by an architect, and there are no additional costs. Delays can be avoided if the contractor is working efficiently. It was a great relief to have an architect capable of inspecting the contractor›s bills and accounts. The contractor will earn at least twenty percent more than the estimated cost. If it is indirectly allowed or tolerated, it will bring peace of mind. If the contractor tries to deceive and earn more, it's easy to find where the voices must be raised and politely disagreed. Straightforward contractors who work for a fair profit are few and far between.

**The Orchard, No. 8, MEG Layout**

# 96

# The Housewarming

The search was underway to find contractors willing to continue the construction work. Raghavan, who had some previous experience and showed some sincerity in discussing with me, was assigned the remaining tasks. Raghavan also said that he was usually reluctant to take up the residual work of a more than half-completed building. Closing the avenues of exploitation gave me some freedom outside the vicious circle of contractors' habits. That is why I agree with Raghavan. We could buy all the materials needed for further construction and agree on a job contract for the rest of the work. Then, the responsibility for the quality of the materials used will be that of the family.

That's how ready-made factory doors, granite flooring, vitrified tiles, floor tiles, Mangalore roof tiles, decorative bricks for exterior walls, and toilet fittings were directly purchased. Teak wood staircase railings were made and brought from Changanassery with Raju's help. Additional beds, sofa sets, chairs, and complete electrical fittings were procured from Kanpur and transported to Bangalore with John's cooperation. The interior, cupboards, TV stand, and bookcases were completed in a separate contract on time. The Italian modular kitchen was also selected, purchased, and installed. Another agreement was entered for electrical wiring, plumbing, and water pipe connections. Raghavan did an excellent job consolidating everything and controlling the workers' engagements. Usually, more cement is used; hence, the finishing works are more costly. Raghavan created an account in that area after calculating and showing the expenditure. After a month of talking and physical verification, the calculation was revised, and a settlement was reached. The contract was happily closed by paying the total contract amount due to him. After completing all the work, the teak planks for the Sacred Heart prayer area design (Roopakkoodu) were installed. Most of the work was completed by early November.

Housewarming was conducted on November 10, 2004, with relatives and friends. In front of the road, we made a shamiana. We served the guests - Raghavan, his staff, friends, relatives, and neighbors- a rich feast like Onasadya. Aparna and Raghavan were rewarded with a good amount of gifts. The amount per the contract has already been paid to them. Everyone who came and attended the ceremony loved the design and construction of the house. They all praised Aparna and Raghavan.

We left the quarters within a day and got into our own home. The household appliances were moved from the quarters to our house within a few days. It was decided to retain the quarters for one more month so that the guests coming for marriage would have sufficient accommodation. Return of the quarters to the government could be done after their use.

It is expected to be interested in making the house more beautiful after the construction and the owners start staying there. An easy decision was to leave the interior decoration and arrangements to the whims and taste of the housewife and the children. They have already started doing that. When the furniture bought from Kanpur was laid out and arranged in the drawing room, there was a sense of satisfaction that the house was equipped with the necessary amenities. One more thing I did for enhanced satisfaction. All three of my brothers have already built their own houses to live in. When I saw Kanpur's sofa set and chairs, I considered buying one set for each of my brothers. I requested John to give the necessary support and order to the shopowners. It was the same design and price I had agreed to. Shipping charges were also reasonable. I could send it directly to them as a February retirement gift. So it was done, happily.

I was happy and lucky enough to go to the office after staying in my home for over a year. My dream was to stay in my own house and go to the office for the last thirty-nine years, which was fulfilled now, though there was only a year left for the superannuation.

There was no irony or contempt in the fact that the opportunity to have a sound sleep after eating dinner and in one's own house with one's family came after forty years. I was thrilled and thoroughly enjoyed it.

The sadness remained that my parents were not with me, sitting there in the right place and sharing the comforts of time and home to achieve contentment. Ammachi was bedridden due to old age and related diseases, causing disappointment and anguish. The desire to live more will decrease if all the wishes are fulfilled. Let it not happen. However, it's important to note that fulfilling desire doesn't necessarily bring happiness, as happiness is a more complex and subjective experience.

"God has put something noble and good into every heart his hand has created. So while living on earth, we must always remember to learn from yesterday, live for today, and hope for tomorrow because time will only show what has mattered throughout our journey." Melanie Klein (British psychoanalyst)

When I went to the native, I sometimes went to see my mother's younger sister (Elayamma) in Chekkidikadu.

I learned from Elayamma that Devasya Chittapan's younger brother, James Achan, had to be rushed to Chethipuzha Hospital recently due to heart disease. After getting well, he did minor contract work in his civil, electrical, and mechanical workshop at the ashram in Chethipuzha without any significant physical problems. I wanted to see him, so I went directly from Chekkidikadu to meet Fr James. After Fr. James Theckethala went to Germany and returned, I saw him for the first time. He was exhausted and had some old-age illness and geriatric syndromes. At the end of welfare inquiries and before leaving and bidding goodbye, I said we would meet again. Three or four years later, another heart attack opened the way for Fr. James to enter heaven.

I had mentioned about James getting a transfer from Pune to Delhi. I used to write occasionally. After marriage, he lived in government quarters at RK Puram, reserved for the Meteorological Department in Delhi. Philo, his wife, also had a job in Delhi.

We all went to Chekkidikadu to attend James's wedding. During that journey on a train, Tony developed a fever and had fits. We requested the services of a doctor who came to the station to examine him and give him treatment.

"James said you had gone there to his house in Delhi."

"Yes, Elayamme, I had been there. They both have jobs, so it was a busy life.

James's child, Jeffy, was brilliant and going to school, and Jenny was getting up and walking. "

Joseph was in Mumbai. He, too, came and returned after marriage. He was taught printing technology and got employment through Fr. James at a printing press in Mumbai. That way, he escaped the struggles in the home village.

Ammini was married and sent to Muttar. They have farming and similar activities there.

James took Thankamma and Susamma to Delhi for employment. When good proposals came for them, they were married off quickly.

Thankamma and Susamma left their jobs in Delhi, came to Changanacherry, and settled there with family after buying property and a house.

We had gone to attend Tomichan's priestly ordination and the first Holi mass.

"Where is Tomichan now?"

"They sent him to Germany. He's the parish vicar of a church there. He often calls here."

"The work of the motor and the paddy milling processes in the mill has now been handed over to Kunjachan. Chittappan is not well. He goes to church. There is no singing like in the past. Once he walks out and comes back, there is tremendous pain in his legs. He has to lie down. Both of us are sitting now. We apply oil and do massages, but it is difficult for me.

"And since Kunjachan's wife is here, she will care for everything in the kitchen ...."

I could not see him when Chekkidikadu Chittappan (December 18, 2004) passed away.

# 97

# MBA at INSEAD

Tony's one-year MBA at INSEAD was without any specialisation. Tony was interested in taking a General MBA and choosing a marketing stream at any multinational corporation. That's how GE Global Operations, Cincinnati, the United States, was selected in the year-end campus recruitment. Everyone who gets a job at GE Corporation will be put on the job only after attending the leadership training for nine months. The Engineering Commercial Leadership Program was one of the world's leading leadership training programs.

This training was the primary recruitment route for university graduates to GE. They were conducted at the Leadership Institute in Cincinnati, Milwaukee. Everyone should be a Lean Six Sigma Black Belt when they finish the training. This training was provided in the hope that the skills of the leaders would grow in the critical activities of the company. Over 25 percent of GE's top leaders started their careers in these programs. Training for Tony began on January 25, 2004. The projects, including the marriage, could be planned and completed on time since the dates were already fixed well in advance.

Joysy got a transfer and moved to New York from JPMorgan in Singapore, where she worked. She lived in New Jersey.

I had twenty months left to retire. Yes, I began counting the months and days since I had many more responsibilities to complete.

When we retire, we stop our work in the office, or the employee asks us to stop the work there. However, some of us may stop working for ourselves for reasons such as voluntary retirement or retirement on medical grounds. When that happens, most of us find new and exciting things, search for something to be engaged in, like other jobs, and even work after retirement. Finding new, meaningful, or more satisfying jobs will be necessary. It can have different purposes, including more financial income. So, it is safe to say that retirement is not the end of anyone's work life. So, if you intend to "retire," the first plan should be to see how you want to spend your time after retirement. That is what is needed to find happiness in later life. Once you have done that, you can retire peacefully.

I discussed these 'future' matters with Leelamma about four months back.

"I felt like telling her in the style of 'Chempenkunju' in the film 'Chemmeen,' "Let us marry off Seema too, then we can enjoy the pleasures of life! ('Nammakkonnu Sokhikanen"). Yes, our dreams will sprout and blossom."

I had promised her that "I would help her with the household chores, including managing the kitchen, when I retire," I repeated the promise, just for her to be happy.

"Hmm, good guy,....

"But if you retire from work and sit in a chair with your hands tied - you'll get aged soon. You may go away soon, Will you ?"

All these are in the policy statement, and we can start implementing it.

You can join the ISO 9001 Lead Auditor training conducted by Zandig Training Institute in Kasturi Nagar. It is a QCI-approved institute. The entire time of five days, and sometimes more, is 40 hours, after which they will issue a certificate upon passing the examination. Rs. 25000 / - is the fee and take leave from office to join the class. Lead Auditor Training will enable you to open other doors after you retire from government. The 9-5 job and 'too much work for too little compensation' are no longer feasible. Isn't it better to do something at your convenience, following the known work rules and ethics?

Busy time is coming. So, priority was given to urgent matters. After paying the fee for Lead Auditor Training, I registered my name, took leave, and attended the class. The classes conducted by Zandig Parameswaran were well understood. Thus, enthusiasm grew to learn and do the things of interest.

I did well in the final examination, and a week later, I got the Lead Auditor certificate sent by QCI. A lot of work was done in the office on the quality system. That's why I was the first in a batch of twelve!

The knowledge and training gained in systematic, independent quality system auditing have greatly aided my office work. The system auditing brought a new vibrancy and enthusiasm to the department, and I have been instrumental in the improvement.

The concerned officers are usually not shown the annual confidential reports after evaluating the officers' performance in the everyday working style of the offices. Those who write the report deliver it to their superior. My superiors, as an exception, called me and showed me the annual report, which, due to various contributions, they had marked the performance of the past year as "extremely outstanding." I have won the favour of my superiors. It was a routine without any extra importance to the government's ruling class. Name a trait that has no personal benefit. It was only a pleasure to receive a rare praise, and a government official should not expect anything more than that. Thanks to Shri RN Padhy and Shri Pulak Sengupta.

They were both particularly interested in my earning excellent ratings for my work performance. They asked me how I could be used for the public benefit of the Department. That's how the following jobs were given to me: -

i. Accepting the audit as an all-India strategy to pursue the regulatory functions, they appointed me to implement it throughout the Department.

ii. I have been directed to periodically update the Department's outdated QMS, QCSR, and AFIO working documents for the last ten years.

iii. Go to other DGAQA-affiliated offices throughout India and share the experience for two days each and teach them our profession more - (in Hyderabad, Koraput, Lucknow, Nashik, and Bangalore)

It was a sabbatical tour - travel on official business - and sharing the experiences with other offices to make their activities more effective. I was proud and happy to be assigned to such a sabbatical tour, usually reserved for high-ranking officials.

Preparations for Tony's wedding were discussed with Sam. The date was likely to be early in January. Construction of our parish St Jude Church building has just begun. So, it was decided that the marriage would occur at the Indiranagar Resurrection Church. I had to go to the church and talk to the vicar about the related matters. DRDO Community Hall, CV Raman Nagar, was booked in advance for the wedding reception. Since the guest list has already been prepared, the invitation cards could be prepared and sent if printed early. We can send letters in advance to the relatives. Many people must plan and make reservations to make their journey more comfortable.

Sam agreed to bring a group from Jamshedpur to prepare the menu and make all the arrangements for the decoration, furniture, etc., as he had done for the DRDO Community Hall reception last time.

## Setback Before the Ceremony

Betrothal should be done before marriage. John's wish to avoid multiple journeys from Kanpur was respected. John also informed me that it was doubtful that many people would come to Bangalore from the native. John told us that there was no need to conduct an informal ceremony for the couple to get hitched before tying the knot in the presence of close relatives and friends and formally announcing the wedding. It has to be announced in each of their churches. All of them could come from Kanpur to Bangalore ready for the betrothal and subsequent marriage, and it was enough to do both ceremonies in Bangalore at our church. It was agreed that all the arrangements would be made in Bangalore.

John had said that Joysy would come to her consent after completing the marriage counselling course that the couple had to attend before a catholic wedding. When Tony was asked to do a similar marriage counselling course, he said that such a facility was unavailable near INSEAD in Paris and would come to Bangalore to do the procedure.

The date was approaching, and the wedding was scheduled for January 3, 2005, one week after the consent. Only when I met with the church vicar, Fr. Benny, at St. Jude Church to ask for his permission did I understand the pretentious stubbornness of the priest, which was unnecessarily causing harassment to us?

A condition was that the certificate of attending the marriage counselling course by both the bride and groom in the recent past was mandatory, and consent was given if they showed the certificates only. It was not enough to show the certificate sometime after the consent and before the marriage!

I expressed the practical difficulties for Tony in attending the marriage counselling course before the betrothal ceremony:-

a) Tony will arrive only a week before the betrothal ceremony after finishing his studies in France. That is the Christmas week. No change was possible for his flight because of his examinations.

b) I requested that he attend the marriage counselling course at his place of study. Still, he could not find a course anywhere near and at his convenience.

Father did not answer me directly but turned to another parish member and justified himself with a counterquestion loudly so that I could hear him.

The counter question was utterly reprehensible and unnecessary.... I heard the reflections of a rather stubborn arrogance when lovingly approached for a compassionate response.

"How will I know whether your children get married or not wherever they go? Go and tell them to register their marriage."

Some people think they have no responsibility to look for solutions to others' problems and only provoke others by showing arrogance.

I should have replied, 'I don't need your permission or recommendation for a marriage registration,' but I remained silent.

A minute later, I said politely -

"Acha, if you are not permitting me, say so. Don't force me to speak in a way that will diminish our respect for Achen."

He returned the invitation card given to him, and I returned home.

Tony was informed of the interruption. He must have called Binoy. When he spoke, I was directed to go to the Bishop's House, meet Fr. Babu, and tell him the information. Fr. Babu was secretary to the Archbishop Bernard Moras. Fr. Babu has been known to Binoy since he was the Political advisor to CBCI President.

I saw Fr. Babu and told him about the issue.

"We will talk to the Archbishop in person and get a decision. The Archbishop is coming to Resurrection Church, Indiranagar, tomorrow morning. Please come there and talk to him at 7 a.m."

We were glad that we got permission to meet the Archbishop.

In the morning, Leelamma and I went to the convent behind the Resurrection Church, where we attended the Holi Mass, which the Archbishop was saying. After the Mass, the Archbishop had breakfast with the other priests and nuns. We waited outside.

A nun asked us, "Did you come to see the Archbishop?" and took us inside. Everyone was sitting at the table and having their breakfast. We greeted the Archbishop, "Good Morning, Your Grace". I did not see Fr. Babu there. Instead, I saw a more familiar Parish Priest of Resurrection Church, Fr. Norman Bernard. When the Archbishop asked for my name, we introduced ourselves by name.

"Have you had breakfast?" His Excellency asked me.

"No, Your Grace."

"Come, sit down, and have your breakfast." The archbishop invited us.

The chairs were brought there, and we shared the table with the Archbishop and had tea. What matters is not what you ate but how, in what environment, and with whom you ate. We were honoured.

When I explained the difficulty of obtaining a marriage counseling certificate, the date of birth, and the obstacles the church vicar mentioned, I also mentioned Tony's church service as an altar boy at the Resurrection Church during his younger days.

The father listened to the problem and could suggest a solution immediately. The Archbishop had Just one look at Fr Norman Bernard in the form of a question, and the answer came.

"I will give you a certificate. But ask Tony to meet me before the betrothal ceremony".

God is great, and God's shepherd is also great!

When I told my parish priest about the solution, he maintained his pretentious stubbornness. He reiterated his arrogance as if it were not a solution!

"Even if you bring a recommendation or certificate from the bishop or the pope, it's hard to do here."

I stood stunned for a minute or two without answering -then I realised that all I had to do was to think and respond.

"Well, Father, I must make a final decision by tomorrow morning, or I will have to look for alternatives. Thank you." and I left the place.

Aren't the bishops and the pope the superiors for this priest? Was it not fair what I did? I have gone through the legal route, and those in need will go to the extremes. Why did he not understand? Is that study not included in their theology? My boiling anger and frustration subsided, and I waited confidently. Everything would be fine.

In the evening, Leelamma said, the Parish vicar's phone came. "Your son's betrothal will be done as decided. I will do it myself as a priest."

I was relieved. I did not have to look for any reason or find fault with anyone. Everyone should know this: no man or priest can stop or control the blessings flowing from above.

Do you remember reading the announcement on the mic during the church festival at Punnapra - "Food is distributed for the priests and nuns in the pandal on the south side of the church and the mankind on the north side of the church..."! (Ch. 15)

# 98

# The Wedding Reception

After completing his MBA at INSEAD, Tony arrived just before Christmas in his new home, in his own house. The light in his parents' eyes and the satisfaction in their minds could be seen reflected in Tony's face. Tony was welcomed by his parents, sisters, and brother-in-law; her eight-month-old baby, Natasha, was with Nita.

Tony bought toys and books for Natasha.

Natasha was her grandparents' most beloved, beautiful, and innocent 'chunni' child. She grew her hair long, wore it, and became a modest Malayalee girl. While Leelamma served Onasadya on a plantain leaf, everyone saw Natasha was more attractive than 'Maveli' and 'Manka' while sitting on the floor.

You must be wondering by reading 'Onam' just before Christmas. There is no need to doubt. Tony did not have 'Onam Sadya' for this year's Onam because he was in France. When he comes home, mommy should prepare Onam Sadya without further delay," was Tony's insistence, whether he came from Singapore, France, America, the British Islands, or wherever. Mahabali does not come for the Onam day; Onam for us is when Mahabali comes!

Although Natasha was accustomed to Hindi as her mother tongue, Leelamma taught Natasha to call her Ammachi. She understood that, and she never called her 'Dadi.' The Malayalee mother, who liked her mother tongue, enjoyed it more. Natasha called me 'Nanu.' Let her call me anything. After all, I'm her grandfather.

The next day, Tony met the Father vicar of the Resurrection Church, Fr. Norman Bernard. After two or three short study sessions, the priest wrote a certificate of attendance for Tony for a marriage counselling course.

John and his family came to Bangalore from Kanpur a day before the betrothal. They stayed at E 34 / 5 DRDO quarters, which I had vacated but did not hand over to the govt. As all the furniture was taken away, it was practically impossible to provide them with any such facility for a short duration, the inconvenience of which John had already agreed as adjustable and adequate. It was ensured that electricity and water supply would always be available. They made arrangements for their food and other things. They had some relatives available in Bangalore.

In some Travancore Christian families, most people know it was customary to have a give-and-take between relatives before marriage. I was particular that no one should make it a topic of discussion because we were all law-abiding citizens, and nobody would gain any reputation by claiming to follow the custom. The wrong custom was not observed in our family history. I had prepared an answer if anyone had raised it as a topic to be considered. That's not all. John and his family were satisfied with the temporary accommodation they were provided with, and we made some inquiries to see if they needed anything more. That was when I could sense that there were some differences of opinion among the family members regarding some trivial aspects of the ceremony, and to cover it up, John said something resentfully. I was unhappy.

Suppose I had heard what I did not like and had not responded appropriately. In that case, John might have gotten the wrong impression that 'Are there such humble people among the Catholics in Kuttanadu?' So, I had to respond. I only remembered what I said for a short time. Leelamma later reminded me as follows (and that I remember)–

"Even if it is true, if you speak in Malayalam, the listeners might think you are quarrelling with them. You should say nothing formally in Malayalam, dear!"

I had heard that John was short-tempered. I had seen him shouting at the rickshaw puller in Kanpur for suddenly coming in front of his scooter. "क्या तुम हमें मरवाओगे?" "(Will you get us killed?)". But in Bangalore, John was perfectly calm, like any father who wanted his daughter to marry and have peace of mind.

It has been said that fathers with eligible spinsters should not get angry. Maybe John heard what I said; he thought it did not matter much and excused me.

The betrothal ceremony of Tony and Joysy took place at St. Jude Church as planned.

After the ceremony, everyone came home and ate lunch. Everyone returned to their homes to come back on the wedding day.

It took two days to go shopping. Tony bought the best wedding sari and dresses for his sisters and other relatives and a little happiness for everyone.

Sam's parents and relatives came from Jamshedpur. The catering team led by Peter's younger brother Thomas also arrived early. They were accommodated in the DRDO guest house at CV Raman Nagar.

All the relatives from native towns and other towns attended Tony's wedding. My 'Brother' came from Pune. Everyone came by train a day before the event.

The elderly relatives were brought on the flight together. Leelamma's mother, Kochuppappan, and Chittamma were all flying in for the first time. Preparations were made for the ceremonies at the church. Seema, Nita, and Tony's cousins did everything to make the ceremony fantastic.

Tony, relatives, and friends had reached the church at the appointed time. Joysy, her friends, and relatives came directly to the church. A few people came from the native place, such as John's relatives and friends.

The wedding Mass was in English, with Fr. Thomas Panakkezham SDB as the principal celebrant for the ceremony. The homily after the wedding was a message that linked Christmas to family life.

About 600 people attended the sumptuous evening reception at the DRDO Community Hall in CV Raman Nagar. We came home with the couple and other relatives. Leelamma marked an invisible cross on the bride and groom's foreheads, garlanded her with a rosary, carried them inside the house, and gave them wine and cake. Marking an invisible cross on the bride's forehead by the groom's mother at the doorstep reminded her that she belonged to God, who loved her very much to be part of this new family hereafter. The bride and groom then went to a room in the Park Hotel prepared for them. Relatives and friends returned to their homes on the next day.

An exciting incident occurred at the old airport when Ottathyckal Ammachi, Kochuppappan, and Chittamma returned to Kochi.

We watched from outside that they had checked in and were going to the security clearance area. A security officer suddenly stopped Ammachi from moving in. Ammachi was segregated aside as if she were a suspected passenger and took out her handbag's contents and checked. The security officer found a handgun in her bag, and he questioned her. Security personnel stood ready, surrounding her for an arrest. On the other hand, the Ottathyckal Ammachi looked at everything calmly, cool as a cucumber, as if nothing had happened. In response to a question from a security officer, Ammachi said –

"Is it a plastic toy for the little one at home to play with? Please don't take it away with you. Give it back to me".

"Okay, but we cannot give it to you, Mother."

"If it's so essential, you take it to your child as my gift; what else can I say ...!"

Whatever the interpretation of the law in the head of the security guards or the faint lines in the law itself, the mother responded well. Then, the journey further was smooth. An inhuman bureaucracy was prevalent that watched everyone with suspicion. Laws must be washed pure in the Ganges of humanity.

Joy came and picked up Ottathyckal Ammachi and others from Kochi airport and went home via Punnapra.

**Daddy, Play With It**

After attending banquets at relatives' homes, Tony and Joysy went to their workplace, Joysy (JPMorgan) to New Jersey, and Tony (GE Leadership Institute) to Milwaukee.

Nita continued her work at Leela Palace. Sam's parents were there to look after the baby. Seema was waiting for admission to the NTU Post Graduate course in Singapore.

Before Tony left, he handed me a laptop computer (HP Compaq Presario) and said-

"Daddy, you will turn sixty next month and retire from government service. You need to be engaged as you desire. This laptop is for you, Daddy; play with it. Over time, you will learn how to use it."

"Thank you, Mone. Yes, I will play with it and learn how to use it. Hopefully, I shall use it beneficially. "

So, at the age of sixty, I started learning about computers. For the rest of my life, I wrote books in English and Malayalam, using only the index fingers of my left and right hands. After that, I don't remember anything I ever wrote with a pen on paper.

Apart from writing books, I have travelled abroad for over 15 years for work and, sometimes on holiday, wrote and submitted reports of all work using the laptop. I can write about it later, after retiring from government service. An essential condition of government employment was that the income should not be from multiple sources simultaneously. Accordingly, I have been working since becoming a more responsible officer, i.e., a Gazetted Officer.

Seema was selected in April for a Master's Degree in Electronics & Biomedical Engineering from Nanyang Technological University, Singapore. Classes started on June 25. As I had in mind earlier, I applied for an education loan from a bank. Having a salary account and getting a loan of Rs 10 lakh from the State Bank of India was not difficult. When it was converted into Singapore dollars, I realised that the amount would not be enough for the fees and the cost of living in Singapore - the price for a year. I was relieved when her employed brother agreed to compensate for the shortfalls. The bankers were deducting the loan amount from my monthly salary in instalments.

Seema started her first-year classes on July 25. When Seema was also sent away to Singapore, and we returned to the 2300 sq. ft house, we realised that the house was too big. With plenty of space for two of us to live, we waited for the children to return, huddling in a corner. The silence that sometimes lingered in the rooms seemed unbearable, but soon it became a habit. The family could happily wait for the next major event to gather together, and then all the rooms would be noisy. As we begin to hear the laughter and cries of grandchildren, the faster the wheels of time turn, the more hope there is for more. The tranquillity may return later, replacing the bustle. Isn't this the fundamental uncertainty in life?

Seema remained at NTU until January 2007. As I had seen the NTU campus and the college, I understood Seema's studies and hostel life better. Seema was accustomed to spending the time alone and studying in the undergraduate classes. After completing her final exams and project work, Seema got a job in the biomedical department of the Republic Polytechnic in Singapore through campus selection.

Before joining the job, Seema came on vacation leave in December 2006 when Tony and Joysy arrived. Seema came to Bangalore, went to Alappuzha, met everyone there, and returned to Singapore to join for the job. That way, Seema also started working as a teacher.

# 99

# For An Adventurous Flying

The Indian Air Force and the National Geographic TV Channel had come up with a plan together to raise awareness about the operation of fighter jet aircraft among the public in India.

I saw what was advertised in the newspapers. -

"Come if you are ready to experience the incredible stunts and adventures in a fighter jet with a trained jet fighter pilot, and if satisfied with your physical fitness, we will give you a chance to fly in a fighter jet. Hold tight as you brace yourself for awe-inspiring views and experience the G-force (gravitational force) and the many manifestations of a fast-moving aircraft. Reach Air Force Station, Jalahalli, at 6 a.m. and register your name for selection tests."

Despite spending an entire career with warplanes, I never had the good fortune to fly in one of them into the sky. The pilots can withstand up to 12 times the gravitational force while manoeuvring in a fighter jet. In rare instances, the gravitational force will exceed 10g, and the pilot will instantly lose consciousness (blackout) and regain consciousness when the gravitational force drops below 10. Their healthy body can do that. Although I knew about the G-Force, thinking this was an excellent opportunity to experience it alone, I went to Jalahalli in our car with Leelamma at six o'clock in the morning. I joined the long queue at the entrance. After entering and registering, the examinations started at 8:00 a.m.

TV reporters and videographers of the National Geographic Channel videotaped the crowd and other scenes. Most people in the queue were young people students, and there were none with grey hairs.

One channel reporter approached me and greeted me as she had not seen perhaps anyone else of my age –

They must have noticed something remarkable with my grey hair or excessive enthusiasm.

"Why do you want to fly in a fighter aircraft? "

I replied-

"People like me work in a department to ensure the safety and quality of fighter jets, and I certify for the safety and quality of the aircraft. So, I have a hundred percent responsibility and confidence in my job. I see this as an opportunity to fly and demonstrate that confidence."

My answer seemed to satisfy them and those standing close by. The next day, the event was telecasted on the National Geographic Channel, and many people watched it.

The first thing I got in the fitness test was a 1.6 km run, which took a little longer to complete, but I managed to run the distance. The Air Force Officer allowed me to rest without doing the rest of the tests. I returned. I was blessed to be able to participate.

On June 22, 2003, George Fernandes, the then-Defense Minister, flew in a Sukhoi-30 MKI fighter jet. After that, the Indian Air Force launched an awareness project to allow civilians to be in fighter aircraft.

From the Lohegaon Air Force Base in Pune on June 8, 2006, President Shri APJ Abdul Kalam became the first Head of State to fly in a Sukhoi-30 MKI fighter jet. He was 74 years old at the time. I tried to fly at the age of fifty-nine!

Before leaving for a sabbatical-like speaking tour to the branch offices of DGAQA, I had to organise and send an answer to the question of how well the recommendations of the COFA Committee had been implemented. Even though these were scientific and technological matters, government affairs were always carried out as usual in the threads of bureaucracy. A few things were done, and there was still much more left. It was always like that.

Having completed all the specific tasks in the office on time, I have reached the critical life stage of retirement. In this phase, one era ends, and the next begins.

During the sabbatical-like tour, I saw many friends working with me in different places and wished them all the best again. It would be a real treat if they all remembered my talks and interactions with them. My technical talks were well-received everywhere. They all greeted me and sent me away with love and affection.

By the time I returned to Bangalore after the trip, the day of my retirement from government service, February 28, 2006, was fast approaching.

I briefed Parameswaran, my colleague, about the jobs to be continued in the office. I have segregated and packed all my personal papers, service files, and diaries separately. I met and said goodbye to most of my colleagues in the affiliated offices. They all gave me warm and loving greetings and words of thanks and appreciation. We wished each other that we would meet again somewhere in life's pathways and remember them with love.

My office honoured me with a fond farewell in a gathering of all the officials and staff members of all the DGAQA offices in Bangalore before the close of business on the pre-arranged day, with a tea party. The boss presented me with a memento.

# 100

# My Farewell

Farewell meetings do not go beyond a simple formality. Although the support to go to the office calmly and peacefully, the spouse might have always given to the person who retires from professional life. Therefore, the spouse deserves respect and appreciation for it. It is most appropriate to allow them to share the gratitude of the organization and the love of colleagues with their spouse and to honour the spouse on the occasion of retirement.

That's why I did act when I got an opportunity. When they retired, I had the opportunity to host dinner for some senior officers in the evening at any hotel or DROMI. On those days, the retired officer was invited along with his spouse. All participants, along with their spouses, were usually the hosts. This time, the people who organised the lunch in a hotel did not consider including their spouses. Therefore, I politely declined the invitation to go to the hotel alone during office hours and join the banquet without my spouse.

Superannuation benefits are the deferred payments my employer or government sets aside and can collect once I reach the designated retirement age. Retirement is stopping work or leaving the job.

I retired from government service after more than forty years of service. The loving authorities described it as an admirable one. I was grateful that I was able to serve. My duty, the duty entrusted to me, was done. Completing active service means that the Government was withdrawing me from public services by saying good words. It is like a leaf falling away or a fruit falling from a tree without self-knowledge as if it is routine. There was a little sadness to it.

In other words, I was giving room to others and was happy that when I retired, I believed those who would come after me would continue the work better than I did. The feeling of people getting together, saying a few words, drinking tea, and parting was one good thing after more than 40 years of service. A step down like this could be difficult for anyone with experience.

After the refreshments and presenting the memento, the boss invited me for a reply speech.

I had prepared for it on the previous day.

"My dear Colleagues,

To this day, I have had a great career and have enjoyed all parts of it heartily. All this was possible by the grace of God. So, let me give thanks to God.

(I am grateful to God ದೇವರಿಗೆ ಕೃತಜ್ಞತೆ ಸಲ್ಲಿಸಿ). I greet my Gurus and the Mahatmas who helped me to enter official life.

I have achieved a lot, and I have professional satisfaction. I was able to keep in touch with very senior officials. They helped me to develop some good qualities. I also believe that I have been able to make some contributions to ensure the quality of the aircraft.

By the grace of God, my official life was happy and peaceful. It is an excellent time to gather here today to talk about non-technical things and have tea together.

During this time, I have had moments of despair and agony. Some moments of fulfillment are always memorable. Moments of pain I did not carry home. I did not blame anyone. It was an extraordinary, serene moment; I will always appreciate it. I want to share it with you.

Dr. APJ Abdul Kalam put his hand on my shoulder. Time was such an occasion, and I will always cherish those moments. He said, "Come, let us go and see how the problem developed on the aircraft."

……..(Walking through the technical workshops, after hearing a brief technical description including the sequence of events that lead to the accident, I lent my ears eagerly to listen to him) –

Keeping one hand on my shoulder and the other pointing to the technicians returning after lunch, he told me -

"Thomas, they are all the Vishwakarma and… You are the Viswaamithra. Thank you. Come, let us go for lunch."

"They are all the Vishwakarmas, and you are the Vishwamitra!"

I will never forget it. Dr Kalam was a gentleman, a scientist, and a great philosopher, so I greatly appreciated him from that time onwards.

(You know, Vishwamitra was a king who attained Brahmanism through penance and replaced the Saptarshis, the rulers - the master, the manager, and the supervisors. Those born and living in the Vishwakarma clan were the builders of the universe - workers and technicians. As a sign of devotion, he is worshipped by all professionals, not just the engineering and the architectural community.)

This is what we need to understand when reading a combination of mythology and quality-

(i) We must be Vishwamitra in our devotion, hard work, and penance to attain quality.

(ii) 'If a technician is to do a job well, the responsibilities and procedures of each, as in the' Process-Quality 'approach, need to be defined. You must guide them in following the procedures.

My colleagues know that I'm often like a busy bee. I'm always so enthusiastic. So, some people ask me, "What will you do after retirement?"

As far as I know, there is something to learn and enjoy every moment. Sometimes stand-up comedians, news readers, sometimes cricketers. So, I'm sure I can happily spend the rest of my life!

I know that I have received a lot of love and affection from all my colleagues here and other field establishments of DGAQA. One thing I would like to say to colleagues is -

We should be able to earn the respect of others and not just ask for it. Only with a more profound knowledge of our work can we achieve it, especially when our main task is to ensure the quality of the aircraft. Safety will always follow where quality leads. We also need to know where the knowledge is available when needed.

I want my superiors to tell me that my junior colleagues deserve more generosity and kindness from you for their outstanding work. Everyone should be encouraged to be better than the classification 'very good' they get during evaluation. Magnanimity is sacrifice, which is more precious than love. Rather than helping others, be kind to those who work according to your desires.

In corporate language, the core competency of our office is now at a very high level. We do our job. As a team, this is our most outstanding achievement. However, for our organization to achieve greater glory, we need to document our mission, vision, and goals more clearly and grow and progress further under the leadership of our Director-General.

Sir, you, my colleagues, and friends have all been very kind to me and have given me your love, affection, and cooperation abundantly and extravagantly. I thank every one of you for that.

'Govt work is God's work.' As I was walking around Bangalore, I saw the slogan "Government work is God's work" inscribed in Kannada and English above the entrance of the Vidhana Soudha. I have always considered that work is my worship of God.

I introduced myself and talked to my colleagues during my service on several topics. But I never told a story or sang a song. On this last day of my service, let me do it once.

'The master went out and asked the workers to come to his field and work for a daily wage. The story is about the salaries received by the workers. Some went in the morning, some came in the noon, and some went in the afternoon. All the workers did their job sincerely in the workplace. In the evening, the master distributed the wages equally to all the workers. Those who came in the morning and worked all day and those who arrived at noon and afternoon were paid the same wages as those who worked all day. Some complained, and some were unhappy. Either others should get less, or they should get more than others. The master replied that everyone was paid a day's wages, and no one was given less. Everyone was delivered a day's wages, regardless of when they came to work. It is the master's mercy, the privilege ..... The master showed more compassion to some. No one was wronged. Some workers thanked their master and left.

I also thank him. I am delighted when I retire from my office on the last day of active service to my nation. The most important thing is to rejoice in what He gives as a reward for serving the country.

I often missed my deserved promotions and career prospects. There is no despair about that. You know, in 39 years, my salary has increased a hundredfold.

Some time ago, I applied for a seat to participate in a local seminar, and today, they have invited me to attend and speak at an international symposium. I achieved this with hard work; I remember it with great pleasure!

I'm singing a song from the movie 'The Sound of Music, with Julie Andrews, and that will be my swan song: -

"For here you are, standing there, loving me, Whether you should,

So, I must have done something good somewhere in my youth or childhood.

Nothing comes from Nothing. Nothing ever could,

So somewhere in my youth or childhood, I must have done something good!"

"I must have done something good in my youth or childhood."

It is also the answer to what I am going to do. Knowledge about Quality Assurance is my strength. I have confidence in myself and look forward to more service to society, the aeronautical community, and humanity.

On behalf of my family, I wish you and your families all the best in the coming days. Thank you for your friendliness and kindness. This love of yours will remain indelibly etched in my mind forever.

I will be grateful to you for this parting gift, kind words, and great respect.

Jai Hind, Thank you, Yours Thomas "February 28, 2006.

Friends and colleagues applauded the reply that this love would last forever in mind.

The day I retired from service was like returning home regularly after duty. The sandalwood-scented garland and the commemorative plaque were placed on the car seat. I drove my Santro home. Personal papers were brought earlier.

The next day, on March 1, like I used to do just before leaving for the office, I took a shower, got ready for breakfast, sat in my usual chair, and read the newspaper. I did not see or read any news about my retirement. Of course, the outside world had not declined or changed a bit. The next day and the next were similar.

# 101

# Services for Quality

I got up and went to the kitchen. My better half used to remind me that "husbands who love their wives help them in the kitchen." I told her she would get the opportunity when I retired from office work. I recalled that the promises were to be fulfilled.

I got a hearty welcome for my new Job. "You can verify the quality of the aircraft and their inspection matters. Those talents can not be used here. I can give you a call whenever I need you here. You go and read the newspaper. Many books are also there on the shelf in the reading room."

My first attempt at an alternate job failed.

Homemakers are reluctant to take an extra pair of hands even for training in their specialized field. And suppose any small jobs are outsourced temporarily. In that case, they will be called to scrape a coconut or two, replace the gas cylinder, or pour water into the plant pots on the terrace.

After 20 days of retiring from my official work, I got a phone call from a Marwari friend running his own business - (Marwari is an Indian ethnic community originating from Rajasthan, not a religious sect.)

"Thomas, what are you doing? Come down if you're not busy, and we will talk."

The friend was a colleague some time ago. Later, he joined a manager in a public sector organisation. After getting some training and experience, these people were interested in returning to the business profession. He was adept at it, skilled in business, and did not spend money on necessities. We should understand that he will have something to gain from us when he calls.

I went and met him. It didn't take much effort for him to subdue me. Being proficient in business, he found my technical training and experience were appropriate for expanding his business.

The quality management system for the aviation, space, and defence organisations I know of was essential for his business expansion into further areas of certification auditing and consultancy. "If you are bored of sitting idle at home after retiring from service, can you come and help me?" It was a sincere request.

"Yes, I can, for some time."

"Enough .."

He was happy. He might have thought if I were not tied up properly, I might jump out of his fence one day. So, he hooked a small prey and threw it to me - "Let me talk to Prof Rao about your monthly salary."

Prof. Rao had a friendly conversation with me. The business owner then asked me-

"How much salary do you need? You need to stay for at least five years."

"Let us see, and I cannot guarantee. Therefore, you can pay me if you wish. I do not wish to continue beyond a point where my continuation is not profitable for your business."

I started going through the Quality Certification or Consultancy business paths the next day. As expected, Quality Certification or Consultancy was the most appropriate business field in which to use the ISO 9001 standard and the Lead Auditor training I completed. I passed the examination. Certification auditing, guidance, and training were all activities in the same area.

When Prof. Rao audited ten or twenty companies in Bangalore, he took me along and taught me auditing techniques and lessons. It provided more experience. Training builds confidence. Auditing training has dramatically helped me understand how the ISO standard has effectively ensured quality in industrial operations and products.

An American aerospace lead auditor who came from America to inspect a business-related certification body gave five days of aerospace lead auditor training to four of us in the office. The training was about the audit process used in industrial establishments manufacturing aviation, space, and defence equipment. After training, we applied for international recognition.

With over thirty years of experience in aircraft quality control work, two Lead Auditor Training Certificates, and audit experience in over twenty companies, I have received international recognition as Aerospace Industry Experienced Auditor of International Aerospace Quality Group (AIEA of IAQG), effective January 2007. I was the fourth lead auditor in India to receive such recognition, being one of only four hundred in the world then.

I audited about fifty companies in India for three years. I have worked as a consultant in over ten companies. The housewife sometimes asked what the financial benefit was. In Tony's opinion, Daddy was getting satisfaction and health, but was it good to work like this for such a meagre income, and why not do anything better? Tony wanted me to think of a start-up organisation.

Was it not necessary for the business owner sometimes to think about how to promote the business and retain an efficient employee? The one who only knew the business strategy and how more money could come from business had no time to consider the employee. Therefore,

I was preparing to demand a reasonable increase in my monthly compensation. Data-based decision-making – with the backing of appropriate arithmetic, was necessary to demand an increase.

Shouldn't business benefits remain roughly balanced for all concerned? For any business to run well at all times, the investment and effort of the stakeholders must be fairly rewarded. Compensation or remuneration to every stakeholder should also be a fair share of total income. When there are differences, when someone creates differences for their selfish interests, there is a loss of collective responsibility and business.

I did 95% of the aerospace consultancy or auditing business assigned to me for over three and a half years. How could anyone justify if I was not rewarded with at least twenty percent of the business benefits? Minor deviations could always be negotiated and agreed upon.

One day, I did an estimate. For the three and a half years I worked, he got the owner a business benefit above 70 lakh rupees. He gave me a compensation of 7 lakhs, including all the perks. It was hard to believe that justice had been done to me. I asked my mentor and benefactor in auditing, Prof Rao, for his opinion. He gave me good advice.

I am not a businessman. I was surprised to find out about his business strategies and ethics. He knew me personally, so he called me. I did not think asking for my help was to exploit me like this. I am ready to forgive. I spoke to him. I started with sincerity.

"I just wanted to know whether my association with you has benefited your business?"

"Yes, of course. We have improved our business. You have been quite helpful. You have contributed a lot. "

"I have been supporting you for more than three years. An increase in my compensation is inevitable; can you consider it? "

Soon after, he turned down the request for a pay rise. I showed him the income and expenditure account that I had written down and said –

"What I asked was perfectly fair."

He stood up and pointed his shaking finger at me. He must have thought that I would get up and run away. I looked at him coolly and smiled. He sat down. Then he angrily responded -

"I know, I am not 'Harishchandra,' the legendary king.' ('Harishchandran' implies 'speaks truth and reality.') However, my business model does not permit me to increase your remuneration - Are you bringing trade union tactics here?" "No. It is elementary arithmetic. Think of it. If you wish, we will talk later. Thank you."

The auditing standard was republished in 2009 after periodic revisions. Based on the revision of Standard 9100, there came an IAQG requirement for all auditors to receive additional auditor training. It applied to all auditors, and further audits were allowed only after passing the exam.

There were no recognised institutes providing revision training in India. Trainers from American or European organisations demanded a fee of Rs three lakh to come to India for training, or the trainees should go to the United States or Europe to get the training and appear for the online exam.

When the trainers come to India, there should be at least eight trainees in a batch to conduct the training.

The business owner was willing to go to the United States and attend the revision training. He was also willing to spend about four lakhs, including fees, for me provided that I continue to stay with the company for at least five years more.

My predetermined response was immediate for such an arrangement, making me a bonded worker for his business purpose.

"I can come along; I can audit for you for five years after passing the exam if you give me double the monthly salary or pay me 20 percent of the income from auditing that I do as a reward for the effort. If you agree, let me know. Otherwise, I will not be coming here anymore. Thank you."

I did not go there after that. Opportunities to meet the business friend, who was a colleague earlier, were rare.

I learned later that an outstanding achievement had come the way of my colleagues. Only a short time before, all my co-workers there received a substantial increase in their monthly salary without anyone asking for it. Sometimes, the influence of righteousness will cause even Satan to oblige!

## 102

# Mother-Eternal Memory

We moved from Pune to Bangalore in 1981. We went to Koraput from Bangalore in 1993 and came back to Bangalore. I retired from work and settled down in Bangalore. He left Pune long ago but went to Pune when Joe Sabi, his brother's son, married. We quickly returned after the ceremony. Even after 25 years of relocation, our love for Pune, my professional life, and family life started in Pune, and we loved it as our second home town. We thought we could visit Pune when the work rush eased. So I called my brother and told him about it. Our plan to travel to Pune was without any specific agenda or mission. He was delighted and added not for two or three days; we could stay there for any number of days. Many of our friends had moved away from Pune. A few have returned to their native village. However, there are still a few old friends like Joseph Scaria, Babu, Vijayappan, Thomas Cherian (Lakshmi) Aby-Thankamma, Thankachi, Johnny, Vijayan Nair, Kuriakose, Jameskutty, Padmanabhan, Madhavan, and Anandaprakash etc in Pune. It was a great hope and consolation that I could meet many of them during this visit.

Seema was going to Pune for the first time. We stayed with Brother. One day in the evening, Babu called all our friends to his house, brought the evening meal, shared it, and arranged for all of us to meet together. Friends also said that we came from Bangalore and did something unusual. Although all those she saw were older people, when she came back, Leelamma noted that going to Pune was like going to our native village; we should go again whenever we get a chance. I said -

"If I continue auditing, we will go to Pune several times."

Tony and his family regularly visit India. The visit to India was not limited to Bangalore. That was impossible; they had to go to Chennai, meet Joysy's parents and siblings, and go to our native place to meet our grandmothers, especially since my mother was ill. Seeing everyone together and closely cooperating with them was a rare opportunity. Children must also get to know each other and get closer to each other for a good family bond.

In the letters of Babychan or Raju, which rarely comes, they write about Ammachi's health condition. Ammachi has almost no memory of the past. Some nerves of her memory were frozen. Most of the time, she remained in bed. She was not able to control some irrational actions and movements. Someone must help her with everything and care for her as for little children; only then could her life be prolonged, at least a little more, without accidents.

You can't go out of the house, leaving your mother alone, and you can't tell when she will go out. It was not possible to even go to church. Once or twice, the priest was brought home to give communion to Mother. She will eat a little if you put the food in her mouth with a spoon. Even if food is scooped with a spoon, she forgets to open her mouth, and sometimes, she needs to be touched and told with great patience to close her mouth. As she had done before, the habit of taking something under her arm and going out - saying, "I will go to our house" has stopped. Often, Babychan took her to the bathroom and brought her back to bed. Reading and speaking have decreased to almost nil. We have been waiting for nearly two months, hoping that the children will come in December and we will go together to visit Ammachi.

We had reserved our travel quite early. We all went to Alappuzha when Sam-Nita, Tony, Joysy and Seema came. I spent a day with my Ammachi in Punnapra. Only when we reached Babychan's house, did we realize Ammachi was entirely bedridden? It felt like an ember was burning in my chest. I did not get the warm kiss of love from Ammachi's usual wet kiss on my cheek to cool my mind and heart. I saw my mother lying in a small room when I went inside. After I called her, she opened her eyes and looked at me but fell asleep again. Then, when she woke up, I saw a part of the smile on her lips and eyes, 'I am happy, my dear, you have brought the children too for me to see them' is what Ammachi thought and tried to tell me.

Babu and his family, as well as Raju and his family, came to Babychan's house. We went to Nedumudi and met Ottathyckal Ammachi there. Seeing Tony was always a great pleasure for Ammachi.

After returning to Punnapra and seeing Kochupappan and Chitamma, I could visit the church cemetery Achayan's grave and pray. After a quick run around everywhere, we returned to Bangalore on the second day. Tony and Joysy had to rush to Chennai the next day to meet Joysy's parents.

It was not easy to return immediately after seeing Ammachi's health condition, but after a week, it was Christmas; Tony and Joysy had to celebrate their first Christmas in Bangalore after marriage. It was not a new celebration, but they came for the holiday with a wish to spend the first Christmas with everyone in the family. That was why they decided to go to Alappuzha and Madras and reach Bangalore before Christmas.

I said goodbye to my mother wholeheartedly. I said silently, "I love you, and thank you, Ammachi". Then we returned to Bangalore. Nothing is enough, no matter how much gratitude and love or how you express it for Ammachi.

We arrived in Bangalore in the morning. In the afternoon, 21 Dec 2006, Babychan's phone call came - Our mother had gone to her heavenly home. May Ammachi's soul rest in peace. Ammachi left after blessing every one of us. Until the next day, Ammachi lay at home, in the mobile morgue, waiting for us to reach. Leelamma and I took an evening flight to Kochi that same day and took a taxi to reach Punnapra.

In time, it was taken from the mortuary. Ammachi was prepared and placed in a decorated box with flowers. Many people, including locals and relatives, attended the funeral. Ammachi's only daughter, Leelamma, and her husband, Thambichan, could not participate in her final journey as she had gone to Saji's place in America. She would be sitting there and crying her heart out.

Just as Achayan's body was carried away, we children carried Ammachi's coffin. We took Ammachi's body to the church cemetery as a celebration.

Ammachi returned to her heavenly home for eternal bliss after giving us love, sacrifice, and endurance. Ammachi is always in our memory, in our midst.

# 103

# Three Cousins

While studying at the Polytechnic, I learned that there were three persons with the same name, 'Kuriakose,' in our family at Anjiliparambil (Kannattumadom's parent family). I realized that the first (eldest) Kuriakose had been to Malaysia for a long time and that he had finally come to Anjiliparambil to see his father after about forty years. He could not come again as after settling down in Thiruvananthapuram, travelling to Kuttanadu was difficult for him. The second Kuriakose lived in Kannattumadom, I knew him as Chittappan, my father's younger brother. After the departure of Theyyamma Chittamma, he sold his inherited land and house at Kannattumadom due to the frequent floods and travel difficulties he faced there. He moved to Mannancherry with his son Manoj. The eldest son of Kuriakose, Joy, lived with his family in Aryat and later moved to Thathampally. After retiring from Kerala Water Transport Corporation, he joined his son-in-law in running the Alpha Academy (entrance coaching institute) in Alappuzha. Another son, Sunny, operated a houseboat service in the tourism sector. When I went to Punnapra in 2009, my Kochuppappan told me –

"Eda, I heard that 'Kuriakochan' was not well in Mannanchery. I am unable to go there alone. Bring an autorickshaw if you can come with me; we can visit him once."

I went to Mannancherry with my uncle to see Kuriakose chittappan. When I saw him face to face, he smiled and was happy. We sat down with him. But he did not know who visited him and did not ask us who we were. Kochuppappan asked him something, which he did not answer.

Mathukutty (second son, working in a railway concrete sleeper manufacturing company in Visakhapatnam, and unmarried) said - Achayan has (rapidly progressive) dementia, i.e., no adequate memory. He sometimes got violent, and it was difficult to stop him, and he quickly got away if he was caught. That was why he was mostly held in a locked room."

The situation that anyone could reach with old age and disease! We said goodbye with sadness in our minds. Soon, the news came that Kuriakose Chittapan had passed away (19.01.2010).

The third Kuriakose was known when AP Kuriakose came to the Carmel Polytechnic Punnapra and taught us English. He was qualified with an MA (English) and Med and taught in another college until then. He was the first cousin of Achayan and Kochuppappan. When I joined the Polytechnic, AP Kuriakose Chittappan's daughter, Maniamma, joined Mar Ivanios College and passed her degree in Biology. After graduation, she joined as a staff in the same college in Thiruvananthapuram. After marriage, she continued to stay and work in Thiruvananthapuram. AP Kuriakose Chittappan bought a plot of land in Punnapra, very close to his cousin's house, and built and lived there. How appropriate for the brothers to live together in the same place! The love and cooperation that started that day lasted forever. After retiring from work, we were always together in social services, family gatherings, catechism, and church activities. Kochupapan informed me when AP Chittapan passed away (11.10.2010).

I prayed for all the three chittappans - mutual cousins - for their eternal peace.

Besides Marwari's organization, several other certification bodies operate in India. After passing the upgrade examination, I can work as a freelancer auditor without permanently joining any institution.

IAQG internationally recognized empanelling of Auditors. The auditors' responsibilities and the controls exercised by the IAQG over them were all the same, and the IAQG determined everything. No age limit was prescribed for doing the work, and one could work as long as he was healthy and able to move around. As long as you work, you need to follow the principles and ethics of audit. Regulations such as impartiality, competence, consistency, and confidentiality were to be followed. The quality management system's knowledge and practical experience were essential for auditing. Violating any principle of auditing or ethics for temporary financial gain would result in a loss of credibility gained up to that point. It was hard to get continual approval from IAQG.

I desired and strived to follow the principles and ethics at all times. Knowledge and practice increase confidence. That's why I considered auditing one of the world's best jobs. There was no need to take home a responsibility or task that caused stress and anxiety. The auditor gets great satisfaction when he audits and submits his findings in a way that adds value to the owner's business.

I wanted to do what I loved myself.

Why should we get anxious about anything that will happen? The sky will not fall if you don't get what you want. Why can't you be relieved that a thousand different ways will open?

Our remedies for anxiety also come from auditing practice, such as thinking and acting maturely. There was no need to advise and correct anyone. It was enough to make others understand what was wrong or what must conform to the criteria. What was the generally accepted and most efficient (best) practice was precisely defined in the international standards (criteria). Suppose you point out that the error is against the instructions. In that case, the owner will further study, search for, and find the best solution for his business.

God asks man to follow the same principles and ethics. Man can use the life and health given by God to achieve spiritual goals. That was why I used to say that auditing work was my worship of God. Only good citizens can become good auditors. Another natural consequence is that good auditors are supposed to be good citizens. Anyway, I am not judging myself or anyone else!

Even if mistakes are found during the audit, no case should be filed, no sentencing, no criticism, no sympathy, no public statements, and no one should be blamed. Do not suggest a solution to anyone. That is the guideline for proper auditing. Even if you know the answers, do not point them out, as doing so would be contrary to the principles of auditing, thereby indulging in consultancy, which is not permitted.

It is sufficient to inform the owner in writing or the institution's most responsible person and provide objective evidence of the nonconformity. There will be a solution. Suppose the owner wants continual improvement for his business. In that case, he will find the answer/solution, whether brought out in a financial or quality system audit. The responsibility of the auditor is over.

The most responsible owner of the company may not be available for an interview during the audit. The audit may be conducted with any authorised representative appointed by the owner. The representative of the institution should accept the findings of the audit. The auditor has no right to dilute the findings for any reason. The findings should be made in writing only after the auditor has explained the things. The auditor can withdraw the findings if the required evidence is submitted before the audit period. Excellent and positive results can be appreciated in a few words. Still, the conclusions, flaws, or mistakes must be reported objectively in writing.

My siblings have been in the auditing business for the last 30 years, and it is a coincidence and God's will that they find their livelihood. No one has chosen the profession. It happened to be their permanent job. They find happiness when they get a job in their native place. They continually updated their eligibility through training, development, and improvement within the limitations and available facilities.

Thambichan also retired from Paradip Port when he reached the age of superannuation and returned home. He retired as an executive engineer at the Paradip Port Trust. He came home, went to Nedumudi, bought a house near his mother's residence, Ottathyckal, and lived there. The site was a large field full of trees, plants, and a little land for paddy cultivation. Good place. Since both his daughters were married, no timely responsibilities were left behind. He got the pension benefits. Life in the village was comfortable. They then spent about three months in San Fransisco, in the United States, with their elder daughter Saaji and family. We had met them before they went to San Francisco and wished them all the best.

They also planned to visit their second daughter, Ansa, and her family in London before returning to India. We met them again after they returned to India.

We had made it customary to honour my brothers, brothers, and co-brothers when they reached the age of sixty as a token of appreciation for the love and cooperation they provided us living in the same generation and extending their goodwill to the whole family. We started with Xavier and Gracy. Then, gifts were given to Brother and Tharamma in Pune. Because of the rare gift, both of them looked surprised.

When we visited Alleppey, it was time to honour Leelamma and Thambichan, and suitable gifts were given to them when we met them on their return from visits abroad. Leelamma was brimming with joy and said, "Kochayan bought something for me after a long time. I am happy."

We were both silent for a long time! Although we always had love and cooperation during the intervening period of life in Orissa, the joy doubled because I could see the old genuine pleasure on the little sister's face.

It came to my mind that in Japan, there is a famous work of art called kintsugi. The name is given to the work of art form, which retrieves what has been shattered and puts it back together. Just as it hides the broken cracks in an inanimate object, forgiving each other and restoring the bonds of companionship also helps repair human relationships. The human relationships thus recreated will be as unique, beautiful, and vibrant as the works of art!

It is a symbolic metaphor for accepting others with their faults and shortcomings or collaborating and accepting each other while knowing our weaknesses and imperfections. Mended relationships have more beauty and value than combined works of art. It is a metaphor for experiencing each other as a rare get-together.

# 104

# Freshwater Fish

Ottathyckal Joy continued his work on the Merchant Navy cargo ship. His family was made up of his wife and two sons. His wife was a teacher at Mankombu School. Children were learning in schools. Everything he earned was invested in the form of agricultural land or backyard.

Joy was always interested in earning more and becoming a local gentleman. Every time he goes to work on a ship, he could return home after at least six months. Then, he was involved in local social and political affairs for four or five months. While waiting for the call to work on the next ship assignment, he considered another investment opportunity that could be done in the tourism sector. An unfinished building near his house in Nedumudi, its owner had stopped the work and was looking for someone to buy it. It could be used for a resort if purchased! He could only pay the total price after completing his next assignment on a ship. He hesitated to give up what came so handy and near to him. Even though he had taken a loan, he insisted on going to work if he could. He also asked me for some money to fulfill that promise. I gave because I could give without much difficulty at that time. The sailor must understand that it was only a small effort on my part to keep the boat of love entangled in the turbulent waves and continue its journey without breaking. That was enough to pay the advance.

Joy returned from work at the end of his term, paid the price, and bought the building. Further work has been completed, the necessary facilities for the resort have been provided, and the resort has been ready for the inauguration. He also renovated his house, making it much more comfortable for living.

Although Ottathyckal Ammachi did not have any significant illness, she had already started showing the fatigue and exhaustion of old age just before she turned 90. The mother anticipated an opportunity for her children and grandchildren to come together. That's how Joy decided to celebrate his mother's 90th birthday, albeit earlier than the resort's inauguration, so that he could set up an occasion for her children and grandchildren to get together. Thus, the resort was inaugurated on a day when everyone could join. Everyone was informed. Dr Philip Mar Chrysostom, the 97-year-old Marthoma Archbishop, was invited as the special guest at the celebrations. His Excellency has always been dear to the listeners for humorously sharing his divine thoughts.

Everyone came again in August, this time in 2015. Even this time, the Nehru Trophy boat race would only be held ten days later.

The accommodation was arranged for all of us going from Bangalore to Alappuzha to avoid too many relatives getting crowded at home. It was always tricky for more than four or five relatives to arrange beds and rooms at any home.

Tony, Nita, Seema, and their family arrived with their parents in Alappuzha a day before the event. We were accommodated at the Rama Varma Club. After breakfast, we went to Nedumudi to see Ammachi in two vehicles. Ammachi was thrilled to see all her children together. Ammachi blessed everyone. The resort was decorated with painting and polishing work, thoroughly preparing for the next day's inauguration event.

The family got together and had dinner at a tourist restaurant on the AC roadside in Nedumudi, where the Kuttanadan unique – freshwater cuisines - dishes like carp, prawns, and duck were served. Everyone loved Kuttanadan dishes. My mother occasionally made the same tasty folk dishes at home years ago! Tony, Sam, and Leelamma liked it most.

Even before the meal on the plate was over, Sam re-ordered something, and he helped Leelamma taste more and enjoy it. Suddenly, Leelamma decided not to eat anything!

Leelamma washed her hands, poured water in her mouth, gargled, spitted, and screamed to escape the difficulties in her throat! The carp's thorn got stuck in her throat and did not come out or go in, no matter how hard she tried. Despite her loud spat, the thorn did not come down from the narrow passage in the throat.

Darkness entered his eyes. Within a few seconds, the Kuttanad dishes' unique flavours disappeared into the night. The shop owner showed me the house of the nearest doctor. Kuttanad's doctor was unfamiliar with the thorn getting stuck in the throat. It was expected to swallow the thorn with a rice ball. How can one tell that to another Kuttanadan girl? The doctor examined and said, "It's hard. It's better to take her to a bigger hospital in the town because it's getting too late at night!"

We went straight to the familiar hospital in Alappuzha. At night, the young doctor on duty examined her at length - not told mainly to take a blood test! -but said, "There are a few complications. You can spend the night here, keep her under observation, and do whatever is possible in the morning."

"That, please...Doctor, are you sure? Aren't there any other ways?"

"That's safe. Is it not a day only? We can do what we can tomorrow."

"No, Doctor, We have to attend an important ceremony tomorrow. We will go home today, rest, and come in the morning. Isn't that enough?"

"No, no. Let the patient be here for the night, under observation. Please admit"

"I shall discuss it with my relatives, and back we'll come. Thank you".

It appeared very strange to me. A thorn in the throat should be kept under observation overnight! Do you watch the thorns coming out and catching with a net? An ordinary person could easily understand what the purpose was.

I went out and consulted with my children, who were waiting anxiously outside.

The doctor's argument was irrational and did not suit common sense. I could not understand the professional ability of the doctor. Have you ever heard a fish thorn getting stuck in someone's throat while eating? If so, how many have been admitted to the hospital and observed for 12 hours to decide whether they needed surgery? In which hospital? It's natural to have the pain and associated discomfort, but does it need so much intensive care?

I never thought the scandal I heard about the hospital would be on such a frightening level. I opened my mind.

No one was delighted with my opinion.

"Let's go and relax, and let us see tomorrow," I said, taking full responsibility for the decision.

Something happened that night. When she woke up in the morning, Leelamma said nothing about the thorn in her throat. A slight pain could be the strain of trying to get the thorn out of my throat with a loud spat. I was relieved that it didn't matter.

("March on, and fear not the thorns or the sharp stones on life's path" - Kahlil Gibran)

"Leelam, what medicine did you take? Where did the thorn go?"

"I just drank some water and didn't take any other medicine."

"However, why did this man have to say such things to the doctor?"

"No, I did not say anything to the doctor. It was to escape from there without saying anything. So today we can attend Ammachi's birthday celebrations. Instead of going there, if we had told your mother -

"'I was in the hospital with the thorn of a carp', You would have to hear Ammachi laughing and saying - "Come on, I'm not that stupid to take me for a game "!

Attending the birthday party, the sisters and nieces asked each other as they greeted and smiled -

"Did you hear that Chechi had a feast with Kuttanadan carp yesterday and went to the hospital?"

"Yes, we had a feast with the carp, and a thorn got stuck in my throat...

"It was enough to squeeze a lemon and drink the juice, not only the thorns but also the duck bone; it will go its way without getting stuck in the throat!"

The birthday celebrations took place in the upper hall of the resort after the resort was inaugurated. Children, nieces and nephews, priests, nuns, friends, and locals greeted the mother. After seeing and hearing everything, the mother and everyone else were happy with a sumptuous coffee feast.

The mother took photos with her children and their family. Another picture was taken with the grandchildren and the grandmother. Everyone wished Ammachi health and longevity. Praising that he would return in the fullness of the century

When the family members returned to their place of residence, saying they would come again on completion of the centenary, they all carried away a heartful smile and a winking look of Ammachi to keep in their hearts forever.

# 105

# Being Busy The Rest Of The Time

After Eleanor's birth in December 2014, Tony bought a more comfortable home in London: # 1 Church Drive, North Harrow. It was close to school and church. It had lovely, beautiful gardens at the front and back. Inside was an open kitchen, three bedrooms upstairs and downstairs, an upgraded garage for one bedroom, and adequate storage space. Tony made further modifications, such as wooden flooring, a full-time heating system inside the house, electrical fittings, upgraded water connections, and a new water closet. The renovations and upgrades themselves became a huge expense.

Every parent must give a token of help, without asking, and blessings when their children buy their own house. It is their responsibility. No one will ask how much was given. There is no need to convince anyone whether you have provided some help or not. Parents should be more magnanimous and generous that their children do not ask or demand help because they better understand the situation.

We were able to provide a token assistance of GBP 15000/-, which could be remembered with pride as we have not yet retired from our jobs.

Tony's contributions to our family's prosperity are numerous, financially and otherwise. Many things were obvious, but some were not easily understandable to others. Not even once did he ask for anything in return. There was no substitute for such aid or responsibility. Happily, Tony heartily accepted it and thanked us. Amazon deliveries came without placing any order on the material front, sometimes through other courier services!

Before leaving Marwadi's business, I had travelled a lot. The daily commute was limited to five kilometres. I could drive to the office to help with his private business. For consultancy projects, wherever they were in Bangalore, they provided pick up and drop facility back home in the evening. The same goes for audits. Travelling to other places - After going to the airport by taxi and plane to the destination, the company always arranges to pick you up from the airport and drop you back at the local airport after the audit work.

If you have to stay at the destination for more than one day, they will arrange for you to stay in a good, clean hotel. Providing such logistic arrangements, whether the job was in Bangalore or any other city in India, was not difficult. There were some difficulties, like travelling and staying away from home. The private businessman, my colleague, did not bother me with any foreign trip. I understood that Marwari would go there himself if there were an audit abroad. He would not give that opportunity to anyone else, not even once. He would take the ways of more income for himself. That was his business model.

No entrepreneur who doesn't want their colleagues to thrive and grow with him has achieved long-term success and steady growth.

Days went by after I retired from a government job, helping an ex-colleague with his private business without any significant gains, imparting a wealth of experience for retail income, and helping many industrial firms improve their quality of management systems.

If you are doing something useful, for your benefit or the benefit of others, or if you are engaged in any occupation or service, in a nutshell, you never know how the days will pass by. Experts say that physical and mental efforts are always reasonable for health.

I used to say, "If you've been involved in something, you will not age quickly."

Or then it would be like many of my colleagues who used to read the newspaper throughout the day and look after the grandchildren at home. They see all the suffering from old age and having some ailment; they appear at least 15 years older than me. Over time, we will get tired of life when we may be unable to do many things without other's help. I have been with Brother in Pune since he said 30 years ago, "We can happily live if we can walk and get on a bus on our own."

How has time changed? Today, there is no need to take a bus to go anywhere!

It does not mean that there is no illness and no medication. I have been taking medicines Dr. Das prescribed at the Sunabeda Township Hospital for almost twenty years. An entire body medical check-up was usually done every year. It was only a matter of time before I started seeing another specialist doctor in Bangalore who treats heart disease and diabetes. He, too, has advised me to continue the medication prescribed by Dr Das. Other drugs were also prescribed in between as replacements. In the meantime, one morning, when I woke up, I felt like everything around me was spinning. Thus, the world revolved around the axis of self. I called Leelamma on the phone, thinking I would fall if I walked downstairs. When I felt like I would fall head over heels, my only plea to God was, "Kindly allow me to finish these current tasks right now."

Shrimati was getting ready to go to church. She heard the mobile ringing when she closed the door and returned to know the information. She made it mandatory to see a doctor. Sam sent his driver, and he took us to the family doctor. When I met the doctor again with a computerized tomography scan report, he said - no matter, in the brain – It was proof that I have a brain - only a few cells were inactive, and there were no other complications. It was a transient stroke. It usually comes up many, many times. Avoid stress, that's all, that's enough. Of the 86 billion neurons, only a few were inactive due to maladaptation or addiction, such as smoking! Or maybe some cells were retaining painful memories, and it was good they became inactive. Subsequently, I never smoked a cigarette.

Four-and-a-half years ago, blood sugar was higher than average, so the doctor prescribed medicines. They are being continued to this day. In short, even if activities and services are resumed, illnesses can come, and the medications are to be continued. Ageing is not at all a pleasure.

Then, as my friend Joseph Scaria from Pune says-

"Thank you for always giving us a bonus, the life after 60, and for extending the time to call us back."

Good people see every moment of life as a gift from God. Achievements, blessings, and everything without exception are seen as every comforting touch of Almighty God. The Almighty is a good master who adds bonuses and wages if you can do more work or services.

# 106

# Departure of a Beloved Brother

It was a very unexpected and shocking piece of news (a bolt from the blue) that Babu's friend from Coimbatore, Rajappan, communicated over the phone one evening in the summer. (12 May 2007)

"Babu was in hospital after an accident when he crossed the road in front of the factory when a motorbike hit him. Two boys who did not even have driving licenses came on a motorbike and crashed into him, dragging Babu for about thirty meters forward. He is in the ICU in the district hospital, has a severe injury, and has not yet regained consciousness."

Putting everything I heard then, I am writing now -

I said, "I am leaving immediately. I will arrive at night. Rajappan should help me there."

I called a co-parishner, a companion, a friend, and a driver, Justin, and Justin came with his Toyota Innova. Leelamma and I left for Coimbatore carrying only the essentials. I informed Babychan, and he picked up Thressamma and left immediately. Rajappan's phone rang again when he reached Hosur - "Babu has gone."

I called Babychan and Raju and shared the pain caused by our brother's departure. The emotional stresses of separation, responsibilities, numbness, and sadness we must go through. Everything is often beyond words! I have to go there and take my brother home and bury his body respectfully. Let's think about the rest later. The thoughts that come to mind cannot be controlled. No road or surroundings were found.

The journey continued with occasional sighs. We have to go through all the emotional stages. We have to think about what is next after Babu.

While growing up, they had two sons who could work and support their families despite their lack of education. There was some cultivation. Then, I tried to contain my grief. After all, I must go back, open my mind and cry! It will help ease the pain inside.

My thoughts lingered around Babu. I remembered the good moments we shared. Those memories can ease the sadness of the mind as time goes on. No matter how much we loved our brother, we could not control his life or prevent unforeseen happenings. Departures create gaps. The irreparable loss will then continue to hurt the heart.

It was past midnight when we reached the hospital in Coimbatore. It has been a while since Babychan and Thressamma arrived from Alleppey. Police had told him we could rest in a nearby lodge and that the diseased body would be handed over to the relatives after a post-mortem in the morning, Babychan informed.

We had been waiting at the door of the hospital since morning. Meanwhile, I spoke to Rajappan and the police constable Amineshwari.

Rajappan said, “I was in the hospital all the time. The doctors did everything they could to save Babu. At about ten o’clock in the morning, after finishing all the essential jobs of the company, he went past the main gate, crossed the road, and went to the tea shop for breakfast. Two boys, vagabonds, were roaming on a motorbike while Babu crossed the road. They saw that Babu was walking across the road and might have judged that they could pass through before Babu could reach the middle of the road and accelerated the motorbike. They collided. Unfortunately, the left handle of the bike hooked Babu’s shirt, and the speeding bike pulled Babu along the road and sped away. Babu’s head might have hit the road in the fall, with more injuries than on his face and hands. The company watchman saw everything from the gate. We ran and took Babu to the hospital.”

The policewoman said, "The driver did not even have a license. We took the bike and put it at the police station. FIR is filed. 'Mahassar' is getting ready. When you get the body, the hospital will give you a death certificate, which you must carry. They will do everything from the hospital until the ambulance."

The body was received after the post-mortem in the afternoon. Thressamma was with tears in her eyes. We, both brothers, picked up Babu's body and left for Punnapra in an ambulance. I was in the driver's side seat to show the route.

We arrived at Babychan's house in Punnapra around 6 p.m. A crowd of relatives and locals were waiting in the house courtyard where a pandal was erected. None of the people gathered had left the shock of the tragedy that had arrived unexpectedly. Many were crying.

I was not strong enough to say anything to anyone. None of the people dared to question the pity and sadness on everyone's faces. Everyone knew everything. Everyone hid their sympathy for Babu's family in their grief.

Preparations were being made for the last rites of my lost brother. Seeing a man who had been wiped out of his mind thirty-five years ago grieving right before him, he must have thought it would be out of place and unfair to ask or say anything to me. Joy looked at me blankly, like he was looking at another lifeless body. 'He looked at me !' was a big event for me, a sign of sympathy or mercy.

"A particle of repentance is enough in the mind, and one is entitled to repentance." That is how I should understand it. I remembered what I read.

"But are you sorry that you are not sorry?"

"Yes, I am sorry that I am not sorry."

(To Every Man a Penny- a novel by Bruce Marshall, quoted by His Holiness Pope Francis in 'The Name of God is Mercy')

For forgiveness to be possible, like a ray of remorse, let in - the door does not have to be opened; only a crack is enough. Just wait. One day, everything will be clear, and misconceptions will change.

When I returned from the church after my mother's funeral about six months ago, I remembered Babu sitting on a steel chair at one end of another pavilion with his hand on his chin and thinking thoughtfully. No one could have imagined that another funeral would be needed here soon.

At that time, Babu was sad that our mother had passed away. How disheartened the rest of the family when both (Ammachi and Babu) suddenly left us recently after Achayan!

Shouldn't Babu's family get any relief from the company in Coimbatore?

"Since Babu was a casual employee (daily wage contract worker), nothing more could be expected," Rajappan said.

The opportunity to go and talk to the company thus faded. It was Kuriachan who put Babu in the Indian Hume Pipe Company, and when I asked Kuriachan to speak to the company management about the relief or compensation, Kuriachan told me -

"You'll get nothing. To help the family, you have to do something yourself!"

Rajappan said he had approached an advocate when he was told to try something like the MACT (Motor Accidents Claims Tribunal) petition I had filed for Joji of Karumadi. Rajappan promised he would do what he needed to do if given the opportunity.

The Mahasar and the post-mortem report were obtained and given to the Advocate. When I went to Coimbatore, I met the lawyer and gave him the necessary documents. When Rajappan brought the employment certificate, I realised how hard Babu had worked to support his family on such a meagre salary. He was a National Trade Certificate (Wireman) holder with outstanding character certificates. Despite all that, Babu got the job as a casual helper from 1976 to 2007. I have never seen him keep his SSLC book. There were two or three books, so he would not show them to anyone. When I asked him about his job or income, he never gave an accurate answer. I was also responsible, but I could not do much about it. Once, when I got angry, I told him I would only eat from his house when he earned his daily bread with sweat. That was my ill-spoken words or the extra sermon. But soon, it became possible. That day, Saju and Soni were playing rubber ball cricket with me in the yard, and Babu and I had lunch together at his house that afternoon.

Although the extra sermon was said to encourage Babu for inspiration, he sadly showed that 'for some reason, he just could not do it,' poor boy! Although he worked hard, he never forgot that insult during his youth mischief; someone 'assumed he was incompetent or not very capable.' He forgave everything he endured and lived and worked hard for his family. Babu never even thought about violence other than he might have blacked out his face and said something to someone. He had no enemies. Still, it is not understood why such a horrendous end has come to him after enduring so much pain. There was no point in blaming anyone. Maybe I am also partly responsible for the hardships my younger brother, whom I loved the most, endured. That's why I have so much pain and sorrow in my heart.

Before returning to Bangalore after the funeral, I talked to Saju and Soni about what they could do to continue living happily.

"If you start something, we can make the necessary retail assistance. I then talked a lot about them completing their degree or starting a job and earning a steady income. But they did not show any enthusiasm for anything. It could be the sadness of losing their father, or naturally, it could be the difficulty of suddenly expressing their likes and dislikes to their father's brother. I do not remember hearing any inspired positive actions or inclinations from the grown-up youth. I saw only a numb look at the surroundings.

Babu's salary certificate from IHP was obtained, and the papers signed by Thressamma and her children were handed over to the Advocate. After talking to Rajappan, the MACT case was filed in the Dharapuram court in August 2007 through Advocate N Karthikeyan. (F / Track MCOP / FTC 1203/11).

Though I had no idea about the progress of the cases in the courts in Tamil Nadu, it was hoped that it would provide fair compensation within about three years.

Whenever I went to Coimbatore for work, I tried to see the lawyer and assess the case's progress. After three years, the case was transferred to the Tirupur District Court. If you call Advocate Karthikeyan once in three months, the answer is that the hearing has been postponed and will be over in another three months. Call two days later; the opponents have not come, and it has been delayed again, etc, were the stock replies. Once contacted, he said the parties to the case should be brought to the next hearing, the date would be announced, and a week later, the next month should be called - so it went on and on.

Babu's departure exposed Thresyamma to unbearable hardships in life. With no regular income and job, financial difficulties increased. The children were just there for the sake of being there and did not give much hope to progress, as they spent time without an objective. She got tired of living alone. Thresyamma's life was frozen when her father, who lived nearby and often helped her, also passed away. Then, I learned of Thresyamma's desire to get married again. It may be the loneliness that has forced her to such a desire. When she told me about it on the phone, she also mentioned the name of a widower I knew, even without asking for his consent. I replied, "Let there be a suitable proposal coming. We can think about it. It is painful for me to take the initiative and send you away to another family".

You are not an extra member of my family. You have at least a little farm to do agriculture. You have two adult sons; I believe they will protect and care for you. But I did not explain anything of that sort. I thought it was better not to aggravate the matter by talking more. Luckily, further, no follow-up happened.

It is good to think that everyone should try to live without forgetting their responsibilities and obligations to their family and find ways to survive any adversities.

When I went to the native place next time, I learned that Saju wanted to study something more and do work. I was happy to know he had this desire. It would be good for him and his mother. Until then, he walked around with his friends, saying he had been studying to complete his degree for over a year. He did not appear for any exam. Saju told me vaguely and hesitantly that he wanted to study and that I should help him pay the fees. I readily agreed that I would pay the entire cost of the installments. I paid the total fees in two or three instalments. He went to Ernakulam to study for a trade certificate in hotel management. He informed me of completing the 18-month course of study, which included some on-the-job training.

Through Nita, Saju got a job in Kochi. Sam's friend Mani worked as a manager in a facility management concern, and Saju started getting a salary. He bought a motorbike, drove it, went to work, and returned. One day, he got into a bike accident and broke his leg. Saju came home from the hospital and rested for three and a half months after spending all the money Tony gave to Thresyamma for her sustenance. Later, he joined his work.

One day, Sam learned that Saju had run away with the company cash and was absent from work subsequently. When I called and inquired, I was told he had taken the money, which was true. Saju thought that no one would ask for the account. When the officials found out, he hesitated to look at their faces and did not go to work. Saju said he would get another job and would soon go to Delhi.

Thresiamma said that Sony was also "interested in learning what Saju learned" and that he could learn if I paid the fees. It was good enough; I was happy to let him live by doing something.

The total fee was paid in two instalments. Sony completed eighteen months of study and went for on-the-job training in North India. Soni once called from there - Work was challenging, and he was suffering; there was no rest, and he felt like running away without continuing.

"It's okay, dear; you have endured so much; it was just a little more time left. If you try more, complete the training, and get the certificate, you will get a good job."

All I could do was comfort him.

When he returned home after the training, I told him to go to Kochi and meet Sam's friend, as Saju did. Sony got the job that Sam recommended for him.

"Daddy, if Sony wants to come to work, let him come; I will call Mani and tell him," said Sam. Sam didn't tell me that I should tell Sony not to steal money and run away like his brother Saju. It is the generosity of the giver. Is it not necessary to have such propriety for the receiver also? At least the receiver should have the generosity to be thankful, no matter whatever independent decisions an adult makes. A word or a gesture - when will they learn such etiquette?

A few months later, Sony quit his job in Kochi without telling anyone. I heard he had joined the tourism department in a big houseboat floating effortlessly down the river.

If Babu had been living, he would have had to endure more grief.

I learned from Babychan that Soni had been in a relationship with a girl who used to come to the church, and Thresyamma had gone to their house to propose marriage. As a formality, Thresyamma has asked Babychan to go to the girl's house whom Sony would marry and discuss the matter with the elders.

As per the advice of his sister-in-law, Babychan went and met the parents of a girl named 'Maya' and talked to her. The girl still needs to complete her education. Parents struggle with limited environments in their living conditions. Babychan told me they don't see a relationship that fits us all. Soni also did not do the work he studied and did not learn anything further; he was doing small chores and agricultural work in the East and West. Why should he make that girl suffer even more by marrying her without himself seeing a stable way of life ahead? Babychan responded that even if we objected, he doubted Sony would listen to us because he likes that girl so much.

My selfish and adventurous nature of assessing the causes and doing the right thing in any crisis came to the fore when Soni appeared in the MACT court in Tirupur. He didn't tell me he wanted to get married or that the proposal was so advanced that he needed my cooperation suitably. Seeing him for the first time after the marriage proposal, even during the 100 km taxi ride together from Coimbatore, Soni, who was free to think and act like an adult, did not speak to me, his father's elder brother. Soni, who had his political views, did not need my advice. Although saddened, I did not say anything until the court proceedings ended. I opened my mind when I got to talk to him outside the court. I thought that Babu's son was mine, too, and I had the obligation to see his welfare.

I was not against love relationships. Was it not enough to be able to do good for the family and the country by standing on one's own feet, developing skills, opening a path for improvement, and subsequently taking more responsibility? That was the question.

It was safe to assume that Sony probably, if not certainly, didn't like this guy's blunt, straightforward, and honest talk and sharing of things with constructive criticism. Shouldn't he ask or say something without countering? What are the ways ahead, and which can this man cooperate with? Wasn't Babu like that? And these can be self-chosen ways. Let something good be happening.

Thresyamma did not call or say anything about the wedding. Sony didn't call either. Babychan said that he was told to inform me.

They thought of me; that was good and enough. Otherwise, who am I - a person destined to do charity for them when necessary?

I couldn't go to Sony's wedding. There was an audit fixed two or three months ago and given to me, and it could not have been postponed even if I had thought about it.

Everyone in the family attended, and I learned the wedding was well done. Maya lived comfortably as Soni's beloved wife and Thresyamma's beloved daughter-in-law for a few days.

Even before the compensation case was settled, it was reported that Saju was more interested in working in Delhi and had learned to live independently. He informed his uncles of his desire to get married, and they sought and arranged his marriage. We were also invited to attend. We went, and everything went on smoothly. Icy Saju, who worked in a hospital in Delhi, is a good girl. They rented a house in Delhi and were in contact with Vakachan and Kuriachan. They gave him the necessary cooperation he needed. When Icy Saju gave birth to a baby boy, Saju took Thressamma to Delhi for childcare. When I went to Delhi, I visited them. The presence of Thressamma at home to look after the child helped Saju do his housekeeping work in WIPRO and Icy her work in the hospital more carefully.

Soni and Maya first came to Bangalore to see us in Bangalore after having a baby – Adam - born to them. They came and stayed only for two days and spent their time together happily. Being happy is more important than being successful.

They didn't want to go to tourist attractions, shopping malls, or the metro while sightseeing in Bangalore; they didn't want to go anywhere. If the older people went with anyone, including the young couple, they would attend the church first. Although our wedding gift to the couple was delayed, Leelamma gave them some amount for their expenditure. They went back happily. Before leaving, I gave Maya my old serviceable laptop and asked her to use it.

I told Soni that if he plans to start any business, job, or venture, think seriously about it and do hard work to succeed.

"I will help you up to rupees one lakh; if you need more, there are institutions like banks that give loans. You can avail them." Sony replied neither in the affirmative nor in the negative. I saw only a blank look as if I had nothing to do with his future! I did not dare to encourage him further.

Suppose the younger ones are less responsive and do not show enthusiasm. In that case, ordinary elders must consider that the youth have much bigger dreams and are looking forward to someone spreading the red carpet on the pathways of life to welcome them.

I remember seeing a Facebook picture of Sony walking along the edge of a paddy field with a red carpet tied to a fishing rod with rope and looking forward to 'Moscow.' It would have been better for him not to participate in violent politics like Periya's.

# 107

# Limited compensation

Advocate Karthikeyan said the case would be coming to an end. The lawyer asked the three who filed the suit to appear. At that time, Thresyamma was in Delhi with Saju. Then I called Sony, took him from Coimbatore to Tirupur, and appeared in court. The judge has asked him nothing. Karthikeyan said he was doing everything he could to wind up the case. Then, when there was no information for a year, I sent a postal order and sought an answer from the court under the RTI Act. One month later, I received the news that the case was decided. After the insurance company has paid the court four lakhs of rupees and interest, the court will hand over the cash to Thresyamma through the advocate.

When inquired, the lawyer said that he was seeking an appeal in the High Court and that if he did so, he would get more compensation and would have to pay the lawyer rupees one lakh in cash for the costs in the High Court and to deliver the enhanced compensation by the judge in the High Court.

I discussed this with Raju and Babychan. There was no difference between their opinion and mine. Nothing can compensate for Babu's life. More compensation will be given to the family by the Almighty God above. What the judge gave here was enough, and no appeal must be filed in the High Court. Karthikeyan did not like that decision.

As Karthikeyan informed me -the insurer took six months to pay the amount in court. By then, the lawyers' strike in the courts of Tamil Nadu had begun, and it took another six months to end. Did they pay the money to the court? When will the court disburse it to you? When I asked the lawyer, he said it was utterly unfair to ask such questions!

The advocate finally said that if we paid the lawyer's fee of one lakh rupees, he could take the money from the court and give it to Thresyamma. The Tamilian lawyer disagreed with deducting the lawyer's fee from the compensation amount and giving the rest to Thresyamma. In that bargain, another six months went by. Then, with Raju's help, Thresyamma and Soni got the cheque from the court after paying the lawyer. Despite paying one lakh rupees to the lawyer, they were happy to have received more than four lakhs in hand. Although it was a small amount, I did not inquire how much was received or how it was spent. Neither did they have the courtesy to inform me. No one needs to remember the hardships many have undergone for years to get the meagre compensation, ultimately for Babu's family's welfare. All others have done their duty. I expected only this much - that an Office for the Dead (Cheriya Opppisu) prayed at the grave of our beloved Babu after the Holy Qurbana for Babu. If it had been communicated to me as such, I could have been contented and overwhelmed with happiness, thinking that a struggle for justice had ended satisfactorily. I decided to wait for the appropriate communication time whenever I remembered this.

As a tree grows and blossoms, every branch and leaf turns towards the sunlight to fuel cellular activities. Similarly, each of us must find our sunlight, the ways and means of life, for ourselves as we grow. That is the law of nature, and it is not right to wait for anyone. As much as possible, do not accept anyone's sympathy and generosity.

After a year, Sony was interested in going abroad. Someone told him that if he paid an agent rupees six lakh, he could get a seasonal fruit picking job somewhere in Portugal (5 degrees C) with a monthly salary of 40,000 rupees (550 Euros)'. He had attached a copy of the letter.

Nothing was written to comment or advise him to accept the offer. So, I requested Raju to advise him suitably. I knew he would do it better than I did!

After some time, I learned that Soni was in charge of the store in one of the Kerala tourism houseboats, and sometimes he went to work there. Farming work also started soon. It was a relief to know that his work for democratic and national progress, like flag hoisting, got him at least a meagre income to run his family.

Saju and Icy flew to Delhi after coming to Bangalore after their marriage. Saju and IC had their baby, Joel, born in Delhi, and the baptism was held in Punnapra. We could attend the function.

Saju and Icy started looking after the family responsibly. Thresyamma was lucky enough to watch Joel grow up. While Thresyamma stayed home looking after the baby, Saju and Icy went to work. They should have considered it, booked a residential flat in Delhi, and paid the advance.

Thresyamma, who could run around the countryside, meet people, and do Kudumbashree activities, could not endure living in Delhi and a closed-door house outside the state for more than a year, along with various illnesses. After going to the hospital for ailments, scanning and x-rays were taken once, and it was discovered that a cyst had formed near her spine. It was like an injury that caused spine pain requiring surgical treatment. The pain did not go away despite the medication. Saju took Thresyamma home in Kerala for the operation if necessary after further tests were conducted.

Thresyamma was examined at Kim's Hospital, Kochi; she underwent surgery and was successfully treated. Babu's children and siblings managed the necessary hospital expenses of around two lakhs of rupees. She recovered well, lived with Soni, and was thought to have almost recovered her health. After the illness and extensive treatment, Thresyamma appeared to have a symptom like depression, perhaps due to loneliness and worry. She was taken to Chethipuzha Hospital, and the treatment was continued there. Staying nearby, Raju and Babychan were always ready to help.

After a year, when the flat was completed, he paid the remaining money and acquired the flat. Saju said that he wanted help from me by lending him two lakh rupees on the condition that he would return it without much delay. The money was given to encourage the person who cared for the family with responsibility. He has yet to return the money even after five years. I have no such expectations or hopes. I would not have written this with concerns if I got his telephone call once after that.

Remembering Babu, I prayed for the peace of his soul.

I wish everyone a Merry Christmas and a Happy New Year. After a long time, I spoke to Thresyamma on the phone. I heard Thresyamma; she was pleased and healthy and spoke lovingly. Thresyamma was also there to celebrate Christmas with Soni and Maya. I happily told her I would visit her when I visit the native next time.

After a few months, Sony called me one day. He quit his job on the houseboat. He was also giving up his career in the cooperative organisation, which he got for carrying a red- flag. Amazon, a multinational company, was hiring for a warehouse in Poland, and Sony got a selection. He was preparing to go soon after he got the ticket and visa.

Well, he has found himself a job of his choice. Saju was instructed to pay Euros equivalent to Rs 50000/-, which Soni said must be held as a reserve in his hands. I was informed that Saju paid the amount to Soni before he departed from Kochi. I wanted to let them know that brotherly love should be expressed when necessary; that was my intention. I was happy that Babu's children worked cooperatively and cared for their mother.

Mothers have a special affection and care for their daughters. It is correct to assume that it is the same in any community. It is like women's interest to wear and keep gold ornaments. Most mothers wish to give at least the gold that they always thought was theirs only to their daughters, out of the wealth they will leave behind in this world when they become eligible for the next world without writing a will or telling anyone in particular. In the Christian families of Travancore, when mothers die, their minnu (thali) is deposited by some family members in the treasury box of the church. Achayans would take the appropriate decision and implement it if they were alive. If a lot of gold ornaments have been earned, their sharing has sometimes been the cause of great conflict among the children.

No one told me that my mother had earmarked any of these jewellery, particularly for any of her grandchildren I could remember. No one even mentioned that such was Ammachi's wish. No one dared to discuss such a topic and had any suggestions. However, I heard the comment that 'someone desired to keep it 'for memory' or 'someone did rightly deserve at least an iota of it.'

Someone kept it, believing he would do what was needed in due time. After attending Saju's wedding, the brothers and sisters were together on the day we returned to Bangalore. There were ten to sixteen grams altogether, just a small chain, a ring, and an ear stud. How do we distribute it? I saw it as a minor problem to satisfy every lady member of the family. I have to find a solution to the problem myself. No one was ready to say anything after gathering everyone and asking for their opinion.

I did not forget any responsibility in this matter. Ammachi's jewellery was handed over to her only beloved daughter. To avoid leaving any discontent or resentment among the ladies, 'the responsible for distribution' himself handed over a small amount to each, saying that it was the share of Ammachi's jewellery that Ammachi gives to her daughters-in-law. May everyone remember Ammachi's love.

After five years of married life, Nita left her job at Leela Palace. She joined Christ University's Hotel Management Department as a teaching staff. As a result of the encouragement of the college, Nita joined the postgraduate course in Hotel Management at Annamalai University, Puthussery. Over time, she thought she could study and write the exam. Nita wanted to learn, thinking it would help her progress, and continued teaching at Christ College. She also received Sam's full support.

The same professor who taught Nita went to Leela Palace, met her, and advised her to accept a job in the college. She found that teaching in the college gave her more leisure time when she considered shift work at the hotel and childcare after returning home. That's how Nita joined Christ College. More responsible, punctual, and consistent - after two years of hard work, Nita passed the exams and earned a master's degree. She could walk with other teachers in the college as a Member of the Faculty. It was an achievement that most people had not achieved after their marriage.

The Sam-Nita couple's second child, my first grandson, Steven, Natasha's little brother, was born on July 12, 2006. He was the first male offspring of the younger generation at the same hospital where Natasha was born and in the presence of the couple's parents

# 108

# Where Is Natasha?

Sam, Nita, Natasha, and I went to Chennai for the betrothal ceremony of Jay, the daughter of Xavier and Gracy. The ceremony was held in Chennai at San Thome Church, officially known as St Thomas Cathedral Basilica.

There was a reservation on the Lalbagh Express for us to return to Bangalore. Fifteen minutes before the train left, we arrived at the station and sat in the designated seat on the train. With her baby - called Sunnu (Steven), Nita sat in the reserved seat, and Nita's mommy was in the near middle seat. Sam got down on the platform with three-and-a-half-year-old Natasha, saying we still had time before the train left. Sam was a tea lover and had tasted tea on the railway platform. I also inadvertently watched people rushing in and boarding the train.

It was just five minutes before the train left the station. Where is Natasha? , I requested Sam to hold her hands and board the train. Where are Sam and Natasha?

"She was here, Daddy. Let me see."

I got on the train, looked all over the compartment, got off, and walked back and forth on the platform, worried about not seeing Natasha. Seeing Sam, he, too, was running back and forth in panic.

I ran from the front engine of the train backward, from the fourth compartment to the twentieth compartment, but could not find Natasha. Darkness entered my eyes.

"Daddy Sam has gone there. Daddy, don't worry, I can look at this part," Nita said, walking towards the engine.

"Daddy, if you see Natasha, call me," Sam ran to the side of Central Station. I ran after him but looked around and could not even see where Sam had gone in an attempt to run forward without hitting people walking on the platform.

I was shocked and frightened and ran out of the Chennai Central Station, thinking someone might have taken my baby. I looked at the taxi and rickshaw stands. My body was exhausted, and I cried as if my head had exploded. With only one or two minutes left for the train to leave the train, I somehow managed to pull away as if I was unable to get back on my feet. I dragged my feet around with a heavy load on his legs.

More weight was on the mind. I felt like I would fall with my heartbeat, but it did not slow down. I turned around and ran, "Natasha.. .." I was calling Natasha out loud without making any sound.

Leelamma asked from the door in the fourth compartment- "Where is Natasha? The train is leaving. Where is Sam?"

I haven't seen anyone, and people were looking at me! People stared at me for no reason.

I ran towards the engine. Suddenly, I saw Nita walking with Natasha on her shoulder. Nita and Natasha both were crying. Sam was just behind and said -

"Daddy, someone has taken her, and when I saw him, he was going towards the engine with the baby on his shoulder." Nita narrated the incident. "Natasha called me and cried loudly and called "Mommy.." I went and stretched out my hands, and the baby jumped into my hands, and the man walked away hurriedly somewhere. With the baby, when I came, Sam came running, looked at me, Natasha came running, called, "Daddy..," and hugged Sam. We did not see where that man went.

My eyes and mind went up to the highest like my mother used to raise her eyes and face to the heavens. I had never experienced so much anxiety, mental anguish, and distress.

The pain in my legs was there until I woke up the next day. The pain in my heart has not yet subsided.

I was shocked to remember, in a flash, what happened in my neighbourhood at Maramkunnil forty years ago. Appachan's first child, playing in the courtyard, suddenly fell into the water on the south side of the field and was found dead after everyone in the house lost sight of the child. I feared that it was about to repeat here. Thank God it has not been repeated here. We got the child back from the wrong hands. What would have happened if Nita had been late for a minute to walk up to the engine side? It took hours for me to regain my balance, and I did not fall; I was lucky that I had been sitting comfortably on a moving train.

I hugged Natasha, kissed her on the cheeks, hugged her, patted her on the head, and cried.... That baby didn't know anything. Natasha hugged Ammachi, taking in the heat of her breath and the rapid beating of her heart. Natasha also cried as she pressed her face to her upper body.

After a few days, Nita learned that there was an attempt to run away with Natasha by the maid at home, and a faithful Bihari boy named Laltan, who was in Sam's house, rescued the baby and brought her back. Laltan saw the maid carrying the baby on her shoulder and calling someone to arrive. The girl went away without coming back home. It was only after one more day that it was realised that the girl had stolen Nita's five and a half sovereigns of gold from the dressing table - gold ornaments such as necklaces and earrings. Nita's carelessness may have caused the loss of the jewellery, but Sam forgave the carelessness as well.

Like the silverware 'gifted' by the generous bishop to Jean Valjean in Victor Hugo's French historical novel (Les Misérables), Sam did not set out on an investigation to add the stolen gold to the maid's wages.

A series of untimely departures continued in the family over the years. It was a sad experience when Kochupapan's eldest son, Bevan Antony, passed away on July 31, 2008. Bevan was teaching civil engineering in Carmel. His daughter - Nissi - lived in Ireland with her family and was a nurse. Baven's sons - Nirmal and Nijo - were studying.

For Baven, it was a continuous battle against his disease. Then, he was fine for about six to seven months. I met him at Sahrudaya Hospital at Alleppey the day before his death. For Bevan's soul to have eternal peace, Babychan recited the farewell prayer, "Jesus, have mercy on me; Jesus, Mary, Joseph, be with my soul" into Bevan's ears. I was praying with him. It was so painful for me to say goodbye to him silently, after which we returned to Bangalore.

Bevan's departure was a cause of great sadness for Kochupapan and Chitamma, who were old and suffering from various ailments. Their younger son Mammachan stayed in Mumbai until his wife's job at the Reserve Bank of India ended. Therefore, Kochupappan and Chitamma spent nearly four and a half years under the care of their daughters and blended their lives with illnesses, treatments, and rest. When Chitamma was bedridden, Kochupappan was always there to help her with all her daily routines. On 08 Mar 2013, when Chittamma left for her heavenly abode, Kochuppappan was left alone.

# 109

# Set Out For Enhanced Services

I started studying for IAQG's AATT exam. Tony paid the course fee of Rs 2 lakh, and the study notes for the 20-day course came through the Internet. After passing the online exam, you must attend the contact classes for four days. I could pass the online exam with 90% marks. Since there were eight students from Bangalore, two instructors came to Bangalore and taught us for four days. On the fifth day, we passed the online examinations in two subjects for two hours each: (a) Knowledge and (b) Application with at least 80% marks for a pass in each subject. The wrong answers had negative marks, so the exams could be passed if we knew 90% of the subjects correctly for each examination. The results came the next day. I passed the tests of knowledge. In the examination of the applications, my score was reduced by two percent, and, therefore, I failed. If you wish to re-appear for the exam, you must pay an additional rupees twenty thousand. I got a month off to study further. With all this money, forty years of work experience, knowledge and personal practices for auditing (Ref ISO 19011: 2011), rules, and more, I have decided that there was no backing down anymore! My confidence increased.

I stayed in Mohali the day before the exam with my friend. Gp. Capt. (Retd) Anand, a sardarji. Anand's wife served me Roti/ Chapati (Indian bread) and lassi) In the morning, she sat nearby and shared her son's educational experiences in the United States. She also mentioned special thanks for the 'Banana Chips' sent by Leelamma to her.

The result came on the second day after the examination. I crossed the hurdle and won on the second attempt. Once again, I am a globally recognized aerospace experienced auditor. All I had to do was to renew my approval every three years. All the doors of the aerospace industry were opened to me. All I had to do was to go there and audit when they called me. The clients, whoever invites us, would bear travel visas and expenses.

Leelamma asked - "Can I come with you?"

"Of course, you must stay at the hotel on the audit days. We can see nature, sites, and other creatures for the rest of the days. I can bear all the expenses."

"If you go to Singapore, you can go to Seema; if you go west, you can go to Tony."

"Yes, we shall; get ready."

Although I left my former colleague's private business, I received a call from another world-renowned firm saying I would be offered a job soon. Two or three months later, I received a call from another two or three major certification bodies with branches in India. Through five certification bodies, the opportunity to audit many countries, including India and many industrial establishments, has become possible for me.

It would have been appropriate for me to work independently and on a contract basis without being a regular employee of any organization. Their call to audit anywhere in the world could be accepted or rejected at my convenience. It's not like working 9 - 5 x 25 days for a monthly salary like I did before retirement. Continuing that way was difficult, and personal time to spend otherwise beneficially would become scarce. Alternatively, suppose I work independently on a contract basis for only ten days a month. In that case, we can set aside what would be sufficient for my use, leisure, and entertainment for the rest of the days. The terms and conditions I adopted and those prescribed by the institutions were similar. Doing the work diligently and legally and enjoying it was most suited. We choose jobs that make us happy. It was rare to do so after joining a government institution for post-retirement employment or entering a private institution.

Two of my younger brothers have been doing auditing work for a long time. They may ask someone close to them whether 'auditing' was a traditional family skill. We have a lot that we should have traditionally got (legacy). Still, we have not just got a job as a newspaper distributor. As was the case in the family, the man in charge of everything decided to achieve diversity instead of one profession of farming or fishing. Like unity in diversity, three brothers are auditors in a branch of the original family! We loved the job and enjoyed it. I got invitations coming from five different institutions. I could accept or reject the job according to my convenience. I have received all offers and am prescribing the same terms and conditions. The auditing job rules and guidelines were the same everywhere, avoiding difficulties. I must do the duties that I only have to perform. Since the dates were planned for two to three months ahead, small changes could be discussed and agreed. I followed the other terms and conditions by complying with the auditing rules. Instead of handling too many standards for auditing, I followed only Aviation, Space, and Defence standards as the single Master where I had the maximum experience. Instead of being a "Jack of all trades, master of none," I thought it was better to be the Master of One and (be the T-shaped person). Anyway, There are too many Jacks around for various other trades!

From 2010 to 2020, I visited ten countries, such as Dubai, England, Japan, Malaysia, Saudi Arabia, Scotland, Singapore, Sri Lanka, and Thailand, for an Aerospace audit. I visited Vietnam and Myanmar for Aerospace standard training. Only in Japan did someone from the local branch of the auditing firm help me translate their language into English. He translated what I was asking in English into Japanese. After hearing the answer in Japanese, he told me the same in English.

The English language was sufficient in all other places. I went to all the places twice or more, and I went to Singapore and England more than six times for Auditing.

I have been a member of the audit team led by Brazilian, German, Indian, Polish, Swiss, Chinese, UK, and USA auditors in some audits. At other times, all those auditors were members of my team.

I went to Israel from the Bangalore office while in service. I went to Nepal on my own without a visa. I took a 20-minute bus ride from Gorakhpur along with Rajasekharan of HAL, walked across the border, bought a tracksuit for Tony at a Nepali shop, and returned. That was in 1992. The border between the countries had extensive barbed wire fencing and security gates on both sides with their respective national flags. Between the high fences of the two countries with the security gates, there was a barren stretch of land, ten to fifteen meters wide, that was 'no man's land,' not belonging to either country.

While in service, I went to Nepal and Israel and left the Bangalore office. In private, without a visa to Nepal, I travelled 20 minutes by bus from Gorakhpur, walked across the border, bought a tracksuit for Tony from a Nepali shop, and walked back. That was in 1992. There are large fences and security gates on both sides of the border between the countries and the national flag of the respective country. Fifteen meters wide barren area between the walls of both countries and the security gates located on the road - no man's land. 'No-Man's Land' was meant to prevent people from jumping the fences from one country to the other. Security did not check whether the visa was available or not, as the entry and exits were for a concise duration.

Audit or training days are scheduled two to three months in advance, and all the logistics arrangements and preparations will begin, with the certification bodies or the beneficiaries doing just that. Accordingly, travel, accommodation, and audits will be confirmed as planned, and return home will be confirmed. Submitting the report a few days after the audits was sufficient. Information travels through computers and the internet everywhere. The post office and postal services were never used.

Auditors must be within the premises of the industry for a minimum of eight hours doing audits. The rest of the day will be spent travelling, staying in a hotel, or preparing a report. There was no time to travel alone, see the sights, or visit any tourist attractions. It was mandatory not to accept anyone's generosity, hospitality, or gift. Then, you can remember the pictures, people, and landscapes you see along the way and capture the scenes on your mobile in the places you are permitted to visit. They will always provide the guests with good food in a friendly and loving environment.

Along with booking accommodation at hotels, there was always a variety of breakfasts offered at no extra cost. We could eat at any mall or restaurant with completely diverse cuisine and flavours for dinner. Communication has always been convenient as mobile phones and the internet have been used since 2006.

After the audit, I could freely visit my children in England and Singapore, visit tourist attractions, and share love with my grandchildren. Being there with them in their life circumstances was possible at least four or five times.

# 110

# Proposals For Seema

Seema registered her name on the Chavara Matrimony website, initiating marriage negotiations. Seema was often asked to describe the features and qualities she expected in her 'would-be fiance.' Still, we received no specific response from her. Seema realised that it was always good to communicate with her parents, as she had learned from both earlier experiences. We responded by adding several candidates to the weekly shortlist, hoping it would be a relationship that suited us. Suddenly, it appeared that the expatriate girls did not get a positive response from the natives. The boys living in the native doing agriculture or work do not get a favourable reaction from the expatriate girls. This generation is very different from the older generation. Any decision would be taken if they had the confidence to know everything. A good family reputation, an economic environment for a comfortable living, and excellent educational qualifications are the reasons for a favourable decision, especially for well-educated, post-graduate girls waiting for a suitable groom. Seema also had a defined opinion on the matter. That's right. That is why Seema checked out what was coming for her without going in search of anyone, without her knowledge or consent.

There were two or three telephone calls from the native place. When we asked about work experience, kinship, or workplace, we realised it did not suit us. The conversation will be closed by saying you can move on to the rest of the matter after letting us know.

A man from Kottayam, Kakkanad, Ernakulam, called and said that his son - who had given his photo and information to Chavara

Matrimony and a software engineer - came on leave from the United States. He wanted to come to Bangalore and see Seema. We welcomed them to come and visit and agreed that it was convenient for us at any time.

The so-called Achayan from Kottayam and his wife came to see Seema. We spoke. They returned, and the next day, his son came. He took Seema to KFC in Indiranagar, drank coffee, walked around, and returned to Kochi. Two hours later, I went to Indiranagar and brought Seema back. For example, at the end of the formal job interview, the American boy went away after saying, "We'll let you know."

The next day, Kottayam Achayan called and said –

"We are ready for further procedures, but before that, we would like to know…." For a moment, I listened without saying anything. He continued.

"You need to specify what you will give to your daughter."

I said, "I'll give what I have to give to my daughter, and I do not think there's no need for a bargain to convince you of that right now."

The city living, the so-called civilized, middle-class mindset, Kottayam (Kakkanad) Achayan may not have liked it; I knew that.

"Okay, I'll let you know in a week. Or call me back a week later. Let me talk to my son." He put the phone down.

Did I say something outrageous to cause his disliking? Did he ask me for the price of his son without discussing the matter with him?

My old illness of sudden anger, I felt it woke up again. I remembered what Ramaswamy once said. "Fathers with daughters should not get angry at all." He had no daughters. Yet, he was not an angry man. His sayings were soft and subtle but assertive. Nobody could deny that, too.

After ten days, I tried to forgive and forget the rudeness I heard to welcome any good news. When I phoned and inquired about the current status, the reply I received made me feel that it was not necessary to ask at all -

'If you were not informed within a week, you should have understood that we were uninterested'!

I presumed that he was only too greedy for money, even in his old age!

I read it somewhere later - I can't remember where it was. However, the concept was remembered. It went roughly like this-

"When you get angry and shout, you have conceded the defeat. An intelligent person sleeps peacefully without thinking much about the subject. When you get angry, the decision you make can often go wrong. You are not insulted when you swallow your selfishness and ego. When someone says, "No, it's not possible," many other avenues open up for you."

I was waiting again for Seema's marriage proposals. There were indications that a proposal was coming from Singapore.

Santosh was one of the founding leaders of Jesus' Youth. His wife, Biji, was an Attorney (Lawyer) for a Singapore-based company and one of the founding directors of Camino Asia, a company founded and run by Santosh. Biji's Malayalee parents lived in Bangalore. E John Thomas retired from the railway service. He has a son, Vinod, who worked in London. There, he pursued a degree in chartered accountancy. Biji and Santhosh met Seema at a Jesus Youth prayer meeting. Biji persuaded her parents in Bangalore to propose Seema for her brother Vinod.

E John Thomas came with his wife to meet us. I was seeing them for the first time. They have not seen Seema. Vinod has not met Seema in person, and Seema has not seen Vinod in London. Some traits of E. John Thomas was similar to me in terms of physical features. Due to the Travancore culture, I was careful to call someone at least two years older than me an 'Achayan.' He did not deny it. We decided to let our children meet each other and express their opinions. They returned happily.

According to his comments, Tony found Vinod, investigated things, and encouraged Seema to go to London. Seema went to London. She also did not expect the opportunity to go to Tony to be a significant turning point in her life. However, the chance to meet and get to know everyone saw each other as a gift from Jesus through the organization Jesus Youth, a blessing for Seema to find a life partner. The fact that Vinod was also actively involved in the organization complemented each other.

The parents' unassuming, innocent comments about their children often give listeners a true sense of their family life- The sense that both parents and children live happily in fear of God and stand firmly on the ground. What else was needed for the two families to agree to an alliance? Leelamma's parents and my parents had a similar conviction. The Almighty should have already reserved such relationships for good people. It will happen in time. And they will join together with great singleness of mind.

Subsequently, everything was so quick. It was decided that the wedding would occur before December, when everyone would take a vacation. Accordingly, everyone came. Although we were often together for various communications, there was no room for disagreement, no curiosity about jewellery or money, no ambiguity like "what to give," and no confusion about where to go, when, and who to lead. Because of this mutual understanding, Achayan got the liberty to ask me at least some money for the wedding expenses only for the groom, and I gladly agreed and gave it.

Seema was always careful and took the time to choose her favourite things from a group. That's why some time was spent on jewellery like necklaces and the design and selection of her wedding dress. Even if one heard that she took more time than her siblings to choose a life partner, Seema has no complaints.

Vinod and Seema married on November 22, 2009, at the Resurrection Church in Indiranagar.

About six hundred people from the offices, relatives, friends, and colleagues from either side attended the grand ceremony.

The reception and dinner were held at DRDO Community Hall, CV Raman Nagar. Sam had arranged for a team to prepare the dinner and serve it. The Sam-Tony partnership organised, presented, and distributed the food. Looking back, I thought the primary responsibilities were neatly wrapped up, and I didn't see anything special to highlight.

I'm looking forward to more critical responsibilities rather than looking straight ahead.

While walking among friends, shoulder to shoulder, shaking hands, we also got a share of the appreciation from the newlyweds. After doing the same greetings two or three times, looking at the faces of those friends, I could see the lack of familiarity on their faces a bit. That's when it caught on - Vinod's daddy and Seema's daddy were of the same height and similar walk. They wore identical glasses and dresses, had similar bald heads and grey moustaches, and aged and looked alike. There was no external difference between them!

Someone might have also said, 'Their beauty was indescribable. '

After marriage, Vinod and Seema moved to London. While Seema could continue working if she returned to Singapore, Vinod completed his MBA in Financial Services and sought a better job in London. Vinod completed his studies but had to wait longer for a better job. After moving to Singapore, Vinod temporarily worked for Santosh's company. Seema was a biomedical engineer (Thomson Medical Center, in Singapore). Seema soon accepted a better job as a field service engineer at GE Healthcare. She worked for two years (2010-2012), travelling on the Metro with engineering tools in her handbag, visiting hospitals, and serving there. Vinod worked as a senior business consultant at Santosh's Camino Asia. They rented one of the flats in Toa Payao and stayed there. Seema soon achieved her status as a permanent resident of Singapore.

# 111

# Completed Desires

Natasha has the reputation of being my first granddaughter. My second granddaughter, Amelia, was born in London on February 22, 2010. With the anxiety and excitement of being a father for the first time, Tony got information from the hospital every few hours. I read Tony's "An Expectant Father," a short story he wrote in his eighth standard. How comparable his anxieties then and his anxieties today!

"I sat there for twenty minutes thinking about what to do next. I got up and walked down the hallway. I did not know why I was doing that. I came back and sat there again. My father looked at me from the hallway and smiled. I thought it was good that he was smiling." He's not going to be a father for the first time."

"I was excited when the young bride told me about an impending guest."

A story begins like that.

"Congratulations, Mr Thomas. Here you are, a healthy baby boy! That is how the story ends.

Twenty-two years later, when the story was significant, and the dream in mind came true, the only thing born was that 'boy' became 'girl.' Both are the same: dream and reality! Isn't the very existence of this universe a recurrence of such situations?

Joysy's parents had already arrived in London for postpartum care. Only after they returned did we have the opportunity to go to London.

I was waiting to collect my visa and ticket. The weather in London was good for late spring and early summer. Trees and flowers were flowering during the monsoon. The hottest, sunniest days provide the best natural beauty, ideal days for sightseeing and travelling. What could be more special than being with Amelia these days, other than the privilege of having the rest of her elderly parents get the rest of their lives?

London was full of parks, gardens, museums, science and technology viewing bungalows, and long farms outside the city, all clean and tidy. The streets were clean and neat, with no vendors and few passers-by. There were no carts or hawkers on the road.

Tony also planned to visit the Vatican in Rome, Italy - with four-month-old Amelia and her grandparents. Tony wrote to bring a Schengen visa (Europe) to facilitate that.

In 2010, Tony and his family lived on the third floor of a multi-story building on the banks of the River Thames. We were there in May and June. The view towards the river was good. Ships and tourist boats were found floating. The water level in the river rose and fell about eight to ten meters -high tides and low tides -which was good fun to watch.

Walking along the river in the evenings was an excellent experience. You can reach the other side by walking through the tunnel at the bottom of the river. Looking at the river from there was another specialty. The wind was blowing so hard that we seemed to be heading back quickly.

We spent two months in London. Then there was the ten-day Italy-Rome, Vatican tour, accommodation wherever we reached, culinary from various countries along the way, a pass to a board for the recreational pilgrimage facilities, etc. Tony had made all the arrangements.

Despite all the good sights and experiences that could be found in the Vatican, there was still so much left to see - the world-famous, we had the sight and blessings of the Pope. We viewed Michelangelo's immortal paintings in the Sistine Chapel. The marble sculpture of Pieta, created by Michelangelo during the Renaissance, was an indescribable beauty of the statue. My experience was that no matter how long we looked at St. Peter's Basilica in the Vatican, we were still in the presence of God. Sculptures, tombs, and classic paintings could be seen all over the area in the capital of the Christian Church. It was a three-hour bus ride from Rome Airport to the Basilica of Saint Francis of Assisi in Umbria, Italy. The tomb of the saint was in the lower basilica. There was another church on top of the hill. We visited both and returned to Rome.

Back in London, once again, in the National Gallery in Trafalgar Square, We visited the Museum of Art, where we spent a whole day looking at so many paintings that we could not finish viewing. Nearby was the National Portrait Gallery. We got off early with a smart card, and most of our trips to see the sights were by tube train.

We first visited London in June 2007. We came back in September. We saw the same thing back again.

At the end of June 2018, I went to Spirit Aero Systems, Scotland, UK, for a week's audit.

Tony told me that if I got off at Heathrow Airport on my way back, Tony would come and pick me up. I had a package for Tony; I took it with the luggage.

Usually, when Tony and his family travel from Bangalore to London, they pack lemon rice, fried fish, and mango pickles. When parents go on summer vacation to stay with Tony, they also prepare the same and take it. This time, there was only an audit for a week, going alone, and there was only a packet of green mango pickles to carry. Other perishables, if taken, might be damaged as they would reach Tony a week later.

While going to Scotland, after landing in Glasgow, I took a taxi to the hotel. I stayed at a hotel in Prestwick, 60 km away. My team lead was Lars-Mikael Johansson from Switzerland. After a week's audit there, in preparation for the return, I took out my suitcase and laid it down on the bed to stack the clothes without bending my back too much. Nothing should have gone wrong; the seal was the same on the bottles. Then I saw the packed bottles and lids were intact, well sealed as they were after packing. The four new banyans, kept in the suitcase without being used, looked like a folded red flag, soaked in the red-colored oil and Kashmiri chilli powder. Surprisingly, I saw cut pieces of green mango in the bottle, like the scooped-out Anchovy fish from the fish basket to the bottle!

After packing, I put down the suitcase and saw that my bed was like a red flag. I pulled out and folded the bedspread safely under the bed, checked out from the hotel, and left the place safely!

I only spent three days (July 2018) with the kids in London (# 1 Church Drive, North Harrow). All those days, Tony and Joysy were on vacation and caring for me at home.

Tony tried hard to wash away the banyan's oil and the red colour but failed. When dry, the bunion became like a saffron dress. If it were torn, it would have been thrown in the garbage. So I returned it to my suitcase and took it home without Tony seeing it!

Occasionally, I repeat the story of 'Uncle Podger Hangs a Picture' by Jerome K. Jerome!

In 2012, I went to Japan while Leelamma was under the care of Seema-Vinod in Singapore. It took 11 hours for a direct flight to London from Bangalore and 8 hours from Singapore to Narita (Japan). Both times, I travelled to Japan on an Air Bus. A 380 double-decker aircraft could carry 850 passengers at a time and flew at 1,000 kmph speed. Airbus A 380 has a wingspan of 80 meters. The journey was pleasant. The days in Japan were freezing, rainy, and foggy. I couldn't see anything beyond

50 meters. The audit was conducted at an engineering company in Narita's industrial estate. They machined turbine blades for high-efficiency Mitsubishi Power Generation gas turbines there. The efficiency and quality of the company were reported in the audit report.

On a holiday between audit days, a Japanese girl, Miss Ayako Mizuno, took me to a nearby Buddhist temple (Narita-san, Shinshō-Ji Temple). It was a 10-minute drive from Narita on an electric train on a private Japanese railway that ran efficiently and on time.

I saw ancient sculptures, pagodas in the typical Japanese style of architecture, and a giant Buddha statue in the temple. When we came down from the temple, there was a drizzle. Mizuno bought me a green Japanese polythene umbrella. I bought tendons with deep-fried shrimp from a small restaurant there for lunch. This classic Japanese one-bowl dish contains oily seafood or steamed vegetables, a delicious combination of tempura (shrimp deep fry) and donburi rice - hence the tendon. One of the most popular ingredients for tendon is large shrimp. Shrimp dipped in cornflour and fried in oil. It tasted good.

While eating at the hotel one evening, I saw a man sitting near the shop's door, grabbing a living freshwater stinging catfish from a large barrel and splitting it in the middle. Without removing the head and tail of the fish, it was peeled and salted, soya sauce was added, fried on a plate, and given to someone to eat.

While having breakfast at the hotel in the morning, I saw someone at the nearby table take sashimi (freshly caught salmon fish cut into thin slices), wrapped with rice balls, held with chopsticks, and put it into his mouth. That was the local diet. I thought I would try one, but I didn't eat it because of laziness or fear of where to go in case of food poisoning. Whom can I say that I got sick after eating sashimi in Japan?

April 03, 2013: Good news from Singapore. Seema became the mother of a baby girl. The baby was named Sarah, which means 'princess'. No wonder the Jesus Youth couple gave their firstborn girl a good name in the Bible with joy and happiness. The monarchy changed, but the children remained the princess and the prince. Parents need not be so-called, but they were always the queen and the king.

Seema's mommy had already arrived in Singapore for postpartum care. The mother and baby were cared for, which continued for a month.

Leelamma had to return from Singapore to solve an emergency at home. The husband had finished all the curries she had prepared for his use. And her poor husband did not like to go to a hotel for lunch or dinner!

Leelamma went alone to Singapore again for the child's baptism. She had announced that if she got a visa and ticket for any foreign travel, Leelamma could boldly travel alone as many times as she wanted. She returned with her husband, who had gone to audit in Thailand and travelled through Singapore en route to India. Sarakutty's baptism was on June 15, 2013, at the Church of Christ the King, Ang Mo Kio. Following the baptism, lunch was served in the church hall for all guests and those involved in the ceremony.

Tony Seema and their family did not come to India for Christmas in December of that year because they had already visited in August 2012. It was also almost time for Joysy to give birth to her second child.

The Tony-Joysy couple's second daughter - Eleanor Thomas, was born on December 27, 2013. Joysy's parents had already reached London for child care this time too. Amelia's baptism was performed in Chennai, so the baptism of her younger sister (Eleanor) was scheduled to take place at St. Jude Church in Bangalore. It was held on August 17, 2014. The granddaughter became a Christian on her grandmother's birthday. All relatives were present for the ceremony. Lunch was served in the church hall.

# 112

# Let not Maternal Relations Break

After Ammachi's departure to her heavenly abode in December 2006, the depth and intimacy of Ammachi's Arakkal family siblings and their children - (my cousins) became less and less intimate. It was not without desire. Each was busy devoting their full time and resources to fulfilling their duties and life's commitment.

Let me pick up the strings of my relationship with my mother's siblings and their children in Kainakari. It will help me join the scattered ends of the string together. Much gratitude and love must be given for the cooperation and love they have given me in my life's journey.

The eldest of my maternal uncles, Valyachayan (A J Varghese 01 May 1984), who lived in Kochi, left this world very early. The aunt lived in Kochi with her daughter (Molly). Now and then, when I was passing through Kochi, I thought I should go and meet her.

Once, when I was in Kochi, I learned that Ammini had come and taken her mother to the hospital. That day, I saw my aunty at the hospital premises. After the exchange of a few words of courtesy, I returned.

About her other children - I will know if I see them directly, even their names - Molly, Bina, Kunjachan (Kuryan), Anto- I think they are - I don't remember. As Kunjunju said - "We all need to build bridges so that you can go there and he can come here."

If you happen to see them, Bina and her husband come and talk directly.

Part 1 stated that my aunty and Kochachan (AJ Job) lived in Delhi with their children. Appachi, their eldest son (AJ Joseph), served in the Military Engineering Service at Pune, Agra, and Ranchi. We were there when his wedding took place in Kochi. Tracy was born after that while they were in Agra. Once on our way to Delhi, we landed in Agra and received his hospitality from my cousin.

When Appachi left the service, he went to Delhi, met his parents, and, with their permission, came to Kochi and settled down. Their only daughter, Tracy, was married off when she completed her education. Appachi acquired a weakness from service and became a liability by habit. One day at home, his foot slipped, and he suffered a brain injury and was treated at the Naval Base Hospital for three to four months. After bringing him home, when I went and saw him, his body was not moving; even though his eyes were not open, his eyes were getting wet, and his lips were twitching. People who were talking from nearby were recognised. Jhansi was helpless.

One day, Appachi left, leaving all his relatives in deep sorrow. (May 14, 2006). Together with his playmate, Kadamattuthara George of Kainakari, I attended Appachi's funeral.

Jhansi became lonely and helpless. After Tracy had finished her studies, she got a job. When Tracy married Sajan Varghese in 2007, Jhansi gave her house in Kochi to Tracy. She ended her solitary life when an ex-serviceman from Chengannur married her.

Kochachan left his wife and children and went to his heavenly home on August 13, 2003. All the children were married and living in Delhi, and only Joji remained in Kochi. Kochachan's body was buried in a cemetery in Delhi itself. When I visited Delhi for an audit, I went to the graveyard and prayed there. The funeral of Philomena, James' wife (Checkkidikadu), was also in the same cemetery.

Vakachan sought relocation from GREF and came to Delhi to work for UPSC. Vakachan's wife, Celine, was in another office.

They have two sons. Vakachan continued to work in the same office after his retirement. He stayed in Delhi. After their studies, Tomichan, Boban, and Binoy worked for NDTV. Over time, they searched, found, and worked for better organisations. Everyone got married and had children. It was difficult for me to accurately tell everyone's names and study status because they stayed at different locations in Delhi, and I could not see them together anywhere. Aunty continued to stay with Tomichan. She stayed with Boban and Benoy for a few days each, but going up the stairs to the house of different children who lived upstairs became difficult for Aunty. A few months ago, Leelamma and I stayed at Vakkachan's house and visited everyone in their homes. I last visited Delhi to see my aunty and all her children in October 2019. On that day, Aunty had a separate room with a TV to watch Holy Mass. She participated in prayers and was able to live without many ailments. I found them very happy when I went to Tomichan's house. The aunty told me that when Tony came to Delhi a few days ago, he went with Binoy and met the aunty. Binoy left NDTV, pursued further studies in reputed institutions, and earned a good name and reputation in the visual media. Binoy got married in Kochi.

We attended his wedding ceremony solemnised by the Archbishop in the Cathedral Church. At that time, Binoy was a media representative in the Catholic Bishops Conference of India. Dr. Manmohan Singh appointed him as a Media Rep in the PM's office when he was the Prime Minister - a political appointment for a specific cause and period. After the elections, when Manmohan Singh's cabinet was dissolved, Binoy had to vacate that political appointment.

One of their sisters, Thankamma, got a job, married, and lived in Delhi. Another sister, Mariamma, worked at the US Embassy in Delhi. After marriage, she left her life due to some personal problem.

Rosamma, the youngest, joined the monastery and became a nun after her $10^{th}$ standard in school. Recently, I heard that she (Sr.Roja) was serving in a school adjacent to the nunnery, which specially cared for and taught autistic children. When she heard about her eldest brother Appachi, I saw tears dropping from her eyes when we were together for some function in Kochi.

I visited Thankamma's house in Delhi just before her elder daughter's betrothal ceremony. Vakachan helped take me to his siblings' houses.

Kunjommachayan, a permanent resident of Kumbalangi in Kochi, was an uncle I was happy to visit and inquire about his welfare occasionally. No matter who walked in, Aunty was just as loving. When Seema was in Thrikkakara College, she used to go there occasionally. Their eldest son, Shajan, completed his education and got a job in Cambodia and Vietnam at a trading company that exported spices. After completing her studies, Sheeba, their daughter, got a job at a school in Kochi. Sheeba was married to Varghese (Palliyan) and had two children.

Shajan was married to Kochurani, a school teacher. They have two daughters, both of whom were well-educated. They went to Shajan's workplace in Vietnam during the school holidays and returned when the school re-opened. That was before the coronavirus epidemic broke out.

Kunjommachayan has been hospitalized from time to time due to his illness. Shajan was on leave while admitted to the Lake-Shore Hospital in Kochi. At the same time, Thambichan was also admitted to Like Shore Hospital after a stroke. Thambichan was brought there for further specialist treatment from the Thiruvalla Hospital, where he was first treated. After a month of medication and therapy in the intensive care unit, his physical ailments improved, but his speech was not completely restored. Later, he went home from the hospital, hoping to recover through physiotherapy. Over time, he regained much of his capability to speak.

Kunjommachayan also recovered and returned home. Leelamma and I went to see them when they were both in the same hospital at the same time. When we saw them, Kunjunju came down from Nashik to see his elder brother, Kunjommachayan.

Kunjommachayan fell ill again and was bedridden. Aunty and Shajan took care of him in the hospital, day and night alternately. On October 15, 2015, Kunjommachayan passed away. I attended the funeral. Fr Thomas Thekkethala, CMI, was the priest who led the funeral Mass and liturgy service. Most of the relatives also came.

Kochurani, Aunty, and her grandchildren spent the days with the memories of Kunjommachayan. Shajan had gone back to his workplace. When I called Aunty on the fifth anniversary of Kunjommachayan's death, which fell during the days of restriction due to the epidemic, she said, "This was how the days went on. I saw the Qurbana on YouTube earlier in the day and prayed. It's hard for me to walk to church in the morning...... Today, we had 'palappam' and meat curry here for breakfast."

My youngest uncle is Kunjunju; many others call him Kunchacko, and he is only three years older than me. He lived in Nashik with his family after retiring from the army.

Part 1 described the heroic stories I knew before Kunjunju joined the army. After his wedding, Kochachan and his family moved to Kochi from Kainakari, and the Arackal house and backyard in Kainakari were sold out. Since then, I have never been to that area or heard anyone talk about the place. I had seen some of Arackal's neighbours, like George Kutty (in Pune), Baby Panavalli (in Mumbai), and Babu Chakkanad (in Kanpur). Chakkanad Babu now lives in Paravur, Punnapra, close to IMS Church.

The Kunjunju's wedding became a milestone that separated the former and later periods. That night after Kunjunju's wedding, our four cousins – Joy, Appachy, James, and me –slept together in my maternal grandfather's room on a mat. I wrote that history in the earlier part. The good memories are not forgotten yet. About a week later, the marriages of Leelamma and myself were arranged with the Ottathyckal family members, the first marriages of the next generation.

Kunjunju got married and went back to the army camp with Aunty. He must have got quarters to live there as a family. When Kunjujun got two months' leave from the army, he became more and more in a dilemma, realising that even though there were many houses of his brothers in Kerala, there was no place for him to stay even for a month with complete freedom - it was not a lack of love. Still, the fact was that none of the brother's houses had enough facilities for that. He used to go to Aunty's house in Perumthuruthi and then return after finishing the leave. When he got a posting at ASC Center, Deolali, near Nashik, after many years, he thought about where to live permanently after retiring from the army. That was how he bought a house and settled down in Nashik. By that time, they had two children, both boys, namely Manoj and Vinod.

There was no close contact with family members. At the same time, they were fully engaged in their life commitments, like children's education, work, marriage, etc. Manoj got a job in Hyderabad, got married, and lived in Hyderabad. Vinod joined the Army service and worked for 15 years. Meanwhile, he married, had two children, retired from service, came to Nashik to live with his parents, and did some small business.

It is written about Ammachi's elder sister (Peramma) and her family, who migrated to Kattappana and Thovala in Part 1. I Wrote about Vakkachi and Ammini. Later, their brothers and sisters, such as Thankamma, Joskutty, and Johnny, were born. They later came to Nedumkandam from Thovala. Ammini was married to Vakkachan, and they lived in Nedumkandam. Their daily work involved the cultivation of rubber, cardamom, black pepper, and tapioca. They resided in Kattappana and Chempalam areas. Sunnychan who came to Bangalore is Ammini's son. (Late) Fr. Jomy Chakkalathara CMI was the son of Johnny. Shiji James, the daughter of Thankamma, got some education, a job, and married.

About Shiji, yes, she was the one who came to our Vaisyambhagom home to help Ammachi and study in the seventh standard at a nearby school. Today, she has a job in a cooperative bank and has two children studying in college in Bangalore.

Sunnichan told us that Shiji's two children, Unni and Juby Maria, were learning in Bangalore. Once, Shiji and his family came to visit our house in Bangalore. After that, Unni and a friend came on a bike on a Sunday. At that time, Unni and his friend transplanted the young shoots of Leelamma Aunty's 'passion fruit' plant, watered and fertilized it, and the vines were made to grow straight.

In the restless race of life's commitments, Perappan, Peramma, and their children, Vakkachi and Josekutty, all were lost to the country, time, and their family members. I met them when I was less than ten years old. I was not lucky enough to see them again for some time. Johnny was sighted in the middle of my mother's funeral, and later, I saw him in Chekidikad for my (Elayamma's) mother's sister's funeral. I learned from Johnny that his son Jomi was a religious studies student. Jomi's younger brother Robin was doing some business in Delhi.

When we met, Shiji said Johnny was now on the path of devotion, had attended all the meditations in Pota, and was a good family man. "His son, the priest, had recited the New Qurbana and later returned to Nagpur. Johnny now has no drinking habits and lousy company like before." Well, wishing the family would not have the experience of his elders, I was relieved.

One and a half months before Seema's wedding, I had sent a letter and card inviting everyone in that family. Maybe just after getting it, Johnny made a phone call to me. It was what Johnny told me in a shallow voice. He was in some significant financial trouble at that time.

"If possible, you should help me by giving me fifty thousand rupees. I will pay it back within a year".

I was in a dilemma. Every resource was being collected to meet the expenses for Seema's wedding. How could I tell Johnny that I would not be able to fulfill all my responsibilities if I gave Johnny a loan? Will anyone believe me? All of a sudden, when there was no give and take until then, and when there was a significant expenditure already planned, and it could not be postponed for a year, how could I say, "A cousin one day asked me for a loan, and I gave it"? Was that much money set aside to be paid immediately or not?

"Johnny, let this wedding be over; some money will come by then. If you say that you need it now, tomorrow, or this week, it won't happen."

"... I have no other option "... I don't know if the phone fell or was suddenly put down! The conversation ended there.

Less than 36 hours later, Sunnichan called and said, "Uncle, Johnny committed suicide. They'll say something about what happened only after the post-mortem."

'I could have prevented Johnny's death.' It was a regret I had for a while. He must have had financial difficulties. After his son became a priest, I was told he started living well.

I first met Fr. Jomi when I went to James's residence for Jenny's wedding.

It was not the first time Fr. Jomi heard such a thing. Later, it came to know that some financial mafia had caught and threatened Johnny. He succumbed to the threats of the disruptive forces.

# 113

# The Book Release

In fifteen years, I have visited over 200 business establishments for audit, consultancy, and training, and I have been able to give them one thousand five hundred days of my life. Many people have been unable to do it, especially after retiring from government service. Not just giving them days but also giving them so much intellectual information about quality systems and assurance procedures. Thus, auditing and training added value to their business processes and helped them achieve their goals. They had accepted more than a thousand days of audit reports submitted to the IAQG. Certificates were issued, approved, and retained by the industry.

Teaching started in 1968 at CME. I had only a handful of teaching notes I had prepared as a remnant of teaching Refrigeration and Air Conditioning to graduate, diploma students in the military, and other veterans for over ten years. The notes were brought to Bangalore from Pune. Everything was codified and collected to make a good book. After giving as much time as possible to the excellent running of the family and the flights, the rest of the time was no longer available. There is no need for any other example of how much knowledge and training can be lost without maintenance. Along with the old newspapers, the bundle of notes went to rebirth.

The first book was easy to compile. I have written articles for the Indian Air Force 'Flight Safety' magazine since 2005. Many readers liked the pieces, which included real-life incidents, inaccuracies in the proper operation and maintenance of aircraft, causation, and lessons learned from experiencing such incidents. Until my retirement in 2006, I published seven articles. The Air Force had asked for the articles to be sent even after my retirement. I wrote for two to three years more. I wrote several essays and papers presented at the seminars and compiled the twenty articles into a book. With all the technical articles, Tony was the one who helped me to give the book the shape of a flower bouquet of goodness by combining elements that captivate the readers throughout. He also published a 'Kindle version' of the book on Amazon. My friend, PP Thomas, printed 1000 copies for readers in India. So, I published my first book in 2010 called 'Safety Follows Where Quality Leads.' The printed copies were almost sold out. The Kindle version is still being bought by people all over the world.

'Safety Follows Where Quality Leads' is my service story. New technical knowledge gained during the effort to ensure the quality of aircraft, mistakes that led to accidents, new methods to prevent accidents and thus ensure safety, previous precautions, technical matters that no one knew much about before but must be put into practice, lessons learned, which if kept alone would be lost, but if imparted, would be of great benefit in the field of technology. All these things have been collected and summarized as much as possible.

When my business friends discovered that I was about to publish my service story, they came up with how to help me. Others accepted a friend's suggestion. Instead of paying the total cost of printing the book, let everyone interested spend a small amount. The author acknowledges their collaboration by publishing a full-page advertisement of their industry on the book's last pages. I could not ignore the excellent suggestion. Those are the advertisements that appear on the last eleven pages of the book.

The second book was inspired by a friend. I was most humbled by the feedback from one of the listeners to their superiors about the intellectual information I imparted during the training days. I felt it was excellent inspirational feedback.

This is what he said -

"This teacher has given us about fifty pages of the subject notes. He spoke about 500 pages of intellectual matter and holds about five thousand pages of right information and knowledge on his head."

Knowledge of five thousand pages in my head? It was a piece of new knowledge for me. Those words were an inspiration to explore it. I wondered how I would dig it. I don't think anyone would invite me to talk about five thousand pages. Or will it not be limited to a class of fifty people even if someone asks me to speak? Why would I not be satisfied by writing it down? Writing like that would be good if I could give to the community that loved me the interest I could give back.

Of course, registering in conjunction with real experiences can be an asset for readers who are technically working extensively, like talking in simple classroom language. Maybe I have a valuable experience that can be passed on to the aerospace community as a legacy. The thought finally worked. Ten years of teaching experience, thirty years of working experience, and a state-of-the-art, world-renowned, quality management system audited after retiring from active service all add to writing a book. Thirty Years of work experience, incorporating the lessons of knowledge that can be imitated, is a book that gives them an understanding of the quality management system that has been adopted by the world and implemented by significant institutions but has not become popular in the industrial sector. No such book has been published in any language in India. A book codified in a way that helps businesses put it into practice, using my consultancy strategy and principles - "minimum documentation, maximum understanding, 100% compliance".

What is meant by legacy - heritage. Treasure may have been given orally or verbally by the great masters of antiquity, or it may have been gold buried in the ground in a clay pot. It is a precious treasure anyway.

Since I have no store of good deeds, no treasure chest, no mass support, no glitter of power, no jewellery box of wealth, no gold or legal rights of large properties, no name, no glory to leave behind in this world for future generations, I want to leave as a legacy, a 'heritage ' including all the good services I have done and written for the country, in the belief that it will be helpful to someone someday. These will provide some valuable information to the existing industry and interested parties.

More than half of the second book was written after nearly five years of experience in auditing. When authentically written with information and experiences, five thousand pages were memorized, filtered, abbreviated, and could be printed into a seven-hundred-page book.

When I approached some publishing houses to print and distribute the technical / management book, they decided that the author's royalty could be only 15% of the sale proceeds. Upfront 50% royalty for distribution through self-publishing, with printing costs paid in advance by the author. If the book is printed as published and self-distributed, like my first book, the revenue may be more than 50 percent. Taking up distribution as a side job when there was no other work to do was a pleasant pastime. That was how I commissioned PP Thomas himself to print the second book. Permission to start a book publishing house - Thomas Orchard Publishers - and the ISBN (International Standard Book Number) for new books has been applied to GOVERNMENT OF INDIA, Ministry of Human Resources Development, New Delhi office. It was all a fascinating new experience.

Tony had already bought the copyright of the 39-page international standard to include in the book for reference. As per my request, it was purchased from the original publishers of the standard, www.sae.org, costing rupees two and a half lakhs. The book "A Complete Guide to Implement AS 9100 C" was released on 06 Aug 2012. The book launch was conducted by Padma Shri NR Mohanty, former chairman of HAL, in the presence of my family members and many invited dignitaries at the HAL Management Academy. Shri Mohanty performed the launch function by handing over a copy of the book to HAL Director (Quality) Sudhir Kumar. Air Cmde. (Retd.) Joseph Varkey delivered the felicitation address. All the dignitaries were presented with a bound hardcover copy of the book. The news of the book's release came in the Malayala Manorama and Kerala Kaumudi dailies. The headline of the news was 'ഭാരതീയ വായുസേനയ്ക്കു കുട്ടനാട്ടുകാരന്റെ സംഭാവന' (Kuttanadu person's contribution to Indian Air Force).

At the launch, NR Mohanty, HAL Chairman (Retd), said, "Quality Management System is a method and discipline that helps us perform our daily activities properly, accomplish our daily tasks, and achieve our goals. This book has unique features - unique expertise, real-world experience, easy-to-use formats, and long-lasting relevance. The author is an experienced professional auditor, master teacher, and trainer, and the book is a treasure trove of knowledge at the guide's fingertips. It applies to all industrial enterprises, including aircraft manufacturing."

A room in the house was full, with a thousand copies printed, and while writing this, only ten or twenty copies of the books remained.

# 114

# Birthday And Book 3 Launch

My children and grandchildren all came together to attend the launch of my second book in August 2012. The last time we stayed in Alappuzha was for the celebrations of Ottathaikkal Ammachi's ninetieth birthday. While returning, we could not stay back to watch the famous Nehru Trophy boat race in Alappuzha. Tony had expressed his interest in watching the boat race at least once at any time. There was a reason for that -

The Boat Race was an annual fair on the River Thames in London. Along with the 2012 London Olympics, Kuttanad's (chundan) snake boats were present for the first time in the River Thames Boat Games that year. It was introduced as a unique attraction. It must have been his interest in seeing the world-famous Nehru Trophy Boat Race at Alappuzha, where the (chundan) snake Boat Race is the main attraction in the boat race held every year on the second Saturday of August. Tony decided to visit the boat race this time while going to Alappuzha. It's Tony's usual practice to have a handful of trips and special events in mind when planning a tour, which is just as important as booking the tickets for the journey.

It was not unusual for Tony and Seema to go on vacation with their families in August. They usually come during the Christmas and New Year holidays. They would run to their parents once or more every year. As the children grew up and started going to school, coming home on vacation became closer to their school holidays. Summer vacation in the UK was from August to September. In Singapore, it was as in India, in April-May. They would consult before deciding on a break in India at any time. "Are you coming here, or should we come there?" "Let's go to Bangalore together for a few days with Mommy and Daddy - what if?"

It is better to plan all the trips together and have the events attended well in advance. As important as booking the tickets for the journey, a few things needed to be done soon after deciding the vacation dates. Now, all travel arrangements are being made through the Internet conveniently, quickly, and reliably.

Tony and his family came to Chennai with tickets to return to London from there. So, he came to Bangalore after visiting Chennai.

For the first time in August, there have been reasons for coming on holiday, perhaps not likely to be repeated. The events scheduled for August were the release of my second book and an essential milestone in Leelamma's life. It was more important than publishing books.

Book launch was on August 06, 2012, 17th August, Leelamma's sixtieth birthday!

Mommy's 60th birthday? No. Tony will not agree. At 39, he refused to see her increasing age. Same thing twenty years later!

"No, you are not of that age, Mommy. You don't look like that ...."

On the morning of the 17th of August, we went to church and prayed, cutting the cake at home and sharing it with all, and Tony repeated the same. The family had lunch at Leela Palace, the highest quality luxury hotel in Bangalore, and wished mommy a long and healthy life. We were at the Leela Palace for the first time. A bouquet of 60 red roses prepared by her children and grandchildren was presented to Leelamma by the chief concierge of the Leela Palace, Nita's professional friend. We all got together and presented a bouquet of congratulations.

We stepped into the world of opulence and luxury and enjoyed a variety of delicacies for three hours –

"It's not about what you eat; it's about how you eat," someone said again.

I did not remember anyone's birthday being celebrated in our family, Kannattumadom. No one has ever noticed such a special day. They have not even told us about Achayan and Ammachi's birthdays. On our birthday, my mother made some special delicacies. One's birth might not have been seen as a special event in the family, but these could not be seen as regular events for others in everyday life.

But can parents see their children's birthdays like that? Maybe that's why, in our family, there was always something special about the children's birthdays if they were near to them. When they were away, they allowed us to talk to them on the phone sometime of the day and wish them well. Same with our birthdays. They also showed particular interest in wishing us happy birthdays on our birthdays and many happy returns of the days when the couples became 'one.' Regardless of who belongs to the family, all birthdays, especially birthdays of new-generation members, have evolved into day-long celebrations. You can't call your grandkids and kiss them on their foreheads; you can't take a piece of cake from their hands and taste it. No matter how far away, we can celebrate by seeing in person (an achievement given by science!), experiencing, sharing, singing, wishing, and filling our hearts with joy. It was comforting to think everyone was around when you were having lunch on your birthday.

Being with them on birthdays, milestones in their parent's lives, and having lunch at least close by is a lot of fun for all children and great satisfaction for parents. Mommy's sixtieth birthday was similar to what happened on Daddy's seventieth birthday.

This five-star hotel ensured the safety and well-being of the guests while enforcing strict hygiene standards and the guests experiencing the beauty of the surroundings. So Leelamma and the children celebrated to have a marvellous and unforgettable experience. Today, in an environment with luxury amenities that were seldom accessible, it has become a lifelong experience that would probably be remembered for a lifetime!

Thomas Orchard Publishers was the publisher of the book 'Manassu Thalarathe,' which contained three short novels by Kochuppappan. The book was added with ISBN and printed by PP Thomas. He wrote the first novel in Malayalam at the age of 92. Before publication, he longed to see the book, which contained some of his autobiographical memories published. I could think in favour. I accepted it as a small thank-you note and gift I could give to my uncle, who benefitted me in many ways.

Rs. Forty Thousand was the expenditure.

"My dear, how can I return it to you?" Kochuppappan used to say that many times.

"No matter, I replied that I had received that amount and more, but Kochuppappan did not believe it. No one would ever believe it."

"How did you get it, and who gave it to you?" Nobody ever inquired.

# 115

# Release of Novel at Ninety

Local MLA Shri G. Sudhakaran came to Punnapra Church on February 20, 2016, and released Kochuppappan's book. The church vicar, some writers from the neighborhood, and family members were in attendance.

Tony congratulated his 'English Valyachan' by giving him a Sheaffer fountain pen. He was so happy and - this is what he told me.

"Special thanks to Tony. I've longed to see a pen like this since I started college. I got it at this age. How far is it possible for me to write something? God bless you both."

When the book was released, Kochupappan observed his parent's memorial day. The Divine Sacrifice was offered and prayed. Adjacent to St. Gregorios Church Punnapra is St. Joseph Poor Home. Lunch was served to more than two hundred senior citizens of the Poor Home. I was lucky enough to be there in the afternoon and participated in it.

In the novel by Kochupapan, in a context of psychological conflict, the protagonist's mother gives the protagonist advice, which elevates the platonic romantic story to a lofty and sublime level.

I tried to remember the connection between the mother's memorial service and the book release.

I arrived in Thiruvananthapuram from Bangalore the previous day to participate in a seminar held there at the invitation of ISRO. Fifty years ago, when ISRO launched the first Rohini RH 75 rocket (Nov

20, 1967), I was working in that organisation. After receiving their hospitality, I stayed at the guest house for the night after the speech. I came to Alappuzha by train the next day.

As a publisher, I praised the novelist KT ANTONY and his novel at the book launch, almost like this.

"Dear friends,

The first person who asked me to give a public speech was Shri PN Panicker, the father of the library movement in Kuttanad. Antony Sir built a good cultural institution in our village under the guidance and leadership of Panicker Sir. The release of three short novels, including one written in the background of establishing our library, occurred today.

Today, it suits everyone who loves the Malayalam language and literature. Let us be delighted and proud.

Antony sir has always been at the forefront of social welfare activities in this region. He has worked for the upliftment of Carmel College since its establishment. After retirement from work, he was in more busy service - in his seventies and eighties. You can tell imaginative stories with humaneness and love in your heart. A good language style will motivate you to write. Age creates no limitations except physically going out, running, and having fun.

When I met him two years ago, I learned that Antony sir was writing stories at ninety. That day, he gave me the manuscript and asked me to read it. I started reading.

I found it all familiar: environments, place, time, language, etc.

There was a time in the 1950s when some considered love stories a sin.

As I read more, I felt nostalgia somewhere, like the library's history. I grew up reading the dialogue I'm familiar with, some of the characters we are familiar with, some of the story contexts, some of the passages we've gone through, some of the vibrations of the mind, a little of the humour, a little of the annoyance - the works of art, the good writings must be like that - all of these can be found in Anthony sir's work, a memory of studying novel literature. Although we only remember part of the story, we remember some moments and sentences with good results. For example

"ഹൃദയത്തിൽ ദൈവത്തിന്റെ കയ്യൊപ്പുള്ള ഒരാൾ " *("One who has the signature of God in his heart")*

"പച്ചിലകൊണ്ട് തുന്നിച്ചേർത്ത ജനിമൃതികളുടെ കൂട് വിട്ടു"....*("Left the nest of mortals stitched with green leaves"...)*

"ബസ്സു വരാനായി രവി കാത്തുകിടന്നു" *("Ravi was waiting for the bus to come.")*

*Don't you remember that conversation we read just a call away from here -*

"എൻ്റെ അച്ചേ വള്ളോം വലേം മേടിക്കാനെക്കൊണ്ടു പോവ്വാണല്ലോ "...*("My Ache is going to get a fishing boat and net.")*

*Although it should not be compared, I could see similar sentences and dialogues in Antony sir's book.*

"ജോണീ, അടുക്കളെച്ചെന്നു പറണോന്നു ഒരു ചക്കര ഇങ്ങെടുത്തേ -"*("Johnny, go to the kitchen and get a piece of jaggery from the thattu.")*

It's a simple story that starts like that.- A simple platonic love story.

The story moves around the ordinary people of the village.

The story smells of life without any tremendous literary synonyms, without blaming anyone, without villains. Three Short Stories That Can Happen - In English, Novellas -

Stories of young people: Love usually starts in adolescence.

Like a calmly flowing river, a good climax. An even better anti-climax.

After writing a small review and handing it back to him along with the script, I said-

"It's the dialogue style of a play - we have to see if it suits the novel."

Antony Sir replied.

"I will correct everything. I want to see this published. Then, the style of the play is my style of writing."

I thought - how good it is to have one's writing style - isn't that the writer's pride? And the main factor that distinguishes good writing.

My father was a journalist. He became a journalist because of his younger brother, Anthony Sir. I have also written some notes, press releases, and articles. I understand the author's desire to publish and see writings satisfying the mind.

When Antony Sir expressed his desire to see the manuscript published as a book, I felt the need to try it.

I approached several publishers.

"If it was written by people past 90, and it was also the first work, today's generation would not relish it." It was also not commercially acceptable to them. I did not understand the answer if a 40-year-old wrote it- please send it. Did it mean those who have experienced romantic success or frustration?

They knew that not even the creator could change the author's age from Ninety to forty.

By then, I had already published two books on aircraft in my technical field. I also used my wealth of experience to publish this book.

Literary works and works of art should be friendly and heart-warming. So, I'm sure you will buy and read this book. Read the whole thing and comment. Respect the writer, the creator. Please accept this book; It is written to entertain you, even when the writer is in the torment of his age.

I wish the author all the best. I hope this ceremony inspires more good writing. I guarantee that everything you write will be published.

Thank you, and greetings to all who have come here to felicitate Antony, Sir. Wishing with love and respect."

During those times, James often visited his children in Bangalore. James' children, Jeffy and Jenny, completed their education and got jobs in Bangalore. James retired from the Department of Meteorology, sold his DDA flat in Delhi, and bought a site with a constructed house in Changanassery. Philo died of an illness three or four years before James retired. Philo was James's good life partner. Whenever I went to Delhi for office work and stayed with James, both sincerely loved me like I was his elder brother. Philo wanted to come to Bangalore and spend time with Chechi. But Philo's wish came true for a short time without coming to Bangalore.

Leelamma went to Delhi and met Philo for a few days and ministered to her, saying, "Let me go and sit by her side for a while before death carries Philo away." ("മരണമെത്തുന്ന നേരത്ത് നീയെന്റെ അരികിൽ ഇത്തിരി നേരം ഇരിക്കണേ"- *Rafeeq Ahmed).*

I went to Delhi thinking it would relieve James a little when the funeral was held in Delhi after Philo departed. The sad news came at the end of the first day of the four-day continuous audit in Bangalore. I had to take leave and withdraw from the audit of the subsequent days. I reached RK Puram by taking the Delhi flight in the morning, attending the funeral ceremonies, and returning. It was not easy to comfort James. How could anyone bear the sadness of having one's children who just completed their studies and were about to join their work, dream of getting them married, and desire to be with them in their lives as support and shade? No one could comfort him. That longing caused great sadness even for his mother.

However, his siblings showed an indifferent attitude towards James, making it more difficult for him to bear the loss. From the time he came to live in Changanassery, the attitude shown to James by his two younger brothers, especially the priest Tomichan, was beyond his tolerance. The giving and taking of ancestral property, house, money, disrespect for elders, resentment, ill-will, etc., might be among the causes, so the family relationship among siblings was shaken and disturbed.

When James came to Bangalore, he often visited us. We exchanged pleasantries. Jeffy's marriage was arranged in Bangalore. Jeffy and his wife worked in the software industry. They lived in a flat in Whitefield. Jenny's marriage was conducted in Changanassery. James's relatives supported Jeffy and Jenny's weddings well. Unfortunately, only two of his brothers continued their non-cooperation with James. Someone else tried to restore peace by interfering in their family affairs but to no avail, as no one was willing to compromise their positions.

Did one of James's brothers suspect even my long-standing relationship with James was a conspiracy against his interests? Or maybe it was a lack of understanding. If not for lack of love, then why did James's brother physically prevent their mother from attending the wedding of her granddaughter Jenny? It was not correct at all.

Praying for the marriage of that motherless granddaughter, I saw his mother with James' request to bless and send the girl away from her son's house while leaving for the church. James had failed earlier and returned, and the adventure I felt when he shared that grief with me brought me to his mother. Elayamma was very interested in coming with me to James's house, and she said so.

It doesn't matter that I was trivialised. But a so-called brother, wearing his dhoti folded up as a sign of disrespect and his head shaking like a buffalo, was standing beside his mother, wringing his hands to stop me. It wasn't easy to appreciate the value and virtue of the human relations such people provide.

"If you take her ...let me see how you do it..." He challenged.

"But, mone, How can I, .. Am I not lying in his shadow, so much feeble me ... living here? If I go without his permission, then what will happen? I don't know... Mone, you go away, it does not matter". Elayamma pleaded.

I had to go back that day with Elayamma's permission.

Checkkidikadu Elayamma passed away on July 1, 2017. I rushed to attend her funeral. Her son, the priest, conducted the funeral services. All her children and grandchildren participated in her funeral.

After Elayamma's departure, my desire to go to Checkkidikadu was almost extinguished.

# 116

# Preparations for a Family Reunion

Binoy is the founding leader of a media organisation called Development Channel, started in Delhi, and a youth wing called 'Leaders For Tomorrow' in connection with it. Binoy promoted a Global Advisory Board with other dignitaries, including Tony (Tony's home as the firm's UK office) and Seema (Seema's home as the Singapore office). Whenever Benoy travelled on behalf of the organisation, he visited Tony and Seema. After the devastating floods in the Kuttanad in 2018, books and stationery were distributed free of cost in many schools in the Kuttanad under the auspices of the Youth Wing.

Binoy informed the relatives when Fr. Jomi Chakkalathara fell ill at the Nagpur hospital and his untimely death the next day. He coordinated the arrangements for the repatriation of the body to his hometown. This activity mainly led to the launch of a WhatsApp group by adding the mobile phone numbers of members of the Arackal family and other friends.

While in good health, Kunjommachayan often wanted to take the initiative to start a group of Arackal family members. Though many have settled in different places in the rush of life, many people would have occasionally expressed a desire to be together and revive the family ties. Such family reunions were common in many families that have grown into organisations having periodic reunions.

Binoy made such a suggestion, especially when he started a WhatsApp group of Arackal family members to make communication easier. When the proposal was discussed, I offered my full support, cooperation, and presence in such reunions. It was decided that representatives would meet in Kochi one day to discuss the details with the other family members and to decide the date and venue.

Binoy took on the task of informing everyone. Everyone was told the meeting was scheduled for May 24, 2019, in a rented hall in Kochi. Thirty-three people attended the meeting, made essential decisions, and determined the collective responsibility for the implementation. Decisions taken were indicated as follows: -

a) Tentatively fix the dates for all family members who live and work in different parts of the world to come together: The weekend after Christmas of 2020. The decision on the agenda and implementation will be made later.

b) The two oldest members have been appointed chief patrons.

c) The adult sons and daughters of the Arackal family and their children and grandchildren should be essential members with equal rights.

d) The Governing Council (nine members) shall be a leadership body of equal rank, consisting of the surviving eldest son or daughter and two nominees of each of the seven children of Arackal Appappan & Ammamma. And that each is responsible for the coordination of their family members. Apart from being the two nominees in the Governing Council, Raju and Binoy have been appointed as the coordinator and chief coordinator.

The following were some of the projects that could be started:-

1. Make preparations for the two-day get-together and determine the location

2. Consolidate a digital directory and family history for release on the day of get-together

3. Intervene in any dispute between family members and try to resolve and make peace.

It was decided to come together again with a determination to work towards the overall goal of having a brotherly, harmonious family that shares and cares for each other in love and spirituality.

The last of the essential start-up projects was started right away! Even before the meeting ended, a family member presented a dispute in their family. Some people who knew about the dispute began a special 'dispute resolution and peace attempt' without ensuring that the parties involved were appropriately heard. I thought that 'it was not right to react or make a meaningful decision without learning things' and simply listening to the whole grief from either side. Therefore, I did not respond, especially since the meeting had ended formally and some persons had left. Some thought that I did not respond adequately to anything!

I was worried and seriously doubted that this might be the beginning of the end! The suspicion was soon confirmed.

A few days later, Binoy informed everyone of the above decisions through WhatsApp. Binoy wrote to me separately that most of the decisions made there were not in line with his interest and were unilateral decisions of the chairperson of the meeting (Kunjunju was the chief patron and chairperson, assisted by me), and therefore, everything should be reviewed!

"Mainly a group of people getting together "just somewhere" once in two years, from different parts of the world, without any structure or rules, without defined responsibilities and duties," That was what my brother had in mind!

It seemed pretty strange to me that someone who had learned so much about the news and media and had acquired the ability to observe and resolve democratic and political issues would be reluctant to incorporate democratic values into interpersonal relationships in a family!

I do not know if there were any plans to start. No one discussed anything for over two years, or I wrote this. Those responsible can find an excuse that the cause of the stalemate was the spread of the COVID-19 epidemic and the conditions for maintaining social distance. Did the intellectuals try to see social distancing as an escape route for psychological distancing? In such a case, they might make bad decisions because they lose sight of the bigger picture.

In the absence of organization and periodic mergers, I think it is appropriate to maintain the same interpersonal human relationships as in the past and to communicate by talking, writing, and using any other medium. If the intended progress is not achieved, why not maintain past relationships?

It's quite a coincidence that this is the weekend after Christmas 2020 when the family was scheduled to reunite. It came out early this year and spread nationwide like the ongoing Covid-19. Uncertainties do not end there.

**Maternal family get-together at Kochi (May 2019)**

# 117

# A Lucky Birthday

It is said to be a real blessing when someone lives to the age of seventy. How many total days have passed in my seventy years of life? Twenty-five thousand five hundred and sixty-six days till today, eleven February 2016. That is all for those who live counting the days. By then, most people believe that old age has set in. Some people carry old age on their shoulders long before that, singing and petting them like children! How many more days are left in my life? I don't know. If I knew, I could calculate. Anyway, no worries. Leelamma reminded me that turning seventy was an important milestone.

What was so special about it? I just asked – "I knew you would prepare a more delicious breakfast, but what? That was what I meant" -

"Need to Go to church in the morning. I have paid for saying the mass ". Good, right, we have to say thanks -

"Ithratholam Yahova Sahayichu , Ithratholam Dhaivamenne nadathy

Onnumillaykayil ninnenne uyarthy , Uthratholam Yahova sahayichu" .... ....

I went to church with Leelamma. We came back. Before setting out on a journey, or as you do immediately after return, I folded my hands in front of Sacred Heart and said, "Thank you, O God."

("So much Jehovah has helped, so much God has led me and lifted me out of nothing, so much Jehovah has helped.")

Touched but not touched, so near, I looked at my mistress; what was the wetness in her eyes?

"Ithratholam ….." What will I give you in return for being with me and sharing my life?

It was a spontaneous action, a deep hug, a kiss that touched the hearts. That's enough, for the time being, to fill the day with enthusiasm and energy!

Happy Birthday greetings would come -"Age is just a number, and you prove it in your special ways. You are an inspiration to many people. Everything about you will always be remembered. We all wish you the best. One of the reasons I love family is because someone like you is a part of it. Happy Birthday, Dear Grandpa/Grandma! May your day be filled with love and happiness for the rest of your life." So, each family member will call, tell, and send WhatsApp messages. If on the phone or Zoom, grandchildren will also come, see, and speak.

What to do next? As Tony calls out on things to do on days like this, lunch can be out and about. All of them - children and grandchildren - come together and eat together; when is that possible? Sometimes Sam and Nita will come today; we can go together, Leelam, call them and tell."

"I told her she would come in the morning with the cake. She hasn't come yet. Come on, let me go and make some breakfast -"

I couldn't say or think anything else. I picked up the newspaper and started reading. Breakfast was just around the corner.

I heard the sound of someone opening the gate.

Leelamma exited the kitchen and opened the main door - "Natasha and Sunnu came together."

Nita and Sam came soon after. No one said anything.

Someone was coming -

Behold! See this Sarakutty, like a watchful cat strolling, Seema and Vinod were just behind. My God, have they arrived, too?

I folded the newspaper, got up from the chair, and I did not reach the door -

Seema and Leelamma were staring at the gate - laughing and calling out - and later found out, putting their fingers to their lips: "Don't say anything, Daddy, shouldn't know" signals had already been given to everyone.

No one said anything. Amelia and Nora held their hands behind their backs, moving like rabbits without opening their mouths or making any noise.

There Joysy was coming, oh my God, Tony was coming too! Everyone came in - the grandchildren all came out and burst out laughing, the candle was burning, the loud noise –

"Happy birthday, Achaayan!"

I saw nothing, heard nothing and all my five senses were exhilarated. Unable to say anything, I stood for a long time, excited and in awe. I bowed and accepted the greetings of my grandchildren.

Happy birthday, dear grandpa! Colourful greeting cards - from Natasha, Steven, Amelia, Eleanor, and Sarah. Like the greeting cards that Tony, Nita, and Seema made in their youth, more beautiful, more diverse pictures, and a new generation of colour pictures full of loving regards!

"Mommy, where was I then?" Reuben once asked Seema.

The heart is cold, and the mind is full! They only saw the happiness on my face and the wetness of satisfaction in my eyes. I prayed with all my heart that they would live long, healthy, happy, and with love forever.

The celebrations began. It was four o'clock when we returned after lunch at the five-star hotel - JW Marriott. The festivities continued at home as well. The flight from Singapore arrived one o'clock after midnight, and Sam went to the airport and took Seema and her family to his house. The flight from London arrived in the dawn at half-past five. Sam himself brought Tony and his family too. Nothing was told to surprise me; the children had known everything, were trained, and got ready to give a surprise.

"I was told she would come at eight-thirty - I didn't even know everyone would be together."

'Surprise' brought great, great joy to Leelamma too.

In January 2017, a soft copy of my third book, 'Implement AS 9100 Rev D for Business Excellence', was published with the Amazon Kindle version. Blue Rose Publishers published the hard copy in Delhi. Wg Cdr DP Sabharwal presented the book to Anand Francis of M/s System Control and formally released it at SIATI Hall. Shri Sreelal Sreedhar, GTRE, Shri. Sastry Veluri, Infosys, Shri V Mahalingam, and fifty other engineers were present. It was written when I went to spend the summer of 2016 with my grandchildren in London. It was written quietly on the days when I did not go out for educational and recreational trips. Grandchildren Amelia and Eleanor and their Ammachi provided immense support.

The first draft, writing, development, revision, and incorporation of the latest quality management system were added to eliminate structure duplication. It was a revised form of the second book, and the content was as expected. It was published after a three-month vacation in London. The self-publishing route was decided because the royalties paid by publishers were meagre. It was sufficient to outsource only the right to print and distribute. Blue Rose Publishers in Delhi was ready for it.

They would look for many ways to sell, and Tony was ready to manage the Kindle version. International Standard Book Number (ISBN) has already been obtained. In March 2017, the third book "Implement AS 9100 Rev D for Business Excellence" was released at SIATI Hall by Kevin Beard, President of NQA-USA, Inc., and HAL Ex-Chairman Krishnadas Nair in the presence of family members and special guests. The latest book has been well-received for two to three consecutive years. The Kindle version on Amazon has been sold in many countries, including the United States, Japan, China, and Europe. Many good reviews came in. Almost all the companies and individuals who supported me have bought and used the book. The book was selected and purchased as a textbook for a postgraduate diploma course conducted by HAL Management Academy. I met Mr. Chaturvedi, the Managing Director of Chaturvedi Technologies, who loved me dearly. When he made inquiries, he wanted me to send copies of the book to a dozen of his business acquaintances, including Directors, MDs, and GMs of various aerospace organisations.

They will look for many ways to sell, and Tony was prepared to manage the Kindle version. The International Standard Book Number (ISBN) has already been obtained. In March 2017, the third book, Implement AS 9100 Rev D for Business Excellence, was re-released in SIATI Hall by Kevin Beard, President of NQA-USA, Inc., and former HAL Chairman Krishnadas Nair, in the presence of family and distinguished guests. "Implement AS 9100 Rev D for Business Excellence" Amazon's Kindle version has sold out in many countries, including the United States of America, Japan, China, and Europe. Many good reviews have come. Almost all the companies and individuals who supported me bought and used the book. The book was selected as a textbook for the postgraduate diploma course conducted by the HAL Management Academy. I met Mr Chaturvedi, the Managing Director of M/s Chaturvedi Technologies Ltd, who was always very friendly with me and behaved kindly and pleasantly. I had already presented a complimentary copy of the book to him. While exchanging pleasantries and telling his opinion about my book, he requested me to send copies to his known friends and familiar dignitaries, such as Directors of some Aerospace organisations, CEOs of some companies, MDs, and GMs of others on his behalf.

I gladly took up the mission. After I saw other colleagues and friends in the company when I was about to leave, Mr Chaturvedi handed me an envelope. When I opened it to see what it was, I saw there was a cheque in it, in my name, for Rs. 90,000 / -

"What do you want me to do, Sir?" I politely asked him. He answered, "Nothing. This one is for you for writing and publishing such a wonderful book. I just wanted to thank you for serving the industry, devoting your time and experience, and helping us. I have also made the 10% tax deduction at source for the payment…."

I did not have enough words to thank him, and I thanked the Almighty. When I left, he said that he would see me again soon. After that, the Corona epidemic spread, and my trips suddenly stopped. One day, when I was under the Corona restrictions, his colleague called me from the company office and said - "Chaturvedi sir will not come anymore. He left us to his heavenly abode!" On the death anniversary day and at the same age as his favourite Guru Sri Ramakrishna Paramahamsa (August 16, 2020, 50 years), the Hindu mystic and spiritual leader attained nirvana! It is still a pity not to be able to see him again. He was indeed a generous person!

A great man named Ramaswamy, my mentor, boss, and best friend, passed away when we were with Tony on the banks of the River Thames on a British summer vacation.

Ramaswamy was not only my guru, guide, mentor, and boss for a while in the office. If I say he was an elder brother, it was also inadequate.

I felt sad and shocked when I saw the emails from Mahalingam and Rajnarayanan (08 Aug 2013). Before leaving for London, I went home to see him in person on the thirtieth of the previous month. His son Venky said that he had gone out - to the native place - for two days. I never thought that such sadness would come when I returned disappointed. I sent out a special request to Nita and Sam in Bangalore. "Go and pay your respects; he was the main reason and instrument for your happy married life. Go and pay obeisance and console Aunty and return." I consoled myself that God would answer even if I prayed from London for the departed soul from India!

I remembered. Achayan disembodiedly told me to go to Ramaswami when I was in a sea of troubles and mental agony. I went there. How easy and calm it was to hear everything from him. How could I forget that Ramaswamy gave me the same peace, tranquillity, and courage to decide what Achayan would have given me if he had been alive?

"What is it? Let it be, Let it be done, let it be good, and these are the characteristics of the times. Why should we lose our life and peace against it?"

After hours of not being hungry, having peace of mind, and having coffee, Arimurukku, and laddu, I made one of the most critical decisions. A storm subsided. That serenity was acceptable to those who lived and to Achayan. Ramaswamy was 'capable of controlling the wind and the sea.'

What was the wind? It was a Delhi relocation order, and the wind could calm down within twenty-four hours, which I had written before. I have seen the majesty of being able to calm down any whirlwind only in Ramaswamy.

"Thomas, go home. Nothing will happen!"

The fuss created by the whirlwind slowly subsided, and the environment helped the streamlined flow of the classes in Tony's final year of secondary school.

While climbing hills or mountains, loose stones or snowfalls hinder the movement forward. There will be anchor nylon ropes that support the upper anchor for safety, which are extremely good at absorbing shock loads and have elastic strength. That kind of security and safety has been provided to me by Achayan, Kochupappan, TC Joseph, and Ramaswamy, the incarnations of goodness. TC Joseph and Ramaswamy have shown that genuinely worthwhile work could consistently be recognised in addition to routine compensation. While giving all colleagues equal respect and viewing them with a high level of maturity, they advanced essential matters. They gave a strong justification without running around and grabbing the recognition. I was privileged to live in the contemporary world where I could avail myself of the generosity of these great personalities.

May the departed souls rest in eternal peace.

The last DGAQA veterans annual meeting attended by Ramaswamy was held on December 2, 2012, at Club House (Diamond Box) hall of Karnataka State Cricket Association Stadium on MG Road. Many of the dignitaries who attended that day were older than Ramaswami. All the officers were our colleagues and friends. What all things he had entrusted to me, like to a younger brother to organise the erstwhile Officers of DGAQA settled in Bangalore! Unfortunately, such meetings would no longer be held.

After returning from London, I met Aunty and Venky and talked to them. Ramaswamy was rushed to Manipal Hospital in the morning due to his sudden ill health. He left shortly after arriving at the hospital. Mahalingam and a few other persons were there to help. Funeral services and obsequies were conducted in association with them.

Visiting London and Singapore in alternate years has become a regular event over the last few years. Tony and Seema made the necessary preparations and suggestions well in advance. The planning was done so that if there was a proposal to go to any other country in India itself, there were audits planned, it could be rejected or postponed at my convenience. It takes six weeks to process for a UK and again the same time for a European (Schengen) visa. All the necessary preparations for the UK trip were made. After getting the UK Visa, the time to apply and process for the European Schengen Visa was inadequate, so it was decided that a visa for only the UK would be enough this time. We arrived in London on a Bangalore (BLR) to London (LHR) British Airways flight at the end of April.

All the fun activities were taking Amelia to school, going to the nearest church most days, and walking down Harrow's streets and nearby parks in the evenings. The streets were lined with flowers, trees, houses of various colours, and adjacent, identical dwellings. Outside busy and clean roads, living inside Tony's new home was in a specially built room with wooden flooring. It was nice to put a chair and table in the corner and write on a laptop; it was almost the same routine on days when we did not go out to see the sights. Summer was perfect there; it started in April, but school summer break began in August. The maximum temperature in summer was fifteen-twenty degrees Celsius. On top of that, the people there took off their shirts and pants, limiting their wear to shorts and T-shirts, Sometimes without even a T-shirt!

Ansa and Vineeth lived an hour away. We went to the couple's house at least once a month because Tony loved long drives, and the kids enjoyed the mutual company. While spending the days jubilant like that, I got a message in the morning of one of those days.

That was during the 2016 visit to London, which had to be cut short before completing the vacation. Kunjunjamma Chechi, wife of Kuriachan of Delhi, expired on May 15. She was in one of the best hospitals in Delhi, under the constant care of specialist doctors, for more than a month - with blood sugar, BP, and other associated ailments. In the last few days, she was in a coma in the intensive care unit. Kuriachan and his sons were always nearby. As the funeral was decided to be held at Champakulam church cemetery, I came to Bangalore. I took a connecting flight to Kochi to go to Champakulam. Cherupushpamangalam, the house Kuriachan bought in the name of Davis, was being used as a vacation home. Chechy's body was brought to this riverside

house in Champakulam. After public viewing at home, checky's body was buried in a specially built tomb at the St Mary's Forane Church cemetery. The untimely death of his wife left Kuriachayan deeply shocked and exhausted. After returning to Delhi, life became completely lonely, non-enthusiastic, and heartbroken for Kuriachan.

# 118

# The Demise of Kochuppappan

Kochuppappan stopped writing anything even before his book 'Manassu Thalarathe' (Three Novelettes) was released. He tried writing by holding his pen between the fingers of his right hand and guiding it with his left hand. He stopped writing when he could not keep the pen between his fingers. Then, the debilitating symptoms of old age became more apparent.

The first and last letter Seema received from Kochuppappan was that he wrote directly to Seema before her wedding, expressing his inability to travel and attend her marriage in Bangalore.

This loss of strength in his body was also evident in the letter he wrote to Seema, telling her not to get upset about him for being unable to attend her wedding. It was the spirit of his writing. - The contents of the letters written primarily to Nita in 2001 and Seema in 2009 were almost similar and as follows:- "God will be with you in your life's path. May your fiance be as good a friend and protector as you desire. May he consider you as a treasure."

He wrote me about his health and the letter to Seema, "I saw a doctor - the ECG was not so good, the cholesterol level is high. Milk was also prohibited, and I experienced more than just vulnerability as a patient. I must consider the risks before venturing into travelling. Others also say the same as an obstacle."

With the help of both hands, I took a long time to get this much written. My hands are not strong enough to write that I will not come. Good luck to everyone.

Yours ever loving, Kochuppappan (Signed) "

Kochuppappan was so loving to Tony, Nita, and Seema, and they called him 'English Vallyachan' in return. They always asked for information about his life progress and health conditions.

When Baven and his mother left, Kochuppappan was utterly alone. He felt a lack of freedom when his daughters looked after him. Although Mammachan's wife retired from the Reserve Bank, she was reluctant to come to Punnapra because they had a flat in Mumbai.

"Life is like a rose plant with beautiful roses in it. It is common to have some thorns in between. We must let go of the thorny issue, especially as we move through life." Kochuppappan used to say.

Every time I saw Kochuppappan, he would pluck one or two thorns of his private sorrows, share them with me, and reduce the intensity of his sorrows.

He used to point out the pitfalls and distinguish between the straight and the wrong ways in life. The cruel selfishness of his daughter-in-law kept his grown-up grandchildren so far away from him that he was deeply saddened. Parents love their grandchildren and want to see them and talk occasionally, not for any financial gain, but to increase their life span with closeness, innocent expressions of love, and words. "Is it greedy to expect at least that much in return for the good deeds done for the grandchildren when we were healthy?"- He used to ask.

The father knew very well that the root cause of the alienation was outdated and due to selfishness. Yet, an average generation could not extinguish it. It perhaps would not get eliminated from his mind since someone's selfishness got tied up to it for life, and he survived, and the scar it created was so deep and hidden. He made his own heart lighter by opening up his heart with the condition that no one else should know the primary cause of the pain.

The root cause was certainly loathsome.

I write it here so that no one in my family shall imitate such an unethical way and never search for the guilty.

"You should tell them that I have forgiven," was his last wish. When he shook hands and said goodbye, I could read the sadness in those eyes that I might not get to meet him again.

I learned that the illness worsened. Kochupapan was admitted to Sahrudaya Hospital Alleppey after the plane landed in Dubai for the audit. That night, Kochuppappan departed to the Heavenly Father's home, leaving all of us who loved him in deep sorrow (25 Sep 2016). On my request to Mammachan, the funeral ceremonies were postponed for two days. I returned to Bangalore and went straight from the airport to Punnapra via Kochi. Within an hour of my arrival, Tony also arrived from London to attend his English Valyachan's funeral. Leelamma had reached Punnapra by train a day before.

Funeral services were held in the cemetery of Punnapra Gregorios Church in the presence of a large crowd of priests, college teachers, Carmel Alumni, and parishioners. As a playwright, director, organiser of the library movement, journalist, and college administrator, his involvement in social work has contributed significantly to raising people's living standards. From 1984 until his retirement in 2002, he worked in the development section of the church, spending time on the Catholic Community Service's Comprehensive Development Project, helping to bring compassion and love to humanity.

He enriched Malayalam drama and literature through his literary works despite the hardships of illness. He worked to shine a light of goodness and life improvement on relatives and the community in the bright light of his individual life. He showed me the way to vocational education. He has chosen my life partner and enriched my family life.

We buried Kochupapan in the cemetery ground, and before returning, I prayed at the tomb of my parents. I had a special mention to my father about his younger brother, who was also brought near his elder brother and permanently placed below the earth even though no one recognised the outward appearance or the externalities of the departed souls!

The next day, before returning to Bangalore, the relatives held a condolence meeting at Kochupappa's house after the prayers at the cemetery. In the meeting, I tried my best not to cry as I mentioned the countless good things he gave to my father and me individually. I could say only two priceless ones. One - by giving Achayan 25 Deepika Newspaper, showing how to bring up and support a family for the next fifty years. Two - by choosing Leelamma as my life partner and showing how to build and support my family. It was tough and challenging for me to suppress the emotions that came out of my heart. I was unable to say all that I wanted to say.

He left having seen the long-term positive effects of two invaluable acts of kindness. God has assigned Kochuppappan to carry out His plans in our lives. He was one of the most respected and esteemed members of the family. A great person who led the Kannattumadom family on the path of renaissance, progress, and modernity, he was a man of the ages and ethos.

Reuben was born on November 6, 2017. Seema had stopped going to the office a month ago and was waiting for the arrival of her unborn baby. Vinod's parents did not want to go to Singapore to assist them because their health conditions were not so sound. Last time, Seema's mommy helped them with Seema's primipara. Seema's mommy also had pain in the limbs and diabetes mellitus. That's why they decided not to seek help from their parents this time. The hospitals and healthcare facilities in Singapore were good. There will always be moral support for mothers. It does not apply to geographical or regional differences. The power of the excellent mind travels unimpeded to the ends of the earth at the same speed as the mind's thoughts. Perform a PESTLE (political, economic, social, technical, legal, environmental) analysis to identify an organisation's or family's external forces and problems. We can evaluate any situation and find a suitable solution.

When everyone came to Bangalore for the Christmas holidays in December, they saw an excellent opportunity to conduct Reuben's baptism ceremony. Vinod's parents had rented out their own house and lived in a rented house at a different location.

They had given their tenant, who had financial capability and political interests, enough time to find another house. But it went on like that for too long. Wayanad Achayan was waiting for a long in the benevolence of 'that man has some difficulties,' 'thought it was every plan of the Lord.' That's when Seema and Vinod were interested in buying a flat and relocating their parents there. And so they did. With a place of their own and a spare house available after being vacated by the tenants, Vinod and Seema didn't hesitate to fulfill their parents' desires. Seema's parents were also very supportive of the said proposal, seeing it as a good idea to reduce the burden of minor ailments and inconveniences for the parents while sitting at different locations and worrying. I deposited Rupees twenty lakhs in Seema's (& Vinod's) account in Bangalore to furnish and make minor modifications to the flat, which was incomplete. Seema thought that Vinod's parents, who would live in that house, should consider it a donation from her. I lacked love and respect for the Achayan, a Kottayam man who asked, 'What will you give to your daughter?'

On the contrary, I had more love and respect for Achayan, a native of Wayanad. The hallmark of dignity is to achieve desired interests through a mature approach without claiming anything with authority. Such people deserve each other's love and respect.

In the same way or more, the like-minded people returned the gift of love. We found out when we saw the new flat. They showed no particular affection for our encouragement to Vinod-Seema, who always behaved as lovingly as ever, always caring and warm-hearted and smiling without saying anything, thanked us repeatedly, and treated us with love and respect.

Ruben's baptism was performed in the parish church near the new flat. Relatives and friends were present. Tony and Joysy were the godparents who helped Reuben fulfill his baptismal promises and would help in his spiritual formation. Godparents are responsible for serving as substitutes for parents, no matter how intense Christians they may be.

After the luncheon in the parish hall, the housewarming ceremony was held in the new flat.

So, the 2017 Christmas season family reunion was one in which Tony, Nita, Seema, and their families participated. All arrived before the baptism date. Christmas celebrations and usual engagements, playful merry-making, laughs, fun, and essential hectic trips – to Chennai and Alappuzha- all went through.

The new year began in January, and everyone returned to their workplaces.

## 119

# More Travels

Everyone loved to travel. It was mandatory for most of us that the travel must fulfill some special needs and requirements depending on the circumstances. But there were generally no opportunities for the entire family to travel together for relaxation and fun. In that regard, relatively more people in our family travel for work and tourism.

From 2017 to the end of 2019, I had to make many trips for other family matters and many trips regarding the audit. I go and return with Leelamma on all such trips.

Sometimes, I may go alone and come back alone, Or we will go together and return each of us by ourselves. All the excursions were together, and we visited different sites and entertainment and made visits in between. Or what's the fun in that? Historical, natural, pure beauty, unique creations of the modern world, the growth of science, glimpses of nature, wonders of the modern world, beautiful sights, life experiences, what life is going round the corner without knowing any of these? Views and perspectives of the external world expand our perspective. Those who want to know, grow, and become extensive travelers visit all such places: all the rest and their consequences. Visiting friends and relatives is a part of family and social life. Tourism is also helpful for good social life.

In July, we attended the wedding of Roymon, Kunjamma's son, in Chennai. Reshma studied, got a job at a major software company, and was ready to find a boyfriend.

I went to Alappuzha in February 2018 to see my mother and returned. In March, Leelamma went alone to Seema in Singapore. I returned after the audit in Malaysia. Nita stayed for a week in Singapore with her children during the summer vacation.

When it was May, I discovered that Xavier was very ill in Chennai, and we went to see him.

Anjiliparambil family reunion was held at the end of May at Punnapra Church. After Kochuppappan left, Anjiliparambil Chittappan was to continue as patron. At the first meeting held after the election of Junior KT Antony (Babychan) as the President, Anjiliparambil Chittappan was felicitated on turning 90 years old.

I went to Alappuzha again in December and met Ammachi. On our way back, we came to Ernakulam. We visited Munnar in a vehicle with my long-time friend and associate Kadamattuthara George and his family. We saw the Suryanelli tea plantation. We saw the tea processing in the factory nearby. We stayed in a Harrison Malayalam guest house and experienced the views and weather of Malanadu at sunrise and sunset. There were fantastic views from the point. As there was no rain, the journey through the canyons was pleasant; George and his wife Ammini gave us friendly company.

Tony's work-related trips were always alone. He used to go on short visits to places like Rwanda, Argentina, Brazil, New York, Singapore, Ireland etc. Tony has been in the healthcare field for data collection and analysis to evaluate the efficacy of particular medicinal preparations, having been a senior advisor in the UK division of the multinational company Johnson & Johnson for more than five years. J&J was a company that developed, manufactured, and distributed effective medications for conditions such as Alzheimer's and Schizophrenia. Janssen's company (pharmaceutical divisions of Johnson & Johnson) was currently conducting a research study on the COVID-19 Vaccine Candidate.

Wherever Tony travels to anywhere, before leaving, after arriving at a destination, and when returning from there, he used to send WhatsApp messages and photos. Being in constant contact with each other was part of Tony's unique personality.

Joysy's field was finance. After earning an MBA from the London Business School, she worked as a Director of Education at Nesta. Joysy was the Edutech Advisor, Entrepreneur, Global Speaker, and a British Parliamentary Steering Committee member. Joysy also travelled to Singapore, Chili, Egypt, Dubai, etc., as a guest speaker and for short visits there.

The Tony-Joysy couple has travelled extensively with their children. Amelia was less than a year old when she travelled with us to Italy, Rome, and the Vatican. Tony travelled that day with a backpack outside, a baby carrier in front of him to balance the weight, and both strapped to his waist on the bus, the tube rail, and the flight. When buying a car, he made sure that the car had a unique fit of a baby seat. When the children grew up, He purchased and used a baby stroller to carry them on the road. When the children grow up, they could go on a journey - without even thinking about "If it is an areca nut, you can hold it; If it is an areca palm... what will you do? "Buy a baby carrier and stroller, and go wherever you want; the journey will be comfortable!

When Eleanor was one year old, the family went to Dubai to celebrate her birthday. They stayed at Hotel Movenpick in Dubai. They took the Metro Rail from the airport to the last terminal, Ibn Battuta Mall, and found the Hotel Movenpick directly in front of them; they stayed there and visited beaches, malls, Burj Khalifa Tower, etc. Loved by children and elders alike, beautiful and elegant Dubai offers the experience of living a dream come true for young people.

Shortly before returning to London after collecting four and a half days of exotic food, scenery, and experiences, Eleanor became ill as she had some allergies. Afterward, Tony returned to London, met a dermatologist, and was treated until cured. It took nearly four and a half years to discover what kind of an allergy it was.

Tony told us that he had booked a room in the same hotel where they were staying and had booked flight tickets to Dubai because the views and accommodation in Dubai were all excellent and were available at no extra cost.

"Daddy and Mommy, go to Dubai for two or three days. Let your fortieth wedding anniversary be the days of another honeymoon in Dubai, and this is done for all your children's happiness."

How can you deny happiness to your children? We went on a four-day excursion from February Thirteen to Seventeen, 2015. We returned after collecting enough exotic food, scenery, and experiences. We dressed in Arabic costumes at the desert resort, like Arab men and women. We watched Arabian belly dancing sitting close to the stage, looked around from the 124$^{th}$ and 125$^{th}$ floors of Burj Khalifa, and ate Arabian food at the mall restaurant. One hundred varieties of dates were found in the Arab world, and we tasted some of them.

We could spend just four or five days without worries and anxieties and without explicitly thinking about what to do. We gave complete rest to mind and body. We spent the fortieth wedding anniversary in Dubai and returned to Bangalore.

We went to London in May to enjoy the British Summer of 2018. The holidays for children also begin at that time. As usual, we were starting to feel this change in circumstances for the better, both mentally and physically. Along the way, I visited the church, school, sidewalks, Kew Garden, and other parks, including the National Museum of Natural History and the Museum of Natural History. We were with Ansa-Vineet and their children one day in their new home; they had a green top garden with an apple tree full of fruits. There were many decorative fishes in the new glass aquarium. Ansa, Vineeth, Eva, and Edward together made a happy family.

Tony said he wanted us to get a European tour visa. However, we could only get a UK visa, and the subsequent processing time for a Schengen visa became much shorter. It took a little longer to process a UK visa this time. So, the remaining time became insufficient to process a Schengen visa. Tony decided to skip the European tour and go to Scotland for one weekend and Wales for another. It was planned as a full UK tour, excluding Northern Ireland. As you are aware, the UK is a united parliamentary democracy and a constitutional monarchy that includes four countries, namely England, Scotland, Wales, and Northern Ireland. Great Britain, the largest island, is named after the country itself.

The journey to Scotland was by a super-fast train from Kings Cross, London. Five hundred and forty km to Edinburgh was covered in four and a half hours, with only one or two shortstops in between.

Tony had a short walk from Edinburgh station to hire a taxi, which he was driving. We went to the hotel, freshened up, and visited various places. We attended the Sunday evening Mass at St Mary's Catholic Cathedral, Edinburgh. There were many churches nearby. The following two days, we covered Edinburgh Castle, the Scottish National War Memorial, and the War Museum; we climbed to Arthur's Seat and the Salisbury Crags. We all enjoyed the tireless travel, food, and rest without worrying about what was happening elsewhere. While walking along the streets, we saw the festivities of the International Festival in Edinburgh.

Camera Obscura and the World of Illusions, Edinburgh, were attractions that appealed to people of all ages. The women and children in our group went to see what they liked most: their images. We could take beautiful city-scape photographs of the streets of Edinburgh from the rooftop terrace. Magic Gallery had a variety of fascinating optical illusions. It was hard not to smile when you saw your reflections in the concave or spherical mirrors. Leelamma told me this after going and seeing the images there -

"I saw my image as a big mango fruit."

I said – "You came to Edinburgh to find the truth!"

Tony and I went to the Scotch Whiskey Appreciation Society to experience the different whiskey flavours in Scotland.

The Scottish Islands are famous for producing Scotch whiskey. These areas, with hundreds of distilleries, have a diverse landscape. There are many leading brands in the world making many flavours and qualities. Scotch is a type of whisky, but it's different from American whiskey (remember the spelling?)! Like champagne, whisky in Scotland is legally distilled if filtered and bottled with at least 40% ABV (Alcohol by Volume).

It is generally spelt "whiskey"—with an e—in the United States and Ireland. It is spelt "whisky"—without the e—in Scotland and Canada. It's not due to a spelling error. The name is based on factors such as the type of cereal grain used in the distilling process and how and where it was produced. (Source: Encyclopaedia-Britannica)

I noticed this ABV percentage in various whisky and whiskeys, mostly kept inside the minibar cabinet at Tony's house as a complimentary gift from friends. By comparing the flavour complexity of a whiskey to 40% and 43%, you can see the evidence and difference in each whiskey. Forty percent may be a compromise, but it helps maintain the integrity of the whiskey.

We went inside to experience the taste of whisky.

"Have you ever tasted different types of Scotch and tried to understand the flavours like an expert? If not, you can go back as an expert!"

These were the words that greeted us at the entrance to the society - the production process takes place in front of you as you step in - you would see working models, and the description ensured a personal experience. In the background, you can see some exceptional landscapes in Scotland.

The production process was described, step by step, as follows -

i. Preparation: Add dried barley and grind. Dust, husk, and debris removed

ii. Mashing: Water is added to dissolve sugars and produce wort, a valuable substance.

iii. Fermenting: Yeast is added, and fermentation turns sugars into alcohol.

iv. Distilling: Alcohol is evaporated, collected, and repeated to increase purity.

v. Aging: Alcohol from distillation is stored in oak casks for several years.

After production, you can see the storage - the most extensive collection of Scotch whisky in the world, some 3 to 72 years old; the wine label walls influenced the view. Lots of glass shelves, tens of thousands of bottles! Let's taste now -

They give you a table to sit on - small whisky bottles lined up in front. "Here are the best single malt bottles to fill your glass," - a British bar owner formally invited. To taste the wine, you need to place a sip (taking only a minimal amount at a time) on your tongue, press your lips together, and slowly inhale through the mouth; then, the experience will give you an idea of the quality of the wine. You can also try Scotch. The flavours are as follows: -

1. Lowland: Colour: Light golden, Smell - Light vanilla freshness, Taste: Fresh fruits, grains & vanilla spices - Light, smooth, lavender

2. Highland: (10 years old) Colour - Burned gold, Smell, Sherry, Vanilla Sweet, Taste - Sweet, Almond Smooth, Lavender, Quick Kick, Satisfactory with a bit of water.

3. Speyside: (10 years old), Colour: Bronze, Smell: Fruit Spice, Smoke, Taste: Forest Fruits, Cream Malt, Smoke Sherry Notes - Slightly smoky red, more intense, severely good taste,

4. Islay: (12 years old) colour: golden syrup, reddish dark yellow Smell: Smell of smoke, seafood, taste - complex smoky red with soft honey and smoke, hard to tell the exact taste.

The Speyside area of Scotland was famous for its single malt whisky sold worldwide. During this visit, I had no intention to immerse myself in the history and heritage of whisky production in Scotland, taste and sample some of the best single malt whisky in Scotland, such as Glenfiddich, and flow with the crowd during this ordeal. Live happily, enjoy the time God has given you, and thank God for all good things. That was the intention. Tony took me and showed me everything.

In any case, sampling a variety of whiskies at a whisky bar or festival was, without a doubt, an enlightening experience.

The Edinburgh International Festival was the annual festival of art on the main streets of Edinburgh, Scotland, for over three weeks in August. At the invitation of the Festival Director, the International Festival invites the best performers worldwide to perform in the arts of music, drama, opera, and dance. They come and add fat to the fair. Founded in 1947, the Edinburgh International Festival was an unparalleled celebration of the performing arts and an annual meeting point worldwide. What I understood was this.

After the Edinburgh Fair, we rested, visited the Edinburgh Palace Archaeological Collection, the Prison, and the Clock Tower, and returned to Kings Cross on the Super-Fast Train.

The journey to Scotland was to the north, and two weeks after, the trip was to Wales. Tony picked us up in his car and drove off. We went straight west, almost up to the beach. It was a fertile land, a beautiful landscape, and a vast and busy highway; only at the end of the five-hour journey could we see slightly narrower roads, hills, mountains, and mixed terrain. Vineet, Ansa, and their family drove with us in their vehicle. We parked on a riverbank, and everyone happily shared the packed lunch, sitting in the lap of nature. We arrived in Wales, rested for the night, went up the hill in the morning, and came down to see the beach and the rocks. The children were pleased to go down to the shallow water on the shore. The next day, we searched on the other side of the hill to see the shoreline. The children ran to the beach. We ate at small restaurants in Wales. Our accommodation was in a private villa specially designed for tourists, with plenty of books to read, cooking facilities for dinner, toys for the kids to play with, bedrooms, and other amenities. It was how tourism developed in a country of scenic beauty like ours. It is possible to prepare some unique attractions that grab attention, all according to the taste of the people who come and stay in these accommodations.

## 120

# Doctorate For Nita, Fish Curry For Dad

A Ph.D., also called a Doctor of Philosophy, is the designation of a graduate-level university degree that a student earns over several years. PhD programs teach students about a specialized field, emphasizing research, analysis, and theory. A person with this degree can work in various fields, including Management.

Jain University, Bangalore, awarded Nita her PhD on August 22, 2018. The graduation ceremony was in September 2018. The festivities had already begun. Seema had come from Singapore to attend the convocation ceremony. On Leelamma's birthday, a banquet at Leela Palace was hosted by Nita to celebrate her PhD with her family. When Leelamma got a large bouquet of rose buds at the Leela Palace, I could see Nita's mom's face blossoming with happy rose flowers.

The moment when Nita received her doctorate from the hands of the university chancellor was a moment of great satisfaction to all, especially to me. Sometimes, the parents were happy when the girls worked hard, studied at least up to a degree, and won. Whether they got a job soon or did not, there was no shortage of education. And it was customary to feel relieved that they were fully qualified to get married and lead a family life. There might have been a need for parents to have further insight into tomorrow. Or there were other limitations involving finances. After Nita got her degree, got a job, and married, unlike customary or ordinary girls, she became more interested in work and her favourite subject. That's why a more punctual and responsible job came to Nita - a job as a college teacher. She happily accepted her new job. She realised that it was mandatory to learn more if she was to continue her passion. Becoming a postgraduate became a special requirement for her job of teaching. % Nita rose to the challenge and wanted to study and become a postgraduate like other teachers. She didn't tell anyone how much she desired and how hard she tried for it. After graduating from Pondicherry University, I learned that Nita, who had lost a year in school at a young age, was pursuing higher studies and could do it more like her siblings. Despite living in a country with meagre education rates for girls, Nita showed that she was different. Nita was incredibly encouraged by Sam, Sam's parents, and her sensible and lovely children.

Nita had already earned a reputation as a good and friendly teacher from college. The authorities were also interested in her prosperity. That was how Nita got nominated for doctorate studies at the college. Nita would be congratulated for being the first doctorate in the family. That's why I frequently inquired about her coursework, paper, and thesis presentation progress and how much fee was to be paid to the University. It was for the realization of this holy moment. Perhaps her family members were happier than Nita. Soon, the college authorities recognised Nita and honoured her with the post of Associate Professor. The Diocese of Mandya and the Annual family gathering at Anjiliparampil honoured Nita with a trophy at a particular felicitation function.

Because there were no other places in the world where our children work and live, non-holiday excursions were all directed to the East or the West. To the East - it takes four and a half hours to Singapore, and to the West - eleven hours to London. There were no friends and relatives who were so loving and considerate elsewhere. How many journeys have been made, alone and together? Will it be similar again?

Corona restrictions have not yet been lifted in India. A new variant of the virus, a new genetically modified species, has arrived. With the third outbreak in London, the lockdown has been extended for another six weeks. Messages were sent today to keep everyone safe. They care so much about their children. Only when this security wait is over will it be possible to travel without fear? Sarah and Ruben wear their school uniforms and go to school wearing masks. The situation there is under reasonable control. Vaccination will begin soon.

Business trips are not pleasure trips, so it is permissible to go alone. Going alone has no meaning if it is not work-related; your life partner will be with you. Working alone and visiting children were rarely taken together because they wanted to finish the work in a few days and return soon. Twice, I had to go to the west and, more times, to the east. So I went west alone in January 2014 for an NQA UK audit and in June 2018 for an Intertek UK audit at Spirit AeroSystems Europe Prestwick, Scotland. I spent four or five days with Tony on the way back from the audit. I went to the east when I spent two or three days in Singapore in various companies and for two weeks continuously at Singapore Airlines Engineering Co at Changi Airport when I audited for Intertek. I used to stay with Seema or go from the hotel to Seema's residence once a week. When I went to Japan, Leelamma was with me up to Singapore. There, the mother met her daughter. When I returned from Japan, I picked up my mother and went to Bangalore.

When Daddy and Mommy started preparing for the usual British summer vacation in 2019, Tony said he had another plan for a trip with his sisters and family. Seema and Nita were looking forward to their "Chachan's Plan."

Therefore, this year's British summer vacation was meant to be a European excursion. When parents, their children, and grandchildren all travel together, it's a headache instead of a mental joy - packing big and small luggage, backpacks, and baby carriers for everyone, wrapped up against the cold with only eyes out, two tired, elderly bodies, their mobile camera, bags of essential medicines - all piled up together. Metro/Subway Systems, international flights, hotel stays, and picnic mobility are, to put it simply, a headache, a hassle, and not necessarily a fun excursion.

"Now, let's go. Let's plan a European tour with Daddy-Mommy next summer."

Yes, that was good. First, you learn about good places, travel facilities, hotels, famous places, popular sights, shrines, tourism, and leisure; come and tell us, we will come next time and after arranging a Schengen Visa.

"But then, I can go and see Sarah and Reuben, Seema often requests. If you say today, she will send you the visa and ticket tomorrow. I can even prepare fish curry for a week; what do you say?"

Leelamma had the instinctual mastery of speed and certainty at the first thought of desires and decisions. Leelamma knows very well that the husband has to decide if there are any shortcomings and correct them.

Leelamma knew very well that it was her husband's duty to decide if there were any deficiencies or shortcomings, CBCI, and he would do that appropriately. I don't understand the reason for delaying things.

"When I take a long time, I am slow,

When my boss takes a long time, he is thorough.

When I don't do it, I'm lazy,

When my boss doesn't do it, he's busy."....

Almost the same is the case here. I might as well agree that I am the boss here!

Do not forget that the mother and children's wishes are always prioritised over anything else. I think I have followed that first principle!

The visa and ticket came from Singapore. Leelamma made a pan full of good fish curry; Kuttanadan Fish curry made with Kudampuli (Garcinia cambogia, commonly known as "Malabar Tamarind") lasts over a week and retains the taste and flavour. Leelamma handed over the fish curry, left her husband alone, and visited Singapore. Sam's Facility Management Services Supervisor assisted in handling and loading her luggage at the airport. The phone rang at seven in the morning - Seema said - "Mommy has arrived."

Sarah and Ruben were happy to wear the new dresses their grandma stitched, which suited them well.

Occasionally, I went out for audit or training. I came back and warmed the rice or made chapatis and ate with delicious fish curry and went to sleep. On the days when I did not go out -

The WhatsApp call always came - "It's late afternoon here; Seema and Vinod have gone to work. What did you eat for breakfast? Don't put sugar in tea, keep rice warm, if the fish curry is done, make some vegetables and eat them, drink a lot of water, not the coloured water! It doesn't mean you don't drink it." Don't you drink sometimes? That's a peg, too. It doesn't matter. I'll bring a bottle when I come, but Seema disagrees, but let's see..."

One day, a special message came - Vinod and Seema decided to move to another house in Singapore. It is a good area, and the property is in a large building complex – a condominium nearby. It has a flat on the second floor, three bedrooms, a swimming pool directly in front and downstairs, and the school and church near the metro station. The distance to the office for both is only half an hour each. The owner, a Chinese man, is selling his flat and wants to move into his villa. Vinod and Seema said they could take their mommy with them today to see the flat again. If the price is reasonable, they consider buying it. They will get a bank loan…."

"Okay, excellent news. Go and take some photos and send them. Discuss the price and let them decide if it is good. It is sufficient to pay the current rent as EMI. At the end of the term, the house is their own."

It is correct to say that they went, saw, and conquered. 'Love at First Sight' itself. It was a fully furnished house. After Mommy saw it, Vinod and Seema saw it as a big dream to own a house everyone liked. A pleasant big hall, kitchen, a small room for the maidservant, bath attached, and small safety grill work needs to be done soon. Reuben climbed on it by the window on the first day itself. There was a good view out from there. In Singapore, it was estimated to cost a significant amount, and the bank would process the loan only after paying twenty percent as an advance. However, having a home was a necessity. Seeing Seema's idea in practice, it was attempted. Seema knew that Dad and siblings would cooperate wholeheartedly. That was right. All of them paid some amounts in advance and in debt. Leelamma returned to Bangalore in March.

SGD Forty Thousand was sent to Seema by Bank transfer on March 27. Everyone went on a European tour after completing the sale deed process in April. To say that you have a home of your own is to say that you have a place to return to wherever you go.

# 121

# To See the World and Share Love

On April 15, 2019, during Summer Vacation, Tony planned to bring his sisters, their families, and all the new generation kids together with his family and travel to European countries. Sam, Nita, and their children flew from Bangalore to London. In contrast, Vinod, Seema and their children flew from Singapore to London. Tony, Joysy, and their children sat in London and arranged for everyone to travel, stay together, and receive the visitors. On the second day onwards, they all went out as tourists together. They visited tourist destinations in France, Italy, Spain, Poland, Switzerland, and Germany in ten days and returned to London. Seema added some information about their travel.

"In August 2018, when the families met in Bangalore, they planned to spend a summer vacation together - starting from London and planning to return after visiting many countries in Europe. Sam, Nita, and their children flew from Bangalore to London. Seema, Vinod, and the little ones arrived in London in the first week of April 2019 from Singapore. Tony and Joysy prepared their home and welcomed all the relatives. They also took the first few days to acclimatise to the cold weather in the UK in preparation for going through the European tour. On Palm Sunday, they boarded an underground train to their first destination, Paris. Mommy's delicious home-cooked delicacies - lemon rice and beef fry - were specially packaged and shipped from Bangalore for them to eat on the go. After spending two days in Paris, including the evening the famous Notre Dame Cathedral caught fire, they left for Milan. From there, they took the famous Bernina Express train from Tirano (Italy) to Chur, the oldest town in Switzerland, covering the scenic route of the Alps mountain ranges. They briefly passed through Zurich, Switzerland, then took an overnight train to Berlin, where they spent two days in Germany, which included Easter Sunday and Natasha's 15th birthday celebrations.

After a short break in Cologne, they flew to Brussels, Belgium, the final leg of their 10-day journey before returning to London. So they embarked on their very tiring but fantastic journey. The following days were spent exploring the beautiful ancient city of London and meeting family and friends.

They visited all the tourist attractions throughout the trip and enjoyed the local food and festivals. They lived together in the places they had stayed during the trip as if they were at home. After two to three weeks of vacation tours, they returned to their homes.

They also resolved to undertake such a family trip to new and never-before-seen destinations at least once in three years. They seem determined to keep their promise, as they have already started exploring the possibilities, even with homework and waiting due to Corona." Covid-19 has upset all preconceived notions and plans.

Seema was scheduled to fly to Amsterdam, Philips Global headquarters, Holland (Netherlands) in early June. She went to Saji-Chiku's residence in the US and spent two days in Holland. Seema returned to Singapore a few days later and received the keys to her new house. The house was modified, minor repairs were completed in July 2019, and the family moved into the new home.

We could not go to Seema's housewarming ceremony. We thought we would go to Singapore on another occasion to relax and have fun with the kids.

I went to Dubai in July 2019 for an audit. Sitting at a bar at the Premier Inn Hotel in Dubai, I saw India lose to New Zealand in the semi-finals of the Cricket World Cup. I could not even read the news in the newspaper the next day about the broken hearts of billions of cricket fans as I returned from Dubai and fell asleep.

I could go to Seema's new home after I completed two or three audits in Malaysia in November. After the audit, the tourist bus ride from Alor Gajah (Melaka) to Singapore was hassle-free. It took about six hours. All passports and visas were checked after entering Singapore. Vinod was waiting at the bus station. Sarah and Ruben warmly welcomed Achayan at their home (9 Rivervale Crescent # 02-30, Singapore 545086). The house that Vinod-Seema bought was lovely. There were generally good facilities, three rooms on the second floor, and a large swimming pool on the ground floor just in front. Reuben and Sarah went there regularly to learn swimming. I was to return to Bangalore two days later.

We saw the Changi Airport's new sights and Christmas decorations before returning from Singapore to Bangalore. It was so beautiful.

Jewel Changi Airport in Singapore is an entertainment and retail mall linked to three passenger terminals. Jewel is connected to the Arrival Hall of the terminals by link bridges. Its centrepiece is the world's tallest indoor waterfall, the Rain Vortex, surrounded by a terraced forest setting. Jewel Changi Airport includes gardens, attractions, dining outlets, and early baggage check-in facilities.

You will likely get dazzled by the sparkles at Jewel with its many underwater-themed elements! Along with the iconic 16-metre tall Prudential Singapore Jewel Christmas Tree at the entrance of the Shiseido Forest Valley, Jewel's Canopy Park, located on the top floor, thrills visitors with many aquatic interactive displays at various attractions and scenic lookouts.

# 122

# Wife's Relations

Ottathaickal Babychan married and could not be with his parental family for long. Ottathaickal Joy bought Thommikunju's land and house in Thundi across the ravine and helped him to live there. Babychan did many jobs at once, and when there was agricultural work in the field, he did farm work on lease. After driving an auto-rickshaw for a few days, Joy bought the land and gave it to his brother Babychan to continue farming. Agriculture was only a source of investment for the sailor. Farming in Kuttanad is not a permanent source of income or employment for many. Natural calamities or floods sometimes affect agriculture, causing losses and sometimes fetching good yields. Babychan had two children named Binu and Liby. Liby finished school, studied nursing, and worked in Kuwait. Liby got married, has a daughter, and continues to work in Kuwait. Binu works as a technician on a cargo ship. His marriage is over. We had also travelled from Bangalore to attend Libby and Binu's weddings.

Josekutty has been in MES service in Visakhapatnam for a long time. On the way from Koraput, we sometimes received hospitality from the Josekutty-Mercy couple. While Mercy was without a job and looking for a job, I gave her the desktop Tony had purchased for me. Mercy took it and practiced an accounting app like Tally. Later, she took it up as a part-time job. Josekutty-Mercy had two children, Jain and Priya, and the children had a passion for music and the arts from an early age while studying in school. They had a conviction of what to work for and live for.

Josekutty later moved on transfer to Chennai. Years later, Josekutty retired from the MES service and came to Changanassery for life after retirement. Josekutty bought a flat intending to stay in Thiruvananthapuram. Still, the builders did not get clearance from the government even after waiting for some time. That was how he bought his house in Arukutty in Kochi and settled there. Jain and Priya had completed their graduations and were already at work.

While preparing for permanent residence in Kochi, Josekutty's retirement benefits were insufficient, like those of any other central government employee. The money invested in the flat was blocked, and he had to buy a house soon and marry his daughter Priya. Mercy was intelligent, trying hard to make both ends meet despite being in debt. There were indeed ways to give back, and she has done it. No one is self-sufficient, and no one is free from encumbrance and responsibilities. Therefore, there is nothing wrong with seeking support from near and dear ones. Isn't it such calculations that keep life moving forward?

The daughter of the Josekutty-Mercy couple, Priya got married shortly after completing her engineering studies and while working for Infosys (2017). Seljo was also an engineer and had secured a job in Sharjah. Seljo and his parents were family friends of the Josekutty-Mercy family from Visakhapatnam days onwards. Priya went to Canada for higher studies. After completing her postgraduate studies, she got a job in Canada. Seljo also flew to Canada and joined Priya soon. Their first child, Shawn, was born in Canada on August 28, 2021.

Priya's brother Jain was working in Dubai after finishing his engineering degree. Jain also married a year later when Priya was on vacation from Canada. Jain was married (December 29, 2018) to Preema, the daughter of Josekutty's friend. Preema is a dentist. In 2019, she got a job in New Zealand after her studies. Jaine was ready to go to New Zealand. A year has passed. Having to stay away and having a flight permitted during the epidemic was a double whammy for the young couple!

We went from Bangalore to attend Priya's betrothal ceremony. At one time, Ottathyckal Ammachi was eagerly waiting to attend Priya's marriage. Thus, seeing Ammachi, who was healthy despite her old age, and many other relatives and friends was doubly sweet when it came to attending local ceremonies like marriage at our homes. When I went to Kandanadu, a place in Kochi, for an audit, Leelamma came with me and stayed with Mercy for two days.

He also bought backwater fish found near the Arukutty Bridge and helped Mercy with cooking and other household chores. After coming to Kochi, Mercy started practicing acupuncture, which she studied with a residential teacher at Punnapra. Then, there was nothing to be jealous of Mercy for finding time to learn and practice treatment. They were a couple who had learned to live efficiently and happily.

Mercy used to go to Nedumudi occasionally to see her mother. She went back after an hour or so. Although she wanted to care for her mother, she feared Joy and could do nothing. Joy often said selfishly, "My mother is mine alone."

After celebrating the age of ninety, she spent two or three more years with her son, Joy, without much illness. Whenever we met and parted, Ammachi was very happy having seen us, and we were much happier having met her again. Joy continued to work as a captain in a merchant cargo ship after a gap of four to five months. It would be four to five months of continuous work each time he went. When leaving, he would say goodbye to his mother, and he would call almost every day; his mother wanted to hear her son's voice when she had breakfast. Joy's wife had gone to school, and his two children had gone out to study. As her health deteriorated, Ammachi found it challenging to stand up, walk alone, and do her things alone.

For some time, Thambichan took Ammachi and protected her. Babychan refused to take Ammachi there because of a lack of facilities in his house. Kunjamma sent a woman from Madras to help Ammachi.

They helped Ammachi for some time. Ammachi was constantly troubled by old age issues and fatigue during the day when no one was at home to help. Joy didn't like his sisters taking his mother home and nursing her even in this exhausted state. But at the same time, Joy was unable to understand and pay special attention to the deficiencies in providing the necessary, efficient, continuous care for his elderly mother in his home. It was only a normal reaction for the sisters to feel sad and disappointed.

Being away from home due to work and being in the middle of the sea, Joy could not hand over those responsibilities and duties to anyone else. It was not for lack of love or willingness to care but because of the stress of life's circumstances. During the 2018 Kuttanad floods, Joy could take Ammachi to Alappuzha by boat and nursed her safely and adequately.

Due to the spread of the coronavirus, we did not get a chance to go and see the parents face to face who were eagerly waiting to see their children and grandchildren despite their old age and fatigue. After Joy went to work, even when there was no other way to see Ammachi in trouble, Mercy and Josekutty went to Nedumudi to see Ammachi, and they allowed us to see Ammachi through a Zoom connection.

On one occasion, when Joy was not there, I noticed Ammachi struggling helplessly without anybody near for help. When the river of life flows calmly to its estuary, where it meets the ocean, any disturbance, natural or otherwise, will cause the river to swell, and turbulence will be generated, disturbing the calmness. Ammachi's situation was similar. My conscience showed me the worries of that mother through Leelamma's wet eyes and quavery and sobbing words full of sadness.

In that case, the most appropriate action was to take a courageous and deliberate action. Josekutty and Mercy were asked to confirm their interest and cooperation. I sent a WhatsApp message to Joy, asking his permission. "As a temporary measure (until Joy arrives) so that mother's health does not deteriorate, should Josekutty-Mercy take her mother home?"

Joy's reply, 'the permission,' was communicated to all concerned. Josekutty - Mercy went to Nedumudi and brought her mother to Arukutty in a taxi. Within a month or two, Mother's health had improved, and she could talk happily and get up independently. Mercy was with her mother for every need. Mercy also saw the days she got to take care of Ammachi as the most fulfilling holy days of her life. Jain and Preema were always there for Ammachi's every little need.

Whether happiness or suffering, the all-seeing, all-controlling Almighty does not allow anything to become too much. That's what happened. She could walk independently, and when it happened again. Mercy was doing something in the kitchen; Ammachi got up and walked to the kitchen, calling Mercy. By the time she reached Mercy, Ammachi had slipped and fallen to one side, barely balancing on the cement floor with no chappals. It was unfortunate, I must say!

Ammachi was taken to a nearby hospital, and she had no difficulty at all. After examining an X-ray of her hips, bringing her to Alappuzha Sahrudaya Hospital was advised. They said that the hip bone had only minor sprains or soft-tissue injuries, and the patient could be taken home after a week of rest.

"I will tell you to get up and walk, and then only I will let you out of here," said Dr. Hegde, who knew the mother and her children comforted all.

We went to the hospital and met Ammachi. Ammachi said that there was no pain or distress and that she was generally happy. The limitation of meeting personal needs while lying down was only considered a difficulty. Still, she said - "I'm glad you all came to see me."

Joy called Dr. Hegde on the phone and requested that Ammachi be discharged only after he came home. Till then, Ammachi should be given proper care in the Hospital itself.

After about two weeks, Joy came, was discharged, and took Ammachi to his home. Ammachi got up and walked outside, returning home.

Joy mentioned a complaint to his political friends and associates that "Ammachi, whom I had been caring like in the palm of my hand, was taken away by her daughters and made her fall and put to bed." No one paid much attention to it. Everyone knew the developments that happened in his absence. No one blamed anyone.

**Some of my published books**

# 123

# Leelamma's Sisters

We attended Xavier and Gracy's son Joe's wedding three years ago in Chennai. We could not go to Kerala to attend his betrothal ceremony. Joe was married to the daughter of Dr. Chacko Palakunnel. Joe's sister, Jay, controlled all the ceremonies. Jay asked me to host the post-wedding reception and take the stage to introduce the bride and groom and their parents to the guests. I did not know the bride's name, educational qualifications, or family details; she gave me nothing in writing. I didn't think it was appropriate for Jay to ask me to do the job, as Joe's close friends, who were much younger than me and knew how to handle the festivities with grace, looked on. Xavier was also just an onlooker and said nothing. Or maybe it was because I don't know why his wife and children banned the laughter that might arise when the brothers get together on such rare occasions. After all, they thought everything should be done according to the children's and the mother's interests, and Xavier did not control anything. So I refused. Jay saw it as a very serious non-cooperation on my part and began criticising it. The non-cooperation that started on Joe's wedding day continued on social media and other occasions when they met. Even though I forgave Jay for her irresponsible behaviour, criticising and reprimanding my wife over the telephone once, along with other misunderstandings, which they assumed, the aversion to Jay did not disappear from my mind.

Xavier and Gracy spent time fondling their grandson (Joe's son) when Xavier became terminally ill. Gracy and Joe worked hard to nurse Xavier back to health for over six months. I met and spoke to him once while travelling from one hospital to another. Xavier was happy—the joy of a father who has fulfilled his duties and responsibilities. Xavier was delighted to know that his family was safe and that they would not have any trouble even after he had left for his heavenly abode.

We were both co-brothers and good friends from when I met him and Thambichan in Dindigul. Ever optimistic and cutting jokes, along with Thambichan, we were the trio throughout our contemporary life and a united force and pride for the families.

I saw him last in October 2018 while he was sitting on a chair and resting at home, awaiting his final days and ready to leave for the last journey. Xavier tried to smile. I looked at the adage that Xavier used to say: if the memories of Bhubaneswar days bring joy to his mind, to see him with a smile-

"Sakkali Sakkali, Pukola Khaibo, Petto Thandi Rahibo" (If you drink pazhangkanji in the morning, your stomach will be fabulous!

Although speaking was difficult, Xavier asked about the three stars that 'Captain' had on his shoulders - Tony, Nita, and Seema.

"Convey my regards to my friend," he said precisely. Xavier called Seema "My Friend" from an early age. That's what Xavier last told me. On the way back, he raised his hand and waved me off.

Along with Thambichan in Paradip and Chennai, Xavier was a colourful presence at all family gatherings and ceremonies. I realized that Xavier deeply loved and was fully committed to Gracy and their children. Towards the end of Xavier's life, Gracy and her children continued to serve him well. But to my understanding, Xavier did not significantly influence Gracy and her children's outlook on life.

While attending the funeral, I could read the sadness of the older man in the trio, in Thambichan's eyes, going away on a never-ending journey.

Kunjamma runs 'an old age home' in Chennai. She has the support of voluntary organizations and the municipality. Kunjamma has appeared as a leader (thalaivi) on public programs and television channels at the political level. For Social Service, Kunjamma has been honoured with a doctorate. She succeeded in life by presenting the weakness of one eye as the power of the other eye - the mind. Wilson was tired of working, found joy in the loving care of his mother and niece, and moved on for days. As soon as she started talking about Reshma's marriage, Reshma revealed that she had already begun trying to alleviate the hardships of her parents. A young man named Vijay, who was interested in her and wanted to protect her, made every effort easier. Vijay got married with the blessings of his parents. When Kunjamma told everyone to gather and conduct her daughter's marriage, the relatives were all happy. The wedding between Reshma and Vijay took place on May 29, 2019, in Chennai and was attended by all.

We were in Chennai for the baptism of Kunjamma's grandson. Vijay Ramachandran and Reshma Thomas named their firstborn son 'Leo Ramabhadran.' After baptism, I saw the baby being laid under the altar in the Latin church. Through this, the family expressed gratitude for God and acknowledged God's love. A unique custom of the people of Israel, offering God the first harvest of their fields, was seen as being imitated here.

My grandfather used to take the first bunch of bananas, the first coconut growing from the coconut tree, and the first sheaf of paddy harvested from the paddy field to the church. It would be set aside for submission to God.

Jews preserve the garment woven from the first wool, which they have cut off from the flock, and the first fruits of his garden as a token of gratitude to God. This ritual called 'Pidyon Haben, in which parents dedicate their firstborn son to God, is a prayer for the firstborn's redemption (atonement and sanctification).

Such ceremonies are not found in Syro-Malabar churches. The 'Pidion Heben' tradition also suggests that the baby must be the firstborn boy laid on the altar and be born through normal childbirth (not a caesarean section). In the modern world, man seeks his comfort and convenience. Therefore, similar meaningful ceremonies, prayers, and offerings to God are not found even in present-day churches.

In addition to the bone disease, Xavier's separation left Gracy debilitated. Before Xavier left, it was a great relief for them to go to the United States together and live there for six months with their daughter. Joe worked for a software company in Chennai, and it was a good job. Joe-Theress couple had a son who was in high school then. While caring for her health and praying, Gracy looked after her grandson and son.

Rosamma worked for a Rolls Royce company in Mumbai for some time. Aniyappan had a job sometimes, and sometimes he did not when his long-term illness became debilitating. Their son Nitin attended boarding high school. After that, he attended engineering degree classes or spent time with friends. Sometimes, he took night rides on bikes on the streets of Mumbai and tried to become a little hero. When Rosamma lost her job, he realised life's hardships. Then Nitin tried to work in a call centre, worked for a few days, and then tried to do business with friends. During the rotation of the wheel of time, he realised that "you can't get a job by studying this manner, Cheriyan Kunje!" (പഠിച്ചിട്ടൊന്നും പണി കിട്ടൂല്ലടാ ചെറിയാൻകുഞ്ഞേ!)

After a while, the course changed. Nitin tried hard and passed the Engineering degree by writing the examinations for the remaining subjects. He recently got a job and started to realize a little more responsibility. He is currently working as an engineer at TCS. It would be Rosamma's prayer and luck if he goes well.

Rosamma now - runs a service that finds small jobs for needy people. She has embraced eternal worship and the practice of the Bible as a way of life. Even though the sense of prudence and appropriateness she lacked right from her younger age remains as such, she shall not be in want of anything.

**Ammachi and her five daughters (2019)**

# 124

# Being A Good Husband

Being a good husband is not a natural trait for most men. Many things can help us to be one -

There is a long list - Being a best friend, being a wife's protector, caring for her, supporting her, respecting her beliefs, showing love to her, acknowledging her mistakes, not losing love, talking things over, taking care of your health, appearance, personality, and dress, and many more. Admittedly, there may be fluctuations in the number of qualities of a husband. But being Leelamma's husband, I always answered every question, like in general qualifying examinations, sure!

I have never been adamant or determined that Leelamma should have no complaints. I do not claim to be such an ideal husband. I had always made love and sincerity a priority in our lives.

Leelamma has always been a good wife to me. I will write more about that later. As I was writing these thoughts recently, I asked Leelamma one thing – "Leelam, can you summarise the qualities and features you like and dislike about me?"

Below is what Leelamma wrote in reply.

"It would not be suitable for someone to say that we have never fought throughout our married life. It has happened at some point in our daily lives.

There was only the thought and prayer of raising children and caring for them in the early days. Suffering and hardships were not an issue at all. I was not particularly eager to inform the kids about our petty quarrel. I knew it would hurt their minds. I have experienced many hardships and difficulties before marriage. Still, my good parents taught me to understand that it was all a part of life. I have never seen a fight between my mother and father.

This man used to live with a rough face on the outside and a tender heart inside. Life experiences and responsibilities as a child might have made him so. I had difficulty agreeing to it after growing up amid love, like a sensitive plant at home. I was ashamed to complain to anyone.

Those who read it might say in their minds that it was my incompetence. Mother's beloved son-in-law was not safe there either. But I did not know how to respond. I was scared. I concealed everything and cried silently without being seen. He is a simple, innocent mind who loves a lot but does not know how to show or express it.

There have been times when I have had the worst pain and grief. Anger and hatred would stay in his mind for a long time. He had no open-minded nature. He seldom tried to see, hear, or console me for my sorrows or hardships.

He will not inform me about money transactions. That is one aspect. Achayan told me when our marriage was confirmed – "He is good and educated. But everyone will have their family traditions, which will also be seen in him. So always pray."

On each occasion, I remembered Achayan's words. But Ammachi said - 'You, being the eldest daughter-in-law of that house, should look after all the brothers and live happily and patiently. Please don't bring a bad name to me, who brought you up with difficulty.

My husband's family is my family, with parents, brothers, and relatives who always loved me. It remained so even today.

I often got addicted to illness by keeping all my mental tension. If I go to any doctor, I will be told It is because I have tension.

Sometimes, I have wondered what the word life partner means. It could all be my childish thoughts. I will not be allowed to comment - He will ask me to be silent. Silence is the character that I do not like in my husband. "There is so much love as the ocean, but unexpressed love is like a coin buried in the ground."

There is a fragrance for the stone lying near the Jasmin flower. The stone does not know where it is lying! "

(Are there two types of love: expressed love and unexpressed love? Isn't all love the same? Either there is love, or there is no love. A lion may show love to a human when it gets food. What is wrong in believing that if one does not show anger or violence, then it is only love? Isn't love a kind of mercy that comes from within? Can't mercy be expressed and given in a thousand ways?

Isn't it love that is given? Isn't it given because there is love? All humans and some animals have love in their hearts and express it sometimes. Is it possible to say there is no love if you don't express it? Love can fluctuate in all beings. A gentleman loves immeasurably but does not necessarily express it as much as others desire.

If a husband and wife love each other, both will know it. They should know it and always desire for it to be expressed. It is not the way for humans, especially wedded couples, to wait for it intentionally to be expressed emotionally or otherwise. It is a kind of pride in oneself or a discriminatory attitude. (Mutual freedom is the unspoken recognition and permission of mutual love.)

"All the isolation and silence made me lose sleep as the babies flew away. After his retirement, the change came when the outside world and more comforts came together.

Despite this, God blessed us to live happily in prayer and cooperation. My husband's nature is that he does not show too much happiness in anything. Daddy is always our children's favourite. He is beneficial to relatives, brothers, and elders. He has no joys and desires of his own. Amid responsibilities, he stood close to God to give an excellent education to children and set good examples. Man is a combination of good and evil. His character traits are strongly influenced by the place where he grew up. God allowed him to practice his ideology that 'work is worship,' and he continues it even today.

I pray that this man of coconut character (with parched, dry exteriors and buttery soft inside) might be my husband in the next life because I have no skills. God is always careful when choosing the right ones to pair. I have entirely forgiven this son."

Now Leelamma complains that 'this man' won't say anything! When Tony heard that, he bought two pieces of 'Alexa,' an Echo in the living room, and the wall mount in the kitchen, and installed them to connect to the Wi-Fi. She does not get enough time to talk to the wifi now! A portable piano keyboard was also bought and given to play and learn songs. She has been practising occasionally - it helps her to be free from the tension!

I don't answer or counter any of her points. It is better not to respond. Sometimes, a silent answer is more beneficial than being vociferous. Life is to be experienced. What is not known today will become known tomorrow. Today's concerns, worries, and thoughts of inadequacy will be experienced in the path of more life. We'll cross that bridge when we come to it. We seldom wait for that. Let's take comfort in the fact that life has reserved certain things for us. Is it right to insist that all the realizations should happen immediately? Shouldn't the satisfaction of giving and receiving anything and the resulting love last a lifetime?

"Love is not something to be asked for. You never get it by asking. Love comes through giving, and it is our echo...!" - Osho (Rajneesh-Chandra Mohan Jain - Indian Spiritual Guru.)

"By this, all will know that you are my disciples if you have love among yourselves." (John 13:35)

Answers to closed questions are limited to 'Yes' or 'No'. You can answer in one word or choose from multiple choice. Points need to be explained when answering open questions. Ask the best open-ended questions to get more detailed answers and knowledge if you need more explanation.

Sometimes, open questions are undesirable for expression. When asked to comment through such an open question, knowing what is right, the questioner expects a simple 'interested or uninterested' answer. Would it be fair to annoy the listener by explaining too much about the cause of disinterest, the risks involved, the pros and cons, and the reason for the change of opinion instead of giving such an answer directly? Mutual disharmony often occurs during a lengthy interaction, giving unnecessary explanations about something poorly understood. Or it would be best to have plenty of time to listen to it all and be patient not to respond. That is my shortcoming.

At work, up to sixty and beyond, I maintained a behaviour that I could talk continuously for eight hours when necessary. I enjoyed it as part of my work. I had no intention of talking less to someone else to compensate for the energy loss. It's also a life experience that such a habit sometimes doesn't seem acceptable to someone close to you.

# 125

# Short-Tempered

I don't deny that I was short-tempered. I have no excuses for that. Maybe it was due to immaturity. In retrospect, I admit I was wrong. I vow not to repeat it. You will also agree that as time passed, as you read more and felt that you gained more knowledge of the world, things changed a little. I learned to control the tongue. It has become necessary to maintain a loving relationship in the path of life with everyone. It is a habit consciously cultivated to understand things and react only according to the circumstances. Sometimes, a complaint of "not saying anything" was another aspect. We also hear comments like, "If you ask something, it will be like that." The answer to that, too, would be silence. Sometimes with laughter, sometimes without even a hint of laughter or happiness.

But -"Angry people are not always wise. If you are always angry or complaining, people may lose faith in you. You lose sixty seconds of peace of mind every minute you are angry. An angry father is cruel to himself."

Who, reading this and hearing it anywhere, can be angry?

"It is good to practice controlling what you do and say when angry. Lack of confidence, inferiority complex, anxiety, mood swings, depression, and despair are the causes of excessive anger. That is what makes many simple problems more complicated. As the causes differ, I must know how to deal with them. For example, I understand that the first way to control anger is to be careful not to talk when angry.

When we get angry, we say something to the person who hurts us with words without giving importance to the love we have in our hearts for him.

There is a need to react or develop an aversion to everything all the time. It's not something that everyone can do, so anger comes when you respond quickly. It can come across as anger to others when you do not fully understand things and react without considering the situation. As a result, things get out of hand. Trying to justify arguments by quoting past stories and sometimes inappropriate things while responding only worsens matters.

That is why it is said that if you learn to control your tongue, you can maintain a loving relationship with anyone. Taking time to understand things and reacting only to the circumstances is an excellent habit to cultivate consciously. Maybe that's what I'm trying to do.

Once in Pune - "Leelam, look here... I have scolded you a lot." Did you forget that? Do you remember why?

At Sunabeda, did I not hit your hand in anger with a hair comb in my hand? Forgot that? Why was that? No claim that I was always right. It was enough to see all these as mere memories in life's journey. None of those was the goal of our life.

Someone told Leelamma that before marriage, I had shown tendencies like throwing things in sight and breaking them, locking the room, sleeping alone, etc., when I got angry. That's how a preconceived notion that 'this man' has been angry from his younger days for a long time has entered your mind.

Leelamma repeats it from time to time without remembering that I had already replied to it -

I will repeat the answer given then.

"Who else had such charming beauty as yours? It was a rumour spread by the esteemed fathers of girls who had no beauty at all - so that no other father should try to give his daughter as wife to this man."

I am happy Thommachi, Leelamma's father, did not believe so.

# 126

# Process Approach And A QMS Way of Life

The following are some philosophical and spiritual thoughts that have often arisen in my mind from the little knowledge I have studied and worked on for so long.

When we meditate or do nothing, thoughts arise about our primary life goals and what we are doing to achieve those goals. Do we live up to our aspirations and the efforts of those who want our growth?

Let us first think about the family and the role of parents and children in family life. In a period full of challenges, my parents not only raised five children but were brought up to be good in society and to be known as beneficial to society and the country. They found a place in many people's minds that was advantageous to a large section of society.

A family is born when a man and a woman become one. Parents in the family love and should love all their children equally. People with disabilities should be cared for more. In the family, the mother and father are the same for children and should be together as parents. The mother is always in the father's shadow and should be so. All mothers wish to be like that. A mother does not have a separate existence as long as the father is alive and together in the family. No mother wants to have an individual existence. A family-loving father would not also want another existence for himself.

Mothers have always led humanity forward with their motherhood and hard work. Apart from being mothers, they were also farmers, labourers, teachers, and professionals, and the women continued to be leaders in the cultural spheres of society. Each section of women has performed essential and controlling duties. It is not justifiable to single out only one group as superior. Aren't slogans like women's liberation and women's supremacy mere amateur trends seen in the complexities of the modern world?

Where it is to be said as the parents, sometimes we address only as Achayan or father. 'Amma/Ammachi' is always with Achayan. Addresses such as Amma or Ammachi come in cases where Amma is to be specifically addressed. Divorce is unheard of in any branch and hierarchy of my family because of the unique characteristic of close-knit and dedicated families.

It is the wish and prayer of every good individual member of a family that ' their father and mother' or 'Achayan and Ammachi' are always together in the family, caring and sharing everything and that they are healthy and maintaining themselves well. Parents are always the lifeblood of the family. Instead of addressing that union of minds separately as 'father and mother,' it is addressed collectively as the father (Achayan) or the mother (Ammachi) for convenience.

Good children love their parents for their whole lives and are always there to help and comfort them. Parents should love their children, too. Parents have a mission to help their children to discover their worth, goodness, and abilities. Parents should also give their children space for themselves until they find their space for comfortable living and becoming independent. Most importantly, children should explore their way of life and share ideas of growth and progress with their parents so that their years of experience in life become a guiding beacon for them. Loving parents are godly, and there is no worship of God without loving parents and understanding their mental strength.

My father used to say if you love your brother, you must love him when he is alive. I want to sincerely appeal that if you love your parents, love them when they are alive. Trust in God begins with loving parents. Trust in God grows when you love your fellow beings.

Rather than saying that children are born from their parents, it is correct to say that they are born through their parents. Children grow up with their parents. They are the Creator's creations.

I call the Creator in my self-fulfillment and ask for this much more. - 'If there is another birth, let me be born as the son of my father and mother, as one of the children of Vavachi and Annamma.'

An essential objective that parents achieve by raising their children is satisfaction. Christians say that the satisfaction of a kingdom of God. Other religious people -faithful- say Moksha or Mukti.

Only when the children grow up and become parents does each of them understand the power and love of a chain of love connecting the three links of 'parents - family - children.' That 'love relationship' brings peace and tranquillity to every person's life. It also makes it brilliant and splendid. As each child gets married and time moves on as a family, this chain link of the 'Parents - Family - Children' - chain of love- continues. The wheel of time is constantly spinning.

Family is also an institution. Family is like an organisation. Most commercial and industrial organisations establish and continue to practice a Quality Management System (QMS) to operate their business and achieve desirable objectives efficiently. There are several processes in a system within the organisation; similarly, there are various processes within a family, and the responsibilities and authorities of all personnel are defined.

Bear in mind that the requirements of QMS are the same as those for any business operation or family function.

One of the basic principles of the quality system in such an organisation is the 'process approach.' If every activity (process) in the organisation is done by the repetition cycle of 'Plan-Do-Check-Act' (Deming's wheel or Deming's cycle), The result will always be acceptable; the intended quality can be ensured, and the desirable objectives and goals can be achieved. Continual improvement is necessary for progress, which is possible by adopting changes and improvements. It is also possible to achieve better objectives and goals. Even if there are mistakes and faults, their causes can be investigated and fixed, and improvements can be made so that the defects and deficiencies never occur again (corrective action). The fact that all this is possible while complying with the existing laws and regulations in the country brings joy to any organization, family, or individual.

In the above paragraph, substitute the word "organisation" (ignore the adjectives, 'commercial and industrial') with the word "family," practice (QMS), process approach ('Plan (includes risk assessment)-Do-Check-Act') desirable objectives and improvements can be achieved.

The above hypothesis may be called a QMS way of life.

Objectives/goals can be both tangible and intangible and are to be measured periodically to ensure that the targets you desire are met for satisfaction. If the targets are not met, appropriate actions shall be taken to meet the targets soon. You can raise the bar for better goals or superior objectives for continual improvements if the targets are met, which is the ultimate success of life.

This 'process approach can be applied on the physical and spiritual levels by observing all the moral and religious norms. The most commendable thing is that one is not against the other; everything is complimentary.

It is a valuable lesson from my fifty years of professional life and the policy I have tried to implement in my work areas. That was my mission in my professional life. Thousands of organisations worldwide have made progress by implementing this process approach.

In my classroom lectures on the applicability of the 'process approach,' things like everyday life, quality, end-to-end (complete functional solution ) capability, ways to overcome crises, and improvements needed for progress, etc., sometimes came up. It was also acceptable to listeners.

One thing is evident in a detailed analysis –

The process approach can be applied equally to good family life and business. The satisfactory functioning of families is the sublime goal of the society and, thereby, of the country.

In this worldly life, each person in the family, and thus each family, is striving to attain their goal. Such effort includes all processes – birth, education, work, marriage, continuing family life, service or contribution to society, ultimate farewell, and so on.

When one process ends, another begins. And when it ends, another one starts. A few processes may begin and progress simultaneously. That is the cycle of repetition. This continuous cycle of processes is the same for an individual or a family. It's a lifestyle that can be started, progressed, and improved at any time for any individual or family striving for the ultimate goal.

I cannot advocate this way of life, this policy, as a replacement for any other. But if you look at it as a commoner's opinion, think more, and act, you may be able to shape a better way of life. I am willing to accept all statements that involve a process approach.

Adopting a quality management system helps improve overall performance and provides a basis for sustainable development.

The potential benefits are:-

— The ability to consistently raise good citizens

- Good citizens benefit the society /world at large
- Considers risks and opportunities before any action
- Provide an example to society for good performance, conformity to defined requirements, and achieving objectives.

Use the process approach PDCA cycle and assess risks while planning activities.

The modern world recognises that there are two ways to achieve the desired goals by resolving the flaws and mistakes -

One – To consider what can go wrong - what errors may occur in any operation in advance (it can be called Operational Risk Management), and thus arrange for necessary precautions (mitigation) to prevent such errors. Check and make sure arrangements are effective (means the planned results are achieved). If such precautions are taken before doing any work, achieving the intended goals without making mistakes is possible. The preconceived notions should be reconsidered at least once a month, and the results should be analysed regularly.

Two - In the journey towards the goal, everything is human effort; therefore, mistakes and failures that were never thought of beforehand may naturally occur on the way. Every error and non-conformity should be analyzed, the root cause should be identified, and corrective action should be implemented. Any human activity will reach its intended effect if mistakes and shortcomings in any field of activity are resolved and moved forward. Defects and the solutions implemented should be reviewed over time to ensure effectiveness. This knowledge will help make all future endeavours even better. Successful leaders learn from failures!

It is the secret to the success of thousands of excellent commercial and industrial enterprises. Roll around, blame others, find out who did wrong, bring criminals to justice - all these are selfish political ways or the law of the land. The laws of the land are essential for a nation's smooth running and for its citizens' welfare and well-being. Such ways of approaching a problem are not a permanent solution to the wrongdoings of family members, and any efforts to contain the problem do not eliminate the problem. Our penal laws are inadequate in providing permanent remedies (corrective actions) for individual wrongdoing. In our penal laws, there is a lack of a lasting solution to the transgressions of individuals and guidelines for upliftment, progress, and permanent solutions. Periodic verification of the effectiveness of the corrective actions is seldom practiced because the focus is always on the containment of the problems and framing of laws against the transgressions.

Any errors or failures in operations may be due to omissions in the design or manufacturing stages, changes in the environment, deficiencies, or errors in maintenance. Inadequate operational skills may also be an anomaly.

Personal life goals, including spirituality, are often defined as 'heavenly kingdom,' 'ultimate salvation,' moksha, and mukti. It can only be achieved through the family. In a good family, when boundaries are set for a growing relationship, steps are taken in an orderly, controlled manner, and mutual support is achieved, family members achieve the family's intended outcomes. And the result will always be flawless.

What we have learned and read is this:-

Spirituality is a process that includes beliefs and precepts and is a very systematic and rational process of conditioning the body and mind toward attaining a goal.

The Bible teaches that the ultimate goal of life is the 'Kingdom of Heaven.' Mukti - liberation - from sorrows, prejudices, fears, sufferings, death, etc., as described in Eastern philosophy, which includes Indian thought, is the same. Our actions and deeds should lead to absolute freedom.

Our actions can build and destroy our own lives. A commoner thinks that he is doing everything for the good. But don't we humans make unintentional mistakes, at least occasionally? Then, we can be reassured that we are real human beings, and it will show us the motivation to live as good human beings, removing our imperfections and mistakes. The essential process is continual improvement.

Just like correcting any mistakes in material or physical activities, the best way to move on from errors in spiritual or nonphysical (morals, ethics, and principles) is to forgive yourself and others. Forgiveness is an act of strength, and forgiveness of others brings lasting happiness. The weak can never forgive and bring peace of mind.

The Quality Management System (Quality Management) is a disciplined way of working that helps us properly carry out our day-to-day activities in our physical life, complete our daily tasks, and achieve our goals. What more is needed to continually improve working for the better quality (goal attainment) of human life, including spiritual life?

WD Deming, a quality guru, views quality as a new way of thinking and life, starting with everyone.

It is the spiritual need of the living to leave behind a contribution with meaning, value, and purpose for future generations to be worthy of that satisfaction, the kingdom of heaven / the kingdom of God, and salvation. I believe that the spiritual satisfaction that comes from giving, by whatever name you call it, is the kingdom of heaven, the kingdom of God, and salvation. To try to be worthy of this spiritual satisfaction is the dharma of human life, the best process approach.

A system to control operational functions, a process approach that is good for human life, and acceptable goals - if we could coordinate and implement these smoothly in life, the human mission would be completed.

Various improvements to the effort by the individual or the family happen due to scientific and technological progress, solutions to problems, lessons learned from best practices, corrective actions, innovations, and so on.

Before any change is adopted, specific considerations must be made - whether the quality characteristics will be met as per requirements, whether desirable objectives will be achieved, and whether improvement will be possible. The purpose and consequences of the change should be analysed, and the availability and mobilisation of additional resources should also be examined. Redistribution of responsibilities and authority may also be necessary. Changes should be implemented systematically.

Learning more about the process approach will help you work efficiently and consistently to achieve the most desirable products and services. Goal setting becomes effective.

Before starting operations, it is essential to understand the following:-

1. The name of the work. (Name and Purpose)
2. Review at regular intervals by considering the likely obstacles that may hinder the efficient and timely completion of the work and the achievement of the objective, and formulate measures to avoid the main obstacles. (Operational Risk Management)
3. Have clear, measurable objectives/goals, outline the plan, set quality standards, determine the means to achieve it, and measure and ensure the objectives are achieved. Suppose you see that achieving the set goals is complex and has obstacles. In that case, it is necessary to immediately review the problems and planned solutions and effectively improve the goals/ objectives.

4. Identify the resources, facilities, materials, tools, and equipment required to start the work and ensure availability and serviceability. (Input)

5. Determine the stages of the work & activities from start to finish.

6. At each stage of the work, accurately describe how to do each job at every stage and check the available knowledge, experience, and skills (How to do?)

7. Find and employ work experience, skills, and competencies in jobs. (Competency)

8. Know the process's result, product, and service (Output).

9. Quality in the outcome/product/service and measure objective/goals - Accurately measure and evaluate whether the intended purpose has been achieved. Record results against the plan(desired result). {Measured results for Quality of Output [measure characteristics] & Objectives}

Find multiple processes in any activity or project. It may be helpful to identify the above essential elements in each process. It will help you complete the tasks without mistakes and achieve your goals.

## 127

# Write-down to Remember

"Men are like wine: some turn to vinegar, but the best improves with age" -Pope John XXIII.

Sam resigned from the company where he had worked for six to seven years to start his start-up facility management business. Eight years of operational / business development experience in the multinational company he worked for enabled Sam to do so. Together with his friend Mani from Chennai, they dreamed of building a good partnership firm through hard work. An appropriate name was given – 'Adaptio' and the organisation was registered. It started well and made good progress in two years. With annual sales of 25 lakhs, the business progressed for two more years. Annual sales reached about 250 lakhs!!

One Sunday, Sam and Nita arrived in their newly bought Innova Crysta car for their company - to pick up Mom and Dad to look at a property and, if it looked good, to explore the possibility of owning it.

We found the Four BHK Villas called 'Assetz Soul & Soil' near Hennur Road as an excellent property, with all facilities, getting ready in one year. It will be completed in December 2020, furnished and prepared to move in, for around two hundred lakhs. Expectations were that about 80% of the cost could be arranged as bank loans.

The model villa house looked like a duplex with upstairs and downstairs, and there was a separate space for parking in the front. An excellent place to live if you have the resources, it was a location that combined nature, environment, and transportation. Even for an investment venture, it would fetch reasonable rents. Sam was interested; however, Nita would have to travel to the college for an additional fifteen minutes. By that time, both children would be ready for college after their school education. Travel and distance were the same for any college. Hospital and church were nearby. Sam booked a villa house, paid a token advance, and proceeded to further processing steps.

On our way back, I was thinking. Sam was confident that he could plan a significant investment. He knows the source of income.

I remembered how Sam promised to show me his right to marry Nita before they married. Those words reverberated continuously in my memory for time and again. Any father who loved his daughter would remember things like that -

"I will continue to work in Bangalore and prove myself economically sound like anyone else serving abroad."

As time progressed, I grew happier. Even though I could not see the perfect results, I at least saw a sincere effort to achieve them.

After the marriage, our daughter got a new family, and the children grew up. With parents and relatives frequently visiting, most of them staying with them, the household needs and facilities for each family member increased. They were now laying the groundwork for fulfilling their responsibilities and creating an environment for the family to grow.

As children mature, the time to fulfill the duties of parents is fast approaching. As loving parents, giving them their rights and sharing the assets they traditionally deserve from parents is customary. Nita also deserves the transfer of the assets and legacy earned by her parents; it is her right to claim them. All children deserve a share of what the parents have earned. Children may not demand it, but it is the parental duty to share as they will depart for their eternal journey sooner or later. It is appropriate to bless them by giving them what is possible when they begin to make significant investments for the growth of their family, and it should benefit them.

Leelamma was also asked for her opinion on the matter and was delighted. I told Sam and Nita -

"If you decide to buy it, we will pay you Rs twenty-five lakhs when the house is finished."

Sam and Nita were happy. No buoyant performance was expected. Nita was not the sentimental type who over-expressed their happiness or sadness. She was not one of those sentimental fools. She was as cool as a cucumber and smiled while sitting in the Car, 'tranquil like the surface of the Ganges river at the deepest point.' Considering the experience, I would not hesitate to say about Sam and Vinod: "They keep their good heads on their shoulders and their feet on the ground."

Within minutes, Tony and Seema knew the information through a WhatsApp message. They saw a photo of the model villa house.

Soon after, Tony also expressed interest in having a four-bedroom villa in the same Soul & Soil complex. It was understood that Tony's interest in owning it was a savings investment option. Sam also spoke to the Assetz group and arranged a villa in the adjacent block. The company building the houses said the property developer will complete it by April 2021. Due to the crisis caused by the epidemic, the construction of the houses was delayed for another year.

Both types of loan processing took place in banks. The advance amount was transferred, and the loan amount sanctioned by the banks against the cost of the villas was transferred to Assetz. The period of loan was twenty years. The banks did not hesitate to start Equated Monthly Installments (EMI) soon after.

When the audit in Malaysia was over on November 14, 2019, I came to Singapore, went to Seema's new house, and met everyone there. After returning to India, I went to a company in Jeddah, Saudi Arabia, on December 8 for three days.

The small town of Jeddah is considered the main gateway to Mecca and has many hotels and restaurants nearby. The Mecca pilgrimage season was over. So there was no rush. Nebin Jose, a manager in that company, said he and his friend went to Mecca disguised by wearing Arabic clothes. They went up to the three stone pillars - known as the Jamarat - Stoning of the Devil – in the city of Mina, east of Mecca, to the point where Muslim pilgrims throw stones.

"I'm not getting anywhere there. I can even say I made it to the main gate to Mecca without changing my clothes."

I jokingly said to Jose, the Nasrani from Kottayam.

I was in Myanmar (formerly Burma) from December 12 to 16. I went to an old Church, St. Mary's Cathedral, on Sunday the 15th and heard the holy Mass in English. It was a ten-minute taxi ride from the hotel, and the Burmese driver spoke to me well. He remembered that our President KR Narayanan married a Burmese girl named Usha.

After returning from Burma, there were no proposals for audits anywhere abroad, and no one wanted me to travel overseas. January, February, March, and April were usually busy periods of industrial production. Therefore, the audit work in India and abroad could have been more extensive. However, there was a complete slowdown in economic activities due to the fear of the spread of Coronavirus disease (COVID-19) worldwide.

In February 2021, a political upheaval broke out in Myanmar (Burma). The army seized power through a coup. Elected members of the ruling party were expelled.

Described as a microcosm of modern Asia, Singapore is a mixture of different cultures and histories. Various foods and cooking methods can be seen, enjoyed, and experienced there. Moreover, Seema often calls out and insists – "Come here - the youngest of your grandchildren growing up are Seema's children here. You can spend time with them, live longer, and feel better than any other treatment, which costs less. If it is in April, then a tourist trip to Singapore, you can stay in Singapore for more days and see the world-class scenes." I was thinking and dreaming. What all human dreams have been put on indefinite leave by the crisis and consequences of the pandemic? We need to hope and look forward to better days.

For a dream trip, there were no hassles like travel plan, mode of transportation, ticket booking, visa, and prior appointment. Choose the time as and when necessary - After the scheduled times for daily routines, put aside the electronic devices and media; there is plenty of time to indulge in your favourite pastimes and travel long distances.

Where should I start, and when? That's when I realised hope and a wish I had given the little boy before. I indeed remembered and showed interest and hope to my younger brother! I should look at the diaries that I kept thinking about - 'If I remember all these things, I can write in detail when I get time'...

From the time I started work until my marriage, I kept diaries. After that, I did not find time to write diaries. Busy with worldly affairs, there was no time to think of anything, as I had been told what to do and when (?). If you open the door of memory, everything will return in a flash. Even a tiny ray of light should create the colours, the movements, like in a kaleidoscope, a constantly changing colourful scene. Longing for that transparency, I started looking over the diaries. Yes, seven colours could be seen.

I believed that I was not that old. Let age take its toll. No one cares. The nerves of memory have not yet begun to numb. I'm praying I don't start having a scary illness like my mother's or that memory nerves can work with warmth for a few more days.

That's when I remembered - My brother Raju had a desire a long time ago. I agreed with him. I had given hope and desire, and it is correct. An obligation that begins somewhere halfway punctuated by a semi-colon and then put off without completion. I could not continue because of the loss of direction but because other urgent and essential tasks (post-retirement jobs) came up. That is how the half-stop was put. I had made up my mind that I would continue when the urgency subsided. Everything is justified because the mind is pure. There are no crooked ways, that is it.

My childhood memories - right before Raju was born - father, mother, family, grandparents, their life at that time, the stories told by grandfather are all of interest to Raju and others. That is why he said-

"Kochayan should write it all down."

Today, the busyness is gone, and the work of writing, another comfortable work, has already started. Now it should be completed as soon as possible. A middle base can be reached after three or four months of empty time in the calendar. Again, if there are empty months and days in the calendar, my brother's desire can be somehow fulfilled after some effort. If only God permitted my well-being as it is. God has granted me seventy-five years. It's a bonus, and asking for more might be unethical and selfish. However, it is all decided by the Almighty. Last time I had a (temporary) transient stroke, I prayed to God, "God, please allow me to complete these present tasks" - what can I ask further today and now? - 'The allotted time is getting over; can you please extend it?' In any case, the only source that will get you if you ask is always at the top!

Before leaving, it is good to pack everything conveniently and arrange them in an orderly for the convenience of those not travelling with you. I am not afraid that someone may complain against or blame me. This thought usually occurs to anyone with a sense of responsibility.

I don't have much, but what I have, what God has prepared for me to keep, should be well organised and arranged for others to use it appropriately. Everything should be left behind with a lot of gratitude to all, and it should all be for the good of those who use it tomorrow.

Where shall I start in good earnest? Nothing is intentionally missed out. I am hiding nothing. Damage and normal wear and tear caused by continuous use are natural and permitted!

The evening is the best time of the day. It is commonly used as an indication of retirement from an official job. Kadamattuthara (Kuttanadan) George gave me the book "Today's Remains" to read. In doing so, George may have instructed me to recall the official explorations, adventures, and unofficial adventures I have undertaken over the past seven decades. The book's theme is the ten years of 'sadness of unrequited love that the protagonist remembers. In any case, it was contextual.

Expeditions may be the most important events. Adventures outside my career and private life are unfamiliar; like love or lost love, every problem can be solved, and every adventure can be included. It can be successful or failed, rare or blocked! Remember one's entire life, as each day begins with brightness at dawn and fades at dusk, changes during the day, and all of us experience the differences in weather.

**Smiles at Sunset**

# 128

# Seventy-Five Years Young

February 11, 2021 - Many thoughts came to my mind when I saw that I am seventy-five years old; Old or young, time will tell. :-

a) Getting old. When you get old, although less energetic than before, as Hemin Sunim writes, 'everything slows down in a busy world,' and we should live more calmly, slowly, and happily.

b) There may always be a thought that there is more to be done, but a message may arrive that it is time to finish your run. Isn't it an example that due to the COVID-19 pandemic, jobs such as quality system audits for the aircraft industry have decreased?

c) Responsibilities are almost completed, and the rest of your duties can be continued with the cooperation of children and grandchildren.

d) Spend time with children and grandchildren by seeing them, being happy, eating with them, and seeing and hearing good things. We should be thankful to the Almighty.

We went to church in the morning to thank God for turning 75 years old, to remember my parents and relatives, and to pray for them. Children and grandchildren were hoping to come, and they all wanted to come and join me. The desires were not fulfilled due to travel restrictions during the Covid crisis. Without warning, my siblings Raju, Tess, Babychan, and Tessy arrived just in time. We all went to church together. Nita and her family had come before lunch. Everyone gave me their love abundantly and a handful of gifts. Tony and his family and Seema and her family have expressed their deep love and congratulations over the phone. The gifts they sent have been delivered to us.

The cake-cutting ceremony was in the afternoon. It was possible to meet and talk to each other through an Asia-Europe integrated video conference in real-time. Saju and Binoy were also seen in the video as mere spectators. I was able to share love and happiness with everyone for some time. Those were priceless moments to remember for a lifetime. Turning seventy-five years old was a milestone birthday and a birthday celebrated by family and friends. Often referred to as the platinum celebration, the gift for this birthday should also be unique because the moment itself was exceptional and rare. More than the expensive gifts like the Apple Watch, sincere love and prayers for good health were given by children and siblings. That was how Babychan wrote and presented a poem felicitating his elder brother on that occasion. Like a king's proclamation- it was printed in golden letters on satin fabric, rolled up in a scroll, and enclosed in a cylinder-shaped casket, Babychan took out the Felicitation Poem and read. Anson Athikalam recited the poem, which was recorded on a mobile phone. The lines of the poem are translated from Malayalam and reproduced below:-

*My brother*

*The family tree sprouted with tender leaves and branches*
*During the season when lot many flowers bloom in colour*
*A few twigs fell and became spirits that rest in paradise for redemption*
*'Takli' the mischievous eldest, grew up to be the cynosure of the house*
*solitary for a decade, the siblings grew later to take your hand in awe*

*shaded to your branch as the safety and shades of siblings*
*headed by the thumb and the five fingers in the hand on*
*the brotherhood forever as by the web of love joining the fingers*

*In the smoothness of natural love, but not losing the firmness*
*Guiding in the tough grind with the genuine lessons of truth*
*All the loving cares of father and mother were shared*

*The sweet memories of living shall ever bloom and never perish*
*Know not with what words do I speak a tribute to you, brother,*
*Along with that of father and mother as an unquenchable lamp*
*For as long as my life remains, keep giving us the oil, oh Lord!*

*May the aura of 'seven and a half decades' of good life increase the brightness of the lamp,*
*May the generations salute you with honour shining in the brightness of the lamp*

*With the thought that there remain a thousand things to be done*
*Let me move ahead until I reach the Lord's presence on the path of my life.*
*(Dedication: Babychan Kannattumadom for all brothers)."*

# 129

# Another Auditor Too Retired

I anticipated the news, but it came too soon that my brother Raju retired after a distinguished service with C&AG at sixty years of age.

Public funds are the wealth of a democratic nation, and the government is responsible for utilising them. The regulatory system is responsible for ensuring that the public funds are used efficiently for the intended purposes as decided by the government and convincing the same to the constitutional institutions. My younger brother Raju was accountable for functioning as a more extensive regulatory system component. After about 38 years of government service, Raju's retirement was another event of pride for the whole family. He was in the same organisation when he joined the job and continued until retirement. He relocated to Gwalior once and to Ahmedabad later and stayed at the outstations for over two years each time. The rest of the time, he was in Thiruvananthapuram, the capital city of Kerala State. Occasionally, I used to tell him that he should still be doing something even after he came home on retirement from work. That was because of the experience I had with its pros and cons. Imparting religious education was a subject of interest to Raju. Everyone had the confidence that whatever he did would be for good.

Babychan, who worked with Raju in the same office, continues to work there in Thiruvananthapuram. He is due for superannuation in June 2023.

COVID-19 spread rapidly around the world and reached India. Lockdown restrictions were imposed across the country. As the lockdown phase gradually eased over time, it relieved people to a great extent. Yet the crisis continued, not for a year, but for two years or more.

Here I am, free from the technology of aviation travel and industrial quality control practices. There are no audits, private training, or academy visits for HAL training.

I feel that the time of COVID-19 with travel restrictions motivated and encouraged me to do my hobbies. I could read at home full time, catch up on world news through television, watch sports matches and cultural events, pray, see my children and grandchildren at least once a week, communicate, and write. Thinking about something or other all the time, except when eating, exercising, or resting. There was still time left, whenever I got time - as Leelamma says - "Let him keep on poking on the computer, but open his mouth and say a couple of words, No; it's not there!"

A loving wife can only say so.

At one point, Ottathaickal Ammachi was very bedridden. A helper was permanently kept in the house for the day-to-day needs of Ammachi's affairs, and the woman took care of Ammachi as best as she could. Sometimes, the housewife in the home reduced the care time for the mother and assigned the woman some other household chores. Due to the extra work, the woman also faced some failures.

If Joy had been at home during breaks from sailing, things would have gone smoothly and without problems. Things worsened when Joy got three or four months of work and left the house. The woman who was hired as a helper was also in more trouble. Ammachi, on the other hand, was tired but fully conscious, and she enjoyed talking to the visitors at least briefly. With the loss of Joy's presence, her mood swings, pains, and difficulties increased. She stopped eating and began to react sharply with desperation. Her mind and body were tired, and she insisted on seeing all the children, indirectly indicating that 'it was time for her to go.' Even without sleep at night, she kept on insisting.

The woman who kept vigil as a helper called Ammachi's daughters and informed them.

Leelamma had only one wish. - "I only want to see my mother once more. I have to go. What if I could not see her anymore?"

If there were any restrictions to travel across the border, we decided to go in Sam's Innova Crysta car, complying with the Corona restrictions and conditions. Nita and Sam also joined for the journey. At night, we reached Thambichan's house. In the morning, everyone went and met Ammachi. We were relieved to find that Ammachi was happy and cheerful. We took a picture together, sat beside her, and said something. To everyone's amusement, Ammachi immediately replied, tit for tat, and her old self was awakened. Ammachi laughed with her toothless mouth open, leaned back, and her right eye not fully open.

Leelamma pointed to her husband and asked her mother - "Ammachi, do you know who this is?"

"Here it is, Oommachan."..Everyone agreed. My mother thought of something and continued -

"Even otherwise, from the beginning, 'Oommachan' is lucky"... The bystanders looked at each other in surprise.

When I saw her last time, I asked, "Do you know who this is, Ammachi?" Ammachi's counterquestion was, "Don't I know my children?"

We were lucky to be able to come and see Ammachi, who was healthy.

"Yes, Ammachi, the luck that Ammachi gave me is still with me!"

Ammachi will understand, won't she? I saw the bliss of self-satisfaction and peace in her eyes!

In the morning, before starting our return journey, Raju gave his Chechi a gift - after remembering that his professional career had started 'Thirty-eight years ago, after having breakfast, blessings, and prayers given to him by Chechi.'

People were eagerly waiting to get back to their everyday routine. Covid-19 restrictions were unlikely to continue for several more months. News from vaccine trials gave the hope that the epidemic would end soon. A couple of vaccines were nearing final regulatory approval.

Only our close friends can stand by us during the good and worst times.

How many of my close friends, well-wishers, and colleagues have disappeared behind the veil of time during the last year and a half of the Covid restrictions? At least some of them could be singled out as outstanding personalities and my benefactors. Air Cmde (Retd) Joseph Varkey, RN Padhy, TS Kani, H Vyasa Rao, JC Anthony and RC Sharma (Kanpur) are among them. The close relatives were Maramkunnil, Appachayaan, and Thommikunju. There's nothing more beautiful than a life fully lived; Your soul lives on in the people you touched.

# 130

# Not Yet Retired

"Learn from yesterday, live for today, hope for tomorrow. The important thing is not to stop questioning." – said Albert Einstein (the German physicist and Nobel Prize winner.)

Let me share some more personal thoughts, often thought out and never revealed to anyone. Simply recording the history in memory would not be a complete exercise without it.

Nowhere is it stipulated that only a leader of the people, a popular leader, a social reformer, a high-ranking figure, or someone who has made many contributions to science and technology can write autobiographical memoirs. Can't an ordinary person write a memoir about his life experiences? Although typical, each person has different life experiences. Every ordinary life story is extraordinary.

A commoner would probably never find such a grand adventure, an eventful and distinguished biography to write. However, the ordinary person can talk about the difficulties he faced, the moments of life he enjoyed, the moments of fulfillment, and the successes and achievements of life. If it satisfies that commoner, wouldn't understanding it add value to any ordinary man? Suppose such methods and planned actions can be replicated in life. In that case, there is no doubt that it will benefit the effectiveness of anyone's life.

Good writers say they get a feeling that urges them to write. Don't similar feelings arise in ordinary people? Writing memories is a desire I have carried inside for a long time.

I remembered my mother-in-law saying, "I am lucky." I immediately understood why she said that. Yes, she gave me my luck, her daughter, as my wife, Leelamma.

Elders are a source of wisdom and strength. We need to revere and respect them always. Respected older people reveal significant meanings in concise words. Ammachi gave me luck, and luck here meant being a lifelong companion, living together, experiencing and sharing each other's joys and sorrows.

Mother said about her son-in-law, not that she was satisfied with me.

Ammachi said, "He...he is lucky". It is enough to see it as a recommendation to the One with the right and authority to say He is satisfied. That in itself was amazing. I may deserve it. It can be described as a conscious conclusion to my mother's continuing affection for me for so long. Ammachi's mind and body have started to know what their weakness was. "Let's come again.., we will see", but the journey came with a sadness of how long. Then Ammachi said - "I can see that all of you children are coming from time to time; that is very happy."

Leelamma has always been with me throughout my family life since marriage. She is my love and my life partner. Our children, grandchildren, and all their precious lives are with us.

I know our children loved and respected us as parents and continue to do so. That's how their children learn to love them as parents when they grow up. They know that. In a joint family, it is easier for children to learn these morals and ethics teach them. Nowadays, everyone lives in different places independently. They meet, cooperate, and interact occasionally. It is highly satisfying that our children always include their babies in their interactions with parents and siblings. Whenever they communicate, it is usual to mention the special love that all babies have for their grandparents. They share small joys - school specials, Natasha's school finals, Amelia's entrance exams, secondary school admission with scholarship, Sarah's Chinese and Hindi studies, swimming lessons,

Sarah's and Reuben's fancy dress costumes, Eleanore's readings and created stories, Steven's football practices after leaving cricket, Reuben's car games, percussion instruments, violin lessons after Amelia's piano, etc. On any special occasion, they sing praises and greetings to Achayan and Ammachi on the phone or video and exchange love and blessings. Being far away, they show it when cutting the cake, eating it alone, and laughing loudly. Achayan and Ammachi are filled with joy, enjoy their being, and long for a long life!

After being diagnosed with COVID-19 as positive, Amelia and Tony took medication to recover. Joysy was taken by ambulance for diagnostic tests and returned after a check-up, for her COVID was negative. It was positive for Sam, and he was admitted to the hospital. He recovered after a few days of treatment, medication, and rest. A photo of Nita wearing a PPE kit and caring for Sam in the hospital went viral on WhatsApp.

Leelamma and I are of one mind and two bodies, complementing each other. Each one of us has our own personality, and it is complementary. Some private thoughts and actions are ours alone, but none have ever been and will never be contradictory. We believe in mutual love, in ordinary good between us both, and sincere reciprocity. Our faults are mutually known, seen, forgiven, and sometimes tolerated. Co-existence and cooperation continue. Mutual criticism has its place, and criticism is accepted with patience. We have no enemies. We do not think that anyone is hostile towards us. We are one and will always be one. There may be some personal weaknesses, but we share the responsibility as long as we understand each other because we are not two but one.

By writing this, I have used my time well during the COVID period. Leelamma also chose drawing and painting as pastimes for good time utilisation. Tony provided canvas and paint. While everyone said the first one was good, Leelamma saw it as a good growth and progression from fabric painting to painting proper on canvas. As soon as we thought of the next painting, Tony sent two canvas sets and suitable paints.

All children should see pictures of mommy on their wall. Leelamma was also happy. Apart from household chores and horticultural hobbies such as gardening and growing vegetables outside the kitchen and on the terrace, this pastime of painting has become a confidence booster apart from maintaining a stress-free mind. She reads the Manorama newspaper on the iPad in the morning, reads parts of the Malayalam Bible, and watches videos on Facebook and YouTube channels of interest for a while. By this time, the housemaid arrives, and it is customary to be on supervision duty for the next two hours. After lunch, she invariably rests by lying down; she swears she has no sleep.

"Just lying down, sometimes I don't even close my eyes. Sometimes, I might snore a little, not as much as you do."

If there are any, Malayalam serials with heart-wrenching stories will keep us alert and awake. Then it is tea time. Then, it becomes time to pursue some other hobby like stitching. Girls like the clothes sewn by their grandmother more than the fashionable clothes they get from the fashion stores. If her back hurts, she applies Kwan Loong oil and lies down until it becomes good. Soon, it will be time to get up and go to the sewing machine to complete the half-finished frock.

Food will be prepared and eaten on time. Insulin and other medicines during breaks, baths, cell phone conversations with sisters, short walks around the premises in the morning, morning prayers on return - she used to go to church when there were no COVID restrictions. We watch movies in the evenings when we have time. While the appeal in Malayalam cinema decreased, the appeal was seen more in Marathi cinema, which has family and social storylines. Marathi, the dialogues can be partially understood as we already heard the words in Pune, and it can be understood a bit better with English subtitles. Authentic reviews were also given about the screenplay, acting, direction, and songs in the movies. The old award movies were not as enjoyable for the mother as they were for the children. Now, the olden themes were all outdated, too. Movies with mythology, violence, war crimes, and unfamiliar dialogues are unacceptable.

Leelamma's lifestyle is characterised by punctuality and discipline, such as prayer and reading scriptures before sleeping. What can I say about myself besides ' The stone near the Jasmine will bear its fragrance too '? But I can assure you that there is nothing like that.

Leelamma is way ahead of me in everything. Lastly, it was when she made good pictures on the canvas and received appreciation from all the family members.

Leelamma walks with me in most of the matters. In other words, I am with Leelamma. It is physically correct, too. As I sometimes walk fast, though I should always be walking along, Leelamma often lags; I have to stay put for her to come up. I then stand for a while until Leelamma joins me. My life partner decides on small things, and we implement them together. Things big enough - to say as significant - are chosen by the almighty and help us to implement them.

I indeed have my say on money matters. It does not mean I objected to my partner's proposals on money matters. I will explain the reasons if I deny it to her.

I have only done what my conscience felt was correct as an ordinary man. I earnestly hope it was like that for as long as I can remember. Every moment of life is seen as a gift from God. Achievements, blessings, and everything without exception are seen as Almighty God's comforting touch and mercy.

# 131

# To Depart Peacefully

When someone asks me how retired life is going, I smile and counter the question, 'Is there such a life?' Then I say - "It could be because I am still working; I have not retired either. I have not retired from work until I am 75; I have not thought about it."

If you meant asking my age, I am seventy-five. Mentally and physically, I am doing small tasks, feel healthy, have slowed down in everything, and walk slowly. I have no massive task before me. Moreover, age is not a measure of mind and self-confidence but of time in years, months, and days.

The first reading of the first work - perhaps the first print of the manuscript - was what my intellectual friend George remembered - after reading the first copy. He is an unregistered fan of Marquez.

"Life is not what one lived, but what one remembers and how one remembers it to recount it." - Gabriel Garcia Marquez.

I listened to it proudly. I believe it is up to the reader to evaluate how the author describes the memoirs. I intend to leave a lasting legacy of sincerity and truthfulness without hurting anyone.

Curved lines of the COVID-19 chart showing daily infections have not touched the bottom yet. There have been several fluctuations, ups and downs. During this period, four or five types of vaccines were developed due to the continuous efforts of scientific research in various countries. Vaccines produced in India – Covishield and Covaxin – were mass-produced, and the entire population was immunised on a priority basis. It will take at least two years to complete the COVID-19 vaccination for this many (139. 2 Crores, May 2021) people. Until then, the use of face masks and other restrictions would continue. Other more virulent variants of the virus have also been discovered. Then, raising their heads like reptiles, the resurgence of the epidemic - the second wave of coronavirus - came without stopping.

In the meantime, many classmates and friends who have studied together at Carmel Polytechnic called me from here and there. It was not easy to see them in person. They decided to come together almost sixty years later and arrange a video conference using the latest information technology possibilities.

We were all proud that Carmel Polytechnic was our parent institution. Most of us are over 70 years old. Given the opportunity, on the evening of September 19, 2020, we met and interacted with about sixty classmates at Carmel College via Zoom from different parts of the world.

Although we were close friends, no one could recognise each other as their age, size, and facial appearances had changed significantly; our relationship with Carmel brought us together.

We all had a lot to talk about, including the current situation, the environment, the weather, the details of our careers, family, the friends we added, the celebrations we had, and the significant impact Carmel had on our lives.

The one thing that came up and that we all valued so much with consensus and excitement was that we wanted to do something together that reminded us of the memories of our Carmel days.

At the end of the discussions, we collected all the memorabilia and memories, including those we can hold or create in any medium. It will help to publish a souvenir for the knowledge of our grandchildren, families, and everyone else. We want to relive the fun and merry days of old when we spent in the bosom of our typical mother 'Carmel.' Even if it is a reincarnation, it is welcome. Carmel Alumni, as souvenirs of the 1961-67 (C, E, M) Batches, let us pass down the souvenir to our posterity.

They all put the task of editor-in-chief on my shoulders, like in the saying, "In the land of the noseless, the broken-nosed man is king."

"I want to wear that as a feather in my cap." I did self-reflection. Since then, I have been making that effort. As a result of three months of relentless effort and reminders, a 100-page, full-colour demi 1/4 size souvenir was ready. The content of the souvenir was the memoirs of classmates who have settled down after service in various sectors. The challenge for the classmates was to recall that particular period of their life after about fifty-five years.

We also planned for the ceremonial release of the souvenir, followed by a full-day excursion in a houseboat at Alleppey.

Due to the second wave of COVID-19 and the imposing of nationwide restrictions, everyone couldn't gather together on the appointed day. With the decision to get together when COVID is under control, we decided to meet the Principal, Carmel Polytechnic, in person and get the souvenir released in a small ceremony. We did that and distributed the souvenir to all members of the alumni.

I have never suffered in life. It does not mean that I did not know suffering. I have known the sufferings of my parents, siblings, and colleagues. I have learned some lessons from all of them. I have often tried many things, even though I never tried hard enough. So, I am always satisfied that my success is commensurate with my efforts. None of my efforts have been sufficient for more tremendous success. I have not lost the confidence that I could have achieved more if I had tried harder.

Life is not suffering. It is a duty. No one can escape from it. So, face the facts; that is the best way.

Exemplary action is being sincere and faithful in all the activities of material life. That's what I've always done.

Some of my interests were turned into goals, and hard work was often required to achieve them, but because they were reasonable goals, I have not felt them as hardships. I had parents, peers, and siblings to help me when I was young. Then, the spouse came and joined me, a lifelong partner. We had many friends to help us and cooperate with us.

I had to leave my siblings and parents, who prepared me for life, and go to another state and continue living there. I was not even twenty-one when I left my home state. I was called, and I went to Pune. My parents found my life partner. We agreed to live together, and we lived in Pune.

After some time, I changed my profession and place of living to Bangalore. The creator completed the structure of my family by then, bringing additional duties and responsibilities to be part of my life. Once, when I was at home with my parents on vacation, I had to say to Achayan without hesitation -

"I have spent more days away from home - in another state - than at home. Now everyone knows that I have more responsibilities. When that happens, naturally, the responsibilities towards home - towards my parents - have decreased a little, I agree. However, I have never forgotten my duties towards them and will never forget them!".

God gave us children in Pune. In Bangalore, the almighty gave them grace and guidelines to prepare them for life and to live physically away from their parents.

Let me conclude that we lived and lived well, quietly, and peacefully. Our children have their own families. We have grandchildren. They grow and learn. Everyone prepares for a dutiful and responsible life.

Our children have given us their love so abundantly and infinitely more. My children always strive for our health and happiness above all their other responsibilities. They always work for spirituality and universal good and well-being.

Although I have retired from my professional life, we continue to be happy. Life is not over. Not enough that we lived.

This is our desire -

Do good, grow in spirituality, live happily, and wish to say goodbye calmly and peacefully. Thank you, and I love you.

Lord, THANK YOU. You have provided me with more than I could ever have imagined. THANK YOU, my parents, who loved me the most, to the hundred people whose names appear in this and to the thousand whose names do not appear. May I lovingly offer you a bouquet of gratitude.

After I wrote the above, I went to London, where my son and family live. I had the opportunity to stay there for two months (2021 Oct-Nov) with the kids, even though it was the cold season. We followed the terms of the COVID protocol during our travel and stay in the UK. We could not walk or wander around seeing the sights. We spent a whole day watching the 'Winter Wonderland' show in Hyde Park. We watched the kids' ice skating. We spent two days with Ansa-Vineet's family.

I learned about Aunty's death (Kunjomachayan) in Kochi that day. Funeral services were watched and prayed through a YouTube video.

When we returned from London in early December, we went to Alappuzha and met our mother. Ammachi blessed us before we returned. At the age of ninety-five, on the 17th of February, 2022, our mother departed to the heavenly home. Funeral services were held on March 2 due to a delay in the arrival of Sailor Joy. The mother's eight children, grandchildren, relatives, and many locals attended the funeral.

Ammachi was the last link in the adult generation that connected a hundred good people. We will never forget the extraordinary personality of the mother, who combined compassion, love, determination, and courage.

www.ingramcontent.com/pod-product-compliance
Lightning Source LLC
LaVergne TN
LVHW041136150826
845673LV00001B/17

* 9 7 9 8 8 9 5 5 6 3 9 1 5 *